The Economics of Defence Spending

Defence spending is both topical and controversial. It raises issues of life and death, protection and security; it is a major issue for every nation, yet surprisingly little has been written about it. This comparative study of the economics of defence spending in countries throughout the world is an important breakthrough in an under-researched area, and it is a valuable contribution to the economics of defence, disarmament, and peace at a time when relations between the superpowers are changing dramatically.

Ten experts report and analyse the variety of international experience, covering the major Western powers, the Soviet Union, Israel, Japan and two key areas of the developing world, the Indian sub-continent and South America. They discuss the various factors and variables that influence a nation's defence spending, showing that since different nations face different threats they differ in their willingness and ability to pay for protection. Some prefer independence or neutrality, while others have joined military alliances; some possess nuclear weapons, while others rely on all-volunteer forces.

An authoritative account of defence spending and policy in both developing and developed countries, the book provides case studies and comparative material for policy-makers, civil servants, and military staffs throughout the world. It will also be of great use to students of economics, politics, international relations, and policy studies.

The Editors

Keith Hartley is Professor of Economics and Director for the Centre for Defence Economics at the University of York. He is the author of many books and articles, including *NATO Arms Co-operation: a Study in Economics and Politics* (1983). Todd Sandler is Professor of Economics and Political Science at Iowa State University. He has written many books and articles, including *The Theory of Externalities, Public Goods, and Club Goods* (with Richard Cornes, 1986). Both Hartley and Sandler are Editors of *Defence Economics*.

The Economics of Defence Spending

An International Survey

Edited by

Keith Hartley

and

Todd Sandler

London and New York

First published 1990
by Routledge
11 New Fetter Lane, London EC4P 4EE

Simultaneously published in the USA and Canada
by Routledge
a division of Routledge, Chapman and Hall, Inc.
29 West 35th Street, New York, NY 10001

Typset by J&L Composition Ltd, Filey, North Yorkshire
Printed and bound in Great Britain by
Mackays of Chatham PLC, Chatham, Kent

British Library Cataloguing in Publication Data

The Economics of Defence Spending: An International Survey.
1. Defence. Expenditure on governments
I. Hartley, Keith, *1940–* II. Sandler, Todd
355.6'22

ISBN 0-415-00161-7

Library of Congress Cataloging in Publication Data

The Economics of Defence Spending: An International Survey/edited
by Keith Hartley and Todd Sandler.
p. cm.
ISBN 0-415-00161-7
1. Armed Forces–Appropriations and expenditures. 2. War, Cost
of. I. Hartley, Keith. II. Sandler, Todd.
UA17.E26 1990
355—dc20   89–49513
                                                  CIP

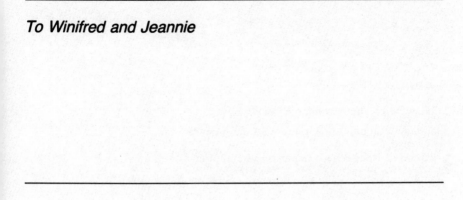

To Winifred and Jeannie

Contents

Contents

List of figures

List of tables

Contributors

Jacques Aben	Université de Montpellier I, Montpellier, France
Shimshon Bichler	The Hebrew University, Jerusalem, Israel
Saadet Deger	SIPRI, Stockholm, Sweden
Dieter Fritz-Aßmus	University of Armed Forces, Hamburg, West Germany
Keith Hartley	University of York, UK
Robert E. Looney	Naval Postgraduate School, Monterey, California, USA
Stephen L. Mehay	Naval Postgraduate School, Monterey, California, USA
Alex Mintz	Texas A & M University, College Station, Texas, USA
James C. Murdoch	Auburn University, Auburn, Alabama, USA
Daniel N. Nelson	Carnegie Endowment for International Peace, Washington, DC, USA
Satoshi Niioka	Kanto Gakuin University, Yokohama, Japan
Louis Pilandon	Université de Clermont-Ferrand I, Clermont-Ferrand, France
Todd Sandler	Iowa State University, Ames, Iowa, USA
Thomas Scheetz	Universidad de Buenos Aires, Buenos Aires, Argentina
Christian Schmidt	Université de Paris IX, Dauphine, France
Somnath Sen	University of Birmingham, UK and SIPRI, Stockholm, Sweden
Ron Smith	Birbeck College, London, UK
Michael D. Ward	University of Colorado, Boulder, Colorado, USA
Klaus Zimmermann	University of Armed Forces, Hamburg, West Germany

Preface

Defence economics is a relatively new and expanding branch of economics. It involves the application of macro- and micro-economic theory to issues of defence, disarmament and peace. There is no shortage of testable hypotheses. Similarly, there are numerous unanswered questions requiring the development of new theories. Studies of defence spending in different countries add to our limited knowledge in this developing field of economics.

Defence is a classic choice problem affecting both rich and poor nations, each reaching its own and often different solution to such choices. Some countries have chosen neutrality and are willing to pay the price; others are members of a military alliance within which there might be opportunities for 'free-riding'. NATO and the Warsaw Pact are examples of major military alliances that traditionally have been in a potential conflict and arms race situation. Some nations, as in the Middle-East and the Indian sub-continent, have a long history of regional conflict with its implications for their defence policies and levels of spending. This variety of international experience needs to be assembled and analysed by defence economists.

By the late 1980s, the superpowers were involved in the arms control negotiations (e.g. INF treaty). But even if the USA and USSR reach arms control agreements, there remain major unresolved issues of defence and security policy elsewhere in the world, ranging from Central and South America, through western and eastern Europe, Africa, the Middle East, India–Pakistan, China, Japan and Southeast Asia. Relatively little is known about the economics of defence spending in different countries throughout the world. This volume aims to add to our knowledge of international experience.

The book is designed for students and general readers interested in defence policy. It is suitable for third-year undergraduates and graduate students in economics, politics, international relations and policy studies. It provides case studies and comparative material for policy-makers, civil servants and military staffs throughout the world.

This volume is the result of a NATO Research Fellowship awarded to Keith Hartley (1986–7), which enabled both editors to meet and collaborate. Work on the volume started with approaches to authors during the second half of 1987. Inevitably, there were delays in finding suitably qualified experts willing to accept our deadlines. Initially, authors were asked for a first draft by mid-1988. Upon receipt, each chapter was read and commented on by both editors. Authors met their final deadlines with varying degrees of success, with revised chapters delivered between late 1988 and early June 1989. We are indebted to all our authors for their support and their contributions to this volume. Others, to whom we are grateful for support and assistance, include Dr F. Welter, NATO; Barbara Dodds, Institute for Research in the Social Sciences; Sue Streeter, Iowa State University; our wives Winifred and Jeannie and our children, Adam, Lucy and Cecilia and Tristan; they bore some of the costs of our interest in defence policy and spending.

Keith Hartley
Todd Sandler

Chapter one

Introduction

Keith Hartley and Todd Sandler

The issues

Defence spending is both topical and controversial. It raises issues of life and death, protection and security. Different nations face different threats: some are involved in an arms race; some have a long history of regional conflicts whereas others are attempting to reduce the arms race through arms control agreements. Countries differ in their willingness and ability to pay for defence. Faced with a major threat, such as involvement in a conflict like the Second World War, nations might be willing to pay highly for protection, allocating a high proportion of resources to their armed forces. But defence is not a free good: like all expenditures, it involves sacrifices of other goods and services, raising controversies about military versus social-welfare spending and whether defence is a benefit or burden to an economy. Such issues arise in both rich and poor countries.

Inevitably, nations differ in their attitudes and policies towards defence. They have adopted different solutions to the defence problem. Some have joined military alliances; others prefer independence or neutrality; some have acquired nuclear weapons; others rely on all-volunteer forces; and some support a domestic defence industrial base to ensure a supply of defence equipment. In other words, there is a diversity of international experience, which was the starting point for this volume.

The approach

The original aim of this volume was to provide an authoritative account of defence spending and policy in a variety of countries, with each chapter written by an expert economist following a standard format. By asking our authors to adopt a similar approach, we planned to produce a genuinely comparative volume. Authors were asked to provide a common data set, to analyse demand and supply issues, and to outline special themes and specific problems facing each nation.

Contributors were provided with a standard outline for each chapter.

This asked them to analyse defence as a choice problem. Choices have to be made about the size of the defence budget (e.g. guns v. butter), and its allocation between nuclear and conventional forces, between manpower and equipment, between various types of manpower (e.g. regulars, conscripts, reserves, civilians), between army, navy and air forces, and between home and overseas locations. We were interested in how each nation had made these choices.

For each country, authors were asked to provide the following:

1 The economic background as reflected in descriptive statistics and general trends in the major economic indicators (e.g. GDP, growth, inflation, unemployment, balance of payments), the government budget and the implications for defence spending and policy for the period 1960–87.

2 The military background between 1960 and 1987, as reflected in the threat, arms races, the armed forces, foreign commitments, membership of alliances and the arms trade (imports and exports).

3 Estimation of the country's demand for military expenditure. Authors were asked to estimate a standard model with military expenditure determined by GDP, the threat, spillovers from allies and other variables such as the governing party or a change in strategy. There was also an invitation to report on any superior model which might be available.

4 The supply of protection or security. This involved supply side issues embracing:
   (a) The supply of manpower, e.g. all-volunteer forces v. conscription v. reserves
   (b) The supply of equipment, e.g. the defence industrial base, imports and exports of defence equipment
   (c) Technical progress in the form of research and development and spin-off
   (d) Questions about the possible burdens of defence spending, e.g. its effects on investment and economic growth.

5 Future contingencies: are there any distinctive features and problems for each country? The suggestions offered included manpower problems and possible solutions to demographic changes in the 1990s; pressure on Japan to abandon the 1 per cent limit on defence spending; the costs to France of maintaining an independent strategic nuclear force; and the implications for the USA of SDI and disarmament negotiations.

For a variety of reasons, not all our authors were able or willing to follow all the details of our standard format. There were problems of data availability, pressures of other work and an understandable desire not to be diverted from current research plans. The international community of academic defence economists is small and the numbers who are expert on any particular country are even smaller! To obtain specialists who were knowledgeable on our various nations required a degree of negotiation and persuasion, with the inevitable trade-offs! Similar difficult choices were required in selecting the sample of nations to be included in our study.

The choice of nations

Given a limitation of ten country chapters, we selected a group of nations with the following characteristics:

1 Developed and developing nations
2 Members of military alliances (NATO, WTO)
3 Nations involved in arms races and regional conflicts (e.g. Israel, India–Pakistan; South America)
4 Nations with nuclear forces (e.g. USA, USSR, France, UK)
5 Nations pursuing policies of independence (e.g. France) and neutrality (e.g. Sweden)

Inevitably, some interesting country studies such as China and South Africa had to be excluded either because of space constraints or the lack of specialist authors. Nevertheless, our final sample comprises a group of nations that amply illustrate the potential contribution of country studies to improving our understanding of the economic determinants of defence spending. We turn now to an overview of each country study, followed by a general evaluation of the theoretical approach to, and empirical results on, the demand for military expenditure.

An overview

The country studies and their ordering have been grouped around the superpowers, Western Europe and other nations. The sample of almost twenty nations and their defence burdens are summarized in Table 1.1. It can be seen that defence burdens vary between 1 per cent and over 25 per cent of national output, with some of the relatively poor countries devoting substantial resources to their armed forces.

The United States (see chapter two) has a multi-front defence strategy with major forces deployed in Western Europe, Japan and South Korea. Various factors are considered as determinants of its defence spending patterns. These include international events (e.g. Korea, Vietnam), elections, changing administrations, public opinion, the attitudes of Congress, domestic economic constraints, the Soviet threat, arms control agreements, inter-service rivalry, alliances and burden sharing. A public choice approach recognizes the importance of the political process in the form of the median voter theorem and economic models of bureaucracy. In their empirical work, the authors test whether domestic economic factors and

Table 1.1 The sample

Nations	Defence share in national output (%)	Date of defence share
Superpowers		
USA	6.6	1987
USSR	12.5	1985
Rest of Warsaw Pact		
Bulgaria	8.0	1985
Czechoslovakia	5.8	1985
East Germany	6.4	1985
Hungary	4.4	1985
Poland	6.0	1985
Romania	6.0	1985
Western Europe		
UK	4.7	1987
France	3.7	1988
West Germany	3.1	1987
Sweden (neutral)	3.0	1985
Other nations		
Israel	25.0+	1986
India	3.6	1985
Pakistan	6.9	1985
Argentina	3.5	1986
Chile	7.1	1986
Peru	4.1	1986
Japan	1.0	1988

the Soviet threat are the most important determinants of desired defence spending. They conclude by referring to the uncertainties for the future resulting from policy changes in the USSR, from possible arms control agreements and from the emergence of other potential superpowers.

The defence spending of NATO members represents their response to the perceived threat from the Soviet Union and its allies in the Warsaw Pact. The substantial defence efforts and burdens of the Warsaw Pact prior to the events of 1989–90 are outlined in chapter three. There are some familiar features of alliances such as differences in burden sharing and varying degrees of commitment to joint military planning and exercises (e.g. Hungary and Romania). It is suggested that in the Warsaw Pact, military commitments have helped to make a bad economic system perform worse. In the USSR, for example, the military has captured most of the Soviet R & D and new machinery production so that the civilian sectors are denied access to technologies that might make them more productive: hence the USSR's own modernization has been sacrificed on the altar of military priorities. However, rather than using arms race models, it is suggested that the USSR's massive military efforts are needed to guarantee power for the ruling communist parties. In return, the military–industrial complex needs the ruling parties to provide them with the prestige, power and budgets to maintain their dominant position and status in society. This chapter provides some fascinating insights and essential background to the changes which occurred in Eastern Europe and the USSR during 1989–90 and the possibility of successful arms control agreements.

Since 1945, the UK's defence policy (see chapter four) has reflected the need to adapt to a changing geographical–political role associated with the loss of Empire and resource constraints resulting from its relative economic decline. None the less, despite changing commitments, roles and new technology, the shares of the defence budget allocated to each of the armed forces have remained remarkably stable. The defence budget buys strategic nuclear forces, an all-volunteer force with substantial deployments overseas (especially in Germany) and, traditionally, has been used to support a domestic defence industrial base. A demand equation is estimated in which UK military expenditure is dependent on US and USSR defence outlays, the Korean War, defence reviews and the NATO 3 per cent commitment. Future contingencies include the possibility of a defence review, the adoption of a non-nuclear defence policy or continuing in the same mode.

In many respects, France is similar to the UK. France (see chapter five) is an example of a nation that is willing to pay for an independent defence policy reflected in its national nuclear forces, a domestic defence industry and substantial forces deployed overseas (e.g. Germany, Africa). Predictably, France has faced similar defence problems to those encountered in other nations such as expensive and rising weapons costs, technical progress and unsatisfactory programmes. A demand for military expenditure equation is estimated incorporating French GDP and the defence spending of the USSR, NATO and a set of African nations. Doubts are expressed about this approach and alternative explanations are explored. For the future, there are problems associated with manpower and the costs of purchasing equipment domestically.

West Germany (see chapter six) is geographically adjacent to France and similar to Japan in terms of its position at the end of the Second World War. Since 1956, it has created modern conventional forces with a substantial conscript element, committed to defence in the NATO region. In relation to debates about burden sharing, the point is made that Germany's defence budget does not reflect the true costs of its military effort (e.g. due to conscription, land and tax exemptions for allied forces in the Federal Republic). It is suggested that Germany's defence spending is determined by a combination of economic, political and military variables. Future military expenditure will depend on such factors as arms control, the role of nuclear deterrence in NATO, US forces in Europe, possibly greater emphasis on costly conventional forces and the opportunities for European solutions in providing and equipping defence forces. Like the UK and France, West Germany will also experience budgetary pressures due to costly new equipment programmes and the problems of recruiting sufficient manpower in an era when defence spending is unlikely to rise.

In our country studies, Sweden (see chapter seven) is distinctive in its adherence to the doctrine of armed neutrality. This requires it to be self-reliant for its defence in terms of forces, armaments production, large reserves of military personnel and a substantial civil defence programme. Empirical estimates of Sweden's demand for military expenditure confirm self-reliance prior to 1973; but in the period of flexible response after 1973, Sweden appears to have relied more on its NATO neighbour, Norway. A conclusion speculates on the defence budget implications of Sweden joining a Nordic Defence Pact as a response to possible US withdrawal from NATO.

Israel (see chapter eight) has a long history of regional conflict. As a result, it has a large defence budget which is influenced by Arab military spending, substantial imports of defence equipment and a defence-dependent economy. A model of military spending is formulated that includes the defence spending of Egypt, Syria and Jordan, war casualties, election cycles, inflation, corporate profits, and the military needs of the Israeli Defence Forces. Whereas defence spending responds to the threat, it is also the Israeli government's most important fiscal instrument for stimulating the economy and influencing elections.

Like Israel, India and Pakistan (see chapter nine) have a long history of conflict. They are relatively poor countries with substantial defence budgets showing the interaction between the poverty trap and the security dilemma, reflecting each nation's perception of the threat. India is possibly the Third World's largest arms producer, whereas Pakistan relies on imports of defence equipment. To the relatively small Pakistan, the Indian threat is dominant. Tests of the arms race model show that it is only relevant to Pakistan and that claims of an arms race on the Indian sub-continent probably reflect political rhetoric.

Informed public choices about defence expenditure and independent research work in the field require a reliable data base. A study of Argentina, Chile and Peru (see chapter ten) contributes by providing a constructive and critical account of the available data and its limitations, so enabling an assessment of the true burdens of defence spending in these countries. Questions arise as to whether defence spending in the three nations can be explained by arms race models or by the needs of internal security, and whether military governments spend more on defence than their civilian counterparts. Stress is placed on the quality of the available data and reservations are made about sophisticated models tested on poor quality data.

Japan (see chapter eleven) is an interesting contrast to West Germany in that traditionally, it has been committed to holding defence spending below 1 per cent of GNP, with its budget allocated to an all-volunteer Self-

Defence Force. However, like West Germany, its defence spending is related to that of the United States and it is a major market for American defence equipment. In view of its limitations on defence expenditure and its successful economic record, Japan is often presented as a classic example of a nation that has not yet experienced the economic burdens and crowding-out effects of military spending.

Estimating the demand for military expenditures

Most of our authors were asked to estimate the demand for military expenditures and empirical results are presented for the USA, UK, France, West Germany, Sweden and Israel, together with India and Pakistan (chapters two and four to nine). The empirical results bear some striking similarities and differences. The estimating equation for military expenditure, ME, has the following general form:

ME = f (income, spillin, threat, economic variables, political variables, dummies)

Income denotes the country's gross domestic product; spillins are the lagged military expenditure of a nation's allies; threat is the lagged military expenditure of a nation's adversary; economic variables may involve the size of the budget deficit; political variables may include the ruling government's party affiliation; and the dummies capture other environmental factors such as the presence of a war or a change in strategic doctrine (e.g. mutual assured destruction, flexible response). In spite of these similarities, differences arise among the various exercises owing to the underlying allocative process, the time period, the 'form' of the variables, the set of economic and political variables, and the dummies.

When deciding on the form of the estimating equation, the researcher may abide by one of two schools of thought. One school insists that the reduced-form equations correspond to a theoretical model of optimization. For example, Murdoch and Sandler (chapter seven) derive their estimating equations based upon the constrained maximization of some policy-making oligarchy, whose interests coincide with those of the nation's constituency. In the Murdoch and Sandler model, the constraint denotes the nation's budget constraint and may depict a constant-cost production transformation function. A second school of thought is more inductive in its orientation and chooses the estimating equation based upon statistical criteria. Both the Looney–Mehay and Aßmus–Zimmermann are examples (chapters two and six). No antecedent maximizing model may exist for equations estimated by the adherents of this second school.

When the estimating equation follows from an explicit maximization problem, the precise form of the equation is very sensitive to a host of factors including the maximizer's identity and viewpoint, the objective

7

function, the constraint, and the time period for which the study is to apply. For example, the maximizer's identity may be that of a ruling oligarchy or that of a voting public. In the latter case, a median voter representation is often used, in which the median voter (identified by median income) decides the outcome of an issue that can be measured along a single dimension. An example would be a referendum taken in a country to decide the level of military expenditure. The relevant constraint would be the median voter's own income constraint equating his income to the sum of his expenditure on private goods and his taxes for the publicly-provided defence goods. Such taxes are often dependent on the jurisdiction's population size, as each individual is assigned a share of defence cost. For some median-voter representations, per capita defence expenditure is regressed against per capita spillins. Other representations call for the share of gross domestic product devoted to defence to be regressed against other share expressions. With the first school, the message is clear: the terms in the estimating equations are determined by the theoretical construct and will change when the assumptions are altered. Even a change in the time period of estimation can change the set of environmental factors owing to theoretical considerations.

Adherents to the second school can select between equations to ensure that their estimations fit the data. Although these estimates often boast better fits than their theoretical counterparts, a clear trade-off is implied, because the underlying process behind the second school's estimated equations is unspecified. Moreover, estimates derived without a theoretical construct should not be compared with those with an explicit construct solely based on statistical criteria. If, for example, the choice of dummies depends on a priori reasoning, then these dummies should not be used by another estimation exercise when the time period differs and the assumptions of the original model are violated.

Many questions and issues with respect to estimating the demand for military expenditure remain. One such question concerns the preferred theoretical model to use in deriving a reduced-form equation for estimating demand. This question could be answered for a given country by constructing two or more theoretical models based upon different viewpoints, agents, allocative processes, constraints and objectives. If the resulting reduced-form equations are nested, as in the Aßmus–Zimmermann or the Murdoch–Sandler chapters (chapters six and seven), statistical tests can discriminate between models. If, however, the reduced-form equations are non-nested, then a non-nested test can be used, provided that the equations have the same dependent variable. In the future, researchers in defence economics will be better able to discriminate between models based upon theoretical and empirical considerations.

Another issue involves the choice between general and specific functional forms to represent the objective function. For example, Murdoch and Sandler (chapter seven) use a general utility function to depict the preference of the decision-making oligarchy. When, however, a median-voter model is used in the literature, a specific utility function (e.g. Stone–Geary) is often utilized to depict preferences. With a specific functional form, the demand equation is identified better; however, most specific forms restrict estimates of key economic parameters such as the income elasticity or the price elasticity of demand. If, say, a Cobb–Douglas utility function is imposed, then key parameters such as the price elasticity of demand must have a value of -1. The use of flexible functional forms, such as the transcendental logarithmic utility function, would allow the investigator to test for restrictions on the function's parameter, thereby permitting the data to determine, in part, the underlying preference structure. To date, empirical studies of the demand for military expenditure either use a general function or else impose a specific form, without regard to the severe restrictions implied. Thus far, flexible functional forms have not been employed.

When allies decide military expenditure, both static and dynamic processes are at work. The burden-sharing approach, whereby an ally determines its defence expenditure based upon the military expenditure (or spillins) of the other allies, is essentially a static maximization choice. Additionally, the 'guns-for-butter' (defence or social welfare) trade-off within an ally's economy is also a static process, in which a central government must decide the share of a budget devoted to various expenditure categories. Both of these burden sharing issues could be represented with a single theoretical model, provided that the optimizing viewpoint and constraints are those of the 'central government'. Dynamic considerations surface when an arms race characterizes the interaction between opposing alliances or adversaries. In fact, allies can themselves be engaged in an arms race – for example, Greece and Turkey in the NATO alliance. Elements of an arms race are shown in the Deger–Sen chapter on India and Pakistan and the Mintz–Ward–Bichler chapter on Israel (chapters eight and nine). If a theoretical construct is to be developed for an arms race, dynamic optimization in the form of optimal control or dynamic programming is appropriate.

As of yet, no theoretical framework has been developed to tie together both the static burden-sharing issue and the dynamic arms race process. Burden-sharing models treat threat (as measured by an enemy's lagged defence expenditure or its stock of armaments) as an environmental factor affecting the static optimization decision; arms race models often ignore the burden sharing issue. Neither approach is entirely satisfactory. Future research must tackle both the burden sharing and the arms race issues with a unified theoretical framework that is dynamic.

Another important issue concerns the distinction between the demand and supply sides of the defence question. The papers in this volume have focused on the demand side, thereby eschewing supply-side considerations. Supply-side considerations require the researcher to build a macro-economic model, in which a nation's income is related to private and public investment and consumption. In particular, the interaction between gross domestic product, investments, and defence expenditure must be disentangled. The empirical work of Smith, Mintz–Ward–Bichler, and Deger–Sen (chapters four, eight and nine) come closest to considering supply-side factors. To account for such interactions, a simultaneous-equation model is needed, in which demand and supply equations are clearly identified. Such an approach would limit the investigator to focusing on a single ally at a time. The supply side also requires a micro-economic analysis of the operation of defence equipment markets. Such markets are often imperfect and characterized by entry barriers so that they are non-contestable.

A final issue concerns the introduction of political variables into the estimating equation. These variables may identify the party affiliation of the government or the length of time between elections. With the emergence of public choice as a field, researchers have paid increased attention to the motivation and constraints of decision-making. No longer do researchers assume that policy-makers are only motivated by the common good. Agents in the political market-place such as voters, political parties, bureaucracies and other interest groups will seek to influence policy. Public choice considerations are clearly germane to the form and estimation of a nation's demand for military expenditure. Although political variables have been added to the estimating equation, their addition has been *ad hoc* with no clear explicit theoretical link. In the future, political variables need to follow from a clearer theoretical structure. In this area and elsewhere, there is the perpetual temptation to resort to measurement without theory.

Terrorism and the demand for military expenditure

Since 1968, terrorism has posed an increasing threat to international stability. Many countries had to allocate a larger portion of their military budgets in the 1980s to curbing terrorism. Terrorism is the premeditated use, or threat of use, of extra-normal violence or force to gain a political objective through fear or intimidation. For political terrorism, the emphasis must be placed on the political goal that the terrorist act, threat, or campaign is attempting to achieve. Terrorists direct their violence and threats at a target group not directly involved in the political decision-making process that the terrorists seek to influence. For instance, the Hezbollah is thought responsible for the kidnapping of Americans in Lebanon – an apparent attempt to force the US to remove its forces from the Persian Gulf and to limit its influence in the region. The kidnap victims were, of course, not directly involved with the US presence in the region. International or transnational terrorism concerns terrorist activities that include participants or victims from more than one nation. Incidents originating in one country and terminating in another (e.g. the hijacking of Kuwaiti flight no. 422 from Thailand in April 1988) are transnational, as are incidents involving the demands made of a nation other than the one at the scene (e.g. the demand by the kidnappers of a French television crew in Beirut that France repay a debt to Iran). In contrast, domestic terrorism does not generate spillovers to individuals or institutions abroad.

Many of the nations surveyed in this volume face significant threats of domestic and transnational terrorism. In 1987, Pakistan experienced 127 attacks conducted by the Afghan intelligence service (WAD) against Afghan refugees and Pakistani citizens. The UK and its troops are targeted by the Provisional Irish Republican Army (PIRA). West Germany experienced transnational threats from the Kurdish Worker's Party (PKK) and the PIRA, and domestic threats from the Revolutionary Cells (RZ) and the Red Army Faction (RAF). Israel is confronted with transnational and domestic threats from Palestinian groups such as the Abu Nidal Organization, the Popular Front for the Liberation of Palestine (PFLP), and the Palestine Liberation Organization (PLO). In recent years, Japan faced terrorist threats from the Chukaku-ha or Middle Core Faction. When, on 28 February 1986, a lone gunman assassinated Swedish Prime Minister Olaf Palme along a Stockholm street, even neutrality was seen to be no protection against terrorism.

As Scheetz points out in his chapter, Chile, Peru, and Argentina are threatened by a host of Marxist–Leninist groups (chapter ten). Chile is targeted by the Manuel Rodriguez Patriotic Front (FPMR); Peru is challenged by the Sendero Luminoso (SL) and the Tupac Amaru Revolutionary Movement (MRTA); and Columbia is confronted by the National Liberation Army (ELN), the Revolutionary Armed Forces of Columbia (FARC), the People's Liberation Army (ELP) and the 19 April Movement (M–19). In Latin America, terrorist groups can be quite large and well-supplied. For example, FARC claims approximately 9,000 combatants and is thought to be funded by profits from the narcotics trade. Given similar ideology, Latin American terrorist groups have united in their own alliances, e.g. the Simon Bolivar Guerrilla Co-ordinator links the Colombian groups under the leadership of FARC, whereas the American Battalion joins left-wing groups in Peru, Chile and Argentina. In Western Europe, the RAF, Action Directe (in France), and the Combatant Communist Cells (in Belgium) have co-ordinated attacks in recent years. Similarly, governments can respond to such terrorist alliances by co-ordinated action involving military and police forces, legislation, diplomacy and sanctions.

Domestic terrorist threats mean that a portion of military expenditure must be allocated for men and equipment to deter country-specific threats and to manage country-specific crises during incidents. When a nation suffers primarily from domestic terrorism, resources allocated to thwart terrorism provide little spillover benefits to its allies, unlike expenditure on strategic weapons or on conventional forces deployed along a probable battlefield such as the Rhine River plain in West Germany. Thus, the demand for military expenditures should try to net out military expenditures of one's allies on purely private, domestic activities (e.g. spending on domestic terrorism) when computing a spillin measure.

In the case of transnational terrorism, a nation's expenditure to thwart terrorism would confer spillin benefits on other nations that face a common threat. Hence, the formation of the American Battalion in 1984 poses a common threat to Peru, Chile, Argentina and other countries. Each of these nation's defence against the American Battalion provides public or spillin benefits to others. The same insight holds for some allies in NATO that confront common terrorist groups and campaigns. For transnational terrorism, the spillin measure for counter-terrorism should include the expenditure of all other countries, regardless of whether they are party to an official alliance, targeted by the same terrorist groups.

Given the escalation of terrorism in the 1980s and the emergence of state-sponsored terrorism, future demand estimates for military expenditure must account for the special characteristics of efforts by nations to thwart terrorism. Terrorism has become a low-level conflict that threatens more than half of the nations of the world.

Conclusion

Economists have allocated substantial professional resources to researching macro-economic problems such as inflation and growth, and micro-economic issues such as industrial economics and health economics. In contrast, and in relation to the size of military budgets, the economics profession has underinvested its resources in studying the economics of defence, disarmament and peace. This volume makes a modest contribution by adding to our knowledge in the field.

Country studies of the economics of defence spending serve at least two purposes. First, they provide valuable data that can be used to test a variety of hypotheses from the economics of defence. This volume provides examples of empirical work for demand and arms race models. Second, they show the diversity of international experience with nations adopting different solutions to allocating scarce resources for protection and security. As the following chapters show, there is a massive research agenda, with different nations providing case study material to test our models and to force us to develop new theories.

Chapter two

United States defence expenditures: trends and analysis[1]

Robert E. Looney and Stephen L. Mehay

Introduction

Either by formal treaty, presidential declaration or executive agreement
the US is committed to provide military support to more than 40 nations
throughout the world. Probably no other barometer of US capabilities in
fulfilling those commitments is so closely watched as the level of its
spending on defence. This is true even though it is debatable whether
measures of input are superior to measures of output, such as readiness or
performance, in gauging a nation's broad defence capabilities. The importance of defence expenditures as an overall indicator of military capability
is highlighted by events of the last decade. An apparent gap in spending
between the USSR and the US in the 1960s and 1970s prompted a rapid
acceleration of US military spending in the late 1970s and early 1980s.

The pattern of defence spending in the US since 1948 reveals a steady
upward trend in real outlays. Real military purchases (in 1982 dollars) rose
$2 billion per year on average between 1948 and 1986 (Higgs 1988: 16).
However, this steady upward trend has been punctuated by three periods
of rapid multi-year build-ups of real military outlays – 1950–3, 1965–8, and
1978–85. All of these mobilization periods have been followed by substantial reductions in real military outlays. For example, the congressional
authorization of $300 billion for fiscal year 1989 represents 11 per cent less
in real terms than spending in the peak year of 1985, and 1 per cent less
than the previous year.[2]

As a result of the complexity of forces underlying the US budgetary
process, single theories have not been particularly accurate in either
accounting for past spending patterns, or in providing insights to future
allocations. At least nine factors have been advanced at one time or
another to account for defence spending patterns (Schneider 1988: 54):

1 international events
2 changing administrations
3 public opinion
4 congressional attitudes

5 domestic economic constraints
6 perceptions of the Soviet threat
7 arms control agreements
8 elections
9 inter-service rivalries

To this list we might add such factors as expenditures by allies, burden sharing among alliance members, and macro-economic stabilization considerations. Clearly, several of these explanations overlap, and they are likely to have had varying strengths and operated in conjunction with dissimilar sets of forces during the various sub-periods outlined above. In addition, the feedback effects from economic performance to future levels of defence expenditures are complex and not well understood.

None the less, all of these threads – domestic budget and political considerations, relationships between allies and external threats – are woven into the final decision on the amount of defence spending. The purpose of this chapter is to develop a model of the relationships between a nation's observed level of defence spending and its economic performance, domestic political status and external spillovers. The chapter starts by reviewing past economic performance of the US economy and how past defence choices have been influenced by economic and strategic conditions. Second, it examines the current position of the economy, recent economic policy developments and forecasts for future growth. Third, it highlights trends in defence spending and discusses current defence policies and trade-offs.

A secondary purpose of this chapter is to estimate a military expenditure demand function for the US using time series data. Accordingly, it assesses the importance of various factors that have been proposed as explanations of defence spending patterns, and then briefly reviews previous models of defence spending from the economics literature. Much of this literature has concentrated primarily on examining the interactions between spending levels of alliance members, principally NATO (Murdoch and Sandler 1984). Although economic models of defence spending are used as a guide to appropriate specification of an expenditure demand function for the US, the main goal of the chapter is not to estimate spillover effects between the US and its allies. Instead, the demand function is specified in an attempt to assess the relative importance of the causal factors in the list above. This section also tests the model of the demand for military expenditures, and discusses the empirical results. Finally, the chapter presents concluding remarks and an appraisal of future directions of US defence spending.

Past performance of the US economy

Although economic considerations seldom directly dictate military strategies, economic realities eventually impinge on the decision process. At one level, military planners mostly ignore economics when devising strategies and determining appropriate force requirements. Ideally, foreign policy objectives are established first, then a military strategy and force structure are designed to meet those objectives. The cost of this force structure determines the defence budget, at which point the economic environment and budget priorities enter the picture (Olvey *et al.* 1984). In reality, this ideal sequence is often completely reversed, as in the recent Gramm–Rudman era. In this sequence, economic constraints and budgetary ceilings dictate the acceptable force-structure options. The alternative selected is the one that best meets the foreign policy objectives.

Regardless of the process whereby foreign policy objectives and military programmes are aligned, ultimately a nation's current real income and future economic growth set important constraints on the fulfilment of basic military strategies – 'in some measure, military power reflects economic power' (US Commission on Integrated Long-Term Strategy 1988: 6). These basic economic parameters not only determine a nation's ability to meet its military requirements but also establish the opportunity costs of doing so. During wartime, of course, nations must mobilize a significant share of the nation's scarce resources for military activities. Both the US in 1944 and Iraq in 1986 devoted over 41 per cent of GNP to military purchases. But even during peacetime strategic choices vary tremendously. Although estimates of Soviet defence spending vary considerably (Becker 1986), by most accounts the Soviet defence burden (as a per cent of GNP) is between 15 and 17 per cent, at least three times larger than the defence burden of the US. Other extremes in defence burdens include poor nations that devote a high portion of their GNP to the military (North Korea, 23 per cent; Syria, 22 per cent; Libya, 18 per cent) and wealthy nations that devote a low share to the military (Japan, 1 per cent; Austria, 1.3 per cent).

Although wide variations in the share of GNP devoted to defence are observed, over time sustained economic growth is necessary to maintain a high level of defence effort. A slowdown in aggregate economic growth constrains the growth of national defence expenditures because the burden of defence spending increases. In a slow- or no-growth environment, the implicit cost of increasing the share of defence expenditures, in terms of foregone capital formation and civilian production, increases sharply.

The relationship between economic growth and defence efforts is underscored by recent events in the Soviet Union. The most reliable data on Soviet military expenditures (compiled by the CIA) indicate that the growth rate of Soviet defence outlays began to decrease after 1977. A major cause of this slowdown was a pronounced slowdown in the growth of the Soviet economy (Brada and Graves 1988). The slowdown in economic growth increased the implicit cost of continuing to divert resources to arms production, something the new Soviet leadership under Gorbachev was

The economics of defence spending

Table 2.1 Performance of the US economy

Year	Growth rate (%)[a]	Unemployment rate (%)	Inflation rate[b]	Federal deficit ($bn)	Trade balance ($bn)
1960	2.2	5.5	1.5	0.3	5,191
1965	5.8	4.5	1.9	-1.4	8,378
1970	-0.3	4.9	5.5	-2.8	5,773
1975	-1.3	8.5	7.0	-53.2	22,984
1980	-0.2	7.1	12.4	-73.8	9,466
1982	-2.5	9.7	3.9	-127.9	278
1984	6.8	7.5	4.0	-185.3	-94,835
1985	3.0	7.2	3.8	-212.3	-101,083
1986	2.9	7.0	1.1	-221.2	-125,684
1987	2.9	6.2	4.4	-150.4	na
1988	2.4[p]	5.4[c]	na	-146.7[d]	na

Source: Council of Economic Advisers, *Economic Report of President*, Feb. 1988
Notes: [a] Percentage change in real GNP, 1982 $.
[b] Percentage change in all items of CPI.
[c] Annual rate for March, 1988.
[d] Preliminary forecast.
na = not available.

reluctant to do. Thus, the real rate of growth of defence – especially procurement – was cut drastically (Ofer 1987).

Economic growth plays an equally important role in constraining US defence efforts. Statistical indicators of the performance of the US economy since 1960 are displayed in Table 2.1. The most notable feature of the economic landscape in the early 1980s was the recession in 1981–3. A trough was reached in 1982 when the unemployment rate peaked at 9.7 per cent, and the economy registered a 2.5 per cent decline in real GNP. Since 1982, however, economic growth has been robust, exceeding that of most other industrialized western nations. By July 1988 the economy had experienced 69 months of economic expansion, and the unemployment rate had reduced to 5.4 per cent, a level many economists believe represents the natural rate of unemployment.[3] The annual growth rate of real GNP averaged 3.8 per cent between 1982 and 1987, exceeding the growth rates of West Germany, Italy, Great Britain and France but falling slightly below that of Japan.[4] As Table 2.2 indicates US growth also outpaced the Soviet economy.

There is considerable debate over the precise causes of the continuous expansion of the economy in the last 5 to 6 years.[5] Some economists attribute the expansion to standard demand-side (Keynesian) economic policies, whereas others trace the expansion to the supply-side policies instituted by the Reagan Administration. The supply-side stimulus was spurred principally by the Economic Recovery Tax Act of 1981, which reduced the maximum tax bracket from 70 per cent to 50 per cent and cut income taxes by about 23 per cent over the 3 years following 1981. Generous provisions for the treatment of depreciation and R & D

Table 2.2 Relative annual growth rates

Period	US	European Community	USSR
1966–70[a]	3.0	4.6	5.0
1971–75[a]	2.2	2.9	3.0
1976–80[a]	3.4	3.0	2.3
1982	−2.5	0.8	2.7
1984	6.8	2.4	1.5
1986	2.9	2.6	3.8
1987	2.9	2.3	1.0

Source: Council of Economic Advisers, Economic Report of the President, Feb. 1988
Note: [a] Measured as average annual growth rate of real GNP (in %).

expenditures also were introduced into the law. The tax cut clearly stimulated investment spending, which contributed to the economic growth record.

However, the rapid growth also can be traced in part to substantial increases in federal government spending. In real terms total spending grew by 30 per cent from 1980 to 1987. The federal tax cuts of 1981 were put in place at roughly the same time that a major buildup in defence spending was launched.

A major concern for the economy has been the federal deficits incurred during this period. Because the anticipated supply-side boost to productive activity from the tax cut was not as great as expected, tax revenues fell short of expectations, producing unprecedented peacetime budget deficits. Until 1982 deficits typically represented less than 1 per cent of GNP; since 1982 the federal deficit has averaged 4.6 per cent of GNP. As Table 2.1 shows, federal deficits grew from $73bn in 1980 to a peak of $221bn in 1986, representing about 5 per cent of GNP and 18 per cent of federal government expenditures. The accumulated debt has caused considerable controversy in the US, including calls for a constitutional amendment requiring a balanced budget. More important was passage of the Emergency Deficit Control (Gramm–Rudman–Hollings) Act of 1985 that mandated automatic spending cuts if progress was not made towards eliminating the budget deficit by 1991.

Regardless of the stimulative effect of deficit spending, there are numerous other macro-economic consequences of the large federal deficit. The low rate of saving since 1982 is explained in part by the high rate of government dissaving, and has been blamed in part for holding down capital formation and long-term economic growth. In addition, the budget deficit appears to carry some of the blame for a growing external deficit. Payment of interest and dividends abroad increased the current account deficit to a record $125bn in 1986. The federal deficit also may have acted as a brake on the recovery of labour productivity (output per manhour). The importance of labour productivity can be seen by its relationship with GNP growth. When labour productivity in the business sector of the economy was growing briskly between 1948 and 1973 by 2.8 per cent per year, real GNP growth averaged 3.7 per cent annually. However, when labour productivity growth fell to only 0.7 per cent annually from 1973 to 1981, the growth rate of real GNP also dropped to only 2.2 per cent. Some improvement has been achieved in labour productivity since 1981, with an annual growth rate of 1.2 per cent between 1981 and 1986 (Council of Economic Advisers 1987), but this remains an important question for the future.[6]

Recent policy developments and prospects

After the stock market crash of October 1987 the US economy appeared to be teetering between the potential for recession on the one hand and renewed fears of inflation on the other. However, consumer and investor confidence recovered quickly and the index of leading indicators has consistently pointed toward continued expansion. Recession fears have ebbed and the economy is projected to grow at roughly 2.75 per cent annually in 1988 and 1989.[7] Mid-term projections show the economy growing at 3.3 per cent annually for the 1989–93 period, a rate which is in line with the post-war average. Indeed, some analysts are predicting the post-1982 economic expansion may last for several more years.[8]

Part of the strength of the economy is derived from continued improvement in real net exports. The dollar has depreciated sharply since March 1985 leading to a 17 per cent increase in exports of goods and services in 1987. Indeed, for the first time since 1980, the contribution to growth of real net exports has become positive. In part the need for additional capacity will stem from export demand. Business fixed investment rose 3.7 per cent in 1987 after a precipitous decline in 1986, and it is forecast to rise 4.4 per cent in 1988.

Despite the recent depreciation of the dollar and the fall in unemployment, inflation has not accelerated. With productivity growth in manufacturing averaging 3.5 per cent per annum, unit labour costs have fallen almost continuously since 1982. The outlook for inflation is good but guarded. Whereas the inflation rate is expected to increase slightly from 3 per cent in late 1987 to 4.5 per cent in late 1989, numerous factors could change that picture rather quickly.

A major policy debate that has surfaced in the US, which has national defence implications, concerns the causes of the reduced competitiveness of US products in world markets. Some analysts argue that the current economic expansion and improvement in exports are due solely to the depreciation of the dollar. They feel that the underlying structural causes of the competitive weakness of US goods abroad have not improved. A part of this problem is that compared to, say, Japan, the US invests far less in civilian R & D.

Other analysts have argued that conditions have improved in American manufacturing and they forecast further improvements in industrial competitiveness. They cite healthy improvements in labour productivity, R & D spending, and investment-to-output ratios. They also cite improvements in product quality control by American manufacturers and the recent restraint in wage demands and increases.[9]

Support for the latter group is provided by several long-term forecasts of positive US productivity growth. The personal saving rate (as a percentage of disposable income) increased somewhat in 1987 to 5 per cent from its near-record low of 3 per cent in mid-1987, and it is forecast to improve further in 1988. Other factors cited for these rosy forecasts are: (a) increases in the age and, therefore, experience of the US labour force; (b) recent declines in energy prices; and (c) increased expenditures on R & D. However, it should be noted that some offsetting factors are at work. Whereas the 1986 Tax Reform Act further lowered the maximum marginal tax rate from 50 per cent to 33 per cent, incentives for investment also were reduced. The Act increased the tax rate on nominal capital gains, eliminated the investment tax credit, and eliminated the generous treatment of depreciation expenses. Thus, gains in productivity stemming from improvements in saving and investment remain a question mark for the economy.

The federal deficit is projected to remain around $150bn for fiscal 1988 and 1989. This implies a neutral fiscal stance and places major reliance on monetary policy to stabilize economic fluctuations. It is also noteworthy that, as a percentage of GNP, the US budget deficit is either less than or about the same as that of Italy, Canada and France, and only slightly exceeds that of West Germany. Moreover, the federal government deficit is in part offset by the surpluses consistently run by state and local governments ($57bn in 1986) and the significant surpluses building up in the social security fund, which are expected to grow from $20bn in 1987 to $46bn in 1989 and to nearly $100bn by 1993.

In summary, economic influences on defence spending will come from two sources – one positive and one negative. The pressure to slow federal spending to meet the deficit-cutting guidelines in Gramm–Rudman will likely translate into no real growth of defence spending, and possibly real cuts through at least 1991. The positive effect will stem from continued growth of the economy, which will likely buoy federal tax revenues and lessen the need for deeper cuts. Of course, factoring in changes in international events and domestic political events, such as the change in administration in 1989, muddies the water but probably does not alter the basic directions determined by economic considerations.

Trade-offs and choices in defence spending

Recent defence policies in the US highlight the interaction between economic constraints and defence strategies. After the Soviet invasion of Afghanistan in 1979, President Carter announced in 1980 that any attempt to gain control of the Persian Gulf region would be considered an assault on the vital interests of the US. Thus, the Carter Doctrine, as it came to be known, imposed a new obligation on US conventional forces already strained to meet existing commitments in Europe and the Far East. Thus, one legacy of the Carter Administration was a huge gap between military obligations and the resources necessary to meet the new requirements (Record 1984).

The Reagan Administration pursued a military strategy that emphasized the ability of the US to wage war simultaneously on several fronts, a concept that was implicit in the Carter Doctrine. The Administration also was committed to expanding and modernizing conventional forces in order to implement this strategy in reality as well as on paper. Thus, Reagan undertook to finance the obligations implied by the multi-front strategy with major sustained real increases in defence spending. In 1981 the Reagan Administration embraced the goal of the US Navy, established as early as 1974, of the 600-ship fleet, including 15 carrier battlegroups, 100 attack submarines and the amphibious lift capability for four Marine brigades. In 1986 the Navy introduced 'The Maritime Strategy', the objectives of which are, in the event of war, to exert global pressure on Soviet naval forces and to strike targets in Soviet home waters and on the Soviet mainland (Watkins 1986). Although the objectives of 'The Maritime Strategy' provide the foundation for the 600-ship fleet, they have been the subject of intense debate and scrutiny (Kaufmann 1987).

The figures in Table 2.3 represent the evolution of US defence expenditures by major mission over the last decade. Following adoption of the Carter Doctrine and the multi-front strategy by the Reagan Administration the share of the defence budget devoted to conventional forces expanded considerably, from 32 per cent in 1975 to 42.4 per cent in 1985. This increase in conventional forces also reflects the outlays necessary to meet the buildup to the 600-ship navy. Note, too, that some increase in the percentage of the budget devoted to nuclear forces has occurred as the Reagan Administration has sought modernization of these weapons systems.

The main missions that appear to have suffered under the recent defence buildup are 'Training, Medical and Other Personnel Activities', and 'Support of Other Nations'. It is noteworthy that the Guard and Reserve Forces have grown proportionately to the overall growth in defence spending in line with adoption of the Total Force Concept in the 1970s. The reserves play an increasingly important role in US

Table 2.3 DOD expenditures by mission – 1975–85 (total spending, $bn, and percentage distribution)

Summary by programme	1975 ($)	1975 (%)	1980 ($)	1980 (%)	1985 ($)	1985 (%)
Strategic forces	7.2	8.25	11.1	7.8	27.8	9.8
General purpose forces	28.1	32.0	52.2	36.6	120.6	42.4
Intelligence and communications	6.3	7.2	9.1	6.4	25.1	8.8
Airlift and sealift	0.9	1.0	2.1	1.5	7.0	2.4
Guard and reserve forces	4.8	5.5	7.9	5.5	15.7	5.5
Research and development	7.7	8.7	11.9	8.3	24.6	8.6
Central supply and maintenance	9.1	10.3	16.0	11.2	24.4	8.5
Training, medical and other general personnel activities	20.0	22.8	29.2	20.5	33.1	11.6
Administration and associated activities	2.0	2.3	2.5	1.7	5.9	2.1
Support of other nations	1.8	2.0	0.6	0.4	0.5	0.2
Total	87.9	100.0	142.6	100.0	284.7	100.0

Source: Office of Management and Budget, *Budget of US Government*, various years

conventional force strategies, and that role is programmed to expand in the future.

Defence versus social programmes

There are numerous ways to represent the relative burden of defence spending on an economy, and the social opportunity cost of defence. In this section military spending is measured as purchases of newly produced goods and services, a component of the National Income and Product

Table 2.4 Shares of GNP (per cent)

Year	Government–military[a]	Government–non–military[b]	Private[c]
1950	5.0	8.5	86.5
1960	8.8	10.7	80.5
1965	7.2	12.4	80.4
1970	7.6	13.9	78.5
1975	5.6	15.4	79.0
1980	5.2	14.2	80.6
1982	6.1	14.1	79.8
1983	6.3	13.5	80.2
1984	6.2	13.2	80.6
1985	6.5	13.9	79.6
1986	6.6	13.9	79.5
1987	6.6	14.0	79.4

Sources: Higgs (1988); *Economic Report of President*, Feb. 1988
Notes: [a] Military purchases as percentage of GNP.
[b] Total government (all levels) purchases as percentage of GNP.
[c] Sum of consumption, investment, plus net exports as percentage of GNP.

Accounts, rather than the budgetary outlays of the Defense Department.[10] Table 2.4 divides GNP into three exhaustive categories – military purchases, other government purchases (by all levels of government), and the residual all-private purchases. Private purchases are composed of the sum of consumption, investment, and net export spending.

Viewed in this light, since 1950 the military share of GNP reached a peak of 8.8 per cent in 1960 and declined for the next 20 years to a low of 5.2 per cent in 1980. The share grew after 1980 stabilizing at 6.6 per cent. It is not clear whether non-defence programmes and the private sector, or both, tend to grow at the expense of defence. The government non-military share grew steadily until 1975, and has fallen slightly since. Conversely, the private share of GNP declined until 1960, where it has remained essentially constant.

Higgs (1988) investigated this issue further and concluded that in the 1948–86 period the government non-military share of GNP gained at the expense of both the military and private share. However, his analysis showed that 'changes' in the military share were almost exactly offset by opposite changes in the private share. A one percentage point 'increase' in the military share of GNP was offset by a one percentage point 'decrease' in the private sector share. A partial explanation for this tendency is provided in Table 2.5, which computes the percentage of federal expenditures accounted for by defence and by federal transfer payments. In 1966, defence purchases were almost 43 per cent of total outlays; by 1980 they had fallen to only 23 per cent. Conversely, transfer payments had risen from 23 per cent of federal expenditures in 1966 to over 40 per cent in 1980. Thus, defence programmes and transfer programmes have reversed their relative positions in the federal budget.

Table 2.5 Shares of Federal Government spending

Year	Federal expenditures ($bn)	Defence purchases (%)	Federal transfer – payments to individuals (%)
1966	145.3	42.6	23.0
1970	207.8	36.9	29.6
1975	364.2	24.6	40.3
1980	615.1	23.2	40.2
1982	781.2	24.8	40.4
1984	895.6	26.1	38.4
1985	984.6	26.3	37.2
1986	1,032.0	26.9	37.3
1987	1,069.1	27.6	37.5

Source: Economic Report of the President, Feb. 1988

Current defence policies

Recent policy initiatives have proceeded along two fronts – one political, the other technological. Diplomatic efforts have produced the Intermediate Nuclear Forces (INF) treaty, which eliminates missiles in western Europe with ranges between 300 and 3,000 miles. Negotiations are also proceeding on START (Strategic Arms Reduction Talks), the goal of which is large reductions in the superpowers' nuclear forces. At the Reykjavik summit in 1986 Gorbachev offered a 50 per cent cutback in nuclear weapons contingent upon the US stopping research on the Strategic Defense Initiative (SDI).

SDI is the technological direction that has been pursued actively by the Reagan Administration since 1983. The defensive system seeks to develop both ground-based and space-based interceptors that would destroy attacking missiles immediately after launch, rather than just before the warheads strike their targets. In 1987 DOD approved a plan to fund six specific projects to be operational by the mid-1990s and built at a cost of $250bn over the entire period (Heppenheimer 1988). This would produce a defensive force, known as Phase I, with the capability of destroying about one-fourth of attacking Soviet missiles. The advantage of Phase I is that it would strengthen deterrence by increasing the uncertainty of the success of a Soviet first-strike. If just one quarter of Soviet missiles can be destroyed, the Soviets must consider the possibility that sufficient US missiles will survive the first strike and be launched in retaliation to destroy considerable Soviet targets.

It is clear that the technological (SDI) and diplomatic initiatives are complementary. By proceeding with SDI development the US will be in a better position to negotiate treaties on new missile systems (e.g. fast-burn rocket boosters) that offer no military advantages to either side once Phase I is in place. Indeed, the current improved climate of superpower relations may be traced in part to American insistence upon continued funding of SDI.

The administration's plans, however, have been forced to yield to domestic budget and political realities. Although Congress authorized $4bn to be spent on SDI in fiscal year 1989 it revealed a strong scepticism of the more exotic space-based interceptors, reducing the allocation to such systems to a meagre $85m for fiscal year 1989. Congress continues to push ground-based interceptors, and allocated $350m for such systems in 1989.[11] In October 1988 the Defense Department acceded to these political and fiscal pressures by reducing the proposed number of space-based interceptors by one-half, and stretching out completion of the first phase of SDI to the late 1990s.

Similarly, the Reagan Administration requested $800m for the multiple-warhead MX offensive system and only $200m for the single-warhead

Midgetman. The Democratic-controlled Congress allotted $250m to each and set aside another $250m for the incoming administration to allocate as it wishes. President Reagan vetoed the entire defence authorization bill in August 1988 and was able to reach some compromises with Congress in the final bill. None the less, the future of SDI and the different offensive systems will be influenced by the party that wins the presidency in 1989. Whereas the Republicans favour the MX and Midgetman offensive systems and SDI, the Democrats oppose all three systems.

The successful negotiation of the INF treaty with the USSR to reduce short- and medium-range nuclear missiles in Central Europe presents some drawbacks as well as obvious benefits. As the number of nuclear weapons held by each side drops, the US and its NATO allies will be forced to turn their attention to conventional weapons. Unfortunately, as Table 2.6 shows, the Warsaw Pact nations maintain a substantial superiority in

Table 2.6 NATO/Warsaw Pact conventional forces, 1987

| | Atlantic to Urals[a] | | Global | |
	NATO	WP	NATO	WP
Manpower (000)				
Active ground forces	2,385	2,292	2,992	2,829
Reserve ground forces	4,371	4,276	5,502	5,348
Ground force equipment				
Main battle tanks	22,200	52,200	30,500	68,300
Artillery mortar	13,700	46,500	24,100	64,000
Anti-tank weapons[b]	10,570	17,650	20,120	24,970
SAM	2,250	12,850	3,000	16,150
Helicopters (armed)	780	1,630	2,020	2,130
MICV	4,200	25,800	8,000	34,400
Land combat aircraft				
Bombers	285	450	518	1,182
Attack	2,108	2,144	5,157	3,119
Interceptors/fighters	899	4,930	1,763	5,265
Naval forces				
Submarines	196	231	238	301
Carriers	16	2	23	4
Cruisers/destroyers/frigates	358	224	400	309
Amphibious	200	100	250	123
FAC	168	238	168	415
Naval air				
Bombers	38	250	38	390
Attack	379	177	621	235
Interceptors/fighters	180	12	264	12
ASW (includes helo.)	535	374	1,179	544

Source: International Institute of Strategic Studies (1987)
Notes: [a] For NATO includes most of Western Europe. For the Warsaw Pact, includes Soviet forces in Moscow, Volga, Ural, and North and Trans-Caucasus Military Districts.
[b] Includes ground-based and helicopter.

conventional forces in Europe. The cost of conventional weapons significantly exceeds that of nuclear weapons, and attempts by the US and its European allies to reduce the gap with the Warsaw Pact will impose greater strains on alliance budgets.

Factors influencing defence spending

This section discusses more fully the factors mentioned in the introductory section as potential determinants of defence spending levels. These factors will be used to specify an empirical model of the demand for defence output.

International events

As might be expected both the Korean and Vietnam wars had a great impact on US defence spending, with the Korean war producing by far the stronger effect. According to Kahn (1982: 47):

> In June 1950, the United States Congress was engaged in a great debate over whether the defense budget should be $14, $15, or $16 billion. Along came the North Korean attack on South Korea. Congress quickly authorized $60 billion, an increase by a factor of four ... that authorization alone represented an enormous military defeat for the Soviets. And yet it was almost three years before the funding was fully translated into increased defense expenditures and corresponding military power ... the fear of an impending Soviet attack on Western Europe – and the attack on South Korea – provided most of the motivation for the 300 per cent increase in new obligational authority.

The Vietnam war produced a less dramatic example of an international event stimulating higher allocations to the US defence budget, as did the Soviet invasion of Afghanistan in December 1979. Other examples of international events affecting defence spending were the activist policy that the Soviet Union pursued during the mid-1970s in the Middle East, Angola and Ethiopia. These actions certainly contributed to the upward trend in US expenditures that began about this time.

Changing administrations – the electoral cycle

The allocation and distribution of federal resources is an inherently political process. A major issue in assessing the United States defence budget centres around the control of the military budget by the executive branch. As Zuk and Woodbury (1986: 446) note, this is done in two ways. First, because a large portion of the defence budget, unlike social security spending, is not mandated by law, the President has wide latitude in formulating the defence budget. The dollars involved in defence spending and the President's ability to influence such spending gain more importance when it is realized that military spending requests from the chief executive are rarely reduced by Congress.

Zuk and Woodbury found that in the years in which Congress cut the total request, the average decrease was 2 per cent and never exceeded 5.3 per cent. And although Congress is prone to make programmatic changes in the defence spending categories of procurement, R & D, and military construction, the fact remains that only twice in the last 30 years has Congress altered executive budget requests by more than 10 per cent in the more important procurement and R & D categories. From this they conclude that the President's proposals are usually approved, and the large sums spent for defence can indeed be used to influence macro-economic conditions.

The best examples of incoming presidents changing defence spending in the post-war era are Kennedy and Reagan, both of whom opted for increased spending. The 1960 Democratic Party platform specifically promised to recast the US military capability to provide forces and weapons of a diversity, balance and mobility sufficient to deter both limited and general aggressors. This concept eventually produced the Kennedy–McNamara strategic doctrine of 'flexible response', which in itself increased defence costs (Schneider 1988: 56). The Reagan Administration is an even stronger example of a new leadership determined to increase defence spending.

In an analysis of US electoral cycles, Zuk and Woodbury (1986) found no support for an electoral-defence spending cycle in the post-war era. In three of the nine presidential contests, defence spending decreased substantially rather than increased during the election year. Moreover, three of the six times defence spending rose, the change was quite modest, ranging from 2.1 per cent to 3.8 per cent. Also, the other three election increases occurred either during wartime or during periods when US–USSR relations were especially bad. In summary, Zuk and Woodbury were unable to find a systematic relationship between defence spending and presidential elections.[12] The implication of these results seems to be that defence spending in the United States is probably not used on a systematic basis by the President or Congress as a macro-economic policy instrument and, by extension, not used for the purpose of winning elections.

Public opinion

In a democratic society electoral competition normally ensures that in the long run some correlation exists between what the public wants and what governments provide. However, between elections elected officials must rely on voter opinion. Perhaps the best example of the link between public opinion and defence expenditures concerns the so-called 'Vietnam Syndrome'. From 1971 to 1978 more Americans favoured cuts than favoured increases in defence spending. The percentage favouring increased spending then mounted very sharply until 1980, after which it again sharply declined.

The factors that may have brought about the downward trend in support for defence spending in the 1980s are many and complex. Among the more important were probably the prolonged and serious recession of 1981–3, a perception that the Reagan Administration was pouring money into the Pentagon while cutting back on social programmes, and growing awareness of the federal budget deficit as a national concern (Schneider 1988: 64). Whatever the reasons, by mid-1985, the American public was in favour of cutting defence spending ahead of a whole host of social programmes, usually by lopsided margins.

As for the direct relationship between public opinion regarding defence spending (increase or decrease) and total authorized spending, spending began to recover in 1975 well before those favouring increases began to outnumber those favouring cuts. However, the plurality favouring more spending peaked in early 1980, about 5 years before total authorized allocations peaked. Indeed the Reagan Administration (and Congress) continued to increase total authorized allocations for about 3 years after the public shifted back to favouring less defence spending. One author concludes that the relationship between public opinion on defence and actual spending is fairly weak:

> spending increases *usually* occurred when the opinion balance was positive; spending decreases *usually* occurred when the opinion balance was negative. But no closer connection has been found. Linkages between the public and defense decision makers clearly had much slack and there is little basis for portraying defense policies as responses to articulate public demands (Higgs 1988: 47).

Congress

Congress plays a significant role in determining defence spending. The executive branch essentially sets the general level of spending by its request to Congress, and the legislative branch normally either cuts or increases the amount requested and some sort of compromise emerges. Korb (1982) has analysed Congressional responses to executive branch proposals for defence spending, and has noted a sharp change following Vietnam. From the outbreak of the Korean War through 1968, the Pentagon enjoyed a special relationship with the Congress in that, compared to the non-defence agencies of the federal government, the Pentagon's budget requests were almost always treated favourably by the legislative branch. Defence cutbacks in this period averaged only 1.7 per cent whereas those in the non-defence areas were more than five times greater (9.2 per cent).

However, beginning with the first budget presented to Congress after the Tet offensive (fiscal year 1970), the legislative branch completely reversed its attitude toward defence and non-defence programmes. From fiscal year 1970 to fiscal year 1975, the Democrat-controlled legislature appropriated more money than the Republican presidents sought in 4 of the 6 years. The total impact of Congress in this period was to increase federal spending by 0.5 per cent. However, it achieved this by slashing a full 6 per cent from defence requests and adding nearly 5 per cent to the non-defence portion of the budget.

Perceptions of the Soviet threat

The very notion of defence conjures up, at least by implication some sort of threat. Clearly the only perceived serious threat to the United States is that posed by the Soviet Union. Beginning in the early 1960s the Soviets undertook a rapid expansion of military capabilities. If one excludes the incremental costs of the war in Southeast Asia, by 1968 the Soviets had forged ahead of the United States in the amount of money allocated annually to defence (Korb 1982: 52). Moreover, because the Pentagon was forced to expend a large percentage of its budget first for prosecuting the war in Southeast Asia and then for paying the additional personnel costs caused by the changeover to the all-volunteer force, the Kremlin began to outstrip the United States in outlays for a wide spectrum of military capabilities.[13]

This situation continued through the 1970s, so that by the end of that decade the gravity of the military threat posed by the Soviet Union began to impress the American people and their leaders. The changing military

Table 2.7 US–USSR strategic nuclear warhead inventory, 1960–84

Year	US			USSR		
	Delivery vehicles[a]	Warheads	Yield[b]	Delivery vehicles[a]	Warheads	Yield[b]
1960	529	1,734	1,812	215	415	475
1965	2,034	4,110	4,433	442	598	2,066
1970	2,255	5,074	4,213	1,891	2,047	6,915
1975	2,145	9,170	3,386	2,458	2,614	6,723
1980	2,040	9,668	3,265	2,645	7,451	4,766
1984	1,986	10,630	2,771	2,728	9,146	5,170

Source: Brada and Graves (1988)
Notes: [a] Aircraft and missiles.
[b] In megatons.

balance between the two nations began to appear in quantifiable measures. For example, as Table 2.7 shows, the US enjoyed strategic superiority to the USSR for many years. But this superiority was lost by the 1970s when the USSR achieved strategic parity, if not dominance.

To deal with this situation the Carter Administration, which had planned to cut defence spending by $5–7bn, actually raised the fiscal year 1979 and 1980 defence budgets by 3 per cent in real terms and pledged to maintain continued real increases of that magnitude for the foreseeable future. Congress, which had been hostile to absolute or relative increases in defence spending throughout 1969–78, ultimately appropriated the 3 per cent increase requested by the administration and urged the President to devote even more resources to areas like strategic nuclear forces and naval combatants.

Arms control agreements

It is impossible to assess the degree to which arms control agreements have affected United States military spending. As one observer has noted:

> When one considers such programs as the ABM, B–1, and Trident – all of which received considerable funding during the first SALT negotiations – one begins to wonder if SALT 1 produced *any* economic savings (Blacker and Duffy 1984: 248).

Here, probably the more significant factor reducing defence expenditures was the general spirit of *détente* that lasted for a period of time in the 1970s.

It may be that the way arms control agreements affect spending is simply not easily observed. For example, the US and USSR are on the verge of a strategic arms agreement (START) that would leave each nation with 6,000 warheads, about one-half of the current US arsenal. Although this agreement would have a minor direct effect on spending, it could have indirect effects. As an illustration, DOD could decide to reduce the number of warheads allocated to the Navy and increase the allocation of land-based missiles controlled by the Air Force, a change in force structure that would require fewer costly Trident submarines. Another possibility is that spending could rise if each side takes steps to better protect their remaining arsenals, such as via the SDI programme in the US.

Inter-service rivalries

Many Washington observers have noted that inter-service rivalries have tended to push defence spending upward. Ball (1980) contends that during the Eisenhower era, the Navy typically asked for more than twice as many submarines as the administration saw fit to authorize, and that in the early 1960s, Air Force requests for Minuteman missiles were for about 1,000 more than the Defense Department would approve. He also states that the Air Force lobby in Congress succeeded in obtaining funds for the manned bomber from fiscal year 1962 to fiscal year 1966 that were over and above those requested by the administration.

Whereas this and other anecdotal evidence is suggestive, it is hardly conclusive evidence that inter-service rivalry has caused US military expenditures to be higher than they otherwise would have been. Apart from specific cases of one service or another pressing for particular programmes to be included in the defence budget, a key manifestation of inter-service rivalries affecting military spending is the drive of each to obtain, preserve and maximize its share of the total.

Schneider (1988) concludes that inter-service rivalries have tended to make the defence budget larger than it otherwise would have been, and tended to maintain the shares of each service near their traditional levels. However, no comprehensive empirical test of this hypothesis has been attempted.

Moreover, there is little reason to expect this factor to have played an important role in defence spending levels as the relative service shares have been stable over time. The Air Force received a larger share (average 35 per cent) than the other services during most of the 1948–85 period, followed by the Navy (31.5 per cent), and the Army (26.7 per cent). The Army's share increased during the land wars in Korea and Vietnam. Finally, the Navy's share has gradually increased from about 30 per cent in the early 1970s to about 34 per cent in the last several years, due to the buildup to the 600-ship navy.

Alliances and burden sharing

A final factor to consider in explaining military expenditures is the manner in which US expenditures are affected by those of its major NATO allies. Olson and Zeckhauser (1966) argued that in alliances the pure public good attribute of national defence and differences in member size combine to create free-riding behaviour by smaller alliance members. These theoretical arguments have added fuel to what has become a major policy controversy – the question of continued US military support of South Korea, Japan and NATO. For example, estimates of the share of the US defence budget devoted to the defence of Western Europe ranges from 50 to 64 per cent (Krauss 1986).[14] The combined wealth of the NATO member nations has prompted many analysts to argue that NATO–Europe should assume a larger share of the cost of its own defence. The US Senate has informally instituted a 'burden sharing initiative' and appointed a special representative who will negotiate with allied nations to increase their share of defence costs.[15]

It should be noted, however, that analysts have also pointed out that defence output is composed of different types of weapons systems, which vary in the degree of publicness. Consequently, some defence outlays may induce complementary behaviour by allies rather than the substitution effects envisioned by Olson and Zeckhauser. Murdoch and Sandler (1984) and Sandler (1988) indicate that burden sharing in the NATO alliance crucially depends on the ratio of private (country-specific) benefits to the total benefits derived from the alliance arsenal. The larger this ratio, the greater the degree to which allies' contributions will match efficient provision levels for defence expenditures. A high proportion of private benefits induces allies to pay for their own share of defence outlays rather than relying on other allies to provide security, because these benefits can be withdrawn at will by the provider unless a payment is received.

When, however, the arsenal provides benefits that are mostly public (alliance-wide) as in the case of nuclear deterrence, greater burdens are placed on the dominant allies with the largest economies. In the case of public benefits, a defence provider finds it difficult if not impossible, to exclude other allies from relying on the defence benefits derived from its arsenal. Those allies with the most at stake become the contributors.

Sandler's work indicates that during most of the 1950s and into the 1960s, the European NATO countries were able to free-ride on the US nuclear deterrence capability. Since the early 1970s, however, it appears that a decline in the role of nuclear deterrence and implementation of the 'flexible response' doctrine as a viable defence strategy has shifted the burdens toward the European countries. Murdoch and Sandler's empirical results are not inconsistent with the hypothesis that the flexible response doctrine has reduced free-riding through an induced complementarity among the jointly produced defence outputs.

Empirical analysis

Several previous studies have specified and estimated demand functions for military output. Most formal models of the demand for military output have employed an approach that involves maximizing a social utility function subject to a general budget constraint (Smith 1980; Murdoch and Sandler 1982; 1984). The Murdoch and Sandler studies yielded important insights by modelling NATO's decision structure as a Nash–Cournot process. None the less, this approach ignored the role of the internal political process in collective choices. Dudley and Montmarquette (1981) attempted to correct this omission by formulating an explicit collective choice model of defence spending. The median voter theorem was employed to derive military expenditure demand functions and to empirically estimate tax-price and income elasticities for defence. Their effort was only partially successful because many of the nations in their empirical sample either were non-democratic or based on proportional representation.

The median voter theorem postulates a single-dimensional issue space in which each issue is decided by a direct vote of fully informed voters. These requirements may appear restrictive especially because most political systems are representative rather than direct democracies. However, Downs (1957) has demonstrated that in a two-party system, electoral competition between the parties produces essentially the same outcome as the median voter theorem.

One key feature of the median voter model that may limit its application at the national level is the assumption (Borcherding and Deacon 1972) that governments supply output at the point where marginal cost equals demand and, in return, obtain a budget equal to the minimum necessary cost of producing the selected output level. Although this assumption may be reasonable for local governments, which ultimately are constrained by the mobility of residents, it is questionable for central governments. Perhaps most important, the median voter paradigm rules out autonomous behaviour by government decision-makers on output and price.

With these weaknesses in mind, Gonzalez and Mehay (1987) analysed military spending utilizing a theoretical framework that stresses the ability of decision-makers to choose between alternative fiscal outcomes. The model integrates the role of bureaux in basic supply decisions and in the determination of defence output (Niskanen 1971; 1975). Gonzalez and Mehay argued that, in contrast with the median voter model, a bureau supply model appears to be more compatible with the expenditure determination process at the central government level.

Because the appropriate conceptual collective choice paradigm for specifying a defence spending model is not settled, in this chapter the question is framed in terms of the budget level achieved by defence decision-makers. This approach is compatible with a Niskanen-type bureau supply model where decision-makers act to maximize budget size. Note that this maximand in the Niskanen model is equivalent to output maximization so long as the marginal benefit of output is positive. Bureaux are subject to the constraint that cost cannot exceed output.[16]

Defence decision-makers are hypothesized to adjust expenditures over time to bridge the gap between what decision-makers consider to be the optimal level of defence capability, and that which exists at any point in time. The optimal level of preparedness is assumed to be a function of events such as the Vietnam war and *détente*, and factors such as domestic economic constraints, NATO responses, the perceived Soviet threat, inter-service rivalries and perhaps the election cycle and/or whether a Republican or Democrat administration is in power.

Obviously each of the factors discussed above makes a priori sense. However, whether or not it makes a significant contribution to our understanding of the pattern of US military expenditures is clearly an empirical issue. A major problem lies in the fact that because of deficiencies in the data, several of the factors are probably not capable of being empirically tested (public opinion, congressional attitudes, arms control agreements and inter-service rivalry). In this chapter an attempt is made to model factors such as the Soviet threat, domestic economic constraints, international events like Vietnam, and NATO burden sharing relationships. The purpose of the empirical analysis is not so much to test the implications of a particular theoretical model of government decision-making as to assess the relative importance of the various demand factors already identified.

The technique adopted here is to evaluate competing hypotheses concerning the relative importance of the factors already identified. Defence decision-making is assumed to be characterized by a partial adjustment process, which can be represented as follows:

$$M_t = \alpha M_t^* + (1 - \alpha) M_{t-1} \tag{1}$$

where M_t is actual military spending in time t, M_t^* is the desired level, and α is the coefficient of adjustment. Thus, observed expenditures are a weighted average of the desired expenditures at t and the actual expenditures in the previous period. We further assume that M_t is a linear function of the factors already mentioned:

$$M_t^* = \beta_0 + \sum_{i=1}^{k} \beta_i x_t^i + \varepsilon_t \tag{2}$$

Substituting equation (2) into equation (1) yields the partial adjustment model:

$$M_t = \alpha\beta_0 + \alpha \sum \beta_i x_t^i + (1 - \alpha) M_{t-1} + \alpha\varepsilon_t \tag{3}$$

In specifying equation (3) for empirical estimation, it is assumed that domestic economic considerations and the Soviet threat constitute the most important determinants of desired military spending levels. The speed of adjustment α is assumed to be a constant. Thus, the primary model to be estimated is

$$
\begin{aligned}
&\qquad\quad + \qquad\qquad + \qquad\qquad + \qquad\qquad - \\
MX_t = {}& a + b_1\, MX_{t-1} + b_2\, REXP_t + b_3\, RUEXP_t + b_4\, UCPI_t \\
&\qquad\quad + \qquad\qquad - \qquad\qquad + \\
&+ b_5\, REVD_t + b_6\, DEF_{t-1} + b_7\, VIET + e_t
\end{aligned} \tag{4}
$$

where MX_t is real US defence spending in year t ($\$$ m), MX_{t-1} is US defence spending lagged one year, $REXP_t$ is expected Soviet defence spending, $RUEXP_t$ is unanticipated Soviet defence spending, $UCPI_t$ is unanticipated US inflation, $REVD_t$ is the deviation from the trend in federal revenue, DEF_{t-1} is the federal deficit lagged one year, VIET is a dummy variable for the Vietnam War period, and e_t is an error term.

The Soviet threat is proxied by the expected level of real Soviet military expenditures. The expected spending variable is constructed by regressing the level of Soviet military expenditures each year on its value for the previous year. This variable should have a positive effect on MX if Soviet spending levels are employed as indicators of Soviet military intentions by US decision-makers and they are able to alter budget requests in response to the perceived threat.

Changes in US domestic economic constraints are also assumed to influence the level of optimal (desired) spending levels by defence decision-makers. Desired spending is further assumed to depend on the rate of unanticipated inflation in the US, the federal budget deficit, and on the revenue side, deviations from the trend in real federal revenues. Inflation concerns are proxied by increases in unexpected inflation. Unanticipated inflation is constructed as the difference between actual and expected inflation, where the latter is obtained by regressing the inflation rate each year on its value for the previous year. If inflation accelerates, it is assumed that budget-makers react by holding down discretionary expenditures, especially defence. Similarly, if the economy is growing more rapidly than projected, the growth of federal revenues will exceed projected levels and discretionary expenditures will tend to grow. The previous year's budget deficit should have an obvious constraining effect on defence spending. Note that since the economic variables, especially REVD, reflect the level and growth rate of the economy, GNP is not included as an explanatory variable in the specification. The basic model also includes a dummy variable (VIET) for the Vietnam War period (equal to 1 for 1967–72, 0 otherwise).

It should be pointed out why some of the potential factors discussed in a previous section were omitted from the specification. The impact of inter-service rivalry could have been measured by each service's share of total defence outlays. However, as these shares have been relatively stable over the period covered by the data, very little variation in the data would have been observed. Similarly, presidential or congressional elections could have been measured by the party in power, but it was unclear which political party has consistently influenced defence spending, and in which direction.

The expected signs of the coefficients are indicated above the variables in equation (4). Data used for the estimation are for the 1965–85 period.[17] Because of serial correlation of the residuals, the model is estimated using the first-order autoregressive iterative (Cochrance–Orcutt) technique. Parameter estimates are presented in Table 2.8.

In column 1 a basic model is estimated that includes as explanatory variables only the Soviet threat, lagged US spending, and a dummy variable for the Vietnam War period. The results of the estimation are fairly robust; the coefficients have the expected sign and are statistically

Table 2.8 Parameter estimates of spending model

Variable	Equation (1)	Equation (2)	Equation (3)	Equation (4)
MX_{t-1}	0.723	0.740	0.935	0.916
	$(4.31)^a$	(8.29)	(14.22)	(14.22)
REXP	0.642	0.844	0.361	0.295
	(2.88)	(6.03)	(5.21)	(3.94)
VIET	28,007	27,580	17,282	14,987
	(2.47)	(5.12)	(3.78)	(2.79)
UCPI	—	−204,497	−247,085	−246,543
		(6.18)	(7.66)	(7.13)
REVD	—	203.85	261.36	232.93
		(3.92)	(5.50)	(4.26)
DEF_{t-1}	—	−67.39	−91.91	−92.94
		(1.86)	(2.74)	(2.77)
NATODT	—	—	5,227.27	6,067.25
			(7.62)	(9.65)
DETENT	—	—	—	−3,073.80
				(1.20)
Constant	−111,300	−159,505	−68,046	−48,071
ρ	0.533	0.629	0.196	0.027
R^r_{adj}	0.622	0.897	0.965	0.974
F statistic	10.90	27.31	73.68	85.67
DW^b	2.86	2.15	2.82	2.56

Notes: [a] t ratios in parentheses.
[b] DW, Durbin–Watson statistic.

significant. The adjusted R^2 indicates that the basic model accounts for about 62 per cent of the variation over time in US spending.

Column 2 in Table 2.8 introduces the effect of domestic economic constraints into the estimation. Again, in all cases the signs of the estimated coefficients are as expected and they are statistically significant. Moreover, this model explains about 90 per cent of the variation in defence spending.

Column 3 introduces NATO members' spending into the model. The NATO variable, NATODT, is measured as the deviation from the trend in total NATO spending (net of US spending), where the trend is established by first estimating a linear trend equation. Again, it is hypothesized that US defence budget-makers adjust the optimal spending levels based on European NATO spending levels. Although the coefficient of NATODT in column 3 is statistically significant, the positive sign indicates that unexpected increases in European NATO member spending tends to induce US decision-makers to increase, rather than lower, their own spending. This provides some evidence that the US does not free-ride on the NATO alliance. Unfortunately, it is difficult to compare these results to those of earlier studies that observed free-riding by the US (Murdoch and Sandler 1982; 1984) due to differences in theoretical and empirical specifications.

Finally, in column 4 of Table 2.8 the impact of *détente* is included in the estimation. DETENT is a dummy variable equal to 1 for the period when cold war tensions were relaxed in 1972–6. The results in column 4 indicate that the period of *détente* had the expected downward effect on US spending, although the coefficient is not significant.

Conclusions

US defence expenditures are likely to level off or decline in real terms over the next 5 years or so. The major factor driving the military build up in the early 1980s – the perceived Soviet threat – appears to be subsiding, or at least is not the burning political issue it was in the late 1970s. Even if it were, fears of increased inflation, concern over budget deficits, and Gramm–Rudman budget-cutting would make any major increases extremely unlikely. This future period of retrenchment confronts defence policy-makers with an unusually large number of challenges.

It is possible that the Gramm–Rudman–Hollings Balanced Budget Act will require deep cuts in defence spending and painful trade-offs both between social and defence programmes, and across different types of defence programmes. For example, if military pay cuts are selected as one quick-fix method of reducing military outlays, force manning and readiness may suffer, as it did in the late 1970s when the military-to-civilian pay ratio fell dramatically. Reduced recruitment and retention may bring renewed calls for reinstituting the draft for first-term personnel, with all of the potential social disruptions.

However, the probability of a serious fiscal crunch will probably be mitigated by the strong economic growth of the US economy. With continued economic growth the economy will continue to generate high growth rates of personal income and federal tax revenues, which should enable DOD to meet primary force structure objectives within the confines of Gramm–Rudman. Moreover, the impact of any cuts on national security will be lessened by the improvement in superpower relations and the apparent willingness of the Soviet leadership to reduce their military posture.

The slowdown in Soviet economic growth provides a partial explanation for why the USSR has agreed to negotiate the INF treaty, to withdraw from Afghanistan, and appears willing to discuss conventional, as well as nuclear, arms reductions. The US defence buildup in the 1980s posed a serious policy dilemma for the Soviet leadership. If the Soviets had followed suit, the cost could have been further economic stagnation of the civilian economy, reduced capital formation, and even lower future growth. This ultimately would reduce the ability of the economy to meet future military requirements. On the other hand, if the Soviets had not followed suit, they may have found themselves at a severe military disadvantage. They appear to have chosen a diplomatic route that reduces any military advantages that the US would otherwise have achieved without unduly raising defence spending requirements in the Soviet Union.

Future US defence directions

Future US defence strategies are, of course, difficult to predict and depend heavily on evolving international relations. The future international climate will depend in part on the policy changes currently underway in the Soviet Union. Some observers have concluded that the new policies of *perestroika* and *glasnost*, and the restructuring of the Soviet economy are signalling an era of benign Soviet foreign policies. Many observers, however, have argued that it is unlikely that the current reform movement will lead the Soviet Union to significantly reduce its military capabilities (Lee 1986; Zycher 1986). They point out that military strength is the only reason the USSR has achieved superpower status. Therefore, they conclude it is dangerous to believe that the poor performance of the Soviet economy will force the USSR to disarm. Unilateral or even bilateral disarmament would reduce the USSR to a second-rate world power, whereas the US still would remain a super ower.

A second area of uncertainty in international relations is the growth of other potential superpowers. The US Commission on Integrated Long-Term Strategy (1988) argues that rapid economic growth in Japan, and the projected growth of China (following their own economic reforms) will confront strategic planners with a future world composed of as many as four, or more, major military powers. It should be added that this multi-polar world will be further complicated by the likely emergence of an economically integrated Western Europe in the early 1990s, which may choose to pursue its own independent security goals. Clearly, the grand US defence strategy that has worked so well since the Second World War will need to be altered to incorporate a wider range of contingencies and international relationships. Strategic planning will require greater flexibility if the US is to attain a military posture sufficiently robust to deal with future superpower alignments.

Notes

1 The materials for this chapter were completed in 1988. The views, opinions and findings in this paper are those of the authors and should not be construed as official policy of any agency of the US government. The authors would like to thank Rodolfo Gonzalez, Todd Sandler, and James Tritten, Commander USN for helpful comments.
2 *The Economist,* 16 July 1988, p. 24.
3 *Business Week,* 8 August 1988, p. 20.
4 *The Economist,* 16 July 1988, pp. 61–2.
5 *Business Week,* 15 August 1988, p. 30.

6 'The productivity paradox', *Business Week,* 6 June 1988, p. 100.
7 OECD, *OECD Economic Outlook,* June 1988, Paris.
8 *Business Week,* 15 August 1988, p. 30.
9 *Business Week,* 8 August 1988, p. 18.
10 DOD outlays include military pensions, which have become the fastest growing segment of the budget. Also, some defence-related purchases originate in government departments other than DOD.
11 *The Economist,* 16 July 1988, p. 24.
12 Zuk and Woodbury feel that their results are consistent with those of Krell (1981), who found the irregular pattern of US expenditures to have been largely determined by two international factors – war and the state of relations with the Soviet Union. The picture is not this straightforward, however, because the war–defence spending relationship apparently varies by type of defence spending.
13 It should be noted that estimates of Soviet spending levels vary widely. Becker (1986) surveys the various methods of estimation.
14 In 1986, the US maintained 250,000 military personnel in West Germany, 75,000 in other parts of Europe, 43,000 in South Korea, and 48,000 in Japan (US Secretary of Defense, 1988).
15 *Navy Times,* 25 July 1988, p. 15. See US General Accounting Office (1988) for a history and evaluation of defence burden sharing initiatives.
16 See Gonzalez and Mehay (1987) for a detailed derivation of the model.
17 Military spending data are in constant dollars and are derived from US Arms Control and Disarmament Agency, *World Military Expenditures and Arms Transfers,* Washington, DC, various issues. Economic data are taken from the International Monetary Fund, *International Financial Statistics Yearbook,* Washington, DC, various issues.

References

Ball, D. (1980) *Politics and Force Levels,* University of California Press.
Becker, A. (1986) *Sitting on Bayonets: The Soviet Defense Burden and the Slowdown of Soviet Defense Spending,* Santa Monica, Calif.: Rand Corporation.
Blacker, C. and Duffy, G. (eds) (1984) *International Arms Control: Issues and Arguments,* Stanford University Press.
Borcherding, T. and Deacon, R. (1972) 'The demand for the services of non-federal governments', *American Economic Review,* 891–901.
Brada, J. and Graves, R. (1988) 'The slowdown in Soviet defense expenditures', *Southern Economic Journal* 54: 969–84.
Downs, A. (1957) *An Economic Theory of Democracy,* New York: Harper & Row.
Dudley, L. and Montmarquette, C. (1981) 'The demand for military expenditures: an international comparison', *Public Choice* 37: 5–31.
Gonzalez, R. and Mehay, S. (1987) 'Economies of size and spillovers in defense spending', paper presented to Public Choice Society Annual General Meetings, Tucson, Arizona.
Heppenheimer, T. (1988) 'Keeping the peace', *Reason* 20: 24–30.
Higgs, R. (1988) 'Guns versus butter and roads: output shares and public preferences in the US: 1939–1986', mimeograph, Department of Economics, Lafayette College.
International Institute of Strategic Studies (1987) *The Military Balance 1987–1988,* London.

Kahn, H. (1980) *US Strategic Security in the 1980s,* New York: Hudson Institute.
—— (1982) *The Nature and Feasibility of War, Deterrence and Arms Control,* New York: Hudson Institute.
Kaufmann, W. (1985) *The 1986 Defense Budget,* Washington, DC: Brookings Institution.
—— (1987) *A Thoroughly Efficient Navy,* Washington, DC: Brookings Institution.
Korb, L. (1982) 'The defense policy of the United States', in D. Murray and P. Viotti (eds) *The Defense Policy of Nations,* Baltimore: John Hopkins University Press.
Krauss, M. (1986) *How NATO Weakens the West,* New York: Simon & Schuster.
Krell, G. (1981) 'Capitalism and armaments: business cycles and defense spending in the US, 1945–1979', *Journal of Peace Research* 18: 221–40.
Lee, D. (1986) 'Arms negotiations, the Soviet economy and democratically induced delusions', *Contemporary Policy Issues* 4: 22–37.
Lee, L. (1987) 'Time to rethink defense', *Challenge,* Mar./Apr.: 15–20.
Murdoch, J. and Sandler, T. (1982). 'A theoretical and empirical analysis of NATO', *Journal of Conflict Resolution* 26: 237–63.
—— (1984) 'Complementarity, free riding, and the military expenditures of NATO allies', *Journal of Public Economics* 25: 83–101.
Nelson, D. and Lepgold, J. (1986) 'Alliances and burden sharing: a NATO– Warsaw Pact comparison', *Defense Analysis* 2, 1: 205–24.
Niskanen, W. (1971) *Bureaucracy and Representative Government,* Chicago: Aldine.
—— (1975) 'Bureaucrats and politicians', *Journal of Law and Economics* 18: 617–43.
Ofer, G. (1987) 'Soviet economic growth: 1928–1985', *Journal of Economic Literature* 25: 1767–833.
Olson, M. and Zeckhauser, R. (1966) 'An economic theory of alliances', *Review of Economics and Statistics* 48: 266–79.
Olvey, L., Golden, J. and Kelly, R. (1984) *The Economics of National Security,* NJ: Avery.
Record, J. (1984) *Revising US Military Strategy,* Washington, DC: Pergamon– Brassey's.
Sandler, T. (1977) 'Impurity of defense: an application to the economic theory of alliances', *Kyklos* 30: 443–60.
—— (1988) 'Sharing burdens in NATO', *Challenge* 31: 29–35.
Sandler, T. and Forbes, J. (1980) 'Burden sharing, strategy, and the design of NATO', *Economic Inquiry* 18: 425–44.
Schneider, E. (1988) 'Causal factors in variations in US postwar defense spending', *Defense Analysis* 4: 53–79.
Smith, R. (1980) 'The demand for military expenditures', *Economic Journal* 80: 811–20.
Stubbs, E. and Nimroddy, R. (1987) 'The Soviet response to Star Wars', *Challenge* 30: 21–7.
US Commission on Integrated Long-Term Strategy (1988) *Discriminate Deterrence,* Washington, DC: USGPO.
US Council of Economic Advisers (various years) *Economic Report of the President,* Washington, DC: USGPO.
US General Accounting Office (1988) *US Defense Burden Sharing with Japan and NATO Allies,* testimony before House Armed Services Committee, Washington, DC.
US Secretary of Defense (1988) *Annual Report to Congress FY1988,* Washington, DC: USGPO.

Watkins, Admiral J. (1986) The Maritime Strategy, Annapolis, Md: US Naval Institute Press.

Wells, S. (1983) 'A question of priorities: a comparison of the Carter and Reagan defense programs', *Orbis*, Autumn.

Zuk, G. and Woodbury, N. (1986) 'US defense spending, electoral cycles, and Soviet–American relations', *Journal of Conflict Resolution*, 445–68.

Zycher, B. (1986) 'Soviet incentives in arms control', *Contemporary Policy Issues* 4: 52–9.

Chapter three

The political economy of military effort in the Warsaw Treaty Organization

Daniel N. Nelson

Introduction

For the USSR and the six East European members of the Warsaw Treaty Organization (WTO, or Warsaw Pact), the economics of defence spending were once largely moot. Soviet hegemony obviated choices that might have been made among East European states based upon their own economic considerations. Poland, the German Democratic Republic, Czechoslovakia, Hungary and Bulgaria acted as junior partners in the Warsaw Pact because their ruling regimes' political futures depended on it, economic consequences notwithstanding. Romania's behaviour, from 1964 distinctive within the alliance, nevertheless had substantial limits to the breadth or depth of its 'independence'.

In this chapter a full treatment of the complex political economy of a multi-state European communist system and its relationship with expenditures for defence is impossible. Nevertheless, it is important to underscore at the outset that the theme of choices and alternatives elaborated elsewhere in this book – the perennial guns-for-butter debate in Western competitive democracies – was less relevant to the Warsaw Pact during most of its first three decades (1955–85). During these decades, the defence policies of member states were inextricably interwoven within the political and economic hegemony of the USSR and the mutual dependencies created by that regional dominance.[1] Romania was the exception to this generalization, but still remained within the Pact, and exercised choice only to limited degrees on specific issues (e.g. relations with Israel or China and arms control). Choices were made at the margins of foreign and defence policies, if at all, effecting modest changes in Soviet use of the WTO for its own security planning.

In the era of Mikhail Gorbachev, this has changed and Eastern Europe and the USSR have become less bound to one another, and their development and maintenance of military forces are now less intertwined. At least through the mid-1980s, however, politically and economically forced defence policies produced high levels of military effort by WTO member states that, in turn, evoked substantial burdens – that is, social, economic and political costs.

Indeed, there are suggestive findings that deteriorating economic conditions may be one of the best predictors of heightened military-related activity in European communist states; rather than defence commitments having economic consequences, economic conditions have consequences for defence preparations and activities.[2] This observation is, no doubt, nothing more than the common-sense notion of reciprocal causation. The linkage between defence and economics in state socialist systems tied together by political dependencies certainly will have recursive characteristics, although they may be difficult to isolate.

Unlike other contributions to this volume, then, this essay has as its focus not economic consequences of military spending *per se*, but the interplay of political conditions that engender higher military effort and associated economic and political burdens. It outlines developments up to 1988, so providing the essential context prior to events in Eastern Europe and the USSR in 1989–90.

Existing literature on the economics of military effort in the WTO

A substantial literature now exists on the Warsaw Pact. An early examination of Soviet–East European relations within the context of the WTO was Robin Remington's *The Warsaw Pact: Case Studies of Communist Conflict Resolution*.[3] Among books in the last decade about the WTO,[4] however, there is very little discussion of burden in the sense of socio-economic trade-offs as a consequence of military effort. And, although there is often citation of statistics regarding extractive military effort (expenditures and armed-forces manpower), only Jones[5] and Simon[6] systematically have used data about an element of military performance (i.e. WTO manoeuvres).

Recent discussion of defence effort and its related burden in the WTO has been very limited. Even the Soviet case, although the statistic is often cited that the USSR has allocated 12–14 per cent or more of GNP to defence, has received less analysis than one might expect. Compilations of data about the Soviet military[7] provide no guide to socio-economic trade-offs, and general discussions of the Soviet economic condition devote little to what might be social and economic consequences of military commitments.[8] The debate about precise estimates of Soviet defence spending has been ongoing.[9] Yet analyses of the burden imposed by such effort remain very few – the out-dated volume on *Economic Performance and Military Burden in the Soviet Union*[10] from which Cohn's article, 'The Economic Burden of Soviet Defense Outlays' was most instructive, Becker's Rand study,[11] a brief exploratory article by Hildebrandt,[12] and studies by Cohn[13] and Bond,[14] both from a Joint Economic Committee volume, *Soviet Military Economic Relations*. There are, to be sure, many efforts to look at the linkage between problems in the Soviet economy and their national security,[15] but such efforts do not tap directly the issue of burden. Other studies such as Mosley,[16] although considering negative aspects of military spending, do not undertake a systematic, long-term analysis that includes hypothesis testing efforts.

Thad P. Alton's work on military expenditures, which has helped greatly to assess levels and trends in one dimension of resource extraction for defence, has constituted the only long-term effort regarding Eastern Europe.[17] There has been, in addition, a modest interest in testing the 'collective goods' theory of Olson and Zeckhauser in the WTO context. The path-breaking comparative study almost two decades ago by Russett[18] addressed such theoretical issues, and included the USSR and Warsaw Pact in his analysis. Reisinger[19] and Oppenheimer[20] are more recent examples of this debate. More descriptive, and with a focus on arms production and military missions apparently assigned to various states' forces, is Condoleezza Rice's chapter in Halloway and Sharp[21] on 'Defense Burden-Sharing'. Rice's effort has the advantage of considering performance as an element of military effort (rather than using extractive measures alone), but offers few comparative or longitudinal data, and makes no effort at testing hypotheses.

The interplay of society, economy and military effort, connoted by the term 'defence burden', has thus been addressed minimally in existing literature about the USSR and Eastern Europe. Yet there is often the recognition that popular dissatisfaction, and the potential for instability, are related to trade-offs between social welfare, economic performance and military effort.

Military effort, defence burden: conceptual distinctions

The Soviet Union and the six East European members of the WTO clearly undertook substantial military efforts through to 1988. The measurement and interpretation of such efforts, however, have been matters of ongoing controversy among military, governmental and academic analysts in the West. Precisely how large the military efforts of individual WTO members are, and the degree to which such commitments can properly be said to engender 'burdens', are empirical questions; yet, what one observes and the kind of data employed to answer these questions depends on a broader conceptual understanding.

Military effort and defence burden, although intertwined, are analytically distinct. Military effort, which has both extractive (taking human and material resources from a society and economy) and performance (conducting manoeuvres, producing arms and exporting them, sending armed forces abroad) dimensions, can involve activities that connote no burden whatsoever. 'Burden' necessarily involves costs to the actor – actually uncompensated utilization of resources or opportunity costs (e.g. labour made unavailable, or productive capacity occupied, due to military needs). Yet some military effort such as exporting arms can provide substantial 'benefits', rather than cost, to a nation-state. Further, the extraction of manpower for the military may not mean, entirely, a 'burden'; construction, harvesting and other economic roles are fulfilled by the regular military in many countries.

To the degree that trade-offs among alternative and sometimes competing goals are a consequence of military effort, defence burden is created. I anticipate that such burden would be measurable via comparisons of trends in socio-economic conditions v. military effort, in investments v. consumption as a share of GNP and in an analysis of relationships between economic performance (GNP growth and productivity growth rates) and military effort. As military commitments rise and fall, do social expenditures or investment/consumption levels change proportionately? What are the apparent trade-offs involved? As various indicators of military effort rise, does a country's socio-economic standing and economic performance suffer? We would be hard pressed, of course, to argue that 'burden' is present if social expenditures – as a surrogate for social well-being – rise as a proportion of total expenditures or of GNP, even as absolute amounts of military spending go up. Likewise, economic growth, coextensive with increasing military effort, would not suggest burdensome consequences. Were social expenditures and economic growth to continue or accelerate, however, it is still possible that a state would be 'burdened' by military effort were that effort to exceed the norm for all nation-states of similar size, population and wealth. In other words, we ought not to look solely within individual states for measures of a concept like 'defence burden', because it is only through comparison that judgements and interpretations can make analytical sense.

I propose, then, to address broad conceptual issues by asking: What are the dimensions of military effort and how can we measure them? What constitutes burden and how can we assess degrees of burden? Such an endeavour will involve comments on variations in each state's military effort during the 1970s and 1980s, as well as aggregate portraits of the Warsaw Pact's commitment to defence in the same period. Defence burden will be tracked over the same span. The emergence of new trade-offs inherent to military effort may become evident in that period, as the maintenance or expansion of extractive and performance levels cost some WTO societies and economies relatively more than others.

Beyond conceptual and descriptive endeavours, I will explore plausible explanations for variation in military effort and defence burden within the Warsaw Pact. From previous studies, I have found that the measures of international tension affect Soviet and East European military commitments, diminishing cohesion as co-operative interactions become more common between NATO and the WTO.[22] The USSR's own allocation of resources to defence may help to maintain a high base-line of effort, but other factors appear to account for variations over time. Most important, 'domestic' political conditions – specifically, public support for the system and leadership turnover may depict the stability or instability of the regime. These would, coupled with measures of a country's economic health, be likely to exhibit a strong linkage with military commitments.[23] Assessments of these relationships are implicit to much of the following discussion.

Military effort: extractive and performance demands in WTO states

Extractive demand

Extractive military effort, as defined here, constitutes the manpower and material resources allocated by authoritative decision-makers to armed forces. Several measures can be used to tap such an 'input' side of military effort. Here, because of their availability and standardized calculation, I employ data reported by the US Arms Control and Disarmament Agency's annual *World Military Expenditures and Arms Transfers*. Three primary indicators are discussed below: 1. military expenditures as a proportion of central government expenditures, or ME/CGE, 2. military expenditures as a proportion of gross national product, or ME/GNP, and 3. armed forces per 1,000 population, or FORCE/1,000.

From these indicators, data through 1985 provide a view of military effort in the Warsaw Pact characterized by continued high or very high levels of extractive effort. When compared with other advanced industrial states using 1985 data, the Soviet Union and four of its WTO allies – Bulgaria, East Germany, Poland and Czechoslovakia – equal or exceed the United States' ME/GNP, which has been in the 5–7 per cent range for the entire post-Vietnam era.[24] The Warsaw Pact, as a region, was – again according to ACDA calculations – second only to the Middle East in its overall ME/GNP ratio; in 1985, the WTO's regional ME/GNP ratio was 10.7 per cent, whereas the Middle East was at 15.6 per cent.[25] The Soviet Union, itself, is said by ACDA to have decreased marginally its expenditures as a proportion of GNP from a high of 13.7 per cent in 1975 to 12.5 per cent in 1985 (see Table 3.1). The latter figure, however, still places the USSR in the top decile of all nation-states; of 144 states for which ACDA reported 1985 data, the USSR ranked thirteenth in ME/GNP. Non-Soviet Warsaw Pact members (NSWP) also have high ME/GNP ratios, with Bulgaria and the GDR placed in the second decile (ranking twenty-second and thirty-fifth in the world), whereas Poland and Czechoslovakia ranked forty-second and forty-third respectively (i.e. in

Table 3.1 Extractive military effort: ME/GNP (per cent)

	1975	1976	1977	1978	1979	1980	1981	1982	1983	1984	1985
Soviet Union	13.7	13.3	13.0	12.8	12.9	13.0	12.9	12.7	12.6	12.6	12.5
Bulgaria	7.9	7.7	7.9	7.4	7.0	7.3	7.2	7.8	8.0	7.8	8.0
Czechoslovakia	5.9	5.7	5.5	5.5	5.3	5.4	5.5	5.8	5.9	5.7	5.8
Poland	5.7	5.3	5.2	5.0	5.1	5.3	5.5	6.3	5.7	5.8	6.0
East Germany	6.0	6.0	5.9	5.9	5.8	5.8	5.9	6.3	6.3	6.3	6.4
Romania	5.7	5.3	5.2	5.0	5.1	5.3	5.5	6.3	5.7	5.8	6.0
Hungary	4.7	4.4	4.8	4.2	4.1	4.4	4.4	4.3	4.2	4.0	4.4

the third decile), and Hungary and Romania fell into the fourth decile with ME/GNP ranks of fifty-second and fifty-third.

When military expenditures are considered as a proportion of central government expenditures, the most recent data suggest a continuing trend in the USSR towards smaller ME/CGE ratios – down to 49.6 per cent in 1985 from a high (in the 11-year period) of 65.3 per cent in 1975 (see Table 3.2). The United States, by contrast, has not devoted more than 30 per cent of its CGE to defence in the same period. Nevertheless, the Soviet government, if Western estimating procedures are correct, still devotes an enormously large proportion of its total spending to its armed forces and, even at the lower figure in 1985, remains easily in the top decile of all nation-states. Afghanistan, Iraq, Taiwan and Vietnam are the only states exceeding the Soviet commitment, and each is either at war, or on a permanent war-footing. (Yugoslavia, too, had a higher ratio, but its federal government has a very constrained budget, in which the military appears disproportionately large.) No East European WTO member has a ME/CGE ratio close to that of the Soviet Union, and most have exhibited a gradual decline over the 11-year span for which data were examined. Yet, Poland (which has surpassed Bulgaria as having the highest non-Soviet WTO ME/CGE ratio) devoted well over 20 per cent of its central expenditures to the military, which places it in the top fourth of all nation-states (ranking thirty-third in 1985) – with the United States – whereas Hungary's ratio of little more than 8 per cent would place it in the lower third (ninety-fourth among all nation-states) of world standards for such a statistic.[26]

Table 3.2 Extractive military effort: ME/CGE (per cent)

	1975	1976	1977	1978	1979	1980	1981	1982	1983	1984	1985
Soviet Union	65.3	61.6	60.6	59.7	56.8	54.2	52.0	48.6	50.1	50.3	49.6
Bulgaria	20.0	22.0	22.5	19.1	18.9	19.4	17.2	18.5	19.2	18.8	18.5
Czechoslovakia	17.6	16.6	16.7	17.5	17.1	17.4	16.5	18.4	17.9	18.0	17.9
Poland	19.6	18.7	17.6	16.0	14.7	13.5	13.0	20.9	22.8	21.7	22.6
East Germany	14.1	13.7	13.3	12.9	12.4	12.0	12.0	12.0	11.8	11.6	10.7
Romania	13.1	12.4	11.3	10.9	9.5	10.9	12.5	18.0	21.0	19.2	18.0
Hungary	8.5	8.3	9.4	8.2	8.0	8.0	7.7	7.9	7.6	7.5	8.1

Other expenditure measures standardized by population (per capita) and by military manpower (per effective or per soldier) have been calculated by ACDA, and suggest corroborative findings. The USSR ranks within the highest 10 per cent of all states on both indices. Indeed, ALL WTO members except Romania rank in the top quintile of 144 countries included in the ACDA report for both ME/capita and ME/soldier (with Romania ranking thirty-fifth and thirty-third, respectively).

On all standard expenditure indices, then, most Warsaw Pact members are far above the median. Only on the index of ME/CGE do two WTO states fall dramatically lower (e.g. Hungary in the 70–80th percentile and the GDR in the 50–60th percentile). Generally, of course, politically stable countries with higher socio-economic levels devote the principal part of their national/federal budget to non-military spending, and it is not surprising that Pact members with a record of stability until the late 1980s, except for the USSR itself, would devote smaller proportions of central government expenditures to armed forces.

But what do such expenditures 'buy'? There are many views concerning what one ought to measure and how such measurement should be accomplished. Division-force equivalents is an artificial construct used by some analysts when considering NATO, by which the varying sizes and armament of ground forces can be standardized. Yet, there remains the difficulty of factoring into any equation varying levels of modernization, mobility, etc.[27] For the Warsaw Pact, because of imprecision about personnel and equipment in specific units, a more reliable gauge of armed forces 'bought' is the more generic statistic of armed forces per 1,000 population.

Military manpower – active duty forces of the regular armed services – is an important gauge of extractive effort (see Table 3.3). Here one finds a continued WTO emphasis on maintaining high levels of active duty personnel, relative to world-wide standards. Although force levels per 1,000 population have dropped slightly since the mid-1970s, a country such as Bulgaria has a proportionately larger standing military than nine-tenths of all nation-states – larger per 1,000 people than the Soviet Union itself. The USSR, East Germany and Czechoslovakia are well within the second decile of a world-wide distribution on active-duty military manpower, whereas Poland, Hungary and Romania are not far behind. Even Hungary, which devotes the smallest (in the WTO) proportion of central government expenditures to military effort, maintains an active-duty force level in the highest fourth of all nation-states (10.9/1,000 in 1985).

Although some changes were evident in the 1980s, leading generally to slightly reduced military expenditures in terms of GNP and CGE and to a modest decline in use of available manpower for the regular armed forces, the portrait of WTO states was still (through 1985) one of well-above world-median levels of extractive military effort. The Warsaw Pact remains

Table 3.3 Extractive military effort: armed forces/1,000 population

	1975	1976	1977	1978	1979	1980	1981	1982	1983	1984	1985
Soviet Union	16.1	16.3	16.2	16.0	16.3	16.5	16.4	16.6	16.4	16.3	16.1
Bulgaria	20.1	20.2	20.1	18.6	18.5	18.3	18.6	19.7	19.9	19.8	19.8
Czechoslovakia	14.2	14.1	13.7	14.1	13.9	13.9	13.8	13.9	13.9	13.8	13.8
Poland	12.8	12.7	12.4	12.3	12.1	11.8	11.8	11.8	11.8	11.6	11.6
East Germany	13.1	13.1	13.2	13.6	13.6	13.8	13.9	14.0	14.4	14.4	14.4
Romania	10.4	10.3	10.2	10.0	9.9	9.7	9.6	10.6	10.8	10.8	10.7
Hungary	11.2	11.1	13.5	10.3	10.3	11.1	11.2	10.3	9.8	9.8	10.9

Source: For Tables 3.1–3.3, US Arms Control and Disarmament Agency, *World Military Expenditures and Arms Transfers, 1987,* Washington, DC: ACDA, 1987

an area characterized by high commitment to armed forces, although as a group these countries do not dip into socio-economic resources to the extent evident among some Middle East or Southeast and East Asian cases.

The distribution of such extractive effort within the WTO has not become more egalitarian during the 1980s, *vis-à-vis* the 1970s. Emphasis on manpower commitments among non-Soviet Pact members predominates, with no East European state making a monetary contribution at a similar level to the USSR save for Bulgaria. Poland's enlarged ME/CGE ratio does not alter the general portrait of an alliance in which the USSR exceeds by a considerable margin the financial commitments in proportion to GNP or CGE of East European members.

Performance demand

Most of the existing studies of 'burden sharing' as applied to NATO omit the performance of military-related activities by states in the alliance. Military forces created or maintained by expenditures are factored into an overall assessment of commitment, but what is done with such forces is ignored. Short of combat, however, important tasks are performed by nations' militaries and/or the military economy that supports them.

First, all states' armed forces conduct manoeuvres – large unit training exercises of varying duration and realism. The frequency of such manoeuvres, plus the frequency of their location on a nation's own territory, help to identify a country's commitment to preparedness. Second, most advanced industrial states send some military advisers, technicians or security personnel to other states. This does not, in small numbers, mean basing units abroad, but rather sending some active duty personnel (usually in civilian attire) to countries with bilateral or multi-lateral security arrangements. Third, industrial economies invariably produce arms for export; arms exports that are consistent with client patterns established by the dominant alliance member must be seen as a form of military effort on behalf of multilateral interests. WTO members export arms to a narrower list of recipients than NATO states, their weapon designs do not compete with one another because all are derived from Soviet origin, and all armament industries are state-owned and party elites make decisions about all sales. Consequently, unlike NATO, arms exports standardized as a proportion of all exports can be indicative of WTO members' military effort as opposed to tapping purely economic motives. Because NATO is an entity that includes states with unilateral world-wide commitments (e.g. Britain in the Falklands, France in Chad) and pairs of states that have had long-standing animosity for one another (e.g. Greece and Turkey), it is more difficult to calculate the distribution of such alliance-related military activities in NATO than it has been thus far for the WTO.

There are many other military activities performed by WTO members about which data can be obtained – but not all states have the potential to undertake such activities. Naval deployments, as opposed to sending military personnel abroad, is indicative of enormous performance effort, but is a dichotomous indicator distinguishing between 'haves' and 'have nots' rather than by gradations of effort. The three indicators used here, however, are generic in the sense of being 'available' military activities for almost all industrial nation-states.

We can infer from these data that East European members of the Warsaw Pact have not been as active in their performance of military tasks as has the USSR and that the distribution of military performance is very different from the distribution of extractive effort. These inferences reflect, in large part, a continuation of the principal findings of such indicators drawn from data over the 11-year period from 1972 to 1982.[28]

Through the early 1980s, the USSR and Northern Tier (East Germany, Poland and Czechoslovakia) were markedly more involved in large unit exercises designed to heighten preparedness. The various 'Friendship', 'Shield' and 'Soyuz' manoeuvres, often conducted with over 25,000 troops drawn from a number of WTO members almost always involved one or more of the Northern Tier. By the mid- to late-1980s, the very large and therefore costly exercises of the previous 10 to 15 years appear to be less numerous. The expense of assembling large quantities of troops and supplies, and disruption to commerce and agriculture, may have encouraged fewer of the multi-division exercises. Also, the 1985 Stockholm CSCE agreement regarding confidence-building measures included language necessitating prior notification for movements of just over a division-sized unit (13,000 troops, or 300 battle tanks for ground forces). It appears that some effort has been made to avoid triggering prior notification of manoeuvres by conducting more exercises of smaller units.[29]

A state's effort to perform military activities may be peripheral within an alliance, and can become largely superfluous to the security of all other alliance members. For Romania and Hungary, participation in exercises and military planning had become almost non-existent in the first case, and seriously constrained in the latter case. Romania, which had ceased to take part in field exercises (and has sent, since the mid-1960s only minimal representation to 'staff' command, control and communications exercises), still has nothing to do with the WTO's preparation for wartime command within the USSR's Western and Southwestern Theatres of Military Operation (TVDs).

Hungary, already with lower extractive effort than its WTO allies, was minimally involved in exercises through 1982, and saw no increase during the next 5 years; Hungarian ground forces participated in only a few large-scale multinational manoeuvres during the 1982–7 period and, by 1988, the potential of Soviet troop withdrawals from Hungary had been raised by Red Army spokesmen and confirmed by the US State Department.[30] The Hungarian Defence Minister, Colonel-General Ferenc Karpati was similarly quoted by Die Welt to the effect that the proposal is part of a three-stage Kremlin plan aimed at eliminating all foreign troops from Europe by the year 2000.[31] The Soviets, one must suspect, judged their divisions in Hungary to be least critical and/or beneficial. At the very least, the record of WTO exercises suggests far less emphasis on maintaining readiness of Hungarian forces, and Soviet troops stationed in Hungary, than that of Northern Tier states and the Soviet groups of forces based in East Germany, Czechoslovakia, Poland and the Western Military District of the USSR.

East European WTO members perform military tasks of other kinds, however, that create different socio-economic and political demands. Two East European countries were recognized by most authorities as having some military personnel abroad, by far the largest contingent coming from East Germany. Although estimates are cloudy, 2,400 military personnel[32] and several thousand technical advisers who assemble and maintain military equipment (radar, communications, etc.) were known to be dispersed around the world. Angola, Ethiopia, Mozambique and Libya are some of the locales where East German regular military personnel were known to have been stationed since the mid-1970s, and they remained in these locales in the late 1980s.[33]

Polish military advisers served in Syria,[34] but my own contacts with individuals who have served in the last decade in the Polish army report carrying out training and advisory duties for the Libyan and Vietnamese militaries in those countries. These individual recollections tend to substantiate, for example, other reports of 'Polish and Czech advisors operating in Laos with Vietnamese forces'.[35]

Aside from the East German case, the number of regular military personnel from East European WTO states serving in the Third World in advisory or training capacities – and, perhaps, occasionally taking part in directing combat operations – were small. Probably fewer than 200 Polish military personnel filled such roles abroad at any single time, and the number of Czechoslovaks engaged in military training/advising in Africa and Asia has been in the same range. Both countries, however, have large amounts of arms sales (discussed below) to states in East Asia, North Africa and the Middle East. With such arms sales invariably go technicians to uncrate, examine, repair, train and maintain more complex equipment or weapons. For instance, Czechoslovakia's sale of six L-410UVP Turbolet transport aircraft to Libya in June 1985 must have included a number of attendant personnel to ensure the operation of the aircraft – a servicing agreement, so to speak.[36] These technicians, not included as military forces abroad *per se*, nevertheless create a *de facto* military presence in other countries.

These 'technicians' who work on military systems or projects, as distinct from active-duty military personnel, appear to number in the thousands. The Central Intelligence Agency estimates that, in 1986, almost 21,000 'military technicians' from the USSR and East European WTO states were in less-developed countries.[37] If these technicians were distributed in roughly the same ratio as Soviet and East European shares of the world arms-export market in the previous year (1985) – 35.3 per cent to 9.6 per cent[38] – then one in five WTO 'military technicians' in the Third World might be assumed to be from East European states, or about 4,160 in 1986.

The USSR and East European WTO members have thus been among the subset of two dozen nation-states with armed forces stationed elsewhere for other than UN peace-keeping purposes. Because our data are imprecise, we can say with certainty only that the German Democratic Republic undertook the largest military effort in this regard, followed by Poland and Czechoslovakia. Arms exports, however, may engender higher numbers of military personnel abroad. If so, any trend towards larger arms exports may portend a higher number of its armed forces abroad.

Exporting arms involves the performance of military activity – the design, manufacture, testing, assembly, maintenance and sometimes the operation in combat of certain weapons systems. To create and retain a capacity for the indigenous production of arms, especially larger and complex weapons versus small arms, is a precondition for sustainable action by a nation's armed forces. States can, of course, export arms to make money. But, as argued earlier, members of the Warsaw Pact do not for the most part compete with one another for customers; they export to the same primary group of client states with which the USSR has established close relations, and provide very similar or identical weapons (e.g. the T-54/55 tank, refitted with new guns and armour, is offered by the USSR and several European states, while the Mig-21, older-generation anti-aircraft missiles, etc. are also standard fare from the entire WTO). The socio-economic demands fostered by devoting large proportions of industrial capacity to armaments that have little role in a world market for hard-currency sales make weapons exports on an alliance responsibility not an economic opportunity.[39]

For the Warsaw Pact as a whole, and Eastern Europe more dramatically than the USSR, the 1980s witnessed a substantial upturn in arms transfers to less developed countries. Eastern Europe, in the aggregate, has tripled its annual average dollar value of arms transfers during the first years of this decade (1981 through 1986) versus the 1977 through 1980 average.[40] From data provided by the US Arms Control and Disarmament Agency one can estimate that Soviet deliveries and agreements of arms throughout the world exceeded those of the United States by a substantial margin in the late 1970s and the first half of the 1980s and continued to enlarge in this decade, but that the USSR's East European allies were increasing arms sales and grants at a faster pace than was Moscow in the 1980s. Whereas total Soviet arms deliveries and agreements from 1977–81 were at $68bn, almost seven times the total amount of East European states, the 1982–6 oviet total of $87bn was 'only' a little more than five times the NSWP states' total.[41] There has been, then, a wider distribution of this form of military effort within the WTO in recent years even as the total amount of arms grants from the Pact rises.

The USSR continued to transfer such a large quantity of arms that, in 1986, more than 18.5 per cent of all Soviet exports were military items (Table 3.4). Moscow ranked second in the world in 1985 and 1986 on that measure; seven of the top seventeen states in arms exports as a proportion of total exports were WTO members and, more significantly, three of the top five.[42]

Arms exports as a proportion of all exports is an important indication of military effort within the economy and society suggesting an element of socio-economic 'militarization'. Trends in arms exports/total exports within each WTO member state have not exhibited dramatic 'net' changes over the late 1970s to mid-1980s. There have been years, however, in which large increases were registered – e.g. Romania's exports of arms in the early 1980s – from which we might infer a country's willingness to perform a more active role in the world arms market. Generally, however, East European WTO states are active suppliers of conventional arms to a well-established list of clients, but they do not participate widely in the world arms market. Poland, for example, had 'ten' known customers outside the WTO for its weapons and military equipment from 1982 through 1986, almost all of which were long established Soviet clients or friends (e.g. Angola, Libya, Cuba, North Korea, Vietnam, Iraq, Syria, Yemen [PDRY], Nicaragua and India). Czechoslovak arms transfers went to fifteen non-WTO recipients, largely overlapping the Polish list, but with the additions of other Soviet friends or clients – Afghanistan, Algeria and Ethiopia, for example. Czechoslovak deliveries to Pakistan and Nigeria represent the anomalies in this pattern, but both were small amounts ($20m and $10m, respectively) of small arms.[43]

Table 3.4 Performance military effort: arms exports/total exports (per cent)

	1977	1978	1979	1980	1981	1982	1983	1984	1985	1986
Soviet Union	19.0	20.8	24.6	21.2	20.5	20.5	19.5	19.7	17.6	18.5
Bulgaria	0.2	0.9	0.6	0.7	1.7	3.2	2.6	5.0	3.7	2.6
Czechoslovakia	6.7	8.1	7.3	6.2	5.1	4.0	4.2	5.2	7.9	5.0
Poland	3.4	4.5	3.3	4.7	7.3	6.2	6.1	5.6	6.2	5.1
East Germany	0.7	0.5	0.5	1.0	0.7	0.7	0.9	1.6	2.3	0.8
Romania	0.6	0.9	0.8	0.8	3.6	6.9	3.0	2.7	3.5	1.4
Hungary	0.8	0.8	0.5	0.9	0.8	1.0	1.9	1.4	1.8	1.3

Source: See Tables 3.1–3.3

All other NSWP states export arms, although Czechoslovakia, because of its traditional role in such an activity, and Poland, because of its industrial size, both transfered a higher net value of weapons and equipment. The Bulgarian effort had risen, interestingly, during the 1980s to become more sizeable than East Germany, Hungary and Romania. Extractive and performance dimensions of military effort in the Warsaw Pact thus provide a convincing portrait of a region making strenuous socio-economic and political demands on itself to create and maintain armed forces. The economic demands were identifiable in budgetary data that revealed that these nations – particularly the USSR and Bulgaria – were among the world's highest military expenditure to GNP ratios. All states in the WTO, however, devoted a high proportion of their output of goods and services to military effort, with no NSWP country lower than the 60th percentile among all nation-states (Romania and Hungary are in that range). Similarly, the ME/CGE ratio was extremely high for the USSR, and all except Hungary and East Germany were among the top third of all nation-states in allocating funds from central government expenditures to armed forces. High force levels of active-duty personnel also resulted in heavy manpower demands, with Bulgaria's military larger, in proportion to the country's population, than nine-tenths of all nation-states. Once again, Hungary and Romania fell behind, but no WTO member was below the 25th percentile in world-wide rankings of force level/1,000 population.

Performance effort was distributed differently within the Pact, as the Northern Tier states conducted more frequent exercises, had more military personnel abroad, and were more involved in the production of arms for export (almost entirely to Soviet client states). Bulgaria, however, participated more in exercises outside its own territory, i.e. its forces trained elsewhere more often than other WTO members, and the former Zhivkov regime committed the Bulgarian economy to an increased level of arms exports in the 1980s that placed it above the much more advanced economy of East Germany.

What Warsaw Pact regimes took from their economy and society to sustain armed forces and what they did with such forces, offers two distinct portraits of an alliance. From both vantage points, however, one can see that the USSR, Poland, East Germany, Czechoslovakia and Bulgaria make consistently heavy demands on the societies and economies they rule. Romania and Hungary have been, on both extractive and performance measures of military effort, less committed to developing or maintaining armed forces; and, of course, Romania has been detached from the Warsaw Pact in most respects (including absenting itself from manoeuvres, refusing to send officers to the USSR for education, seeking alternative sourcing for weapons systems, etc.).

In the context of the WTO, then, socio-economic demands made on behalf of military effort are onerous in some member states – the USSR and Bulgaria for extractive measures, and the Northern Tier for performance indicators – but are sufficiently low in Romania and Hungary that they may properly be labelled as 'the periphery' of the alliance.[44] In Romania, however, the Ceausescu regime up to 1989 placed heavy demands on the army by insisting that it assume economic roles (construction, management of enterprises and harvesting), while increasingly bringing high-ranking officers into top state and party positions. A caveat, then, is appropriate; lower than 'average' extractive and performance military effort by a member of the Warsaw Pact does not imply a reduced importance of the army within the socio-economic and political life of a country. Indeed, as in Romania, until the demise of Ceausescu the inverse seems to have been true. When dicussing the choices and trade-offs that are now being made by WTO members, party–military ties will be an important component.

The burden of military effort in the WTO: choices and costs

Defence burden, unlike military effort, implies a trade-off or cost; whereas security as a 'collective good' may be enhanced by whatever commitment is made to military preparations, social welfare and economic growth are not necessary by-products of manpower and material resources expended in the military sector. Indeed, there may be hidden cumulative costs to extractive and performance effort over a long period of time.[45] Concomitant with socio-economic costs may be political burdens that are seen in diminished public support for the system, heightened conflict and violence among competing strata and segments of society, and a reduced capacity of the party to ensure its leading role. Military effort is not, in other words, a benign collection of resources and commitment to certain actions. Rather, in communist party states, extractive and/or performance effort was the bane of state socialist economies, and a proximate cause to haemorrhaging legitimacy of such regimes.

Socio-economic burden

Socio-economic conditions of Warsaw Pact states, seen in the aggregate, may obscure such observations. When ranked on a number of social welfare and economic performance variables in the late 1970s and early 1980s, some WTO members dropped substantially when compared to other nation-states (see Table 3.5). The precipitous fall of Romania from among the most highly 'developed' quintile of all nation-states into the 'top third' is only the worst of several poor performances. Czechoslovakia, East Germany and Poland also saw their socio-economic standards diminish relative to world-wide comparisons in this brief span. A small drop in Bulgaria's ranking, or small rise in that of the USSR may not tell us much about their socio-economic conditions because changes were slight. Hungary, through the mid-1980s, was the only country in the Pact to see a clearcut rise in socio-economic conditions relative to world standards – but this gain, of course, has dissipated during the late 1980s.

Table 3.5 Socio-economic standing of WTO members

	1977	1980	1983
Soviet Union	24	25	23
Bulgaria	26	31	28
Czechoslovakia	20	27	32
Poland	27	34	35
East Germany	14	19	25
Romania	31	35	45
Hungary	29	28	24

Source: Ruth L. Sivard, *World Military and Social Expenditures*, 1980, 1983, 1986, Washington, DC: World Priorities; rankings among all nation-states

Using comparative rankings that aggregate many indicators, however, sends contradictory signals regarding defence burden (i.e. the costs imposed by the high levels of military effort discussed above). For Romania, none of the constraints on extractive and performance effort insulated the country from a political, economic and cultural disaster invoked by the chaotic autocracy of the late Nicolae Ceausescu. On the other hand, Hungary's restrained military effort must be considered when explanations are sought for the maintenance of a 'Kadarist consensus' in social and political terms even when economic performance began to diminish in the early 1980s. That Hungary's socio-economic standing within the world avoided, through 1983, the decline evinced elsewhere in the WTO may have been partly due to a cap on military effort in most dimensions. Lower defence commitments may have contributed to Kadar's ability to hold on as long as he did (i.e. until spring, 1988).

In the Polish case, however, one encounters again the difficulty of assessing burden incurred because of military effort from an aggregate perspective. Obviously, the large extractive and performance efforts undertaken by the Polish regime did not 'cause' Polish socio-economic decline. Instead, Poland's considerable extractive effort included larger ME/CGE ratios since the martial law period, as well as continued high levels of performance effort, seem inextricably intertwined with the ongoing national crisis. Because of the political insecurity of the communist regime in Poland, military effort increased when socio-economic crises surfaced. Yet such added commitments of resources when coupled with heightened activity by military and security forces, had debilitating effects: they cost billions of zloty, disrupted domestic transport and communications, lowered the availability of foreign high-technology imports, and exacerbated already bad relations between the regime and workers, intellectuals and students. Polish communists could not point to their greater support for the armed forces as a panacea; raw power exhibited by more armoured personnel carriers and more frequent exercises had no salutary effect on the country's problems, at the core of which was the regime's lack of legitimacy and the failure of a centrally-planned, state socialist economic system.

For the most advanced NSWP members, East Germany and Czechoslovakia, the heavy demands imposed by their military commitments, especially in terms of performance effort and force levels/1,000 population, were coextensive with falling socio-economic standards through 1983 when ranked against all nation-states. Once more, however, we encounter contradictory evidence insofar as neither East Germany nor Czechoslovakia, relative to GNPs and Central Government Expenditures, undertook the level of military effort exhibited by other WTO allies.

If, however, one examines more specific data, the intimate link between military effort, defence burden, and the political insolvency of European communist regimes begins to emerge. Expenditures on education and health, for example, suggest that the proportion of GNP allocated to these social arenas was most constrained when elements of military effort increased. Further, such increased military effort appeared to coincide with challenges to the regimes' political futures.

In Table 3.6, it is evident that Romania, Poland and the Soviet Union had small or non-existent increases in health and education expenditures/ GNP during the late 1970s and early 1980s, whereas the net changes for Bulgaria, Czechoslovakia and Hungary were substantially larger during the same period. Although these calculations should be regarded as approximations rather than precise measurements, it is not counterintuitive that the two East European countries confronting the largest negative trend in public attitudes during the same period – Romania and Poland[46] – also increased military expenditures/CGE by the biggest margin among WTO states in 1982–5 (see Table 3.2). Military spending as a proportion of GNP in the early 1980s rose as well in both countries *vis-à-vis* mean levels for the late 1970s (see Table 3.1). Such a linkage is not, of course, applicable to WTO members alone; the tie between lower social spending, especially in education, and higher defence budgets has also been noted among the US and its allies.[47]

Table 3.6 Health and education expenditures as proportion of GNP (per cent)

	1977	1980	1983	Net change
Soviet Union	7.2	7.5	8.0	+0.8
Bulgaria	5.9	6.2	8.3	+2.4
Czechoslovakia	6.2	6.1	8.6	+2.4
Poland	6.9	7.6	7.8	+0.9
East Germany	6.2	8.9	7.5	+1.3
Romania	4.2	6.9	4.2	—
Hungary	6.2	7.8	8.3	+2.1

Source: Author's calculations using data from Ruth L. Sivard, World Military and Social Expenditures, 1980, 1983, 1986, Washington, DC: World Priorities

One 'cost' of bloated military effort among WTO members, then, was tightened budgets for health and education (and, perhaps, other social expenditures). Yet, neither dimension of effort is likely to be the origin of a burden imposed on society. Instead, the causal chain can be traced to a Leninist party regime's own fears when confronted by a population that no longer believes that the system performs adequately, and no longer expects the ruling party to resolve problems. These fears for its own political survival, to be discussed further below, brought the party elites to first drain social expenditures in order to pay for heightened performance effort, i.e. to employ once again raw coercion to retain power against popular antagonism. Increased expenditures and manpower levels may follow, but military/security activities will be first to show the effects of political turmoil.

Burdens of defence, according to John Erickson, were 'felt keenly' in other respects among WTO states, 'not merely in terms of money expended but also in the opportunity cost of displaced manpower and displaced resources'.[48] As is well understood for market economies, however, the 'relative merits of "butter" and "guns" were by no means clear-cut':[49]

A nation's military expenditure can stimulate industrial production and hence reduce unemployment, and defense industries can be developed into a thriving export sector. The civilian economy can benefit significantly from the military's technological research and development. Military service can also have a modernizing influence in developing nations as people are exposed to new skills and discipline.[50]

These positive effects of extractive military effort, even if present, are certain to be diminished when performance effort rises and generates ancillary demands on society and the economy – using transportation and communications while at the same time producing nothing, consuming energy and other expendables, returning little, and directing productive resources into inefficient uses.

Soviet military outlays and activity have not translated into the civilian economy. Worse yet, from Gorbachev's standpoint at least, has been the tendency of extremely heavy defence commitments to deplete technological resources in civilian sectors – the 'sapping of the economy's innovational energies', according to Stanley H. Cohn.[51] Rather than a military economy proceeding at its own pace, preventing diffusion of technology to non-weapons applications, the Soviet defence production sphere backed by an 'overriding priority . . . and the effective political support',[52] the defence production sphere drains the economy's 'technological and innovative energies'. More specifically, the military has had priority access to 'the best quality raw materials . . . the best industrial workers, and the most advanced machinery', as well as a 'disproportionate share of research and development . . . diverted from civilian purposes'.[53]

Across the Soviet economy, this absorption of innovation and technology by the military sector has had grievous effects. No matter how one gauges Soviet output and input productivity from the mid-1960s through mid-1980s, it is certain that, concomitant with a slowing of GNP and industrial output growth, there was an abysmal record of declining capital productivity. According to Richard Kaufman's calculations, the USSR exhibited during the Brezhnev years a consistent and unenviable pattern of negative growth in both output per unit of input and capital productivity.[54] As the value of goods produced by the USSR per unit of input has diminished, it has been unable to keep pace with accelerating technologies of the Japanese, West Europeans and Americans. Indeed, the USSR remained far behind these Western developed market economies in the proportion of basic industrial products incorporating recent technologies (e.g. oxygen steel accounted for 29.6 per cent of all Soviet steel produced in 1982, whereas it was 62.1 per cent of the US total, 73.4 per cent of the Japanese total and 80.9 per cent of the West German total).[55] Soviet imports of technology and technology-based products, moreover, actually declined as a proportion of all USSR imports from OECD countries between 1970 and 1982 (from 22.8 per cent to 9.32 per cent), meaning that exogenous sourcing for technology was evaporating as well.[56]

In the WTO generally, extractive military effort explains only a negligible part of variance in economic indicators. Yet, higher 'performance' levels (all three indicators) have exhibited a statistically significant negative association with measures of economic growth (see Table 3.7). Interestingly, the frequency of joint manoeuvres appears to have had the strongest negative association with economic performance in WTO countries – a relationship that may imply both the economic disruption and out-ofpocket costs of heightened military activities. That these associations are relatively weak, of course, is due to the many structural explanations for communist systems' economic lethargy in the 1970s and 1980s; military effort certainly plays a marginal explanatory role when looking at the entire alliance over a lengthy span. One can be confident, however, that military commitments have 'helped' to make bad economic systems perform worse.

In the USSR, this detrimental effect can be seen clearly. Despite a high rate of investment from 1965 to 1980, Soviet producer durables – machinery to be used in manufacturing – declined substantially as a proportion of all Soviet machinery output, whereas machinery intended for the production of military equipment rose greatly. If there is a sector of the Soviet economy 'gaining' in terms of technology, it is obviously the military economy as it receives a higher and higher proportion of new equipment and machines. Such diversion of new technology to the military meant that rising investment levels (from 24.2 per cent of GNP in 1960, 30.6 per cent in 1975 and 34 per cent in 1983 – larger than any Western country except Japan, which spens only 1 per cent of GNP in defence) did not augur well for productivity in consumer and civilian manufacturing sectors. That the military captured most of Soviet research and development, new machinery production, etc. does *not* mean that defence production was any more efficient, but that the civilian sectors are denied access to technologies that might make *them* more productive. Indeed, the Soviets' usage of machine tools becomes less efficient as complexity increases, suggesting that the diversion of newer technology from most of the economy makes workers, managers and planners less familiar with such machines when and if they see them.[57] The remainder of the industrial and consumer economy are falling further behind as time goes on, with less of a claim on new production techniques and equipment.[58] This, at least, was

Table 3.7 Military effort and WTO economies, 1975–85: bivariate correlations

	Arms exports/ total exports	Joint manoeuvres	Forces abroad
GNP growth rate[1]	−0.13	−0.20[a]	−0.07
Capital productivity[2] growth rate	−0.11	−0.13	0.03
Income per capita[3] growth rate	−0.12	−0.16[b]	−0.04
Number of observations = 77			

Sources: [1] US Arms Control and Disarmament Agency, *World Military Expenditures and Arms Transfers*, 1986, 1987, Washington: ACDA; [2] *U.N. Economic Survey of Europe*, Geneva: U.N., various years; [3] *U.N. Economic Survey of Europe*, 1987–88
Notes: [a] Significant at $p < 0.10$.
[b] Significant at $p < 0.05$.
Joint manoeuvres as proportion of Soviet total.
Forces abroad as a proportion of population.

the choice that had been made by the Brezhnev regime from 1964–82, and the trade-off has only now begun to be reversed.

Ruling party elites in Eastern European and the USSR unquestionably were required to make choices that 'sacrificed' some social expenditures and some economic modernization in order to manage the elevated military efforts maintained for several decades. That requirement arose because of politically determined economic policies insisting on centrally planned state socialism, and because of the political insecurity of these regimes. I will return below to the matter of ties between political 'costs' and military commitments. The choices and trade-offs, however, merit emphasis.

For European communist states, we have seen some evidence in a confined period of time (principally the late 1970s and early 1980s) of diminished public support in Eastern Europe, heightened extractive and/or performance effort, and diminished social spending forming a complex nexus in some cases. The more one focuses on specific arenas of public expenditure, the more such trade-offs are revealed. And, in the Soviet case, there are a number of assessments to the effect that the USSR's own modernization – its ability to diffuse technology, and therefore to enhance productivity throughout the civilian manufacturing and consumer sectors – were sacrificed on the 'altar' of military priorities.

Yet, we may be seeing only part of the story. Steve Chan, indeed, has recently noted that Bruce Russett's *What Price Vigilance?* of almost 20 years ago revealed the cumulative economic consequences of military spending.[59] Instead of examining cases within a narrow temporal span, Russett examined longitudinally the impact of variation in defence spending across nations. To the degree that military outlays decreased capital investment apart from an immediate decrease in personal consumption, Russett's calculations suggest permanent losses to the American economy (or other economies). Dollars lost to capital investment are losses that reverberate throughout the economy for years, expanding in effect with each year.[60]

For WTO members, this longitudinal impact must be assumed as well. Put simply, the USSR and most members of the Warsaw Pact exacerbated their already inefficient economies by imposing severe demands on national resources; they have, indeed, mortgaged their futures. Whereas in developed market economies that engaged in military effort beyond their willingness to pay for it (i.e. with a reduced standard of living), huge deficits and a mounting national debt are readily apparent. For the USSR, and its East European allies (particularly in the 'core' WTO of Bulgaria plus the three Northern Tier states), the future was mortgaged by diminishing potential for socio-economic advancement.

We have already noted, for example, the negative effects on social spending and technical innovation. GNP growth rates, consequently, have been neither consistent nor as high as some NATO members. More important, NATO members achieve comparable GNP growth with substantially less investment. Since 1961, Eastern Europe had average annual GNP growth rates smaller than the European Community average except during 1971–5, whereas the share of national income used as net investment (accumulation) in communist Europe almost always exceeded 20 per cent, and sometimes has been over 30 per cent. The USSR's fixed investment as a proportion of GNP has exceeded all OECD countries except Japan over the 1960–80 period, but was substantially behind all principal capitalist states in terms of GNP per capita. Lagging factor productivity has been a persistent feature of the Soviet economy.[61] Although the handicap of centrally planned state socialism lies at the core of such inefficient Soviet and East European economic performance, and only a negligible proportion of variance in GNP growth rates can be accounted for by military effort, the added weight of military priorities contributed to underdevelopment for the countries of the WTO that had not already achieved levels comparable to the rest of Europe.

Political burden

Political burdens are less tangible, but no less damaging. There are two dimensions of political costs associated with the heavy commitment of national resources over a lengthy period to armed forces – disruption of intra-elite cohesion through the emergence of a military/security challenge to civilian authority, and the distancing of elites from masses. One might think of these as burdens or costs imposed on both 'horizontal' and 'vertical' planes within communist systems.

Within the 'establishment' of communist states – inside the *nomenklatura,* and especially at the apex of it – the weight of extractive and performance military effort drove wedges between civilian and military/security elites. There are, of course, no simplistic dichotomies that would denote individuals in such a way. Nevertheless, in the absence of clear-cut international threats about which there is a broad consensus, the priorities discussed above coupled with sacrifices in social programmes and technological progress in the non-military sectors of the economy will be debated and rejected. As such debates intensify, exacerbated by mounting evidence that socio-economic costs are imposed via the onus of long-term elevated defence commitments, the symbiosis of civil–military relations will begin to unravel.

Ruling communist parties, of necessity, retained close relations with their country's military forces. The revolutionary army, after all, 'was' the party in the early histories of communist Yugoslavia, Albania, China and Cuba – and, for the Bolsheviks, their seizure of power on 7 November 1917 would have been short-lived without the Red Army. The Bolsheviks, themselves, were portrayed as an 'army of revolutionaries, with their mobilization efforts seen as akin to military activity'.[62] It was, as well, the Red Army that made it possible for communist regimes to control areas now within the Warsaw Pact, and armies of the USSR and other Warsaw Pact members, acting domestically or to intervene in the affairs of their socialist neighbours, that ensured the survival of such regimes for more than four decades.

Communist parties, in other words, need the army's loyalty because the army ties current elites to an erstwhile revolutionary past and, in some cases, to the vague appeal of nationalism. But, ultimately, the ruling communist parties need the military to guarantee their rule, both through raw coercive power and through the performance of some functions that the party cannot alone accomplish – mass mobilization and socialization, often coupled with roles in economic management or production.

Conversely, communist militaries needed the Leninist parties that ruled in Warsaw Pact states, with officers gaining status and prestige from their intra-party roles, and the general staff having another tool – party discipline – with which to control younger officers and NCOs. The operating principles of Leninist parties – those of democratic centralism and of the *nomenklatura* – both helped to assure military commanders that the society and economy will comply with demands made or orders given. The military's linkage with the ruling party, although once organic, became largely utilitarian. Although it is true that the Red Army, or other communist armies, were themselves 'endangered if the party-state collapsed',[63] it is also evident that the horizontal symbiosis between party and army in communist party systems was not a necessary consequence of one-party authoritarianism or state socialism. Cleavages can develop between the two institutions over resource allocations, foreign policies and military doctrine.

How might such divisions arise? Among East European WTO armies, national identity is subsumed within the Pact and, were hostilities to occur, within the Soviet Western and Southwestern Theatres of Military Operation (TVDs). If one assumes that the militaries with the 'healthiest' collective psychologies are those confronting nationally-defined external enemies, then it follows that NSWP armies will be troubled by their pre-programmed role as adjuncts to Soviet-directed goals. Even more troublesome must be the higher probability (i.e. higher than combat against NATO forces) that they would be employed under Soviet direction to intervene against a neighbouring member of the WTO where political events untenable to the USSR were taking place. Undoubtedly, the most unappealing role, but the highest likelihood of all, is domestic repression[64] – to halt protests by an ethnic minority, to disrupt workers' strikes or student demonstrators, and to provide if necessary the institutional support for a junta when the party has ceased to rule. All of these actions have been taken by East European armies and, to the degree that communist parties lose public legitimacy, the scenario of combat against their own people becomes increasingly possible for the region's armed forces.

Thus, the military effort undertaken by non-Soviet members of the WTO did *not* contribute to the political cohesion of elites within East European regimes. Horizontal cleavages formed not only between the leadership and those sectors denied resources because of military priorities, but also between the party leadership and the armed forces because of the roles the latter must fulfil. Benefits from high extractive effort may be seen by non-Soviet military officers as small compensation for the continued denial of national command authority, the dangerous scenarios of intervention against a neighbouring state or of domestic repression, and the sapping of military professionalism through the assignment of tasks such as youth socialization and construction and management of enterprises.

Large and long-term military effort simultaneously engenders a distended bureaucracy, swollen to accommodate and absorb the manpower and material resources extracted for the armed forces, and to plan and implement performance demands placed on the military. Although the term 'military–industrial complex' has been applied to the Soviet Union,[65] there was more accurately a national security establishment in the USSR, with branches in WTO members. This establishment encompassed, beyond the military itself, at least nine defence industry ministries in the Soviet case.[66] The military (specifically the Soviet General Staff) was at the core of a national security establishment because of the extraordinary primacy concerning military matters achieved during Brezhnev's tenure. While civilian policy-makers may have maintained the selection of high-level officers, 'strategies, doctrines, and force postures' were the domain of the General Staff.[67]

The degree to which the Gorbachev leadership and the CPSU can exercise its leading role over the burgeoning apparatus of the military economy and the domain of military expertise carved out by the General Staff is difficult to assess. It may be sufficient to note, though, that Mikhail Gorbachev and his principal advisers concerning *perestroika* (e.g. Abel Aganbeygan) have implied on numerous occasions the need to reduce the military's hold on a huge proportion of the GNP and central government expenditures. With 'sufficient defence' being a euphemism for such reductions, Gorbachev and his Politburo supporters face an uphill struggle to wrest any substantial resources from the military. Other efforts to strengthen – to re-establish – civilian control of the military was evident in July 1988 when, after the CPSU Conference of June, Foreign Minister Eduard Shevardnadze proposed that the Supreme Soviet oversee all military/defence production and make decisions about troop deployment abroad.[68]

Conflicts of institutional interests and challenges by an alternative power centre such as a national security establishment are not, to be sure, solely attributable to the military effort of communist governments. The intricate relationships between dimensions of military effort and various political costs ought not to be oversimplified such that extractive or performance commitments are independent variables, and measures of political change are seen as dependent variables. The issues on which intra-elite cohesion and consensus begin to founder were present regardless of defence spending, manpower demands, and military activities of the armed forces. In the Soviet case, for example, the choices between reform and reaction, 'Western' modernization or Russian nationalism, even if not always stark, nevertheless pervade debates about military policy, and divide those who command the armed forces and manage defence industries. Socio-economic malaise and political insecurity contributed to higher defence efforts, but the long-term consequences of such expanded commitments to the military may provoke other political weaknesses while hindering the economy. If military effort was seen as a means by which to protect the 'socialist community' of communist party states from internal collapse, then the treatment became little better than the ailment. It was to protect the Party from 'chronic fundamental disorder' of its own system that 'inordinate resources' were channelled into the military.[69] After decades of such 'inordinate' effort, however, ruling parties in WTO states confronted no less daunting policy problems, having faced a voracious national security establishment and military economy accustomed to their consumption of large proportions of GNP and central government spending.

Instead, the strenuous military effort undertaken by WTO members (and particularly the 'core' group of the USSR, the Northern Tier, plus Bulgaria) over many years added urgency to already extant policy debates within the elite stratum. Onerous defence commitments have not helped mitigate structural problems within state socialism or heal the political wounds of events such as the 1953 East German uprising, the Hungarian Revolution of 1956, the Prague Spring in 1968, or numerous expressions of Poles' antagonism toward a communist regime.

Doubtless unnerving to party elites was the tie between high socio-economic levels (and therefore expectations) and political turbulence, and the concomitant association between negative economic and political conditions and military effort.[70] Neither of these associations was a good omen for European communism. High socio-economic levels were accompanied by higher degrees of political change and unrest, whereas poor economic performance by communist systems seem to have been associated with a perceived need to raise commitments to, and activity of, the armed forces. Yet, those heightened military efforts produced little of economic or political benefit to insulate the ruling elite stratum from their own failures. By the late 1970s and early 1980s, the cumulative drain on socio-economic performance due to structural characteristics of state socialism, exacerbated by sustained elevated military effort, placed the European communist systems under greater pressure for fundamental political change.

Nowhere was that stress more evident than at the mass level of communist party systems. As heavy defence outlays were made in most WTO members, the distance between elites and masses grew perceptibly. Once again, military effort did not itself created mass antagonism. Heavy extractive and performance military effort, however, placed severe strains on a vertically-integrated political system. Most of the burden of a country's military commitments fell squarely on the shoulders of men and women who are conscripted to serve, and on consumers who must make sacrifices, whether consciously or not.

Many sources of data, both attitudinal and behavioural, enabled leaders of European communist systems to infer the disaffection of populations they rule. Public-opinion surveys, commissioned by Radio Free Europe but conducted by professional polling organizations, used ersatz national samples drawn from among East European travellers to Western Europe. These studies tended to indicate a substantially negative evaluation of the performance of 'socialism in practice' among most inhabitants in the region.[71] Studies conducted in some East European states in general corroborate those findings. A CBOS national poll of 1,300 people in late 1987 revealed that 80 per cent of Poles had entirely negative opinions about the current government, whereas 60 per cent thought that reasons existed for 'a serious explosion and open social conflict'.[72] Elsewhere, behaviour as much as attitudes revealed the public disapproval that, in a sense, surrounded party headquarters. The open formation of informal groups or unofficial associations that pressed for an expansion of public debate about leaders and policies was a feature of all European communist systems, except for Romania. This widening of organizational latitude was much more constrained and their activities more quiescent in Czechoslovakia and the GDR than in Poland, Hungary and the USSR itself. Nevertheless, in combination with attitudinal indicators, such behaviour suggested an evaporating mass confidence and a strong popular pressure to respond to public preferences and concerns.

The possession of large, modern armed forces did nothing to halt these changes in communist states. Indeed, in the USSR and Eastern Europe, the military effort by WTO members itself became an issue interwoven with environmental concerns and opposition to nuclear energy (as is the case among West European and North American peace activists). Contacts and co-operation among dissidents in the USSR and Eastern Europe 'are steadily deepening and multiplying',[73] with topics such as conscientious objection, human rights, autonomous trade unions, and other issues becoming avenues for co-operation.[74] Both in Czechoslovakia and in the GDR, public debate and demonstrations surfaced in 1987–8 on demilitarization, nuclear disarmament and broadly anti-war sentiments.[75]

Political elites in WTO states thus found, by the 1980s, that their acquiescence to, or enthusiasm for, some of the world's highest levels of military effort did little to make communist party regimes of the region more secure. The political legacy of elevated extractive and performance commitments was a less cohesive party elite, exacerbating existing policy debates, and an unwieldy and threatening national security establishment. Further, WTO regimes' relationships with the masses became more, not less, distant and volatile as the public evaluated the performance of communist systems very poorly, and as political activism began to focus – openly – on opposition to conscription, nuclear arms, and militarism.

Conclusion

Soviet and East European defence commitments have been, relative to world standards, enormous. Although the variation of military effort in the WTO was real and important, even Hungary and Romania extract more resources and perform more military-related activity than do most nation-states. Were one to confine comparisons to Europe – thereby 'controlling' for some nebulous historical/cultural variables, and narrowing the socio-economic range of states involved – WTO members *still* have records of much higher extractive and performance effort than NATO members.[76] Even the extractive effort of Hungary exceeds most NATO states except Greece, Turkey and the US. Performance effort is also generally higher in the Pact; Hungary's low effort in the early 1980s was exceeded only by Belgium, the United Kingdom, Turkey and the US (plus France, outside NATO's military structure).

What we saw in the WTO, then, was no mirage. That which was taken from the East European and Soviet societies and economies, plus extensive military-related activities, engendered demands that were heavy at all times, and debilitating if cumulative effects are considered.

Some of the consequences *are* social and economic – diminished social spending, depleted human and material resources, and stunted technological innovation or diffusion outside the defence industries. But the 'real' costs of a military *carte blanche* for so long are political.

The military, state defence production ministries and the huge managerial stratum of the military economy together became the rogue elephant amid the party elite. On that horizontal intra-elite plane, the symbiosis between party and army, an organic unity at the outset of many communist states, began to break down, with shared interests (system maintenance) papering over differences in policies and personnel.

Military leaders, however, knew that civilian elites need them in many respects, and thus arrogated to themselves final control of weapons research/development/deployment, military strategy and tactics, and military cadre. Party control over military-related decisions slipped away as Politburos continued to see their own security as dependent on large and active armed forces and attendant defence industry. Of course, as long as the USSR undertook no broad and all-encompassing reforms, the political uncertainty of European communist regimes could only become worse, heightening intra-elite frustration and paranoia, playing directly into the hands of the General Staff, and NSWP militaries quite willing to be seen as needed. Mikhail Gorbachev is trying to reverse this slippage of party authority in military matters, and achieved some early and fortuitous victories (e.g. replacing Defence Minister Sokolov with the much more junior Dimitri Yazov) but the defence budgets have yet to suffer deeply from *perestroika*.

The wider political cost, and that which carries the most long-term potential for systemic disruption, has been the disaffection between party and masses to which military effort has contributed. We cannot isolate the degree to which taking manpower and material resources added to the severity of public alienation. We do know, however, that negative evaluation and generalized pessimism about existing communist systems' performance attended the emergence of dissent across the region that concentrated on issues pertinent to the military – nuclear arms and energy and conscientious objection, for example. Further, the systemic performance about which East European and Soviet citizens were so negative was hindered greatly by the priorities given to the military spending, military manpower, and defence industries' raw material and technological needs.

In all of this there is a painful lesson – too late for application in the USSR and Eastern Europe – that political systems learn and unlearn: armies, no matter how magnificent, are no guarantor of security and well-being. The effort to maintain and to employ armed forces at levels far beyond defensive needs reveals more of the political insecurity of regimes than external threat. Ironically, an obsession with military strength over past decades in the WTO did nothing to enhance that security, while sacrificing national wealth and wasting human resources.

Notes

1 Valerie J. Bunce, 'Neither equality nor efficiency: international and domestic inequalities in the Soviet bloc', in Daniel N. Nelson (ed.) *Communism and the Politics of Inequalities*, Lexington Books, 1983, pp. 5–34.
2 Daniel N. Nelson, *Alliance Behavior in the Warsaw Pact*, Boulder, Col., Westview, 1986, esp. pp. 71–107.

3 Robin A. Remington, *The Warsaw Pact: Cast Studies in Communist Conflict Resolution*, Cambridge, Mass., MIT Press, 1971.
4 See, for example, Robert W. Clawson and Lawrence S. Kaplan, *The Warsaw Pact: Political Purpose and Military Means*, Wilmington, Del., Scholarly Resources, 1982; David Holloway and Jane M.O. Sharp (eds) *The Warsaw Pact: Alliance in Transition?* Ithaca, NY, Cornell University Press, 1984; Kennan Institute, *The Warsaw Pact and the Question of Cohesion: A Conference Report*, Washington, DC., The Wilson Center, 1985; Christopher Jones, *Soviet Influence in Eastern Europe: Political Autonomy and the Warsaw Pact*, NY, Praeger, 1981; A. Ross Johnson, Robert W. Dean and Alexander Alexiev, *East European Military Establishments: The Warsaw Pact Northern Tier*, Santa Monica, CA, Rand Corporation, 1980, R–2417/1–AF/FF, Dec.; William J. Lewis, *The Warsaw Pact: Arms, Doctrine and Strategy*, NY, McGraw-Hill, 1982; Ronald Linden, *Bear and Foxes*, East European Monographs, 1979, Boulder, Col.; Daniel N. Nelson (ed.) *Soviet Allies: The Warsaw Pact and the Issue of Reliability*, Boulder, Col., Westview, 1984; Daniel N. Nelson, *Alliance Behavior in the Warsaw Pact*, Boulder, Col., Westview, 1986; Teresa Rakowska-Harmstone *et al.*, *Warsaw Pact: The Question of Cohesion, I, II*, Ottawa, Ministry of Defense, ORAE, Feb. and Nov. 1984; Jeffrey Simon, *Warsaw Pact Forces: Problems of Command and Control*, Boulder, Col., Westview, 1985; Stephan Tiedtke, *Die Warschauer Vertragorganisation: Zum Verhaltnis Von Militar-Und Entspannungspolitik In Osteuropa*, Munich, R. Oldenbourg Verlag, 1978; Ivan Volgyes, *The Political Reliability of the Warsaw Pact Armies: The Southern Tier*, Durham, NC, Duke University Press, 1982.
5 Christopher Jones, *Soviet Influence in Eastern Europe: Political Autonomy and the Warsaw Pact*, NY, Praeger, 1981.
6 Jeffrey Simon, *Warsaw Pact Forces: Problems of Command and Control*, Boulder, Col., Westview, 1985.
7 John M. Collins, *U.S.–Soviet Military Balance 1980–1985*, Washington, DC., Pergamon–Brassey's, 1985.
8 Goldman, for instance, devotes only a couple of paragraphs to the issue of defence spending. See Marshall I. Goldman, *USSR in Crisis: The Failure of an Economic System*, NY, Norton, 1983.
9 William T. Lee, 'Soviet defense expenditures in an era of SALT', United States Strategic Institute, Report 79–1, Washington, DC, 1979 and 'Estimates of Soviet defense spending': statement prepared for Select Committee on Intelligence, House of Representatives, US Congress, 5 Sept. 1980; compare with Stanley H. Cohn, 'A reevaluation of Soviet defense expenditure estimates', Stanford Research Institute Working Paper, 1976; Central Intelligence Agency, 'Estimated Soviet defense spending: trends and prospects', SR–78–10121, June 1978; and 'The estimated cost of Soviet defense activities, 1965–1980', paper presented at Workshop on Soviet Military Economic Relations, Congressional Research Service, Washington, DC, 7 July 1982.
10 Stanley H. Cohn, 'The economic burden of Soviet defense outlays', in US Congress, Joint Economic Committee, *Economic Performance and Military Burden in the Soviet Union*, Washington, DC, US Government Printing Office, 1970.
11 Abraham S. Becker, *The Burden of Soviet Defense: A Political–Economic Essay*, Santa Monica, CA, Rand Corporation, Oct. 1981, R–2752–AF.
12 Gregory C. Hildebrandt, 'The dynamic burden of Soviet defense spending', in US Congress, Joint Economic Committee, *Soviet Economy in the 1980s*, Part I, Washington, DC, US Government Printing Office, 1983, pp. 331–50.

13 Stanley H. Cohn, 'Economic burden of Soviet defense production: qualitative and quantitative aspects', in US Congress, Joint Economic Committee, *Soviet Military Economic Relations*, Washington, DC, US Government Printing Office, 1983, pp. 192–207.

14 D. L. Bond, 'Macroeconomic projections of the burden of defense on the Soviet economy', in ibid., pp. 180–91.

15 H. S. Levine and B. Roberts, 'Soviet economic prospects and their national security implications', paper presented to the NATO Workshop on National Security Issues After the Twenty-Seventh Congress of the CPSU, Brussels, Nov. 1986.

16 H. G. Mosley, *The Arms Race: Economic and Social Consequences*, Lexington Books, 1984.

17 Thad P. Alton *et al.*, *Estimates of Military Expenditures in Eastern Europe*, Washington, DC, US Arms Control and Disarmament Agency, 1973; Alton, 'Military expenditures in Eastern Europe: some alternative estimates', in US Congress, Joint Economic Committee, *Reorientation and Commercial Relations of the Economies of Eastern Europe*, Washington, DC, US Government Printing Office, 1974; Alton, 'East European defense expenditures, 1965–1978', in US Congress, Joint Economic Committee, *East European Economic Assessment*, Part 2, Washington, DC, US Government Printing Office, 1981; Alton, 'East European defense expenditures, 1965–1982', in US Congress, Joint Economic Committee, *East European Economies: Slow Growth in the 1980s*, Washington, DC, US Government Printing Office, 1985.

18 Bruce Russett, *What Price Vigilance: The Burdens of National Defense*, New Haven, Conn., Yale University Press, 1970.

19 William Reisinger, 'East European military expenditures in the 1970s: collective goods or bargaining offer', *International Organization*, vol. 37 winter, 1983, pp. 143–55.

20 Joe Oppenheimer, 'Collective goods and alliances: a reassessment', *Journal of Conflict Resolution*, vol. 23, 1979, pp. 266–79.

21 Condoleezza Rice, 'Defense burden-sharing', in Holloway and Sharp, 1984, op. cit.

22 See Daniel N. Nelson, 1986, op. cit., Chapter 1.

23 See Daniel N. Nelson, ibid., Chapter 30.

24 US Arms Control and Disarmament Agency, *World Military Expenditures and Arms Transfers, 1987*, Washington, DC, ACDA, 1987, p. 5. The Central Intelligence Agency and Defense Intelligence Agency estimated in April 1988 that Soviet defence spending absorbed 15–17 per cent of GNP as compared to 6 per cent for the US. See the discussion of such data in R. Jeffrey Smith, 'Is Gorbachev shifting from guns back to butter', *Washington Post National Weekly*, 1–7 Aug. 1988.

25 ibid., pp. 5–6.

26 ibid., pp. 38–9.

27 Congressional Budget Office (CBO), 'Alliance burdensharing: a review of the data', Staff Working Paper, June 1987, pp. 11–12.

28 Nelson 1986, op. cit., pp. 88–94.

29 For a discussion of the Stockholm agreement on confidence (and security) building measures (CSBMs), see Richard Darilek, 'The future of conventional arms control in Europe – a tale of two cities: Stockholm and Vienna', in *SIPRI Yearbook, 1987*, Stockholm, SIPRI, 1987, pp. 339–59. SIPRI's tabulation of the frequency of notifiable military activities in 1987, and projections for 1988, suggest lower-than-average East European participation as compared with

previous compilations reported by Jeffrey Simon (1985). See SIPRI, pp. 379–81. Soviet military manoeuvres for 1987 were on par with prior years, but 1988 may reveal a substantial decline in ground forces training as with naval deployments.

30 Soviet General Gelyi Batenin was reported to have confirmed at a Warsaw Pact Political Consultative Committee meeting in July 1988 (in Warsaw) that such a proposal on conventional force reductions could be 'expected'. An unnamed US State Department official 'predicted . . . that the Soviets are readying to pull out their 65,000 troops in Hungary', William Echikson, 'Gorbachev in Poland: great expectations', *Christian Science Monitor*, 11 July, 1988.

31 *Die Welt*, 11 July 1988.

32 Ruth L. Sivard, *World Military and Social Expenditures, 1987–1988*, Washington, DC, World Priorities, 1987, p. 13.

33 Sivard, 1987, ibid., p. 12.

34 Sivard, ibid., p. 12.

35 Daniel S. Papp, *Soviet Politics Toward the Developing World During the 1980s*, Maxwell AFB, Ala., Air University Press, 1986, p. 353.

36 International Institute of Strategic Studies (IISS), *The Military Balance, 1986–88*, London: IISS, 1986, p. 210.

37 Central Intelligence Agency (CIA), *Handbook of Economic Statistics, 1987*, Washington, DC, CIA, 1987, p. 126.

38 ACDA, 1987, p. 10.

39 M. Checinski, 'The cost of armament production and the profitability of armament exports in Comecon countries', *Osteuropa-Wirtschaft*, vol. 20, no. 2, pp. 117–42.

40 CIA, 1987, p. 112.

41 US Arms Control and Disarmament Agency (1987), op. cit., p. 131.

42 ibid., p. 36.

43 ibid., pp. 127–30.

44 Nelson, (1986), op. cit., pp. 108–22.

45 Hildebrandt (1983), op. cit., p. 334.

46 Radio Free Europe, East European Audience and Opinion Research, 'Political legitimacy in Eastern Europe: a comparative study', Mar. 1987.

47 'The high price of America's arms buildup', *The National Journal*, 9 Apr. 1988.

48 John Erickson, 'The Warsaw Pact – the shape of things to come', in Karen Dawisha and Philip Hanson (eds) *Soviet–East European Dilemmas*, NY, Holmes & Meier, 1981, p. 161.

49 Vladimir Sobell, 'Perestroika and the Warsaw Pact military burden', Royal Free Europe Research, RAD Background Report, no. 103, 7 June 1988, p. 2.

50 ibid., p. 2.

51 Stanley H. Cohn, 'Economic burden of Soviet defense expenditures: constraints on productivity', *Studies in Comparative Communism*, vol. XX, no. 2, summer, 1987, p. 145.

52 ibid., p. 145.

53 Richard Kaufman, 'Economic trends and defense burden issues in the United States and the Soviet Union', in Thomas Lucid, Judith Reppy and George Staller (eds) *The Economic Consequences of Military Spending in the United States and the Soviet Union*, Ithaca, NY, Cornell University Peace Studies Program, 1986, p. 67.

54 Richard Kaufman, 'Industrial modernization and defense in the Soviet Union', paper presented to the NATO Colloquium, 1–3 Apr. 1987, pp. 4 and 6.

55 Ronald Amann and Julian Cooper, *Technical Progress and Soviet Economic Development*, NY, Basil Blackwell, 1986, p. 13.
56 Morris Bornstein, *East–West Technology Transfer: The Transfer of Western Technology to the USSR*, Paris, OECD, 1985, p. 120.
57 Gregory Hildebrandt, 'Comparative efficiency of U.S. and Soviet defense efforts', in Lucid *et al.* (eds) *The Economic Consequences of Military Spending in the United States and the Soviet Union*, NY, Cornell University Press Studies Program, 9 and 10 May 1986, pp. 78–9.
58 Daniel Bond and Herbert Levine, 'The soviet machinery balance and military durables', in US Congress, Joint Economic Committee, *Soviet Economy in the 1980s: Problems and Prospects*, Washington, DC, US Government Printing Office, 1982, Table 1.
59 Steve Chan, 'Military expenditures and economic performance', in ACDA, *World Military Expenditures and Arms Transfers, 1986*, Washington, DC, ACDA, 1987, p. 34.
60 Bruce Russett, *What Price Vigilance: The Burden of National Defense*, New Haven, Conn., Yale University Press, 1970.
61 For real GNP growth, see CIA, 1987, p. 39; for net investment as share of national income in the early 1980s, see Jan Janous, 'Macroeconomic adjustment in Eastern Europe in 1981–83', in US Congress, Joint Economic Committee *East European Economies: Slow Growth in the 1980s*, p. 41. Comparisons of Soviet and OECD economies are presented in Stanley Cohn, 'Measuring the impact of Soviet defense spending on technology', in Lucid *et al.* (eds) *The Economic Consequences of Military Spending in the United States and the Soviet Union*, pp. 18–19.
62 Amos Perlmutter, *Modern Authoritarianism*, New Haven, Conn., Yale University Press, 1981, p. 91.
63 ibid., pp. 56–7.
64 See my discussion of such probabilities in 'The measurement of East European WTO "Reliability"', in Daniel N. Nelson (ed.) *Soviet Allies: The Warsaw Pact and the Issue of Reliability*, Boulder, Col., Westview, 1984, pp. 6–10; see also Daniel N. Nelson, 'Mobilization potential and the Warsaw Pact's southern flank', in Jeffrey Simon (ed.) *Force Mobilization in NATO and the WTO*, Washington, DC., National Defense University Press, 1988.
65 Vernon Aspaturian, 'The Soviet military–industrial complex: does it exist?', *Journal of International Affairs*.
66 Julian Cooper, 'The civilian production of the Soviet defense industry', in Ronald Amann and Julian Cooper (eds) *Technical Progress and Soviet Economic Development*, Oxford: Basil Blackwell, 1986, p. 32.
67 Condoleezza Rice, 'Soviet military policy under Gorbachev', comments at Kennan Institute, 3 May 1987.
68 Reuters Dispatch, cited by US Air Force *Current News*, 26 July 1988; also cited in 'The USSR this week', *Radio Liberty Research Bulletin*, vol. 32, no. 31, 3 Aug. 1988, p. 3.
69 Sobell (1988), op. cit., p. 3.
70 See Daniel N. Nelson, 'Socio-economic and political change in communist Europe', *International Studies Quarterly*, June 1977, pp. 359–88; see also, Nelson (1986), op. cit., Chapter 3.
71 Radio Free Europe (1987), op. cit. Also, see Daniel N. Nelson, *Elite–Mass Relations in Communist Systems*, London: Macmillan, 1988, pp. 106–16.
72 Jackson Diehl, 'The Poles give a whole new perspective to "approval" ratings', *Washington Post Weekly*, 18–24 Jan. 1988.

73 'A chain of change in Gorbachev's empire, *The Economist*, 21 May 1988, pp. 53–4; see also Brian Morton and Joanne Landy, 'East European activists test glasnost', *Bulletin of the Atomic Scientists*, May 1988.
74 *The Economist*, ibid., p. 54; see also, John Tagliabue, 'Network of dissenters expanding in east bloc', *New York Times*, 22 Mar. 1988.
75 Peter Martin, 'Independent Peace Activity Intensifies', SR/8, 3 June 1988, *RFE Research/Czechoslovak Situation Report*, vol. 13, no. 22, 3 June 1988, pp. 7–10.
76 Daniel N. Nelson and Joseph Lepgold, 'Alliances and burden-sharing: a NATO–Warsaw Pact comparison', *Defense Analysis*, vol. 2, no. 3, 1986, pp. 205–24.

References

Alton, Thad P. (1974) 'Military expenditures in Eastern Europe: some alternative estimates', in US Congress, Joint Economic Committee, *Reorientation and Commercial Relations of the Economies of Eastern Europe*, Washington, DC: US Government Printing Office.
—— (1981) 'East European defense expenditures, 1965–1978', in US Congress, Joint Economic Committee, *East European Economic Assessment*, Part 2, Washington, DC: US Government Printing Office, 409–33.
—— (1985) 'East European defense expenditures, 1965–1982', in US Congress, Joint Economic Committee, *East European Economies: Slow Growth in the 1980s*, Washington, DC: US Government Printing Office, 475–96.
Alton, Thad, P., *et al.* (1973) *Estimates of Military Expenditures in Eastern Europe*, Washington, DC: Arms Control and Disarmament Agency.
Amann, Ronald and Cooper, Julian, (1986) *Technical Progress and Soviet Economic Development*, NY, Basic Blackwell.
Aspaturian, Vernon, 'Is there a Soviet military–industrial complex: does it exist?' *Journal of International Affairs*.
Becker, Abraham S. (1981) *The Burden of Soviet Defense: A Political–Economic Essay*, Oct., Santa Monica, CA: Rand, R–2752–AF.
Bond, Daniel L. (1983) 'Macroeconomic projections of the burden of defense on the Soviet economy', in US Congress, Joint Economic Committee, *Soviet Military Economic Relations*, Washington, DC: US Government Printing Office, 180–91.
Bond, Daniel L. and Levine, Herbert (1982) 'The Soviet machinery balance and military durables', in US Congress, Joint Economic Committee, *Soviet Economy in the 1980s: Problems and Prospects*, Washington, DC: US Government Printing Office.
Bornstein, Morris (1985) *East–West Technology Transfer: The Transfer of Western Technology to the USSR*, Paris: OECD.
Bunce, Valerie J. (1983) 'Neither equality nor efficiency: international and domestic inequalities in the Soviet bloc', in Daniel N. Nelson (ed.) *Communism and the Politics of Inequalities*, Lexington, Mass.: Lexington Books.
Central Intelligence Agency (1978) 'Estimated Soviet defense spending: trends and prospects', June, SR 78–10121.
—— (1982) 'The estimated cost of Soviet defense activities, 1965–1980', paper presented at Workshop on Soviet Military Economic Relations, Congressional Research Service, Washington, DC: 7 July.
—— (1987) *Handbook of Economic Statistics, 1987,* Washington, DC: CIA.
Chan, Steve (1987) 'Military expenditures and economic performance', in ACDA,

World Military Expenditures and Arms Transfers, 1986, Washington, DC: ACDA.

Checinski, M. (1975) 'The cost of armament production and the profitability of armament exports in Comecon countries', *Osteuropa-Wirtschaft* 20, 2: 117–42.

Clawson, Robert W. and Kaplan, Lawrence S. (1982) *The Warsaw Pact: Political Purposes and Military Means,* Wilmington, Del.: Scholarly Resources.

Cohn, Stanley J. (1970) 'The economic burden of Soviet defense outlays', in US Congress, Joint Economic Committee, *Economic Performance and the Military Burden in the Soviet Union,* Washington, DC: US Government Printing Office.

—— (1976) 'A reevaluation of Soviet defense expenditure estimates', Stanford Research Institute Working Paper.

—— (1983) 'Economic burden of Soviet defense production: qualitative and quantitative aspects', in US Congress, Joint Economic Committee, *Soviet Military Economic Relations,* Washington, DC: US Government Printing Office, 192–207.

—— (1986) 'Measuring the impact of Soviet defense spending on technology', in Thomas Lucid, Judith Reppy and George Staller, *The Economic Consequences of Military Spending in the United States and the Soviet Union,* Ithaca, NY: Cornell University Peace Studies Program.

—— (1987) 'Economic burden of Soviet defense expenditures: constraints on productivity', *Studies in Comparative Communism* XX, 2 (Summer): 145–61.

Collins, John M. (1985) *U.S.–Soviet Military Balance, 1980–1985,* Washington, DC: Pergamon–Brassey's.

Congressional Budget Office (CBO) (1987) 'Alliance burdensharing: a review of the data', Staff Working Paper, June.

Cooper, Julian (1986) 'The civilian production of the Soviet defense industry', in Ronald Amann and Julian Cooper (eds) *Technical Progress and Soviet Economic Development,* Oxford: Basil Blackwell.

Crane, Keith M. (1987) 'Military spending in Eastern Europe', *Rand Report* R–3444–USDP, May.

Darilek, Richard (1987) 'The future of conventional arms control in Europe – a tale of two cities: Stockholm and Vienna', in *SIPRI Yearbook, 1987,* Stockholm: SIPRI.

Diehl, Jackson (1988) 'The Poles give a whole new perspective to "approval" ratings', *Washington Post Weekly,* 18–24 Jan.

Die Welt (1988), 11 July.

Echikson, William (1988) 'Gorbachev in Poland: great expectations', *Christian Science Monitor,* 11 July.

The Economist (1988) 'A chain of change in Gorbachev's empire', 21 May, pp. 53–4.

Erikson, John (1981) 'The Warsaw Pact – the shape of things to come', in Karen Dawisha and Philip Hanson (eds) *Soviet–East European Dilemmas,* NY: Holmes & Meier.

Goldman, Marshall I. (1983) *USSR In Crisis: The Failure of an Economic System,* NY: Norton.

Hildebrandt, Gregory G. (1983) 'The dynamic burden of Soviet defense spending', in US Congress, Joint Economic Committee, *Soviet Economy in the 1980s: Problems and Prospects,* Part I, Washington, DC: US Government Printing Office, 331–50.

Holloway, David and Sharp, Jane M.O. (eds) (1984) *The Warsaw Pact: Alliance in Transition?,* Ithaca, NY: Cornell University Press.

International Institute of Strategic Studies (IISS) (1986) *The Military Balance, 1986–88,* London: IISS.

Johnson, A. Ross, Dean, Robert W. and Alexiev, Alexander (1980) *East European Military Establishments: The Warsaw Pact Northern Tier*, Dec., Santa Monica, CA: Rand Corporation, R 2417/1–AF/FF.

Jones, Christopher (1981) *Soviet Influence in Eastern Europe: Political Autonomy and the Warsaw Pact*, NY: Praeger.

Kaufman, Richard S. (1986) 'Economic trends and defence burden issues in the United States and the Soviet Union', in Thomas Lucid, Judith Reppy and George Staller *The Economic Consequences of Military Spending in the United States and the Soviet Union*, Ithaca, NY: Cornell Peace Studies Program.

—— (1987) 'Industrial modernization and defense in the Soviet Union', paper presented to the NATO Colloquium, 1–3 April.

Kennan Institute (1985) *The Warsaw Pact and the Question of Cohesion: A Conference Report*, Washington, DC: The Wilson Center.

Lee, William T. (1979) 'Soviet defense expenditures in an era of SALT', Report 79–1, Washington, DC: United States Strategic Institute.

—— (1980) 'Estimates of Soviet defense spending', statement prepared for Select Committee on Intelligence, House of Representatives, US Congress, 5 Sept.

Levine, H.S. and Roberts, B. (1986) 'Soviet economic prospects and their national security implications', paper presented to the NATO Workshop on National Security Issues After the Twenty-Seventh Congress of the CPSU, Brussels, Nov.

Lewis, William J. (1982) *The Warsaw Pact: Arms, Doctrine and Strategy*, NY: McGraw-Hill.

Linden, Ronald (1979) *Bear and Foxes*, Boulder, Col.: East European Monographs.

Lucid, Thomas, Reppy, Judith and Staller, George, (eds) (1986) *The Economic Consequences of Military Spending in the United States and the Soviet Union*, Ithaca, NY: Cornell University Press Studies Program, 9 and 10 May.

Martin, Peter (1988) 'Independent peace activity intensifies', SR/8, 3 June, *RFE Research/Czechoslovak Situation Report* 13, 22: 7–10.

Morton, Brian and Landy, Joanne, (1988) 'East European activists test glasnost', *Bulletin of the Atomic Scientists* 44, 4 (May): 18.

Mosley, H.G. (1984) *The Arms Race: Economic and Social Consequences*, Lexington, Mass.: Lexington Books.

National Journal (1988) 'The high price of America's military buildup' 20, 15 (April): 972.

Nelson, Daniel N. (1977) 'Socioeconomic and political change in communist Europe', *International Studies Quarterly* 21, 2 (June): 359–88.

—— (1986) *Alliance Behavior in the Warsaw Pact*, Boulder, Col.: Westview.

—— (1988) *Elite–Mass Relations in Communist Systems*, London: Macmillan.

—— (1988) 'Mobilization potential and the Warsaw Pact's southern flank', in Jeffrey Simon (ed.) *Force Mobilization in NATO and the WTO*, Washington, DC: National Defense University Press.

—— (ed.) (1984) *Soviet Allies: The Warsaw Pact and the Issue of Reliability*, Boulder, Col.: Westview.

Nelson, Daniel N. and Lepgold, Joseph (1986) 'Alliances and burden-sharing: a NATO–Warsaw Pact comparison', *Defense Analysis*, II 3 (autumn): 205–24.

Oppenheimer, Joe (1979) 'Collective goods and alliances: a reassessment', *Journal of Conflict Resolution* 23: 266–79.

Papp, Daniel S. (1986) *Soviet Policies Toward the Developing World During the 1980s*, Maxwell, Ala.: Air University Press.

Perlmutter, Amos (1981) *Modern Authoritarianism*, New Haven, Conn.: Yale University Press, p. 91.

Radio Free Europe, East European Audience and Opinion Research (1987) 'Political legitimacy in Eastern Europe: a comparative study', Mar.

Radio Liberty, 'The USSR this week', *Research Bulletin* 32, 31 (1988) Aug. 3.
Rakowska-Harmstone, Teresa, *et al.* (1984) *Warsaw Pact: The Question of Cohesion*, I, II, Feb. and Nov., Ottawa: Ministry of Defense, ORAE.
Reisinger, William (1983) 'East European military expenditures in the 1970s: collective goods or bargaining offer', *International Organization* 37, winter: 143–55.
Remington, Robin Alison (1971) *The Warsaw Pact: Case Studies in Communist Conflict Resolution*, Cambridge, Mass.: MIT Press.
Rice, Condoleezza (1984) 'Defense burden-sharing', in Holloway and Sharp (eds) *The Warsaw Pact: Alliance in Transition*, Ithaca, NY: Cornell University Press.
Russett, Bruce (1970) *What Price Vigilance: The Burdens of National Defense*, New Haven, Conn.: Yale University Press.
Simon, Jeffrey (1985) *Warsaw Pact Forces: Problems of Command and Control*, Boulder, Col.: Westview.
—— (ed.) (1988) *Force Mobilization in NATO and the WTO*, Washington, DC: National Defense University Press.
Sivard, Ruth L. (1987) *World Military and Social Expenditures, 1987–1988*, Washington, DC: World Priorities.
Sobell, Vladimir (1988) 'Perestroika and the Warsaw Pact military burden', Radio Free Europe Research, *RAD Background Report*, no. 103, 7 June.
Tagliabue, John (1988) 'Network of dissenters expanding in east bloc', *New York Times*, 22 Mar.
Tiedtke, Stephan (1978) *Die Warschauer Vertragorganisation: Zum Verhaltnis Von Militar-Und Entspannungspolitik In Osteuropa*, Munich: R. Oldenbourg Verlag.
US Arms Control and Disarmament Agency (ACDA) (1987) *World Military Expenditures and Arms Transfers, 1987*, Washington, DC: ACDA.
Vanous, Jan (1985) 'Macroeconomic adjustment in Eastern Europe in 1981–83', in US Congress, Joint Economic Committee, *East European Economies: Slow Growth in the 1980s*, Washington, DC: US Government Printing Office.
Volgyes, Ivan (1982) *The Political Reliability of the Warsaw Pact Armies: The Southern Tier*, Durham, NC: Duke University Press.

Chapter four

Defence spending in the United Kingdom

Ron Smith

In 1985 the UK ranked fourth in the world in terms of military expenditure (ACDA 1988), was one of the five overt nuclear powers who make up the permanent membership of the UN Security Council and had forces deployed around the globe. But despite these indicators of importance, it had become a marginal player in global politics, no longer the Great Power it once was. Post-war British security policy has been dominated by the need to adapt to a changing geo-political role, to loss of Empire and to relative economic decline. The process of adaptation was not smooth. There was deep ambivalence about the appropriate relationships to Europe, to the US and to those many parts of the rest of the world where it had historical links and economic interests. There were also recurrent reappraisals of the appropriate balance between resources and commitments. As Kennedy (1988: 482) puts it, the 'divergence between Britain's shrunken economic state and its overextended strategical posture is probably more extreme than that affecting any other of the larger powers, except Russia itself'. In this light, it is appropriate to begin with the economic base before proceeding to the security superstructure perched precariously on top of it.

Economic background and prospects

The macro-economy

After the Second World War, the British economy performed well by its own historical standards, but dismally by comparison with its competitors. As a result economic performance was a constant constraint on defence policy. UK GDP grew at a rate that was only about half the OECD average; the UK share of world exports fell from around 20 per cent to 8 per cent; and the share of imports in domestic demand steadily increased, turning what was once the 'workshop of the world' into a net importer of manufactures. Poor trade performance produced a fragile balance of payments, which inhibited expansion. Unemployment rates crept steadily up during the 1960s and 1970s, and inflation accelerated to 25 per cent in the mid-1970s. Britain's poor record in innovation, quality and industrial relations was notorious. OREP (1988) provides a good review of the UK's long-run economic performance.

Even the windfall of North Sea oil, which appeared to remove the balance of payments constraint, proved to have dismal consequences: an appreciation of the exchange rate led to a sharp contraction of manufacturing output during the severe recession of 1980. Following the election of Mrs Thatcher in 1979, and the implementation of the monetarist medium-term financial strategy, unemployment increased to over 3 million, but inflation, after initially accelerating sharply, fell to below 5 per cent. From the depths of the recession, productivity also rebounded sharply. Some, for instance, the Chancellor of the Exchequer in his spring 1988 Budget speech, claimed that the British economy had been transformed. Not only was productivity growing faster than in other major industrial countries, but also Britain was expanding its share of world trade, had low inflation, falling unemployment, and was likely to show the first budget surplus since 1969, despite the cut in basic rate of income tax to 25 per cent. However, following the 1988 Budget there were signs that the economy was overheating, inflation was starting to rise again and the balance of payments was moving quickly into deficit; signs that prompted a sharp rise in interest rates.

Given the conflicting indicators, it is too early to say whether the British economy has been transformed: there have been false dawns before. In any event, economic constraints are likely to interact with the escalating cost of weapons and overextended commitments to shape the defence budget during the next 5 years as they have done for the past 40 years.

The defence budget

Figure 4.1 shows UK military expenditure as a percentage of GDP over the post-war period. The main features are clear, the demobilization after the war, the rearmament for Korea, the slow decline through to 1979, and the initial buildup under Mrs Thatcher, who implemented the previous Labour Government's commitment to NATO for 3 per cent growth in real military expenditure. This commitment was ended in 1985 and the share of GDP devoted to defence is projected to decline until 1991. In 1986–7 defence took 12.6 per cent of public expenditure, compared to 13.1 per cent for health, 13.3 per cent for education and science, and 32 per cent for social security.

In international terms, Britain has devoted a smaller share of GDP to the military than the USA, but substantially more than her European competitors. Within NATO, the UK share of military expenditure in GDP (4.7 per cent in 1987, down from a recent maximum of 5.4 per cent in

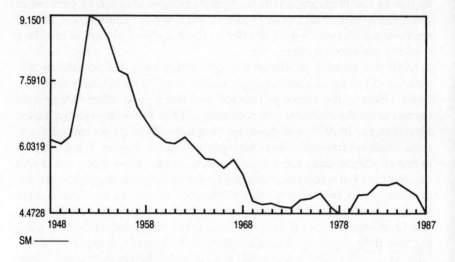

Figure 4.1 UK share of military expenditure in GDP

1983–4), is beaten only by the US at 6.6 per cent and Greece at 6.3 per cent; whereas France at 4 per cent and Germany at 3 per cent are substantially lower. The UK, France and Germany each spend roughly the same amount in total, each about a tenth of the US. The exact ranking between the three is sensitive to exchange rate variations. Between 1985 and 1987 the ranking in both total and per capita expenditure changed from UK, France, Germany, to France, Germany, UK.

The smooth movement of the time series in Figure 4.1 disguises the frantic quality of defence decision-making. John Baylis in Edmonds (1986) provides a review. Again and again the interaction of a weak domestic economy and escalating weapons costs meant that Britain had to review its commitments. The major reviews were by: Sandys in 1957 ('Defence: outline of a future policy'), when conscription was abolished and plans were made to substitute nuclear for conventional forces; Healey in 1966–8 ('The defence review'), which planned withdrawal from East of Suez, and a shift of focus towards Europe; Labour in 1975–6 ('Our contribution to the price of peace'), which planned further concentration on the continental commitment; and Nott ('The UK defence programme: the way forward') in 1981, which planned to cut-back on naval forces. Hartley (1987b) uses a public choice framework to examine the determinants and impact of these reviews.

In practice, these defence reviews often did no more than outline a future policy that failed to materialize or chart a way forward that was rapidly reversed. For example, in February 1966 it was declared that the UK would not undertake major operations without allies; provide military assistance outside Europe unless given every facility; or commit herself to any operation beyond the range of land-based aircraft; and that given these limitations Britain no longer required aircraft carriers. Sixteen years later, aircraft carriers were used in a major operation without allies to launch an opposed amphibious assault outside Europe. The Falklands/Malvinas War also led to the reversal of Nott's plans to cut back the Navy.

The outcome of this process of review and reversal can be characterized as either an unresolved Hegelian dialectic, in which the thesis of budgetary inadequacy and antithesis of cost escalation generate continued contradictions rather than a synthesis of sustainable commitments; or as a Newtonian dynamic equilibrium, which manages to maintain a subtle and impressive balance between the opposing forces operating on it. Both Greenwood and Freedman in Baylis (1985) emphasize the contradictions, whereas Williams in Roper (1985) emphasizes the equilibrium.

Military background

Strategy and forces

UK defence policy centres around the NATO alliance and its response to a Soviet threat. Although the UK has welcomed the changes introduced by Gorbachev, it regards it 'imprudent to rely on a sustained change in Soviet attitudes' (SDE 1988: 1), and its military doctrine remains determined by the NATO deterrence strategy of forward defence and flexible response (SDE 1988: 2).

The UK contribution to the alliance consists of four main roles: the 'independent' nuclear deterrent; ground and air forces in the Federal Republic of Germany; naval forces in the North Atlantic; and defence of the 'home base', the UK, against Soviet attack. In addition the UK has a range of other commitments, including those outside the NATO area. The UK has attempted to maintain 'balanced forces' capable of meeting all these commitments. The projected cost of these commitments in 1988–9 was £1,072m for the deterrent, £4,090m for Germany, £2,583m for naval forces, £2,162m for the home base, and £848m for out of area, leaving overheads not attributable to particular commitments of £8,457m.

The deterrent is provided by four Polaris submarines, due to be replaced by Trident submarines in the mid-1990s. The Continental commitment is met by the 55,000 soldiers of the British Army of the Rhine, and the 12,000 RAF personnel with squadrons of Tornado, Jaguar, Phantom and Harrier aircraft in Germany. This is envisaged to be an armoured war, and in the UK and Germany, there are 300 Challenger and 900 of the older Chieftain tanks to fight it. The naval functions are met by 3 ASW aircraft-carriers, 14 destroyers, 35 frigates, 15 nuclear attack submarines, and 42 mine-hunters/sweepers. The numbers are taken from IISS (1987).

Out of area in early 1988, the UK had ground forces in Hong Kong, Belize, Gibraltar, Cyprus, Brunei and, of course, the Falklands, as well as on training and exercise missions elsewhere (SDE I 1988: 20–1). Naval functions, such as fishery protection (memories of the 'Cod Wars' with Iceland), protection of the North Sea oil installations, and the 'Armilla patrol' of warships and mine-sweepers in the Gulf, are met by ships diverted from NATO acitivities. Within the UK, troops have been on active service in Northern Ireland since 1969. The forces are also used for search and rescue and in industrial disputes (SDE II 1988: 57–8).

Table 4.1 The UK defence budget

	1966–7	1976–7	1979–80	1986–7	1988–9 (plans)
Total expenditure					
£bn (current prices)	2.2	6.2	9.2	18.5	19.2
£bn (1986–7 prices)	19.1	16.2	16.2	18.5	17.5
Composition (%)					
Nuclear strategic	4.8	1.4	1.5	4.7	5.6
Naval forces	14.2	12.9	13.2	12.9	12.6
Land forces	17.7	18.6	18.4	17.1	17.8
Air forces	16.8	16.1	17.1	18.2	17.8
R & D	12.7	12.4	13.4	12.4	11.8
Other	33.8	38.6	36.4	34.7	34.4

Total expenditure and the functional division of the defence budget are shown in Table 4.1. The 1986–7 price figure, which uses a defence-specific deflator, peaked in 1985–6 at £18.9bn and is planned to be £17.4bn in 1990–1. 'Other' includes reserves, R & D, training, support and stocks; if these elements were split down by service, and nuclear strategic forces allocated to the Navy, the service totals for 1985–6 would be £4,190m Navy, £4,181m Army, and £4,548m RAF; with £4,371m, £4,673m and £4,536m projected for 1988–9, all in current prices. After allowance for the fluctuations caused by large investment programmes, such as the delivery of Tornado, the stability of the share of the budget that each service has received over the post-war period is quite striking. This would be expected from the economics of bureaucracy, because bargaining among equally influential players tends to start from some status quo. Against this, over the post-war period there has been a general trend towards increasing central control and reducing service autonomy. The latest step in this direction being the major reorganization of the MOD in 1984. Edmonds (1986) discusses the higher organization of defence.

Strategic nuclear forces took their maximum share of the budget, at 6 per cent, in 1965–6 during Polaris construction, then fell below 2 per cent in 1970–1 and stayed there until 1980–1. The purchase of Trident means that they are likely to take a rather larger share in the future. The January

1988 estimate for the cost of Trident in 1987–8 prices is £9.043bn, compared to the 1981 estimate of £10.85bn. Of the total, 33 per cent is accounted for by the submarines, and 12 per cent by the missiles. The £/$ exchange rate is of course a major influence on these estimates as 36 per cent of the cost will be spent in the USA, HCDC (3 1988). So far, the project appears to have been relatively well managed, and to have stayed under control; although the long strike at the submarine manufacturers, VSEL, in the summer of 1988, may cause some slippage.

The budget figure for strategic nuclear forces understates the cost of the UK nuclear weapons, excluding R & D and non-strategic weapons for instance. Theatre nuclear forces include Tornado, Buccaneer and Sea Harrier aircraft delivering the WE177 free-fall bomb; helicopter delivered US nuclear depth bombs; and US tactical warheads fired from Lance missiles and artillery. The replacement of the free-fall bombs by an air-launched missile is under consideration, possibly to be developed jointly with France or the US. HCDC (7 1988) discusses the modernization of these systems.

The share taken by equipment purchases fluctuates with procurement cycles. It was around 30 per cent in 1949 and 1971, and over 45 per cent in the early 1950s and mid-1980s. The projected figure for 1988–9 is 43 per cent, compared to 22 per cent for forces' pay and allowances, and 11 per cent for civilian pay. Britain adopts a relatively capital intensive military posture. Whereas it ranks fourth in the world in military expenditures, it ranks only twenty-first in size of armed forces. The number of regular service personnel showed a post-war peak of 872,000 in 1952, during the Korean War; then fell steadily with the abolition of conscription touching 320,000 in 1978 and remaining steady since. The time series for service and civilian personnel employed by the Ministry of Defence is shown in Table 4.2.

The concentration on NATO, with its focus on Europe and the North Atlantic, developed slowly over the post-war period; and as it did, the fifth role, capability to meet 'post-imperial' responsibilities outside the NATO area, declined in importance, being treated as a residual in budgetary terms. Whereas before 1970 around 20 per cent of expenditure was directed outside Europe, after 1974 it fell to less than 5 per cent. Instead, equipment and forces designated for NATO roles are used to meet out-of-area demands.

The budgetary and policy emphasis may have been on NATO roles, but the extensive military activity was in non-NATO roles. British service personnel have died in action in almost every year since 1945: in the Korean and Falkland wars; in the large number of decolonizing conflicts such as Palestine, Malaya, Kenya, Suez, Cyprus, Borneo, Aden and Oman; and since 1969 in the Civil War in Northern Ireland. The Falklands War cost about £1.2bn in 1982–3, and the cost of the subsequent defence of

Table 4.2 Personnel employed by MOD

	Regular forces	Civilian personnel
	(000s)	
1950	690	296
1955	803	328
1960	519	322
1961	474	326
1962	442	326
1963	426	290
1964	423	285
1965	423	277
1966	416	275
1967	417	275
1968	409	273
1969	383	263
1970	373	258
1971	368	253
1972	371	275
1973	367	273
1974	349	267
1975	338	267
1976	337	266
1977	330	259
1978	321	251
1979	315	248
1980	321	240
1981	334	230
1982	328	217
1983	321	209
1984	326	199
1985	326	174
1986	323	169
1987	320	164
1988	317	145

the islands fell from £873m in 1983–4 to a projected £145m in 1988–9. The cost of the Northern Ireland campaign is not separately detailed, but it is likely that the main budgetary burden falls on the Civilian Account (compensation, subsidies, etc.) rather than the military account. The military, of course, suffer the cost in casualties. The 1987 figure of 11 service personnel killed (8 of whom were in the local Ulster Defence Regiment) was well down from the 48 deaths in 1979, though there was an upsurge of IRA attacks in 1988.

Arms trade

Britain produces the bulk of its own weapons. Imports have traditionally accounted for about 5 per cent of the equipment budget, rising to 10 per cent in recent years, whereas 15 per cent goes to the British contribution to collaborative projects, such as Tornado produced with Germany and Italy. The most significant import is that of strategic nuclear missiles, Polaris and Trident, for which the warheads and submarines are produced in Britain, though using some US technology. This use of US technology has meant that the UK required US approval before being able to offer to sell nuclear submarines to Canada. However, dependence on US systems has meant that Britain acquired its nuclear capability very cheaply; certainly compared to France, who chose to develop it independently. Whereas, France has had to devote between a quarter and a third of her budget to nuclear programmes, it has cost Britain, on average, less than 5 per cent of a similar total. Whereas Trident is very good value for money, like a Rolls-Royce it still might not be affordable: the opportunity costs in terms of reduced conventional weaponry and a higher defence budget being greater than the benefits. One other significant import was that of the Boeing E3 AWACS aircraft after the failure to develop the Nimrod AEW despite an investment of almost £1bn and 10 years' work. Seven AWACS will enter service from 1991, replacing the existing Second Ward War vintage Shackleton aircraft.

UK military exports rose substantially from around £2bn in 1984 to about £2.6bn in 1987. Of particular importance to UK sales is the Saudi Arabian A1 Yamamah programme, with 1985–6 orders of £5.5bn and 1988 orders of £10bn for Tornado and other equipment. About 80 per cent of Britain's arms sales are to the Third World and around half to the Middle East and North Africa. Unlike France, Britain has not chosen to design its equipment primarily in the light of export prospects.

Demand for military expenditure

There is now a large empirical literature devoted to explanations of military expenditure. This literature is reviewed in Smith (1988b), which also compares a range of equations for UK military expenditure, starting from the models used in Smith (1980b; 1987) and Murdoch and Sandler (1984). Both of these models used tight theoretical specifications, deriving their equations from constrained maximization of welfare functions. An alternative, more empirical, approach involves beginning from very general equations, which allow for a variety of functional forms, dynamic effects, economic and strategic influences and political factors; then searching for restricted versions of these that pass a wide range of misspecification tests and can dominate alternative models in terms of nested and non-nested hypothesis tests. The preferred equation, obtained after such a 'general to specific' specification search is given in Table 4.3.

The equation has an 'error correction' form, explaining the share of military expenditure; the implied hypothesis that the price and income elasticities were unity could be easily accepted. All the coefficients are

Table 4.3 The demand for UK military expenditure. Sample 1949–87; dependent variable, the change in the UK share of military expenditure in GDP (ΔSM_t).

Variable	Coefficient	t statistic
Intercept	−1.32	−4.0
Change in the US share, ΔSA_t	+0.19	7.5
Error correction term, $SM_{t-1} - SR_{t-1}$	−0.15	3.8
Korean War dummy, KD	+1.22	6.6
Defence review dummy, RD	−0.47	−4.8
NATO 3% commitment, N	+1.24	2.4
Standard error of regression	0.1635	
$\bar{R}^2$	0.8576	
Misspecification tests for		
serial correlation: $F(1,32)$	0.14	
Functional form: $F(1,32)$	0.57	
Normality: $\chi^2(2)$	3.0	
Heteroscedasticity: $F(1,37)$	0.53	

Notes: SR is the share of military expenditure in Soviet GNP.
KD = 1 in 1952, 0 otherwise; RD = 1 in 1957, 1968 and 1969;
N is the value of ΔSM implied by the 3 per cent growth commitment,
$N = SM_{t-1} (0.03 - G_t)/(1 + G_t)$, 1979–85, 0 otherwise; where G_t is the growth rate of real GDP.
Estimation was carried out using DataFIT and details of the tests can be found in Pesaran and Pesaran (1987).

significant. This model passes the four misspecification tests shown in Table 4.3. It also shows structural stability over a range of sub-periods. A similar model also fits well to French data. Smith (1988b) contains a full discussion of the econometrics.

The model suggests that the UK adjusts its share of military expenditure to remove deviations between its share in the previous period and a long-run target share based on the Soviet share of military expenditure in GNP. There are substantial measurement problems involved in estimating the Soviet share, and the series used is based on the figures given in ACDA 1988. The long-run target for the UK share is the Soviet share (which was 12.5 per cent in 1985) minus 8.6 per cent (given by the intercept divided by the coefficient of the error correction term). The hypothesis that the long-run coefficient of the Soviet share was unity could be easily accepted.

In addition, the UK tracks changes in the US share of military expenditure. The significant positive effect of US military expenditure conflicts with the 'free-riding' result found in previous studies, which showed negative effects of either US military expenditure (Smith 1980a) or NATO expenditure (Murdoch and Sandler 1984). It is possible that those models, which used the values of US or NATO spending in the previous period were picking up the negative lagged impact that arises from the change effect.

Finally there are political influences from the Korean War rearmament that increased defence spending, defence reviews that reduced it, and the NATO commitment that increased it. This model sheds no light on how provision for defence interacts with other elements of public expenditure, a question that has been examined using a dynamic complete demand system (Dunne *et al*. 1984).

The supply of protection

The defence burden

Kennedy emphasizes how difficult it is for a once Great Power with inherited military commitments and an overburdened economy to judge the balance between defence, consumption and productive investment and says of Britain: 'As with most decaying powers, there is only a choice of hard options' (Kennedy 1988: 483). Spending on defence may increase current security only at the cost of damaging the economic base that provides the foundation for future security provision.

The role of Britain's high military expenditure (relative to its European competitors) in explaining its poor growth performance is hotly debated. Chan (1987) provides a survey of the general literature on the effects of military expenditure on growth. There are a range of possible transmission mechanisms. Military expenditure seems to depress investment (Smith 1980a). It consumes half the UK public R & D budget (CSS 1986) with little evidence for any significant technological spin-offs (Maddock 1983). It is associated with foreign commitments that impact adversely on the balance of payments, though this is offset to a certain extent by arms exports. It may have Keynesian demand stimulation effects if the economy is operating below its 'natural' rate of activity. It may also have micro-economic influences on industrial structure by changing the technology and incentives available to firms.

Estimates of the impact of military expenditure on growth thus naturally differ. The results will depend on the specification of the model, which transmission mechanisms are allowed for; the type of data, time-series or cross-section; the assumptions about *ceteris paribus* conditions, such as how other policies adjust in response to the changes in military expenditure; and the estimation method and sample adopted.

The range of estimates can be illustrated with a personal selection. Dunne and Smith (1984) calculate the effect of reduced military expenditure on the UK economy using simulations of a large econometric model. These results suggest that, after allowing for all the feedbacks, a reduction of the share of military expenditure in GDP by 1.5 per cent would increase GDP by 0.5 per cent, assuming that total public expenditure was kept constant. Martin *et al*. (1987) provide estimates of small simultaneous equation time series models, for the UK and France, explaining growth, unemployment and investment. These results suggest that military expenditure has a small direct positive effect on growth, but a strong negative effect once the feedback through investment is taken account of. However, the total multipliers are implausibly large (−2.4 to −6.9) and differ substantially between the restricted and unrestricted reduced forms. Smith (1978) provides estimates for a three-equation cross-section model, which also gives a direct positive effect, but a net negative effect once the feedback through investment is allowed for. Though here the multiplier is more plausible: a 1 per cent increase in the share of military expenditure reduces the growth rate by 0.13 per cent.

The value of the multiplier will not be independent of other circumstances. It is more likely to be positive if there is excess supply, as in the 1930s. It will differ between wartime and peacetime, because of differences in the population's willingness to sacrifice consumption. However, if an average value of around −0.13 per cent were a reasonable summary of the position of the OECD countries in the post-war period, this would suggest that the difference in military expenditures between Japan and the UK only accounts for a fraction of the difference in their growth rates, albeit an economically significant fraction.

Personnel

In 1986–7 the UK fielded 320,000 regular forces, and 317,000 reserves from a population of 56.8m (5.1m of whom were males between the ages of 18 and 30) and an employed labour force of 24.5m. Volunteer forces seem likely to remain the rule. Britain does not have a political tradition of peacetime conscription, nor is there any strong pressure for it within the armed services, thus the return of 'national service' does not appear to be high on the political agenda. Currently, the combination of demographic factors, high unemployment and competitive pay scales has meant that recruitment is not a problem. However, the MOD expect that the reduction in the number of young people coming into the labour market, and economic expansion, will make recruitment more difficult (SDE 1988: 52), and they are taking measures to encourage trained personnel to stay longer in the forces.

Whereas the number of service personnel has remained relatively constant in recent years, the number of UK based MOD civilians has fallen sharply from 248,000 in 1979, to 167,000 in 1986, and a projected 145,000 in 1988. The proportion of non-industrial workers in the total has risen from 46 per cent to 56 per cent between 1979 and 1989. The reduction has been achieved by privatizing the Royal Ordnance Factories, bringing private management into the Royal Dockyards, using private contractors for a range of functions previously done by civil servants, and making a variety of efficiency improvements and cosmetic accounting changes. In the process there has been a contraction of the research establishments, with the number of scientists employed falling from 10,700 to 6,400 between 1979 and 1987.

In addition to the military and the civil servants, MOD expenditures generate an estimated 515,000 jobs in industry, and arms exports a further 110,000, through direct and indirect employment effects. The total number of industrial jobs dependent on defence expenditure has fallen from 710,000 in 1978–9 to 625,000 in 1985–6 (SDE II 1988: 61).

Equipment

Military equipment is expensive, the Trident programme will cost half as much again as the Channel tunnel and unit costs increase rapidly between generations. Type 22 frigates were four times as expensive as their Leander predecessors, and the Type 23, which was intended to be simpler and cheaper than the Type 22, has proved much more expensive than predicted. Given the large amounts of money involved, it is not surprising that equipment procurement and the structure of the Defence Industrial Base, have been matters of concern throughout the post-war period. Recurrent problems with cost and time overruns and the failure of systems to meet specifications, led to the 'Downey' reforms in the 1960s, which specified a decision structure for each stage of the procurement process; the 'Rayner' reforms of the 1970s, which led to the setting up of an integrated Procurement Executive; and the 'Levene' reforms of the 1980s, which introduced a more commercial approach. A similar cycle of procurement reform is apparent in the US (McNaugher 1987).

The recent performance failures have involved time and cost overruns on the Chevaline re-entry vehicle for Polaris, various torpedos, the Foxhunter radar for Tornado, and most notably the systems for the Nimrod Airborne Early Warning aircraft. These have been the subject of a series of critical reports by the House of Commons Defence and Public Accounts Committees, and by the National Audit Office. HCDC (5 1988) discusses the general problems associated with procurement and reviews progress on nine current projects. It also discusses the internal MOD report on project management, 'Learning from Experience', which was commissioned after cancellation of Nimrod.

The current reforms, announced in MOD (1983), and implemented by Peter Levene, the Chief of Defence Procurement since 1984, involve the increased use of competitive tendering from a much wider range of firms, the replacement of cost-plus by fixed-price contracts, and changes in the structure of the MOD Procurement Executive, to attribute responsibility and to make it a more demanding, better informed customer. The philosophy behind these changes and the efficiency improvements that have resulted are described in Levene (1987). The complex theoretical issues associated with defence procurement are reviewed in Smith (1988a). The policy resulted in competitive contracts rising from 30 per cent of total value in 1979–80 to 64 per cent in 1985–6; before falling back to 53 per cent in 1986–7 and 50 per cent in 1987–8, as a result of a few large projects, such as Trident, for which competition at the prime contractor level was impossible. SDE I (1988: 31) cites savings over initial budgetary estimates of £105m on eleven projects.

The scope for competition is limited by the prevalence of domestic monopolies. Products where there is a single UK producer include: major airframes and missiles, British Aerospace (BAe); ordnance and small arms, Royal Ordnance, now owned by BAe; tanks, Vickers; torpedos, GEC; nuclear submarines, VSEL; large aero- and marine-turbine engines and nuclear propulsion units, Rolls-Royce; and helicopters, Westland. Until 1979, government policy encouraged concentration in the defence industries to exploit economies of scale and scope, particularly in systems integration, culminating in the formation of BAe, and British Shipbuilders (BS). Since 1979, BAe, BS warship yards, Rolls-Royce and Royal Ordnance, have been privatized. As has been the rule, they were not privatized in a way that would encourage competition. The partial exception to this is the warship yards, where there is now some competition in the building of frigates. It is not clear that this competition is sustainable since there is substantial over-capacity in warship-building. The MOD argued strongly, on grounds of competition, against the 1985–6 GEC attempt to takeover Plessey. The Monopolies and Merger Commission accepted this argument and blocked the merger. Their report (1986) is an important source of information on the defence market. In 1988 GEC made a further attempt in conjunction with Siemens.

Where domestic monopoly prevails, competition can only come from abroad. This inevitably threatens the large and previously heavily protected British Defence Industrial base (DIB). The issues in the maintenance of such a base are reviewed in Hartley et al. (1986). They point out that while the need for a DIB is widely asserted it is rarely justified. To do this requires specifying the objectives, such as security of supply in crisis, national independence and economic spin-offs, and assessing the alternative ways of meeting them through inventories and strategic stockpiles, long-term contracts, diversification of supply, and industrial policy. In this light, long lead-times may make production capacity irrelevant in the short duration conflicts that are most likely. Independence may be an illusion given the complex international inter-dependencies that exist in the construction of weapons. Nor is there any evidence of long-term economic benefits from the maintenance of a DIB protected from foreign competition. The paper concludes that weapons should be procured competitively within an alliance framework in order to meet security requirements. This should be done without concern for the

DIB, unless specific defence requirements for a particular domestic capability can be documented. The list of capabilities that can meet this criterion is very short.

Developing the appropriate alliance framework for the evolution of defence industrial structure remains a matter of concern. In the UK the issue surfaced in the dispute over the future of the Westland helicopter company. The acquisition by United Technologies Corporation (Sikorsky) of a substantial holding in Westland was seen by some as threatening both Britain's technological independence and links with Europe. This somewhat arcane controversy over an unprofitable little company provoked the resignation of two Cabinet ministers (Freedman 1987).

At a European level, the Independent European Programme Group (IEPG) is trying to open up and rationalize procurement. Despite a major report, 'Towards a Stronger Europe', produced by an independent study team chaired by Vredeling, progress is slow. There is widespread agreement on the problems: unnecessary replication of R & D; inefficiently short production runs; excess capacity which is underutilized; proliferation of unstandardized and non-interoperable equipment; and highly constrained defence budgets (Hartley 1983; 1987a). There is virtually no agreement on how to implement the solutions. These would require each country making concessions in sensitive areas; concessions that current political markets cannot deliver. Even among those who favour stronger European institutions, common procurement policies and industrial rationalization, there are worries. The model of the Common Agricultural Policy and the fear of a European Tank Mountain, to join the Butter Mountain, haunts the discussion!

Future contingencies

Future prospects can be examined under two scenarios: on the basis of current policies, or on the basis of alternative policies. The primary issue about current policy is whether it is sustainable. The long-term costings, which the MOD uses to plan for future commitments, appear overcrowded. Trident, AWACS, the EH101 helicopter, MLRS, the European Fighter Aircraft (EFA), tank modernization, amphibious warfare capability, the NATO frigate and many other items are jostling for space in a restricted budget. The Commons Defence Committee pointed out the dangers and predicted a defence review by stealth (HCDC 1985). This is achieved by 'salami slicing', cutting small amounts from a range of programmes and 'shifting programmes to the right', postponing dates for development or deployment. There have been some efficiency savings in procurement that help, but identified savings are small relative to the size of the problem.

So far, the MOD has survived longer without a major defence review than many outside commentators thought possible, but whether it can postpone a serious review indefinitely is questionable. Despite the success of the Levene reforms, and the attractions of fixed-price contracts, it is unlikely that cost overruns have been abolished. The fixed price ALARM (air launched anti-radar missile) project has already had to be re-negotiated (HCDC 5 1988) and in the future EFA looks particularly vulnerable.

Serious review means consideration of commitments, asking which might be surrendered. Trident is now well advanced, £1.5bn had been spent and £3.5bn committed in May 1988, and spending is continuing at around £1bn a year (HCDC 3 1988). Thus cancellation would not save a lot of money. Bringing troops back from Germany would involve a large short run cost in providing barracks and facilities for them in the UK, and would raise problems with allies and treaty commitments. Thus the candidate is likely to remain the one chosen by Nott: naval forces. Although the MOD retains the declared aim of a fleet of around 50 destroyers and frigates, the rate at which it is ordering frigates is more consistent with a much smaller navy by the mid-1990s (HCDC 6 1988).

In terms of alternative policies, the central question is the nuclear issue. For the Labour Party defence remains a sensitive issue with its 1989 review suggesting a change in its commitment to unilateral nuclear disarmament. Anyhow, given past performance – between 1964–70 when they proceeded with Polaris deployment and 1974–9 when they developed Chevaline and did the initial planning for Polaris replacement – some would question whether a Labour Government would actually implement a unilateralist policy.

There is a wider political argument against Trident in that it constitutes a massive, unnecessary and destabilizing enhancement in nuclear capability at a time of improving relations with the Soviets; it complicates future strategic arms control initiatives; its independent use would be incredible; and it diverts resources from more important improvements in conventional weapons. The anti-nuclear argument also expresses concern at UK exposure to retaliation in its role as 'an unsinkable aircraft carrier' for US forces. The alternative policy would involve efforts to create a European nuclear-free zone and to develop non-provocative defence strategies. There is a substantial literature on all these issues, for instance the discussion in Baylis (1985) and Roper (1985), but with the recent reduction in international tension, they seem to have become matters of less concern to the general public. The traditional Labour Party demand that military expenditures should be reduced as a share of GDP to around the European average of 3.5 per cent, seems to have been dropped: thus it will remain Treasury parsimony, rather than Socialist principle, which constrains military expenditures.

In conclusion, it seems likely that British defence policy will continue in the same mode, reactive rather than directed; dominated by the need to respond and adapt, albeit reluctantly, to changing external circumstances – economic, geopolitical and technological – and to changing internal constraints.

References

ACDA (1988) *World Military Expenditures and Arms Transfers 1987*, Washington, DC: US Arms Control and Disarmament Agency.

Baylis, John (ed.) (1985) *Alternative Approaches to British Defence Policy*, London: Macmillan.

Chan, Steve (1987) 'Military expenditures and economic performance', in *World Military Expenditures and Arms Transfers 1986*, Washington US Arms Control and Disarmament Agency.

CSS (Council for Science and Society) (1986) *UK Military R & D*, Oxford: Oxford University Press.

Dunne, J. P. and Smith, R. P. (1984) 'The economic consequences of reduced UK military expenditure', *Cambridge Journal of Economics* 8: 297–310.

Dunne, J. P., Pashardes, P. and Smith, R. P. (1984) 'Needs costs and bureaucracy: the allocation of public consumption in the UK', *Economic Journal* 94, Mar.: 1–15.

Edmonds, Martin (ed.) (1986) *The Defence Equation*, London: Brassey's.

Freedman, Lawrence (1987) 'The case of Westland and the bias to Europe', *International Affairs* 63: 1–19.

Hartley, Keith (1983) *NATO Arms Co-operation*, London: Allen & Unwin.

Hartley, Keith (1987a) 'Public procurement and competitiveness: a community market for military hardware and technology', *Journal of Common Market Studies* XXV, 3, Mar.: 237–47.

Hartley, Keith (1987b) 'Reducing defence expenditure: a public choice analysis and a case study of the UK', in C. Schmidt and F. Blackaby (eds) *Peace Defence and Economic Analysis*, London: Macmillan, 399–423.

Hartley, Keith, Hussain, F. and Smith R. P. (1986) 'The UK defence industrial base', *Political Quarterly* 58, 1: 62–72.

HCDC (1985) *Defence Commitments and Resources*, Third Report of the Defence Committee 1984–5 (vols I–III), HC 37, London: HMSO.

HCDC (1988) Reports of the Defence Committee Session 1987–8: 3rd Report *The Progress of the Trident Programme*, HC 422; 5th Report *The Procurement of Major Defence Equipment*, HC 431; 6th Report *The Future Size and Role of the Royal Navy's Surface Fleet*, HC 309; 7th Report *The Statement on the Defence Estimates*, HC 495; London: HMSO.

IISS (1987) *The Military Balance 1987–1988*, London: International Institute for Strategic Studies.

Kennedy, Paul (1988) *The Rise and Fall of the Great Powers*, London: Unwin Hyman.

Levene, Peter (1987) 'Competition and collaboration: UK defence procurement', *RUSI Journal* 132, 2: 3–6.

McNaugher, Thomas, L. (1987) 'Weapons procurement: the futility of reform', *International Security* 12, 2, autumn: 63–104.

Maddock, Sir Ieuan (1983) *Civil Exploitation of Defence Technology*, Report to the Electronics EDC, London National Economic Development Office.

Martin, S., Smith, R. P. and Fontanel, J. (1987) 'Time series estimates of the macroeconomic impact of defence spending in France and the UK', in C. Schmidt and F. Blackaby (eds) *Peace Defence and Economic Analysis*, London: Macmillan.

MOD (1983) *Value for Money in Defence Equipment Procurement*, Defence Open Government Document, 83/01, London: Ministry of Defence.

Monopolies and Mergers Commission (1986) *The General Electric Company PLC and the Plessey Company PLC*, a report on the proposed merger, Cmnd 9867, London: HMSO.

Murdoch, James and Sandler, Todd (1984) 'Complementarity, free riding and the military expenditure of NATO allies', *Journal of Public Economics* 25: 83–101.

OREP (1988) 'Long run economic performance in the UK', *Oxford Review of Economic Policy* 4, 1, spring.

Pesaran, M. H. and Pesaran, B. (1987) *DataFIT: An Interactive Econometric Software Package*, Oxford: Oxford University Press.

Roper, John (ed.) (1985) *The Future of British Defence Policy*, London: Gower.

SDE (1988) *Statement on the Defence Estimates 1988*, Cm 344, I & II, London: HMSO.

Smith, R. P. (1978) 'Military expenditure and capitalism: a reply', *Cambridge Journal of Economics* 2: 299–304.

Smith, R. P. (1980a) 'Military expenditure and investment in OECD countries', *Journal of Comparative Economics* 4: 19–32.

Smith, R. P. (1980b) 'The demand for military expenditure', *Economic Journal* 90, Dec: 811–20.

Smith, R. P. (1987) 'The demand for military expenditure: a correction', *Economic Journal* 97, Dec.: 989–90.

Smith, R. P. (1988a) *Buying Weapons: Defence Procurement in the UK*, Birkbeck Discussion Paper in Economics 88/6.

Smith, R. P. (1988b) 'Models of military expenditure', *Journal of Applied Econometrics*, forthcoming.

Chapter five

Defence spending in France: the price of independence

Christian Schmidt, Louis Pilandon and Jacques Aben

Economic background and prospects

Since 1960, French defence policy has been quite specific. The end of the colonial wars and the change of political power have led to a complete reorganization of French national defence and, in particular, to a new definition of the military defence concept. In 1960 and 1964, the French Parliament accepted reluctantly the idea of a national nuclear force, named first of all *force de frappe*, then *force de dissuasion* (the latter being more acceptable politically). This new concept permitted the removal of French armies out of the integrated military organization of the Atlantic Alliance, which had become necessary because of the tensions between the French Government and NATO (since 1956 at least).

These different options found expression in a smooth military equipment policy, aiming first of all at the construction of the *force nationale de dissuasion* with three constituent parts: Mirage IV bombers, Plateau d'Albion GLBMs, and Redoutable-class nuclear submarines with SLBMs (1960–72). Then, with the regular up-dating of these weapons, came the construction of tactical nuclear forces (later named *pré-stratégiques* to underline their governmental nature), and the complete renewal of conventional forces. This priority in equipment is so emphasized that in 1988 the arms procurement section of the military budget (*Titre V*) exceeded day-to-day expenditures (*Titre III*): 52.1 per cent v. 47.9 per cent (Figure 5.1).[1]

This chosen policy has taken the form – very traditional in France since 1945 – of planning, or rather, in military jargon, of programming.[2] From 1960 to 1983, five *Lois de programmation militaire* were voted, with the aim to 'cover' progressively the whole of military expenditures. However, in 1987, with the sixth law, this appeared too ambitious a purpose and it was decided to programme only equipment expenditure (Table 5.1).[3]

As an economic power France is a medium-size country: 550,000 km^2 with 55 million inhabitants, i.e. a density of 100. In 1987 the French GDP per capita was FF94,882 (i.e. $15,814). From the Second World War

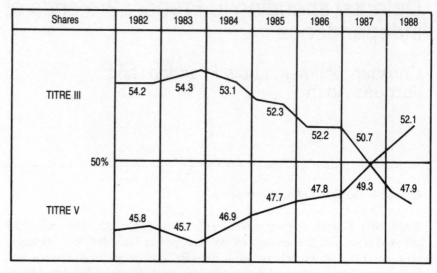

Shares	1982	1983	1984	1985	1986	1987	1988
TITRE III	54.2	54.3	53.1	52.3	52.2	50.7	52.1
50%						49.3	
TITRE V	45.8	45.7	46.9	47.7	47.8		47.9

Figure 5.1 Shares of equipment and other costs
Source: SIRPA, Ministry of Defence

Table 5.1 The laws of military programmes (Les lois de programmation militaire)

Dates	Stated resources (resources inscrites)	Number of programmes (nombre des programmes)
1960–4	One-third of programme authorization (Le tiers des autorisations de programmes)	16
1965–70	Two-thirds of programme authorization (Les deux-tiers des autorisations de programmes)	25
1971–5	Totality of programme authorization (La totalité des autorisations de programmes)	31
1976	—	—
1977–82	Totality of payment credits (La totalité des crédits de paiement)	39
1983	—	—
1984–8	Totality of payment credits (La totalité des crédits de paiement)	40

Source: Ministry of Defence

onwards, the real French GDP has grown at an average rate of 3.86 per cent, so that the real GDP per capita could grow at about 3.13 per cent per annum. Such an economic growth allowed for an expansion of military expenditures and for achieving the successive equipment programmes, reducing at the same time the 'burden' of military expenditures on GDP: the ratio of military expenditure to GDP declined from 6.1 per cent in 1960 to about 3.8 per cent in 1988, after 3.35 per cent in 1974 (Figure 5.2).

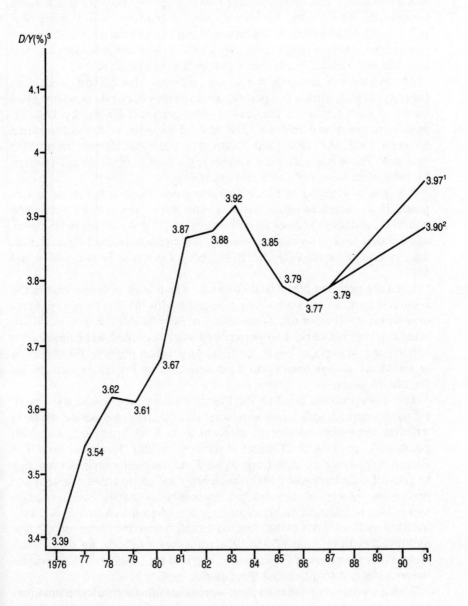

Figure 5.2 French defence shares
Notes:
[1] Assumption: +2 per cent growth in defence spending.
[2] Assumption: +1 per cent growth in defence spending.
[3] D/Y is defence spending as a share of *Produit Intérieur Brut Marchand*.

This is not to say, however, that the evolution of military expenditures was satisfactory and that the successive programmes were successfully completed. After 1970, the inefficiency of military programming was pointed out by Members of Parliament, and even by Ministers. Each new programme was designed to make up for the gaps of the preceding one and to avoid new delays, but it seems that problems remained.

The reason was certainly not a consequence of insufficient production capacity. In fact, during this period, the unemployment rate was multiplied by six at least (from 1.7 per cent to 10.5 per cent) leaving by 1988 2.5 million workers unemployed. The rate of capacity utilization declined between 1963 and 1968, and followed a continual decline from 1973 onwards. There has only been a slight revival since 1984, though perhaps by 1988 there were signs of a real expansion.

Nor was it a matter of productivity, because the hourly rate of labour productivity increased at the average rate of 4.49 per cent between 1960 and 1979, and again at 2 per cent from 1980 to 1988. As for the productivity of capital, it grew at an average rate of 4.4 per cent between 1951 and 1973, 4.6 per cent between 1973 and 1979, and 3.7 per cent between 1979 and 1984.

Even the problem of the trade balance, which is a traditional clue in the French economy, does not seem connected with the question of military expenditures. The French armaments industry is third in the world for arms exports, with about 10 per cent of world exports[4] and French arms exports are on average five to ten times larger than imports. Finally, arms exports have always been up to 5 per cent of total French exports during the last 15 years.

The main problem faced by the French military programme was one of inflation coupled with erroneous forecasts. During the period 1960–83 inflation continued: its average rate was as high as 7 per cent, with high points of 15 per cent in 1974 and 14 per cent in 1981. However, even if in France it appears that (rigorously defined) military inflation is not superior to general inflation (Aben 1981), such rates are easily able to destroy the purchasing power of any budget especially as public budgets adapt themselves to inflation and because they are often the instrument of anti-inflation policies. After the first oil crisis, when the price of oil was multiplied by three from 1973 to 1974, things went so badly for the defence budget that Members of Parliament stated that the training of pilots was no longer sufficient to guarantee their own safety.

Perhaps worse than inflation itself were misleading forecasts on inflation, and, more generally, on its evolution. Inflation rates were almost systematically underestimated and the adjustments rarely managed to balance current expenditures with the new growth in prices.[5] A direct increase would have meant raising tax rates but this threat in fact never materialized. A relative increase was just as difficult in the context of economic crisis, with increasing unemployment everywhere (in 1973–6 and especially after 1982).

Military programmers are faced with another problem of forecasting that concerns the specific price of armaments or, rather, armament systems. The acquisition of these systems not only reflects an inflation due to the growth of factory prices, but they also become rapidly outdated due to technical progress. One of the keys to the difficulty is unknown (or partially unknown) technological progress. The history of French military programming is littered with examples of uncompleted armament programmes due to inadequate forecasting of prices (e.g. Plateau d'Albion GLBMs; Pluton SRBMs).

In 1988 the situation was scarcely more favourable, although the overall economic situation was clearly improving, inflation having receded from 14 per cent per annum in 1981 to 3.5 per cent by 1988. However, what is more important is that the difference between French and foreign rates was drastically reduced – for example, the difference with the Federal Republic of Germany was only 1.7 per cent by mid-1988. The French Franc exchange rate has been relatively stable over the past few years, even if interest rates were substantially reduced, following the inflation rate (but they remain at a higher level, in real terms, than foreign ones: between 2.4 and 3 percentage points higher). Above all, economic activity has been sustained over the past months, with the result that the unemployment figures are stabilized and that job offers are now growing. Even the national fiscal resources were more than predicted in 1988, so that the public debt was reduced.

Description of forces and strategic doctrine

In order to carry out the tasks that France has assigned itself in different parts of the world, French military forces have been organized differently. France, as the only European nuclear power on the Continent besides the Soviet Union, has divided its forces into several special branches. Within each of them the traditional distribution between the army, the navy and the air force has given way to a more general distinction between 'nuclear' and 'conventional' forces (see Table 5.2).

Nuclear forces, in turn, fall into two categories according to their aims, which are defined in the French doctrine of deterrence (*doctrine française de dissuasion nationale*) whose description is provided below. The two categories are 'strategic forces' and 'pre-strategic forces':

(i) *Strategic forces* in 1987–8 were comprised of:
— six nuclear-powered ballistic missile-armed submarines (SSBN), each with 16 missiles whose single M4 warheads are now being replaced by multiple M20 warheads (6 heads);

The economics of defence spending

Table 5.2 Allocation of military expenditures
Average percentage of Titre V (%)

	1970–5	1976–82	1983–6	(1987–91)
Common forces	32.21	30.88	27.83	28.01
Air force	24.77	24.27	25.08	24.54
Army	21.96	23.45	24.27	23.66
Navy	19.81	19.22	21.00	21.99
Police (gendarmerie)	1.24	2.17	1.82	1.79

Relative shares of nuclear (strategic and pre-strategic) conventional and space forces (shares of Titre V)

Period	Nuclear	Conventional	Space
1970–5	35.57	64.43	–
1976–82	31.64	68.36	–
1983–6	32.59	67.41	–
1987–91	32.00	65.98	2.02

Source: Ministry of Defence

— 18 silo-based missiles located on the Plateau d'Albion, south-east France. Here again the replacement of M4 by multiple M20 warheads is being carried out;
— 2 squadrons of Mirage IV bombers fitted out with medium-range air-to-ground missiles with nuclear charges. This force has a logistic support that comprises 3 KC 135 tanker aircraft; 2 Transall aircraft as well as 8 training aircraft; 7 Mirage IIIB and 1 Mystère Falcon 20P; 3 AWACS will soon be added so as to improve the alert network of the system.

(ii) *Pre-strategic forces*

These are deployed among the three forces (i.e. army, air force and navy). As far as the army is concerned, it comprises 32 Pluton 112-mile range rockets, which will be replaced by Hades missiles – striking range 280 miles. The navy has 38 Super Etendard fighter-bombers equipped with ASMP missiles. The air force comprises 5 squadrons, three with 45 Jaguars, one with 15 Mirage IIIE equipped with AN 52 weapons, and one with 13 Mirage 2000 equipped with ASMP.

The strategic and pre-strategic units are manned by a total of 18,000 persons; with 8,450 persons assigned specifically to the pre-strategic units. Slightly more than half of the overall personnel is employed by the air force (10,200).

Conventional forces, 1987–8

The army comprises 336,000 men, including 185,000 recruits (conscripts) and 40,000 civilians – 6,000 women are distributed among the different categories. An original feature of the army is what is called the Rapid Task Force (*Force d'action rapide* – FAR), which comprises 47,000 men and is composed of one division of paratroopers, an airborne naval division, a cavalry division, an infantry division and an airborne infantry division. This unit is equipped with 241 helicopters armed with Hot missiles. To this should be added the 8,500 men in the Foreign Legion. The army also has 305,000 reservists available on call.

The navy comprises 73,500 men distributed as follows: 46,580 men in regular service, 19,510 recruits and 7,410 civilians – 1,700 women are assigned to the various categories. The fleet consists of:

— 24 submarines, 4 of which are nuclear-powered attack submarines armed with Exocets;
— 43 surface vessels (cruisers, destroyers, frigates, etc.) and 2 aircraft-carriers, to which must be added 38 accompanying ships.

The naval air forces comprise 9,000 men and are equipped, apart from nuclear weaponry, with Breguet Atlantic, Alizé, Falcon and Navajo aircraft and Alouette and Lynx helicopters, and can use Exocet, Martel, Sidewinder, etc. missiles. In addition, 400 men, divided into 5 commando squads, belong to the navy.

The air force includes 100,548 men divided into 58,494 regular airmen, 36,398 recruits and 5,656 civilians, with 5,600 women belonging to the various categories. Besides its nuclear resources, it is composed of 13 attack squadrons of Mirage aircraft (IIIC, FIC, 2000), armed with various types of missiles, as well as 19 transport squadrons of DC8, C160, etc. and 193 helicopters (Alouette, Puma, Seyer Puma, etc.).

To complete all these forces, it is necessary to add the National Police forces, comprised of 88,194 men, divided into 77,170 regular members, 10,092 recruits and 932 civilians – 1,400 women are to be found in the various categories. Equipment consists of combat cars, coastguard patrols, light reconnaissance aircraft and helicopters.

In the same way, other services such as the coastguards, though not belonging to the military forces, play a part in defence and are supplied with appropriate equipment, i.e. ships, planes and light helicopters.

Thus, as far as France is concerned, a comparison between the fighting strength and population is in the ratio of 14:100. France's position, as illustrated by its military forces, shows another distinctive characteristic, namely, that France is also active overseas. This entails the following distribution of forces (air force–army–navy):

— 50,000 men in the Federal Republic of Germany
— 8,000 in the West Indies and French Guyana
— 3,300 in the Indian Ocean
— 9,500 men in New Caledonia

— 5,000 in Polynesia
— 1,200 men in the Central African Republic
— 1,900 men in the Republic of Chad
— 3,900 in Djibouti
— 1,750 men in the Lebanon (FINUL–UNIFIL)
— 1,200 men in Senegal
— 500 men in the Côte d'Ivoir
— 500 men in Gabon

Such a situation quite obviously leads us to consider the strategic doctrine governing the use of these forces.

The strategic doctrine

The first goal of French defence is to maintain the identity and independence of the country. That is why it adheres to the principle of self-decision at this level, while closely co-operating with its allies within the Atlantic Alliance. This explains why France, being outside the integrated military organization, has a strategy of nuclear deterrence of its own.

This strategic doctrine has been conceptualized over many years. Since the first French nuclear explosion in the Sahara in 1960, the concepts for its utilization have changed in some regards. From 1960–74 approximately, the doctrine was to use the nuclear strategic weapons as final recourse against the enemy. However, since the middle of the 1970s, much has changed with the rise of technology and the introduction of tactical weapons now called pre-strategic (Pluton and Hades).

Consideration needs to be given to the unique nature of French nuclear doctrine. Thanks to the asymmetric power relationship with the Soviet Union, the French doctrine was labelled as *dissuasion du faible au fort* by General Poirier, one of the doctrine's fathers. In order to characterize such a doctrine, its two main tenets must be remembered: (i) nuclear weapons are not battlefield weapons and they are not meant to be used during the battle at any level (contrary to US doctrine on nuclear weapons); (ii) major cities are the only targets for nuclear strategic missiles (which excludes any counter-force strategic option as in US doctrine).

From the beginning until the mid-1970s, the actual nuclear weapons have provided an exact translation of the French doctrine. After that time, however, new short-range nuclear missiles have been added to the strategic ones. These do not, of course, modify the hard core of the doctrine. As pre-strategic these weapons are not to be used on the battlefield but must be understood as an ultimate warning for the enemy.[6]

France is diversifying its strategic forces in order to avoid sudden technological breakthroughs. This is the reason why France, for example, considering the relatively reduced extent of the national territory, abandoned its plans to develop a mobile missile.

Finally, a problem has long been raised as to the so-called pre-strategic nuclear weapons. Together with strategic weapons, as explained above, they play a part in deterrence. French deterrence is a package, from which no particular type of nuclear weapon can be extracted. As a result of this, the pre-strategic weapons have *not* been designed to succeed conventional ones by providing a further step in war escalation. According to their very name, they are to be used at the beginning of the nuclear process. They are not, and they cannot be, weapons for use on the battlefield: hence the notion of an ultimate and unique warning being attached to their use.

As far as conventional weapons are concerned, the strategic doctrine is that they complement nuclear weapons. The first mission assigned to these arms is to make sure that the French nuclear system cannot be bypassed. The structure of the army emphasizes the bonds of solidarity uniting France to its allies. The fact that French forces are present in some areas of vital interest for the Western world (the Lebanon, Chad, the Gulf) is widely acknowledged. It is in this way that France intends to fulfil its duties towards other states, particularly the African states to which it is bound by treaties of aid and protection.

Similarly, within Europe, French strategy does not only fit into the framework of the Alliance, but more particularly into that of the Western European Union (WEU). Thus, the most appreciable advances in strategic matters have been realized within the bilateral framework of Franco-German relations.

Bound by the 1963 Accords, France and the Federal Republic of Germany have built up several common institutions such as a defence council, a land brigade, joint plans of armament, etc. Intent on tightening its defensive co-operation, France has extended the field of intervention of its Rapid Task Force (FAR) to the whole territory of the Federal Republic, even envisaging a possible nuclear cover of this same territory.

France is also working at strengthening its bonds with Great Britain, the Alliance's third nuclear power. These joint arrangements are worked out only within the framework of the Atlantic Alliance and are by no means intended as a substitute for it. On the contrary, France is doing its best to avoid a fatal loosening of the ties between the United States and Europe; the latter, however, will not exist as long as it is unable to secure its own defence.

The demand for military expenditures

The analysis of the trend in French military expenditures suggests three specific features, namely: (a) a nuclear hardcore connected to the deterrence option; (b) a defence industry providing almost all the arms procurements for national military needs; and (c) a military presence area in Africa related to historical background. Each feature has its own incentives and is determined by different factors. Furthermore, from the point of view of the international threat, it is true that the nuclear deterrence component of the French defence system is related to the Soviet Union and the countries of the Warsaw Pact, whereas a part of the conventional forces is devoted to the African area. So, in spite of the crudeness of such a classification, the disaggregation of French military expenditures into two sub-sets (nuclear and high technology, on the one hand, non-nuclear and standard technology on the other hand), would be convenient, assuming their determinants are largely independent. Unfortunately, the empirical data do not allow following this method-ological option, in order to provide a relevant equation for the demand for military expenditures.

Given these limitations, the demand equation that is proposed here, is a tentative exercise to apply a standard model to French data. Six variables were selected in order to explain the demand for military expenditures:

GDPFRA = French National PIB (*Produit Intérieur Brut*)
MILESSUR = Soviet military expenditures
MILENAT = aggregate NATO expenditures (except France)
MILEAFR = aggregate Allied African countries' military
             expenditures (except Chad and Mauritania)
MILECHA = military expenditures of Chad
MILEMAU = military expenditures of Mauritania

PIB has been chosen as an index of national economic wealth because the French *Lois de programmation militaire* are computed by reference to it. In order to measure the threats, Soviet military expenditure (MILESSUR), on the one hand, and the defence outlays of the major African allies (MILEAFR), on the other, are selected. First, as has been noticed, the French defence system is mainly organized around these two types of threats. Second, it has been assumed, following the lines of Richardson's model, that the amount of the military effort against a potential enemy can be used as a measurement of the threat. Third, a set of African countries (MILEAFR) has been chosen because France is committed via treaties to provide for their military assistance. This is the case for the Central African Republic, Chad,[7] Gabon, Mauritania, Niger, Senegal and Togo, whose military expenditures are aggregated. Finally, the defence budgets of Chad (MILECHA) and Mauritania (MILEMAU) have been isolated. The amount of both is approximately 50 per cent of the total, because military intervention occurred during the period studied (1965–78).

The equation for the level of French defence spending (MILEFRA), which has been estimated, can be written in the following form:

$$\text{MILEFRA} = C + a_1\text{GDPFRA} + a_2\text{MILESSUR} + a_3\text{MILENAT}$$
$$+ a_4\text{MILEAFR} + a_5\text{MILECHA} + a_6\text{MILEMAUR} \qquad (1)$$

All the data used for military expenditures have been gathered from SIPRI (constant 1973 dollars). Concerning the French GNP, we used the OECD evaluation in current French currency, changed into the constant 1973 dollars using an IMF deflator. Our main concern is to use a homogeneous series of data. The use of SIPRI's figures also allows comparison with other countries studied in this volume, but limits the sample available to the period 1964–77, because of the change in the base used by SIPRI in 1977, which induced discontinuity. Furthermore, discontinuities can be observed after 1978 in the series of some developing countries shown here. In spite of all these limitations, the above equation has been estimated on the statistical data discussed above, using ordinary least squares methods.

In a first step, MILEFRA has been regressed on each of the six explanatory variables for the period (1964–78),[8] assuming a year-to-year correspondence between MILEFRA and the explaining variables. It appears that only four of them are statistically significant (see Table 5.3). The coefficient of MILEAFR was not significant. As regards MILECHAD, its correlation with MILEFRA is negative, and the test of significance very poor, especially after corrections. Therefore MILEAFR as well as MILECHAD were excluded at the end of this stage. The main result of this first investigation can be summarized in the following way: no statistically relevant relationship can be demonstrated with the data used between French military expenditures and the budget of African countries benefiting from French military assistance. However, this general statement has an important exception. MILEMAU, on the contrary, is closely linked to MILEFRA. It should be underlined that during the period French assistance to Mauritania was approximately one-third of the global amount of military assistance in the area.

The poor results for MILEAFR can be explained by different factors. The value of statistical material used to compute the aggregate could provide part of the explanation.[9] This does not mean, however, the falsity of the assumption about a relationship between threat in Africa and French military expenditures during the period, but shows difficulties of extracting it from the defence budget. Indeed, a part of military assistance is not computed in the defence budget but elsewhere. Furthermore, the classical decomposition of the French defence budget does not leave space for military intervention, which could explain more particularly Chad's case. It also provides a basis for understanding the extreme contrast between MILECHA and MILEMAU *vis-à-vis* MILEFRA. The kind of French intervention was quite different in each case. Whereas the military was explicitly called out by the Chad Government on very specific occasions,[10] assistance to Mauritania was implicit and continuous during the overall period. Therefore accounts were easier to find in the French defence budget as a consequence of military assistance in Mauritania during the period studied.

Table 5.3 French military expenditure

Variable	Coefficient	Standard error	t statistic
Constant	3 818.3228	1 246.8673	3.6023331
GDFRA	0.0234335	0.0053346	4.3927361
MILESSUR	−0.0377445	0.0190300	−1.9834247
MILENAT	0.0269923	0.0060946	4.4288973
MILEAFR	−6.0540218	12.766524	−0.4742107
MILECHA	−47.216859	29.116303	−1.6216639
MILEMAU	28.422399	13.893953	2.0456669
R^2	0.963491	Mean of dependent variable	8 991.667
Adjusted R^2	0.919680	SD of dependent variable	460.1548
SE of regression	130.4113	Sum of squared residuals	85 035.52
F statistic	21.99210	Log likelihood	−70.22277

Notes: Sample 1964–78; 14 observations; dependent variable is MILEFRA.

Table 5.4 Further statistical results

Variable	Coefficient	Standard error	t statistic
Constant	6 172.1175	540.14469	11.426786
MILESSUR (−1)	−0.0638105	0.0144301	−4.4220521
MILENAT	0.0134050	0.0035705	3.7543358
MILEMAU	34.741342	4.0702447	8.5354432
GDPFRA	0.0216673	0.0036184	5.9881237
R^2	0.985955	Mean of dependent variable	9 284.615
Adjusted R^2	0.978933	SD of dependent variable	690.2248
SE of regression	100.1821	Sum of squared residuals	80 291.61
F statistic	140.4040	Log likelihood	−75.18126

Notes: Sample 1965–78; 13 observations; dependent variable is MILEFRA.

The second step was to improve the statistical results by the introduction of time lags between the dependent and some of the explanatory variables and to correct for autocorrelation. At the end of the process, the best results were obtained with a lag of one year for MILESSUR and no time lag for the other variables (see Table 5.4).

Some dominant features emerge from Table 5.5, which corrects for autocorrelation. From a statistical point of view, even though they provided slight improvements, they did not change the meaning of the results. However, the explanatory power of MILESSUR, GDPFRA and MILENAT looks very strong. The reason is not the same for GDPFRA on the one hand, MILESSUR and MILENAT, on the other. Other studies have proved that a positive relationship exists between the dynamics of French military expenditures and national economic growth (Smith 1980; Fontanel 1980; Fontanel and Smith 1985; Martin *et al.* 1987). Such observations are to be related to a long-term phenomenon, and the selected period is definitely too short to throw light on such types of link. Nevertheless, the French defence budget does not reveal a statistically strong dependence from growth indices in the long run. The correlations between MILEFRA and international variables, such as MILESSUR and MILENAT, are not unexpected, but the sign of the coefficient is more unusual in both cases. They give indirect arguments in favour of bureaucratic versus international models to explain French arms dynamics.[11] In addition to the reasoning developed to support the superiority of internal bureaucratic models, it must be pointed out that a disconnection between a physical evaluation of Soviet military forces and its economic computation exists. Therefore a better index would be the stock of Soviet weapons, rather than the flow of Soviet military expenditures. As regards MILENAT, the existence of a positive coefficient is not so surprising. Indeed, France left the NATO military staff during the studied period and organized an independent defence system. Viewed, however, from a geopolitical point of view, the strategic relationship between France and NATO is a more complementary than a substitute one. However, according to SIPRI's data, negative econometric correlations would also be obtained with US military expenditures, at least during the last part of the period studied (1970–87).[12]

Two main features emerged from the econometric results and have to be explained, namely the negative sign of the relationship between MILESSUR and MILEFRA, and the high degree of correlation between MILEMAU and MILEFRA, which contrast with those of other selected variables (and even more with MILECHAD).

Concerning the close statistical relationship between MILEFRA and MILEMAU, this is partly the result of the French military assistance mainly during the end of the period under review,[13] and partly the consequence of 'coincidence' in the profile of the trends in both countries.

Table 5.5 Corrections for autocorrelations

	Observations	Constant	MILEMAU	MILESSUR (−1)	GDPFRA	MILENAT	d	R^2A	F
No correction	13	6,172.1	43.741	−0.0633	0.0217	0.0134	3.16	0.979	140.4
		(11.4)	(8.5)	(−4.4)	(5.99)	(3.75)			
AR(1)	12	5,547.1	32.542	−0.0725	0.0247	0.0172	2.89	0.986	160
		(13.38)	(−8.3)	(−10.91)	(5.47)	(3.75)			
AR(2)	11	561.4	32.236	−0.0732	0.0248	0.0168	2.19	0.987	136.5
		(11.5)	(17.99)	(−11.5)	(13.36)	(5.61)			

Notes: Dependent variable is MILEFRA; AR(1) and AR(2) are first- and second-order autoregressive equations; figures in brackets are *t* ratios; R^2A is adjusted for degrees of freedom.

Indeed, according to SIPRI's figures, but in a more determinative way, Mauritania's military expenditure stayed quite constant from 1964 to 1974 (between $3.3m and $3.8m) and rose quickly from 1975 to 1978. Obviously, the magnitude of MILEMAU is without any comparison with MILEFRA, but the time schedule was in fact the same in the two countries.

Turning to MILESSUR, the observed negative coefficient may be spurious due to the comparison of two independent trends in the Soviet Union and in France. With regard to the evaluation of military expenditures in USSR, we have to be very cautious. However, according to SIPRI's figures, the Soviet military expenditures rhythm of growth is more rapid from 1964 to 1969 (about 38 per cent) than after 1970 (officially $1,000m per annum). If we look now to the evolution of French military expenditures, the temporal profile was the reverse. The data provided for 1965 were about the same as for 1969 (respectively 8,446m and 8,739m constant dollars). Indeed the share of military expenditure as a percentage of gross domestic product has declined during this sub-period from 5.6 per cent to 4.2 per cent. After 1974, an inflexion was observed because the increase was about 20 per cent in constant dollars from 1975–8. Therefore the only argument that can be stressed following so statistical a treatment is an indirect confirmation of the lack of a significant relationship between the Soviet military expenditures and the French defence budget.

Finally, in spite of satisfactory statistical tests, the proposed demand equation for MILEFRA fails to provide a convincing economic and political explanation. Therefore some alternative approaches should be proposed in order to find a better explanation for French defence dynamics. First of all, some indications can be found in studies about the statistical determinants of French military expenditures using data analyses (Pilandon 1982). Furthermore, a theoretical game framework has been developed to describe the dynamic process (Schmidt 1986). Three players are isolated, namely the Defence Minister, the Finance Minister (responsible for the national budget) and the Prime Minister. The game itself is played only by the first two players, the Prime Minister acting as an arbiter. More precisely, each of the two players reveals his national demand and then refers to the Prime Minister's arbitration. The decision of the Prime Minister at the end determines from outside the game the effective budget to be voted by the Parliament. At the first stage of the process, the proposals of the Defence Minister and the Finance Minister are viewed as the consequences of non-cooperative strategies (in the NASH sense). The whole system is computed as a dynamic one, with an incorporated memory corresponding to the Prime Minister's arbitrations in past sequences of the process (annual budgets).

Such a model is obviously difficult to test in empirical data. In any case, in contrast with the regularity of the trend from 1965 to 1972, the relatively strong increase observed after 1973 could be imputed to a change in the Prime Minister's arbitration, which has induced a change in the expectations of the two players. Another advantage of this model is that it produces a relevant picture of the net impact of international variables in the dynamics of French military expenditures. Indeed, in this model the demand equation from the Minister of Defence takes into account the variables used in the estimated equation (cf. equation (1)), whereas they are excluded from the demand equation of the Minister of Finance. The equations proposed are respectively

$$\Delta MILEFRAD = a_{11}x_1 + a_{12}x_2 + a_{13}Y_1 + a_{14}Y_4 \tag{2}$$
$$\Delta MILEFRAF = a_{22}x_3 + a_{23}Y_2 \tag{3}$$
$$\Delta MILEFRA = a_{31}Y_1 + a_{32}Y_2 + a_{33}Y_3 \tag{4}$$

$\Delta MILEFRAD$ and $\Delta MILEFRAF$ are the national defence budget's annual variations offered by the Minister of Defence and the Minister of Finance respectively. $\Delta MILEFRA$ corresponds with the actual defence budget's annual variation induced from the Prime Minister's arbitration.[14] x_1 represents the military expenditures of French adversaries (i.e. MILESSUR in equation (1)), x_2 the French military interventions in the African area (i.e. MILEAFR in equation (1)), and x_3 the French GNP (GDPFRA in equation (1)). Y_1 and Y_2 are the national demand for annual military expenditures prepared by the Minister of Defence and the Minister of Finance respectively; Y_3 is the effective demand emerging from the Prime Minister's office, and Y_4 is the value conventionally equal to ΔY_3 in order to obtain a differential system of order one.

The present situation would be well pictured in such a model. Indeed, despite the rigidity of the programmes, some flexibility is provided mainly by the expectations of the Minister of Defence *vis-à-vis* the Prime Minister's arbitration and a related optimization. A correct basis for the computation is obviously the past series of arbitration. Unfortunately, this sample cannot be used at the present time because of the new Prime Minister and the existence of a *Loi de programmation militaire* voted by the past majority.[15] Therefore, the novelty of the case is better illustrated by the game approach than by the standard equation.

Economic problems and future trends

Is defence a burden for the French economy? In order to clarify the economic impact of military expenditures on the French macro-economic variables, the available studies are not numerous and their results are not conclusive until now. Roughly speaking, the evolution of the GDP does not appear to depend strongly on that of military expenditure. Rather, military expenditure seems to exert only a weak indirect influence upon consumption, while at the same time tending to place strains on the basic building of fixed capital. In the short run, a weak positive relationship has been observed between military expenditures and the rate of growth which seems to be corrected in the long run by a reverse effect due to the negative impact on civil investment through a substitution mechanism (Fontanel 1982; Martin *et al*. 1987). As to its influence on the French labour force, it is slightly beneficial in the short or medium term, mainly via arms procurement expenditures (Aben and Daures 1981; Aben and Smith 1987), thus increasing demand. As far as foreign trade is concerned, military expenditure seems to have two opposite effects: a positive effect on exports and a neutral one on imports. On the contrary, the rate of exchange of French currency seems to be pulled downward whereas inflation would appear to be stimulated, thus generating a self-contradictory movement (see pp. 93–7).

Moving to the reverse relationship between the French economy and the need for national defence according to the principles previously recalled, several questions emerge for the near future.

First, the question of the supply of manpower is actively discussed nowadays among military spheres, and especially between the Ministry of Defence and the army, navy and air force. This is due to the fact that the need to develop military equipment combined with the rising cost of manpower generates a reduction of the day-to-day expenditures (Figure 5.1: *Titre III*). The possibilities of a substitution between the day-to-day expenditures (*Titre III*) and the arms procurement expenditures (*Titre V*) have been used in favour of arms procurement during the last *Loi de programmation* (see Table 5.1). Such opportunity risks may be limited for the near future in spite of some optimistic forecasting.[16] However, wages are still a significant part of the defence budget: 33.9 per cent in 1987, and defence remains until now one of the major employment managers among the administrative sectors with 699,460 employees in 1987, only 630,000 of whom are actually producing goods and services corresponding to the defence sector *sensu stricto*. They represent 3.2 per cent of the total number of employed people and 16.4 per cent of those who work in a non-market sector. One should notice that some of them are civil servants. These civil servants now number 138,000, approximately 20 per cent of the total. Historical considerations explain such a situation. The number of civil servants in defence administration is slowly declining from 155,000 in 1960. No fundamental change is to be expected in the near future.

The question of the global volume of manpower is not a new problem, because the total number has been reduced year after year from the beginning of the 1960s: in 1960 there were almost 1,200,000 persons employed by the defence administration. From that time, the annual rate of decrease has on average been 1.9 per cent. Nevertheless, this decrease was made possible first by the end of the colonial wars, then by a strong growth of defence labour productivity. For example, nuclear forces, with about 20 per cent of the global French military expenditure, only employ 5 per cent of the defence manpower. The problem today is seen from another viewpoint, that is to say an optimum answer to the various facets of defence missions. From 1975, different studies have been produced in favour of a modernization of the management in the army, navy and air force. More precisely, a *Mission de modernisation des armées* was created in 1975 in order to promote rationalism in manpower management (Blandin and Ravier 1977; Schmidt 1981a). The system of 'programme targeting management' is now applied to almost all military forces.

Military staff are paid on the same scale as civilian staff, but with specific subsidies. In 1975 there was a complete reorganization of careers for military staff including a new wage scale. This transformation was followed by a substantial global rise in the wage bill and, after a period, by small adjustments through additional subsidies. Until now, military staff salaries are not that bad in comparison to those of average civil servants. However the constraints on the defence budget now adopted, especially for *Titre III*, do not preclude the reopening of a wage problem for the future.

Finally, one of the original characteristics of French defence is that conscription remains an important part of military recruitment. In 1987, there were almost 253,000 conscripts, i.e. 43 per cent of military personnel. In 1966, they numbered 664,000 representing 64 per cent of military personnel. In 1970, the figures were respectively 293,000 and 49 per cent, therefore a smooth decrease of conscripted military personnel can be observed in the medium term (with the exception of the 1972–8 period). This quantitative trend is reinforced by the fact that an increasing number of operational units are professional soldiers, such as the *Force d'action rapide*. Therefore in that field also the question set by conscription is more a qualitative one, more an issue about the content of the military training and its adjustment to the actual defence needs, than a quantitative one. Some attempts to apply a cost benefit analysis to this topic in order to compute the opportunity cost of conscription demonstrates that the economic argument in favour of the cheapness of conscription is not undebatable. According to such computations, the effective cost of conscription would be between three and four times its budgetary evaluation (Galitzine 1989). Nevertheless, there will probably be no massive revision of the French concept of recruitment because, even if the question of conscription is raised periodically, no government, for obvious political reasons, will probably take the risk of completely suppressing it.

Another series of issues focuses on arms procurement. The share of arms in the 1988 defence budget was 41 per cent of the total expenditure. As the largest part of this is produced by French industry, the defence budget has become year after year an industrial budget, inducing a direct impact on some major companies by means of R & D financing support. A specific administrative institution, the *Délégation générale à l'armée* (DGA) plays a leading part in the resource allocation process.[17] According to official figures for 1987–8, the Defence Ministry supports 37 per cent of the public R & D in France. In 1988, R & D provided by the Ministry of Defence is around FF30m. The largest part are utilized by industrial companies (I.A. FF18m). Such figures depict the actual part of defence in French high technology dynamics. Furthermore, according to the National Accounting System, about 67 per cent of the military purchases from French economy is located in the industrial sector,[18] which provides a rough measurement of the industrial impact of the defence budget.

The future, however, is not without problems. The rate of increasing cost for R & D must always be revised upwards[19] with two main consequences. First, a smooth increase of arms imports especially for certain kinds of sophisticated material too expensive for home production (e.g. AWACS), and second, the consequences of high cost tend to reduce French arms' competitiveness in export markets. Indeed, the decline of French arms exports from 1984 (FF61.8m) until 1987 (FF27.3m) cannot be imputed to the cost argument alone, but also to the modifications acting on the world markets especially for the last 3 years, which have certainly worsened the negative consequence of the observed cost and price increases (Schmidt 1987b). During the period 1982–5, 66.3 per cent of French arms transfers were marketed to the Middle East countries and only 10.7 per cent to Western European countries. From 1985 until 1988, however, the Middle East countries have become more reluctant, for financial reasons, to buy French material and the price competition in the European zone is fiercer. Reduction of exports have, in turn, a negative effect on military R & D, because of the growing share of self-financing. Therefore there appears to be a risk of a vicious circle developing, unlike the present trend of restructuring in the arms industry (Dussauge 1988).

To summarize the economic constraints on a future defence budget, the following main features should be emphasized: (a) a reduction (or at least remaining at the same level) of public expenditures as a proportion of GNP, (b) a political priority for education and research expenditures, (c) a limit to substitution between *Titre III* and *Titre V* in the defence budget, and (d) an acceleration in development unit cost for military materials. Combining these constraints forces a re-examination of the *Loi de programmation* on the part of the political authorities. Nevertheless, the future of French military expenditures is strongly dependent on one unknown variable and on one control variable.

The unknown national rate of growth for the next 5 years, is indeed a key variable. Let us remember that the present *Loi de programmation militaire* voted by the Parliament in 1987 was based on a trend of 2.8 per cent yearly rate of real growth until 1991. Actually the framework for decision-making under constraints (a), (b), (c) and (d) would be quite different with a national rate of growth above 3 per cent as nowadays, or just 2 per cent because the necessary choices among a large range of costly programmes are left open in the current *Loi de Programmation*.

The control variable is rather a political one and concerns the public management of education in national research priorities. As one can observe, a way to make (a), (b) consistent with (d) would be to consider the military R & D (or at least the fundamental research) as a component of education and research priority. According to the data provided, some arguments do exist in that direction. Such an interpretation, however, reopens the classical debate on the relative spin-off between the military and civil sectors. From our point of view, a conclusive end is out of reach for the French case, because of the close overlaps between civil and military activities in dominant industrial firms in aerospace and electronics. The balance between military and civil activities measured by the share of cash-flow, computed on the average of the last 5 years, varies from Dassault (91 and 9 per cent), Aerospatiale (55 and 45 per cent), Thompson SA (45 and 55 per cent), and MATRA (33 and 67 per cent). With the exception of Dassault, the main companies in these sectors have tried to combine the advantages of both military and civil activities. An incentive for military activity is the public financial support for R & D. However, the net impact on civil activities of a reduction in such public financing is not easy to estimate. Moreover, this is only one aspect of a more general problem facing French defence policy, namely, the need to make some difficult choices.

Notes

1 In the French defence budget, expenditures are allocated according to two main categories, i.e. *Titre III* for all the maintenance activities, and *Titre V* for equipment. No specific category exists corresponding to 'military intervention'. This feature can explain the difficulties in imputing such an expense (see CHAD, pp. 103–6). The respective evolution of these two components is a key to the budget policy followed by the defence administration. The following table summarizes their annual average variation in percentages:

Period	Titre III	Titre V
1970–5	+ 3.2	− 0.5
1976–82	− 4.3	+ 4.7
1983–6	− 1.2	+ 0.8
(1987–91)	–	+ 6.0

2 Three different levels are singled out according to the time schedule, namely the 'Plan' (long run, i.e. between 15 and 20 years), the 'Programme' (middle run, i.e. around 5 years) and the 'Budget' (short run, i.e. 1 year). Such distinctions

bring to light the specific role of the *Lois de programmation*: to co-ordinate the whole decision-making process from the planning activity to the budgetary final act. It must be underlined that from 1960, the military programme takes a legal form as a law voted by the Parliament.

3 The evolution of the *Lois de programmation* is seen from two points of view: the effectiveness and the extension of their contents. The first point is based on the distinction between the *autorisation de programme* and the *crédit de paiement*. Schematically from 1960 to 1975, all the expenditures listed in the *Lois de programmation* took the form of *autorisation de programme*. After 1977, they were changed into *crédits de paiement*. From the second point of view, the first three *Lois de programmation militaire* only covered equipment needs (i.e. *Titre V*). From 1977 to 1987, they were extended to all the defence expenditures (i.e. *Titre III* and *Titre V*). The present *Loi de programmation* (1987–91) returned to taking into account only *Titre V*.

4 Only major arms are computed in these estimations, which represent about 40 per cent of the national production. Among the materials delivered, air and ground are the more prominent (see Kolodziej 1987).

5 These distortions in the *Loi de programmation* are to be imputed to two major sources. First, a weak relationship with the French Plan. Second, a global target expressed in terms of a share of public expenditures. The *Loi de programmation militaire rectificative* (1977–82) had tried to correct the second bias in referring the target to the PIBM (*Produit Intérieur Brut Marchand*) as it is computed by the French accounting system. For the first source, a tentative linkage has been experimented in the fifth *Loi de programmation* (1984–8) between the National Plan and the military programme. Nevertheless, the normative feature of the *Loi de programmation militaire* also features in the optimistic views discussed here.

6 From the point of view of the strategic doctrine, the pre-strategic weapon is to be connected to the hypothesis of a pre-emptive attack, which is not to be understood as an attack in the conventional meaning, but as an advanced part of deterrence behaviour. Nevertheless, it must be pointed out that the strategic interpretation of the nuclear pre-strategic forces is not exactly the same for Pluton and for Hades, because of the difference of the range (80 km Pluton versus 350 km for Hades).

7 During the period reviewed, France had no formal military assistance treaty with the Republic of Chad. Although MILEAFR might be regarded as an alliance variable, it is interpreted as a threat variable.

8 MILECHAD; coefficient: −25.167269; standard error: 53.931180; t statistic: 0.4666553; two-tail significance: 0.673.

9 According to SIPRI's figures, 1965, 1968, 1972, 1975 estimates for Chad's military expenses are uncertain and based on the budget figures; as well as 1975 and 1976 estimates for Central African military expenditures; 1976, 1977 estimations for Gabon's military expenditures; 1975 estimates for Mauritania's military expenditures; 1976 for the estimations of Niger's military expenditures; and 1964, 1965 for estimates of Togo's expenditures. Furthermore, SIPRI does not provide any figures for Chad, Central Africa and Gabon after 1977.

10 During the period under examination, French troops intervened in Chad first between 1972 and 1974 and afterwards between 1976 and 1978. Obviously such intervention went on beyond this time.

11 See the distinctions promoted by Hollist 'Alternative explanations of competitive arms process: test on four pairs of nations', *American Journal of Political Science*, no. 2, May 1977. On the one hand, some paradoxical results

are found, testing international French military expenditures' dynamics (equation (1) p. 102), whereas a first estimation of bureaucratic data seems more reliable (see p. 109).

12 A clear distinction must be introduced between (1) the trend of military expenditures in NATO's European countries, (2) the trend of US military expenditures. The time profile of French defence expenditures is practically the same as for the others, NATO's European countries (stabilization between 1964 and 1968, and slight increase during the 1970s) contrasting with the time profile of the USA (long run declining trend from 1968 ($103,077m at 1973 prices)) to 1978 ($71,477m at 1973 prices). The positive relationship between MILEFRA and MILENAT is then a positive average rate of growth observed in both aggregates during the whole period (1964–78).

13 From 1975 to 1977.

14 The model's dynamics can be specified in the following way. In order to determine their strategies, the Minister of Defence may adopt a minimization criterion such as ΔMILEFRAD − ΔMILEFRA, and the Minister of Finance a maximization criterion such as ΔMILEFRA − ΔMILEFRAF consistent with the reasonable hypothesis ΔMILEFRAD $\geqslant$ ΔMILEFRA $\geqslant$ ΔMILEFRAF. As an arbiter, the Prime Minister does not have any strategy in the game and his decision is fully dependent on a_{31} and a_{32}, a_{33} respective weights. Anyway, according to the French political institution MILEFRA is both the Prime Minister's arbitration result and the actual defence budget, because the Prime Minister's proposal is voted by the Parliament.

15 The problem is still more intricate. The Socialists have indeed voted the *Loi de programmation des équipements militaires 1987–1991*, which was adopted by the Parliament during Spring 1987 with a large majority (536 votes for and only thirty-seven against at the French Assemblée Nationale).

16 Following the *Loi de programmation des équipements militaires 1987–1991*, *Titre V* would represent more than 53 per cent of the total defence budget. Such an estimation is, however, highly disputable because of the rigidities of *Titre III* (Aube-Martin 1987).

17 The *Délégation générale pour l'armement* (DGA) is a genuine French institution. It is a governmental agency, whose purpose is to establish links between the military staff and industrial companies. In addition to this general mission, the DGA is in charge of more specific tasks, as, for instance, R & D co-ordination, financing support to the arms industry control and co-ordination in arms export policy. With 25,000 servants the DGA is a decisive partner of the French arms policy (*La Délégation Générale pour l'Armement face aux défis de l'avenir* 1987).

18 According to the French accounting system, the sub-sector 'equipment' received the largest part of the defence budget. In dynamics, one of the consequences of increasing *Titre V* versus *Titre III* over the last 10 years was obviously to enlarge the impact of military expenditures on this sub-sector. A reverse evolution has been observed during the period for the energy sector, whose share was regularly reduced from the defence demand relating to the *Titre III* relative decline.

19 A discrepancy has been observed between the supply side practically correlated to the GNP trend and the cost of the arms programmes because of the technological jumps from generation to generation in arms systems (sometimes more than 25 per cent). Furthermore, 80 per cent of the global cost is determined by the preliminary studies. The possibility of correcting the tendency at a later stage is then small. Therefore, underestimated expectations drastically pull up the programme's costs.

References

Aben, Jacques (1981) 'Désarmement, activité et emploi', *Défense Nationale*, May.

Aben, Jacques (1986) 'La défense nationale face à l'inflation', mimeograph *Fondation pour les Etudes de Défense Nationale*, Paris.

Aben, Jacques and Daures, Nicolas (1981) 'Défense nationale et emploi en France', *Cahier du Séminaire Charles GIDE* XV, de Montpellier University.

Aben, Jacques and Smith, Ron, P. (1987) 'Defence and employment in the U.K. and France: a comparative study of the existing results', in Christian Schmidt and Frank Blackaby (eds) *Peace Defence: an Economic Analysis*, London: Macmillan.

Artru, Yves (1987) 'La mission de modernisation de l'administration des armées', *Revue Française des Finances Publiques*, no. 19.

Aube-Martin, Philippe (1987) 'Le budget de la défense', *Revue Française des Finances Publiques*, no. 19.

Bailly, Maurice (1987) 'La programmation des équipements militaires', *Revue Française des Finances Publiques*, no. 19.

Blandin, Henri and Ravier, André (1977 1980) 'Vers une gestion prospective par objectif: la mission de modernisation des armées', *Défense Nationale*, Dec.

Collet, André (1989) *Armements, mutation, réglementation, productions connexes*, Paris: Economica.

DGA (1987) *La Délégation Générale pour l'Armement face aux défis de l'avenir*, Paris: FEDN.

Dussauge, Pierre (1985) *L'industrie française d'armement*, Paris: Economica.

Dussaug, Pierre (1988) 'La baisse des exportations françaises d'armement et ses répercussions industrielles', *Défense Nationale*, Jan.

Fontanel, Jacques (1980) 'Formalised studies and econometric analysis of the relationship between military expenditure and economic development', United Nations.

Fontanel, Jacques (1982) *Analyse économique du couple Dépenses Militaires – Développement économique*, Cahier du CEDSI, no. 1, Faculté de droit de Grenoble.

Fontanel, Jacques and Matiere, Jean-Pierre (1983) *Rôle des dépenses militaires sur la croissance économique de la France*, Cahier due CEDSI, no. 3, Faculté de droit de Grenoble.

Fontanel, Jacques and Smith R. (1985) 'Analyse économique des dépenses militaires', *Stratégique*, no. 3.

Galitzine, Georges (1989) 'Les implications économiques de la conscription et de l'armée de métier', thèse doctorat, University of Paris IX, Dauphine.

Hollist (1977) 'Alternative explanations of competitive arms process: test on four pairs of nations', *American Journal of Political Science*, no. 2, May.

Kolodziej, Edward A. (1987) *Making and Marketing Arms*, Princeton: Princeton University Press.

Martin, Stephen, Smith, Ron P. and Fontanel, Jacques (1987) 'Time-series estimates of the macro-economic impact of defence spending in France and U.K.', in Christian Schmidt and Frank Blackaby (eds) *Peace, Defence and Economic Analysis*, London: Macmillan.

Pac, Henri (1986) *Politologie de la défense nationale*, Paris: Masson.

Pilandon, Louis (1982) 'Analyse quantitative et causale de dépenses militaires à partir de quelques résultats économétriques', mimeograph, University of Clermont-Ferrand I.

Schmidt, Christian (1980) 'L'économie de la défense en France', *Revue d'Economie Politique*, Dec.

Schmidt, Christian (1981a) 'L'appréhension économique du service de défense nationale: I le système des hommes', *Défense Nationale*, Oct.

Schmidt, Christian (1981b) 'L'appréhension économique du service de défense nationale: II le système des armements', *Défense Nationale*, Dec.

Schmidt, Christian (1986) 'Esquisse d'un modèle du dynamique des dépenses militaires française construit en forme de jeu de NASH', *Revue d'Economie Politique* 1.

Schmidt, Christian (1987a) 'A la recherche d'une économie politique des programmes d'armement', *Chroniques SEDEIS* 6, June.

Schmidt, Christian (1987b) 'Les marchés internationaux d'armement en question', *Chronique SEDEIS* 11, Nov.

SIPRI (Yearbook 1964–87) *World Armaments and Disarmament*, London: Taylor & Francis.

SIRPA (1987) *Loi de programme relative à l'équipement militaire pour les années 1987–1991, Données générales*, Paris: Ministry of Defence 1988.

SIRPA (1988) *La défense de la France*, Paris: Ministry of Defence.

Smith, R. (1980) 'Military expenditure and investment in OECD countries, 1954–73', *Journal of Comparative Economics* 4.

Chapter six

West German demand for defence spending

Dieter Fritz-Aβmus and Klaus Zimmermann

Introduction

In the Federal Republic of Germany, comparable to almost all industrialized countries and similar to many developing countries during the past decade, a remarkable amount of the available resources is taken up by defence expenditures. Although the economic impact of this spending is considerable, and despite the fact that providing defence capability is a very noticeable burden to the German community, the economic discussion of defence issues and the analysis of defence spending in particular is rare. Most problems in the economic debate of defence expenditure remain untouched.

In consequence of this deficiency the purpose of this chapter is twofold. First, we present and discuss the basic facts and figures of Germany's defence spending during the period 1960–87. For analytical reasons it seems necessary to begin with a selective description of the economic and military background. Our primary attention will be focused on the demand issue of national security. Initially, we offer a model, which appears reasonable for the estimation of a military expenditure demand equation. Finally, the attention will be extended to some considerations on the future prospects of West German defence spending, particularly in the wake of the recent INF Treaty.

Second, we are particularly interested in analysing the public choice process concerning German defence spending. We try to evaluate the influence of political factors, such as the centre-left or centre-right orientation of the governments, and above all the international environment, in particular the NATO membership and the international economic dependence. The last factor seems to be especially relevant for small open economies like the Federal Republic of Germany, where the government because of the international dependencies is somehow in limited control of decisions. These dependencies lead to a situation where the government has to take over some responsibility with respect to income maintenance and support, which requires the implementation of expenditure programmes for social security, health care, education and unemployment benefits. Under fiscal constraints the indicated strategy of 'internal compensation' has unavoidably to collide with external commitments, for example, towards the alliance, and consequently and above all with defence expenditures. Wherever it is possible we try to investigate the political economy of this strategical conflict and to assess the likely direction of future trends.

The economic background

Economically the Federal Republic has experienced a series of shocks during the last decade. The 'Wirtschaftswunder' (economic miracle), throughout the post-war period the basis of German self-esteem, is now a thing of the past. However, it still is impressive to remember the rapidity of the post-war recovery and the high rates of economic growth achieved until the early 1960s. For example in 1987 Gross Domestic Product (GDP) in current prices has been 20 times as high as in 1950 and almost 7 times as high as in 1960. Using constant 1980 prices GDP expanded 2.3 times since 1960. Nevertheless over an almost 40-year period the picture of the rate of economic growth is one of gradual deceleration. Following the high rates of expansion observed in the 1950s, when the annual average growth rates of GDP reached 8.2 per cent, the growth of GDP declined to 4.6 per cent in the 1960s, to about 2.8 per cent in the 1970s reaching its lowest growth rates during the early 1980s (0.7 per cent) and increasing recently only slightly to a still moderate 2 per cent.[1]

The turning-point of development has been the early 1970s, when a number of events significantly changed the international and domestic situation facing the West German economy. The new system of floating exchange rates led to an upward movement of the effective DM exchange rate of almost 30 per cent between 1972 and 1976. At the same time a change in the income distribution in favour of the labour share occurred, which was related to a corresponding fall in the rate of return on investment. In addition Germany was particularly hit by the impact of the first oil price shock on world trade. The German export growth rate declined from 8 per cent per annum in the years before 1973 to half that rate thereafter. Altogether this has contributed to the decline in the rate of growth of capital formation in the 1970s, and to a slower rate of increase of the 'productive potential', estimated by the German Council of Economic Experts (Sachverständigenrat, SVR) to have fallen from 4.5 per cent prior to 1973 to under 2 per cent after 1980.[2]

Whereas the growth rates have not been satisfactory during the last decade and surely have not reached the aims of the 1967 Law on Stability and Growth,[3] the Federal Republic enjoyed a relatively low and stable rate of inflation during the whole post-war period. The consumer price index

Table 6.1 West German economic performance, 1960–87

Year	POP	GDP	GDPCAP	GROWTH	CPI	URATE	INF	GSGDP	GEX	GDEF	BALPAY
1960	55.4	302.7	5.464	7.5	48.0	1.3	na	32.8	na	na	4.8
1965	58.6	459.2	7.836	3.1	54.1	0.7	3.2	36.5	64.2	−0.1	− 6.2
1970	60.6	675.3	11.143	6.9	61.0	0.7	3.5	39.1	88.0	0.4	3.2
1975	61.8	1,026.9	16.616	4.5	82.0	4.7	5.9	46.2	158.8	−35.0	10.0
1980	61.6	1,478.9	24.008	−2.3	100.0	3.7	5.4	47.5	215.7	−27.6	−28.5
1985	61.0	1,831.9	30.031	2.0	121.0	9.4	2.2	45.3	257.1	−27.7	44.5
1987[a]	61.1	2,012.6	32.939	1.8	121.1	8.9	0.2	45.5	268.5	27.8	79.5

Sources: SVR (Council of Economic Advisers), *Annual Assessment* (various issues)

Notes: POP: German population (m); GDP: Gross Domestic Product (DMbn); GDPCAP: Gross Domestic Product per person; GROWTH: Percentage change of GDP; CPI: Consumer Price Index (1980 = 100); URATE: Unemployment rate (%); INF: CPI's yearly change (%); GSGDP: Government's share of GDP; GEX: Government expenditures (DMbn); GDEF: Deficit of the federal budget (revenues–expenditures, DMbn); BALPAY: Balance of Payment (DMbn); [a] preliminary.

(CPI) indicates the extent to which not only the level but also the fluctuation of the inflation rate is significantly less in Germany than elsewhere. Of course this was one of the main factors that helped to stengthen the competitive position of German industry, offsetting the adverse effects of the upward pressures on the DM exchange rate. In addition, by reducing import prices due to the currency strength, this helped to sustain a lower rate of domestic inflation.

The economic miracle of the German economy from the early 1950s to the late 1970s is connected with an outstanding performance in foreign trade. Until the early 1970s the faster volume growth of exports compared to imports, facilitated by the advantageous exchange rate, led to an increase in size of the trade surplus. After the first oil shock vigorous export growth was combined with a restrained growth in imports. However, the external performance after the second oil shock was less satisfactory and the balance of trade turned sharply into deficit. After a recovery in 1982 the current account of the balance of payments, as seen in Table 6.1, was recently trimmed through the combined effect of a strong DM exchange rate and a period of increasing domestic demand. Drawing attention to the export side, Germany still is the world's largest exporter of goods and services.[4] In contrast to Japan, for example, its export product structure is heavily specialized in investment goods, which embody advanced technology and human capital, but remarkably less 'young technologies'. It appears that Germany particularly has lost ground in world markets in medium R & D-intensive sectors. On the other side, a substantial proportion of exports is produced by a small number of branches, particularly the machine-tool, road vehicle, chemicals, electrical goods and iron manufacturing industries. This makes it susceptible to changing terms of trade but at the same time accelerates the necessary adjustment process. Recently the sharply improving terms of trade pushed the surplus on trade in 1987 to DM117bn, despite a decline in the value of merchandise exports.[5] The gain resulted entirely from steeply falling import prices. All in all there are signs of increasing difficulties in the export sector, where growth itself is slowing and where the rapid appreciation of the DM combined with mounting exchange rate uncertainties will lead to a deterioration of the export performance.

The labour market is clearly the weakest point in West Germany's recent economic performance. During the post-war period up until now there always have been large imbalances, characterized from labour shortage during the 1960s to the present high unemployment, as seen in Table 6.1. The large inflow of foreign workers until the first oil shock in 1973 provided a kind of balancing mechanism for the period of labour shortage. The number of foreign workers reached a peak of 2.5m in 1973, then falling quickly to 1.9m in 1979 as a result of the recession. The number started to recover again, now being close to around 10 per cent of total labour force.

The real problem of the labour market began in 1981 with an abrupt upward movement in the unemployment trend reaching its peak in 1985 with 9.4 per cent. This large increase reflects the retarded adjustment to the economic slowdown and an insufficient net employment creation, but in addition it reflects a remarkable overall demographic trend, which is already in operation. Although birth rates have been high during the post-war period, the native population of the Federal Republic has been declining since 1972. What now puts pressure on the labour market is expected to relieve the situation in the coming years.[6] For now, labour force is still picking up vigorously, increasing at a rate of around 200,000 annually.[7] At the same time this neutralizes the steepening of the employment trend, considering the fact that the number of employees rose by nearly 530,000 during the last 3 years. Nevertheless, the difficulties of the labour market seem to have reached their peak, getting some relief at least from the foreseeable demographic development in the years to come.

Finally, the structure of the public sector has to be analysed. Between 1960 and 1987 overall government expenditure, which includes federal, state and community budgets, rose faster than GDP, leading to an increase of government share (GSGDP) of GDP from 32.8 per cent to 47.5 per cent in 1980, falling again to around 45.5 per cent in 1987. Government revenue on the other side rose less rapidly, indicating a significant move into deficit. Following a long period when deficits and surpluses in total offset each other, the deficit became substantial in 1975 with almost DM30bn, as the economy moved into recession after the first oil price crisis. A second leap can be observed after the next oil shock, when the deficit increased again sharply to over DM37bn. Since the government change-over in 1982[8] the deficit is moderating somewhat despite the strength of the recessionary forces, but is expected to increase significantly again in the near future due to the dynamics of the social security system, which will continue to rise in main sub-areas such as health insurance, unemployment benefits and pensions at rates well in excess of GDP's growth rate. Taking into consideration the announced tax reform partly in operation at the time and in total effect in 1990, which is supposed to relieve tax burden all together by around DM45bn, and adding some other external uncertainties to the planning of the federal budget such as increasing contributions to the European Community, one does not have to be a clairvoyant to foresee the accumulated problems ahead. As a result there would seem to be little room for greater expansion of total government expenditure.

To sum up, prospects for the end of the 1980s and beyond are surrounded by an unusually high degree of uncertainty. The slowdown of German export markets combined with a decline in business confidence points to a worrying lack of growth dynamics.[9] The virtual elimination of inflation, one of the major achievements of the economic policy during the past years, will turn towards a more unfavourable price picture. The pick-up of price increases will even be accelerated by the effects of the planned drastic increase of some excises. The labour market will be characterized by persistently high unemployment, despite the recent trend towards labour-market flexibility and a significant increase in employment. More-over, the external adjustment process does not seem to result in a reduction of the still sizeable current external account surplus. Finally, in spite of the considerable progress which has been made in consolidating the federal budget over the last years, high downside risks can be seen for the future.

Table 6.2 West German economic trends, 1990–2010

Year	POP	LFORCE	EMPL	UNEMPL	UNEMPL (%)	GDP (%)	EXP (%)	IMP (%)
1990	60.4	29.1	25.6	2.3	9.3	2.3	3.6	3.5
2000	59.1	27.2	26.0	1.0	4.1	2.6	3.9	4.1
2010	55.9	25.9	25.5	0.4	1.6	2.3	3.4	3.6

Source: Prognos-Report No. 12
Notes: POP: Population (m); LFORCE: Labour force (m); EMPL: Total employment (m); UNEMPL: Unemployment (m); UNEMPL (%): Unemployment in percentage of total labour force; GDP (%): Growth of GDP (annual change in percentage in constant 1980 prices); EXP (%): Export (annual change in percentage in constant 1980 prices); IMP (%): (annual change in percentage in constant 1980 prices).

A more medium- and long-term forecast for Germany is offered by the newest Prognos Report,[10] which gives some interesting supplements to our analysis and prediction. As seen in Table 6.2 the basis of this forecast is a most unique demographic development. The German population will shrink from around 61 million in 1987 to less than 56 million in 2010, caused by a sharp decline of the 20-year-old age group and younger. This trend will affect the whole social and economic basis of the Federal Republic and will generate an aggravating social and economic adjustment process. In addition there are three external factors, which seem to determine the future trends in economic development. The scarcity of resources will be painfully felt more and more, particularly concerning the environment and energy. The complexity of the international involvement of the Federal Republic will further increase, especially in the European Community, causing constraints on national decisions. Finally new techni-cal and innovative developments will require an additional deepening of the structural changes, which are already in operation. All these external factors will induce in the long run vehement adjustment processes concern-ing individual and collective behavioural patterns, political objectives and the organizational and institutional framework. In the past the repression of similar adjustment processes has already caused a social polarization, limiting the potential economic development of the Federal Republic. All in all this process will be the key to the long-term economic development. If a new social consensus on the adjustment question is not established in the near future, the much needed new dynamic growth period will not occur; but if there is a consensus, a long-term growth in the 3 per cent range seems possible.

The military background

The basic limit to Germany's defence spending is by all means the special nature of its recent history. Naturally the prospect of rearmament provoked suspicion and emotional conflicts among the future allies, and an ambivalent attitude among the German people itself. On the other hand influential circles in the West, mainly in the United States, wanted West Germany to participate in the Western military effort. Consequently the Federal Republic was invited to join NATO, contributing a national army to be integrated into the forces of the Alliance.[11] The accession became effective on 5 May 1955. Today the Bundeswehr, which was finally established in 1956 with a basis of 6,000 men and a budget of DM3.4bn,[12] may no longer remain an issue with its Western neighbours. Nevertheless, there are certain built-in limitations to German defence contribution. The most important one is the constitution itself which, as a result of the First and Second World Wars, limits the role of the armed forces to defensive action, extended exclusively to the NATO region.[13] Another limitation is the signing of the 1968 Treaty on Non-Proliferation of Nuclear Weapons, which stopped the discussion about nuclear armament. This at the same time meant the acceptance of an important reduction of the Federal Republic's strategic military role and a commitment to rely on NATO's nuclear deterrence.[14] As a result the German forces take part only in one of the three interlocking elements known as the NATO Triad. They have to provide conventional forces strong enough to resist and repel a conventional attack on a limited scale, and to sustain a conventional defence in the forward areas against large-scale conventional aggression.[15]

After the NATO commitment to a forward defence along Germany's eastern border the FRG does not have the alternative of relying too much on others to make up for shortfalls in its own defence capabilities. Therefore Germany produced in a relatively short period and with high defence outlays in the 1960s and 1970s an obviously well-equipped force in NATO.[16]

The basic structure of the Federal Armed Forces (Bundeswehr) provides for a force of 495,000 soldiers during peacetime – 332,000 of them (67.1 per cent) form part of the field army deployed in 12 divisions providing half of the forces of NATO's central army group. The naval force of 36,000 men (7.3 per cent) operates 24 submarines, 7 destroyers and 91 naval aircraft, whose mission is to defend the Baltic and part of the North Sea.

Table 6.3 West German armed forces, 1965–87

Year	TAF	DUR	SARMY	SNAVY	SAIR	SHIPS	SUBS	TANKS	ACRAFT
1965	428	18	306	35	98	10	11	na	650
1970	455	18	326	36	104	11	11	3,300	1,080
1975	491	15	345	39	111	11	24	3,700	585
1980	490	15	335	37	106	11	24	3,826	707
1985	495	15	336	36	106	7	24	4,662	708
1987	495	15	332	36	109	7	24	4,887	708

Sources: IISS, *The Military Balance* (various issues), NATO Statistical Service
Notes: TAF: total armed forces (1,000); DUR: duration of conscript service; SARMY/SNAVY/SAIR: manpower army/navy/air (1,000); SHIPS/SUBS/TANKS/ACRAFT: number of destroyers/tanks/submarines/combat aircraft (including naval aircraft).

An air force of 109,000 men (22.0 per cent) and 617 combat aircraft provides more than 30 per cent of combat air strength in central Europe.[17]

The Bundeswehr is a mixed force of 55 per cent volunteers and 45 per cent conscripts. This system of compulsory military service ensures a representative military force and a constant supply of recent trained reservists. Altogether, when the reserves are included Germany is able to mobilize 1.34m troops in a relatively short period.[18]

To achieve this effective defence capability the financial contribution of the German taxpayer to its national security has been significant. The most commonly used method to measure defence burden in an international comparative way is to take the ratio of defence expenditure to GDP.[19] As seen in Table 6.4, the FRG's defence spending as a share of GDP rose from just under 4 per cent to 4.3 per cent, due to the set-up of the new established forces, before declining since 1980 to around 3.2 per cent. The explanatory pattern is similar to that of other European countries and is supported by the shift of the ratio of defence expenditure to the Central Government Expenditure (CGE). Since 1960, the share of governments' expenditure going to defence has been cut back, remaining since the mid-1970s at a constant but still relatively high level. In the column DE/PER of Table 6.4 the per capita burden is given, which illustrates a significant increase during the analysed period, being now within the range of comparable NATO nations.

These remarkable changes over the last three decades can be explained by various factors. First, the federal armed forces have only been established since 1956 and consequently the increase of the outlays during the buildup period had to be significant. Second, the economic miracle in Germany loosened the financial constraints and allowed the defence

Table 6.4 West German defence expenditures, 1960–87

Year	DEFEX	DEFCON	DEFUS	DEFBER	DE/PER	DE/CGE	DE/GDP
1960	12.115	17.836	6.665	12.889	120	na	3.9
1965	19.915	40.063	10.955	22.176	187	31.0	4.3
1970	22.573	37.865	12.418	25.790	205	25.7	3.3
1975	37.589	45.932	20.679	45.506	336	23.7	3.6
1980	48.518	48.518	26.692	61.096	434	22.5	3.2
1985	58.650	50.200	32.266	73.862	529	22.8	3.2
1987	61.551	50.010	33.862	77.632	554	22.9	3.1

Sources: Data are based on NATO Statistical Service and SVR 1987/88
Notes: DEFEX: defence expenditure (NATO definition, current prices, DMbn without Berlin support costs); DEFCON: defence expenditure (1980 prices, DMbn); DEFUS: defence expenditure (constant 1980 US dollars using 1980 period average exchange rate); DEFBER: defence expenditure including Berlin support costs (DMbn); DE/PER: defence expenditure per person (in 1980 prices converted to US dollar using 1980 average exchange rates); DE/CGE: defence expenditure as a percentage of total central government expenditure; DE/GDP: defence expenditure as proportion of GDP.

burden to increase dramatically up to a certain level. Third, under the pressure of recent economic slowdown of growth rates and together with changing political circumstances a sharp cut in projected spending and a reduction in real terms occurred. The interesting question to be answered later is whether these declines indicate a cyclical adjustment to short-term economic problems or a tendency toward systematic defence cutbacks. Another interesting question to investigate in this context is Germany's role in the NATO alliance. However, it seems extremely difficult to evaluate its contribution to the alliance. To consider the Federal Republic's share of total NATO outlays, which rose steadily from just under 5 per cent in 1960 to almost 11 per cent in 1975 before settling back to roughly 8.1 per cent in 1987,[20] does not help too much, as most criticism of the German effort focuses not on the level of current defence expenditures but on the trends implied in the recent budget decisions. Simple comparisons of different countries' proportion of defence spending to their GDP cannot answer this question. Germany spends a noticeably lower proportion of its GDP on defence than the US or some other European allies. Yet it is well known and worth considering that the German defence budget, in particular, does not reflect several important but less clearly identified burdens. Because of their nature it is difficult to assess the true costs of these additional burdens, but nevertheless they are politically relevant. The most significant difference between the FRG and, for example, the US and the UK is Germany's conscript army, whereas the other two employ expensive all-volunteer armies. There are no budget adjustments for the lower pay levels permitted by a conscript force. In addition the land and tax exemptions provided for allied forces and different host-nation support do not enter the FRG's national budget. The value of the provided land is estimated at DM40bn and the yearly benefit for allied troops amounts to DM2.5bn.[21] Another factor to mention is the presence of around 400,000 allied forces in Germany,[22] which are supported with free facilities and substantial subsidies. Not accountable are the apparently high social and environmental costs for the FRG as a host nation if considering, for example, the more than 5,000 training exercises per annum or the yearly 580,000 military flights in Germany, which include 68,000 hours of low flights.[23] Not added to the defence expenditures, but considered as an important part of its national security spending is Germany's high amount of financial contribution to Berlin, which added up, for example, to more than DM16bn in 1987.

When these factors are added in the national defence budget the Federal Republic compares favourably with other European allies, although it falls short of the US commitment to defence of around 6.7 per cent of the GDP.[24] On the other side figures recently released by the Pentagon indicate that the US military spending attributed to NATO is very nearly comparable to Germany's spending level.[25]

Demand for West German defence spending

In the pursuit of national security the Federal Republic has dedicated a large share of its nation's resources to the purpose of enlarging and maintaining the defence sector. While discussing the economic and military background some causal patterns for the defence expenditures became obvious. Nevertheless it seems valuable to investigate now in detail the determinants of these spending levels to explain why such a substantial proportion of the limited national resources are spent on defence. On the basis of the developed theoretical model a defence expenditure demand equation for the FRG will be estimated and tested.

Determinants of defence spending

Governmental budgeting is problem-solving by way of a choice process. To organize the discussion of this approach two significant dimensions have to be included: the decision-making process within the governmental system and the relative influence of the internal and external environment.[26] As the purpose of this section is directed towards the demand analysis of defence expenditures, the further investigation will be limited to the potential influences of the internal and external environment on the spending level and shares. Several factors will be hypothesized as explanatory determinants of the defence budget and its changes over time.[27] The potential factors have been deduced and constructed from various national and international statements on defence and are transformed to the German environment. Not all of them can be used for a testable theory of the demand for defence expenditure; nevertheless they show that defence expenditures of the FRG are determined by a combination of economic, political and military variables.

Table 6.5 Potential determinants of West German defence spending

Variables	Internal environment	External environment
I. Economic factors	Income Economic stability Military–industrial complex	Dependencies on international trade and foreign resources
II. Political factors	Composition of government Interest groups	pressure and commitments	International political
III. Military factors	Own capability Military doctrine	Threat Alliance spillins

Economic factors

The economic factors are the obvious starting point in most studies on public expenditures. Little expertise is required to hypothesize that there is a positive relation between the growth rate of national income and the growth of the defence expenditures. Nevertheless the obvious differences of growth rates are remarkable. Using, for example, 1980 constant prices, the German defence budget virtually doubled its volume since 1960, while at the same time GDP increased by more than 149 per cent. In addition there seems to be empirical evidence that the defence share is positively co-related with per capita income.[28] An explanation could be, that the higher a country's level of income, the greater the threat of an enemy's attack.[29] In conclusion it is obvious, that the national income and its growth rate represent important determinations of defence spending. Therefore GDP can be viewed as a possible income variable in the demand function.

Economic stability is a second variable influencing the volume and composition of defence expenditures. In particular, fiscal constraints, caused by the instability and accompanied by growing budget deficits, increase the political readiness and economic necessity to reduce or redistribute defence spending funds. A first look on the data supports this expression, nevertheless the hypothesis remains preliminary.

Another factor frequently mentioned but never investigated in full is the influence of a domestic arms industry, which may develop persuasive power to influence decision-makers to agree to additional military expenditure. This seems to happen particularly during times of high unemployment or with the argument of international technological competition.[30] However, the influence of the military–industrial complex on defence spending, though definitely important in the industrialized countries,[31] unfortunately cannot be tracked down to a testable data set. The same problems occur with the external factor 'dependencies on foreign resources and international trade'. It seems plausible for the German case that a high degree of international economic dependence may contribute to the level of defence spending. The protection, for example, of the international resources and trade routes during a crisis, seems to be costly and would increase the demand on the defence outlay.[32] On the other side, the extremely high dependency on international trade implies an internal compensation to secure the capability of competition, which collides strongly with external commitments and in consequence with defence expenditures.

Political factors

Defence spending has to be evaluated not only according to its economic impacts, but also with respect to its political impacts. Therefore a second set of variables for the explanation of the determinants of defence expenditure involves the political factors.

Probably the most important factor within the set of political determinants is the political preference for the 'composition of the government'. Whether a country's government is generally dominated by a leftist or by a conservative party provides an important hint to the relative degree of change in the size and structure of the defence budget. In the Federal Republic, like the United Kingdom,[33] there are differences in the party's attitudes against and preferences for expenditures on military and non-military goods as well as in their attitudes towards allies, international pressure or commitments, military strategy, disarmament negotiations, or even the up-dating of weapons. However, the periods of rising and falling real defence expenditures have coincided with centre-left and centre-right government.

Related to political preferences are the factor 'interest groups' and their influence on government decisions. The social democratic party (SPD) seems to be more influenced traditionally by the working class and trade unions, and recently in addition by environmental groups and the peace-movement. The liberal (FDP) and the conservative parties (CDU/CSU) rely relatively more on support from well-fixed voters and, concerning our subject, seem to be in addition more influenced by, for example, the interest of the establishment. Both political preferences as well as interest groups appear to have a strong influence on the level and particularly on the general structure of the public budget. One could expect that a change in the composition of the government would have a noticeable impact on the allocation of the financial resources between different expenditure groups or even the overall budget level.

Some remarkable findings concerning this question can be derived from an earlier study,[34] which analyses the substitution effects between selected expenditure groups of the FRG's public budgets during the 1970s and 1980s.[35] The results of this study are somewhat surprising, at least for those who assumed that political variables would have substantial impact on structural changes in public budgets. The expectations of major or even revolutionary changes in budgetary policies by the change-over from a centre-right to a centre-left coalition in 1969 turned out to be a 'fiscal illusion'. During the analysed period only 1.3 per cent of the federal budget has been redistributed. The result of the substitution analysis for the long period indicates that public budgets in the FRG, including the defence budget, are more stable and rigid than expected. Political factors only have weak impacts on the structure of public budgets, structural variations are rather caused by economic and in particular by institutional factors.

Nevertheless a second finding of this study illustrates the losing position of the defence expenditure group compared to other expenditure groups. By analysing the substitution effects with regard to the structural changes of the public budget during the analysed period (1963–78) it can be clearly seen that the defence budget had to bear the main burden of the recognized budgetary redistribution. More than 72 per cent of the redistributed budget volume has been 'financed' by the defence budget, essentially in favour of social security (28.3 per cent of the redistributed volume), public finance management (25.4 per cent), public enterprise (21.5 per cent), education (16.1 per cent), healthcare (2.3 per cent) and public safety (0.9 per cent). Obviously the budget volume of defence expenditure has been used in the dynamic sense as a disposable fund for financing the 'internal compensation' and especially as a source of financing the enormous increase of social spending during the analysed period.

Military factors

The most important influences on the demand for military expenditures derive from the military factors themselves. The principal dynamics behind the determination of the defence sector's endeavour for an optimal spending level is the evaluation of the state's security position. This position reflects a favourable or unfavourable balance between the expected 'threat' on one side, and the country's 'own capabilities' in combination with the 'spillins' of possible allies on the other.[36] It is likely that a discrepancy between the desired and actual position leads to the corresponding request for a modification in the present spending level. Taking the external environment first it is presumed that the national security decision-makers are analysing the international surrounding with the objective of defining a possible 'threat' as well as the 'spillins' they may expect from other countries. The first evaluation concerns other states' capabilities, the second, and maybe more important, tries to generate information on the intentions in terms of hostility as well as co-operation.[37] The combination of these two critical elements is assumed to represent the perceived threat and spillin[38] within the external environment directly influencing the calculation of the spending level. The strategic external environment generally depends on the power of the nations, the geographical positions and political commitments. For Germany being a non-nuclear flanking member of an alliance, the threat is clearly determined by the intentions and postures of the United States and USSR. The military spending of both countries will be included in our demand function for Germany. Consequently, threat plays an important role, too, in evaluating the 'own capability'. The traditional indicator of capability is a country's stock of arms, though it also depends on manpower, up-dated technology, readiness, training, morale, etc. Nevertheless the defence sector primarily compares equipment and forces available to Warsaw Pact and NATO, which plays an important role in decisions about deployment and procurement.[39]

These decisions have to be seen, of course, in the context of 'alliance spillin' and existing 'military doctrine', as both elements do have significant influence on the behaviour of and demand for a country's spending level.[40] The most important economic issues have been the burden sharing debate and, associated with it, the free-rider behaviour of allies relying on the defence spending of others.[41] The analytical foundation of this normative approach is based on the theory of public goods, which allows an inside look into the basic idea of alliance behaviour and its coherence.[42] Germany as a NATO member for instance shares the pure public good 'deterrence' with its partners, which relies on a credible threat of retaliatory punishment against possible offenders. The benefits of the good 'deterrence' are non-rival in consumption, which means that additional allies can simultaneously share the deterrent umbrella without reducing the benefits to existing allies. The characteristic 'non-excludability', which determines the optimal provision of a good either by the private or public sector, applies whenever an attack on an ally inflicts unacceptable damage, for example, on the economic external environment of the ally providing the deterrence.[43] In this situation deterrence has the quality of a pure public good, which induces free-rider behaviour in the sense that the larger allies would shoulder the defence burdens of smaller partners. As a result smaller allies contribute a suboptimal allocation towards defence. In addition it is even likely that an ally's increase of defence expenditures will cause a decrease of another ally's military expenditure. Particularly this hypothesis will be tested in estimating the demand equation for the Federal Republic, to examine the degree and possible change of free-riding and the actual influence on the defence spending level, which seems to have been of some importance especially when relying on the doctrine of Mutual Assured Destruction (MAD).

During the late 1960s a more flexible strategic concept was developed and adapted by NATO. The basic intention behind the new doctrine 'Flexible Response' is NATO's ability to deter and to counter military aggression of varying scales in any region of the NATO area. This can be secured only through a wide range of forces equipped with a mixture of conventional, theatre nuclear and strategic nuclear weapons.[44] To explain the behavioural change concerning burden sharing and the free-rider problem after the installation of the new doctrine, Sandler and others have put forth the joint product model.[45] They came to the conclusion that the new doctrine has caused a major change in the NATO allies' demand for defence spending,[46] particularly as the European allies have to be prepared to meet any aggression by themselves, maybe with certain reservations concerning the flanking allies. Consequently they can no longer rely primarily on nuclear deterrence by the NATO members USA, UK, or in special cases France, but have to increase expenditures for their non-nuclear, conventional arsenals. Flexible Response therefore causes a 'complementarity' between nuclear and non-nuclear arsenals as they have to be deployed and used in conjunction, which reduces the extent of free-riding and thus influences the closing of the share gap between the defence burdens paid by the smaller and larger NATO allies. In regard to Germany we can predict that it will have to respond in a different way to the expenditure behaviour of other allies. Increases in an ally's defence spending should theoretically induce an increase of Germany's own defence spending. Nevertheless the flanking location of the Federal Republic has to be stressed, whose forward areas in connection with the strategy of 'Forward Defence' require a substantial number of conventional and theatre nuclear forces stationed close to the flanking border of the alliance.[47] If the hypothesis, that 'Flexible Response' induces structural changes of the allies' defence expenditure pattern, this should be significant, too, for the German demand equation of defence spending. Therefore the new doctrine will be included in the next section's estimation of the demand function.

Estimation of the demand for defence spending

The model
The discussion of the defence spending's determination indicates that Germany's national security depends on a variety of economic, political and military factors from both the internal and external environment. Considering the fact that not all of the analysed variables can be transformed into a testable form, the theoretical discussion yields the general form of the German demand equation for defence spending with five primary variables:[48]

GDS = f(INCOME, ECOSTAB, THREAT, SPILLIN, GOVCOMP) (1)

The estimation of the response variable GDS, the German defence spending, is based on the common nominal NATO data,[49] recalculated to annual real spending figures (1980 is the base year) expressed in billions of constant US dollars using the 1980 exchange rates.[50] This approach, used for all monetary variables included, ensures that the variations in the nominal data are transformed to real changes, giving the opportunity of direct comparisons with other countries' data.[51] The Gross Domestic Product (GDP) is used as a measure of the Federal Republic's yearly INCOME.[52] Concerning this measure we assume that GDP and GDS are positively related, which means that the demand for GDS is expected to rise with a growing GDP. As a possible indicator of economic stability (ECOSTAB) the deficit of the federal budget was chosen because of its potentially high pressure on the defence budget. A growing deficit (DEF) should limit any increase of the defence budget or even induce a decreasing defence spending.

The starting-point of every discussion about defence spending is usually the perceived THREAT. In the German case THREAT is measured by the estimated Soviet military expenditure (SUDS), as the Soviet Union bears the main burden within the Warsaw Pact.[53] We expect that there is a positive relationship between THREAT and GDS. The counterpart to THREAT in the framework of the state's security position is the perceived SPILLIN. For Germany the spillin variables are measured by the defence spending of its NATO allies (NATODS). To obtain more detailed information we selectively consider the defence spending of France (FDS), as the French–German relationship shows certain symptoms of an alliance within the alliance. The defence spending of the main ally USA (USDS) is added, and the defence spending of a modified NATO (NATODS1), in this case the sum of the real defence expenditures of the United Kingdom, Italy, Belgium, Denmark, the Netherlands and Norway is also included.[54] Presuming that Germany is a free-rider, its defence spending should be negatively related to its allies' military expenditures, which implies that an increase in spillin causes a decrease in GDS. To enable an optimal reaction time to the spillin and threat variations, all spillin and threat measures are lagged by one year to account for the sequential response attributed to Nash-type reaction.[55] Spillin, therefore, is the allies' defence expenditure in the previous year. A negative coefficient on these variables would indicate a free-riding behaviour of the Federal Republic. In addition to the spillin variables dummy variables (D) are added to identify statistically the predicted structural change of defence spending in West Germany concerning the flexible response doctrine. D SPILLIN is SPILLIN multiplied by zero before 1974 and by one after 1973. Murdoch and Sandler have statistically identified 1974 as the best shift year.[56] If the impact of the doctrine of flexible response is consistent with our assumption, a structural shift of German spending behaviour should occur.

A second dummy variable is included independently in the equation to

Table 6.6 Description of the variables

Variable	Description
GDS	German defence spending in 1980 prices, converted to 1980 average period exchange rate ($bn)
GDP	Gross domestic product in constant prices ($bn, 1980 = 100)
FDS	Defence spending in France in 1980 prices, converted to 1980 average period exchange rate ($bn), lagged one year
NATODS	Defence spending of a modified NATO, including USA, UK, Italy, Belgium, Denmark, Netherlands and Norway, in 1980 prices and 1980 average period exchange rates ($bn), lagged one year
SUDS	Defence spending of the Soviet Union, expressed in 1980 prices and in $bn, using the SIPRI conversion method, lagged one year
D	Dummy variable for NATO change of strategy, equal to zero for 1960–73 and one for 1974–87
D1	Dummy variable for composition of government, equal to one for 1960–70 and 1984–7 and zero for 1971–83

Sources: NATO Statistical Service, SIPRI *Yearbooks* (various issues) and IMF, *International Financial Statistics* (various issues)

identify a possible impact of differing government coalitions on GDS. $D1$ is equal to one for the years 1961–9 and 1983–7 and zero for the years 1970–82.[57] If the images concerning the parties involved in the government composition are not some kind of a political illusion, a structural change of some significance should be recognized.

Empirical results: 1961–87

From the pool of potential predictor variables the demand equation for defence spending can be written in the form:

$$\text{GDS}_t = \beta_0 + \beta_1 \text{GDP}_t + \beta_2 \text{FDS}_{t-1} + \beta_3 D\text{FDS}_{t-1} + \beta_4 \text{USDS}_{t-1}$$
$$+ \beta_5 D\text{USDS}_{t-1} + \beta_6 \text{NATODS1}_{t-1} + \beta_7 D\text{NATODS1}_{t-1}$$
$$+ \beta_8 \text{SUDS}_{t-1} + \beta_9 \text{DEF}_t + \beta_{10} D1_t + \varepsilon_t \qquad (2)$$

where ε_t measures the error and the βs are coefficients estimated by applying ordinary least squares (OLS) to the model. Data have been prepared for the period 1961–87, giving 27 observations.[58]

Equation (3) contains the regression coefficients (t ratios in parentheses) estimated for the complete ten variable model with an R^2 of 0.981.

$$\text{GDS}_t = 13.399(5.599) - 0.008(-1.580)\ \text{GDP}_t + 0.469(0.884)\ \text{FDS}_{t-1} -$$
$$0.089(-0.148)\ D\text{FDS}_{t-1} - 0.098(-5.025)\ \text{USDS}_{t-1} +$$
$$0.072(3.108)\ D\text{USDS}_{t-1} - 0.142(-0.610)\ \text{NATODS1}_{t-1} -$$
$$0.244(-0.853)\ D\text{NATODS1}_{t-1} + 0.237(6.244)\ \text{SUDS}_{t-1} +$$
$$0.056(1.112)\ \text{DEF}_t + 1.121(1.327)\ D1_t \qquad (3)$$

Although the selected predictor variables appear to be useful in explaining the demand for defence spending, there remains the question of whether there are specification errors of any kind and whether all predictor variables included in the initial model are of significant relevance. The relatively high R^2 indicates a good fit between response and predictor variable, the equation is significant at the 0.01 level, and the Durbin–Watson (DW) coefficient is reasonably close to 2. Using the usual selection criteria we tried to reduce our model to the best specification of German demand for defence spending.[59] Based on several statistical tests $USDS_{t-1}$ and DEF_t were dropped from the initial equation (3). That yields as the final equation (t ratios in parentheses):

$$GDS_t = 10.8504(6.8021) - 0.0064(-1.3136)\ GDP_t + 0.5778(2.6518)\ FDS_{t-1}$$
$$- 0.5117(-3.0147)\ DFDS_{t-1} - 0.0958(-7.4380)\ NATODS_{t-1}$$
$$+ 0.0495(2.6498)\ DNATODS_{t-1} + 0.2115(6.7826)\ SUDS_{t-1}$$
$$+ 0.9056(1.2075)\ D1_t \qquad\qquad (4)$$

$R^2 = 0.976$ DW = 2.23   degrees of freedom = 15   cases = 27

All estimated coefficients of the final equation (4), with the exception of GDP and $D1$, are significant at the 0.005 level, the R^2 is high and the DW is in a reasonable range. In summary equation (4) appears to be the best estimation of the Federal Republic's demand for defence spending.

Discussion of the results

The coefficients measure Germany's marginal responses to changes of each of the seven selected variables. Surprisingly, the coefficient for GDP is neither positive nor significant at a reasonable level. The estimated GDP coefficient of -0.0064 implies, for example, that a dollar increase in real GDP causes a 0.6 cent decrease in real defence spending, holding all other factors constant. Nevertheless, the insignificance of the GDP coefficient does not allow such a conclusion: rather it indicates that Germany's GDP is not a significant determinant of its defence spending behaviour. This confirms the hypothesis, and earlier findings,[60] that West Germany's policies of 'internal compensation', as discussed earlier, are colliding more and more with its defence expenditures. Therefore, national security will not be relieved of the financial pressure even with growing GDP and expanding public budgets.

The estimated values of the SPILLIN and $DSPILLIN$ coefficients are all significant and provide evidence that structural changes in Germany's response to allies' expenditures occurred after the adaptation of Flexible Response. The reaction after 1973 is calculated as the sum of the corresponding coefficients. The values of NATODS and $DNATODS$ show that Germany reacted negatively during the MAD period on NATO members' defence increases. A \$1 increase of real NATO spending causes a 9.6 cent cut in German defence expenditures, keeping the other factors constant. The marginal response since 1974 is estimated to be -0.0463 ($-0.0958 + 0.0495$). This indicates that during the flexible response era the Federal Republic is less responsive to spillins, which means that Germany, although being a non-nuclear flanking nation, reduced its free-riding behaviour concerning the NATO. This evidence supports the hypothesis that the new doctrine reduced free-riding and induced complementarity.

Another very interesting result is given in the estimated FDS and DFDS coefficients. During the pre-1974 era, Germany responded positively to defence increases of its closest European partner France. The value indicates that a $1 increase in France's military activities would cause an increase of German defence spending by 57.7 cents. Nevertheless during the post-1973 period the responsiveness to the French spillins changed remarkably to a marginal reaction of 0.0661 (0.5778 − 0.5117). Obviously there is no recognizable marching in step any more between France and Germany, maybe due to the expanding costs of the French nuclear forces and its overseas commitments. This seems to support the hypothesis that the French–German connection has to be considered more and more as an alliance within the alliance. At least the results discussed indicate that the close political relations together with the growing French spillin, based on nuclear deterrence, facilitates a change towards a free-riding behaviour as observed within other alliances.

Finally we consider the estimated coefficient of the Soviet defence expenditure $(SUDS_{t-1})$, which is significantly and positively related to German defence spending. However, bearing in mind the problems of the Soviet data, this finding should be used with caution. The last result is based on the dummy variable $(D1)$, which represents the change of the government party composition and its implication on the structural change of the dependent defence spending variable. The coefficient indicates that the composition of the German Government and its changes do have a noticeable influence on the demand for defence spending, supporting the impression that the centre-right government has forced a positive shift in the demand for defence spending.

Future prospects

Considering the findings of the estimation of the demand for defence spending West German military expenditure faces a critical period. There will be enormous military pressure, particularly from the alliance and the USA, to increase Germany's financial contribution to Western security substantially. This pressure will even be intensified by the presumable direction of the alliance's strategic reassessment in the wake of the INF Treaty. Contrary to the military demand there will be growing economic and political pressure to reduce the defence burden. This pressure reflects the almost classical guns-versus-butter issue, but in addition, it represents a totally new quality, the changing public perception of the military threat in a generally warming East–West climate.

On the military side the recent conclusion of an agreement to eliminate intermediate-range nuclear forces (INF) brings into relief a series of issues with profound implications particularly for West German defence spending. These issues include questions over the future of nuclear deterrence; the future relationship between nuclear and conventional forces; the absence of a so-called 'Gesamtkonzept', a conceptual arms control framework; the future of US–European relations; and the dissension on a strategic reassessment.

None of these issues facing the Federal Republic is more insidious than the question over the future of deterrence in post-INF Europe.[61] Although acknowledging the fact that the treaty may be a major arms control breakthrough that could eventually help promote a comprehensive strategic arms agreement, West Germans are concerned that they might have to take the greater risks, more than all the other NATO allies. Although the agreement bans deployment of missiles with ranges from 500 to 5,500 km, it leaves some 4,000 battlefield nuclear weapons on German soil, only able to reach East and West German territory, thus 'singularizing' West Germany in a possible confined nuclear conflict in Central Europe. As a result, the nervousness regarding nuclear deterrence seems to be growing and a West German consensus in favour of total nuclear withdrawal, the so-called triple-zero option that would remove all remaining short-range nuclear weapons, is predictable.[62] The triple-zero option seems to be attractive for the whole political spectrum, as the conservatives are against them for nationalistic reasons, and the left for disarmament purposes.[63] Therefore the question of nuclear deterrence and of singularization will be of paramount importance for the alliance cohesion in the near future, and in consequence of West German national security.

In addition West Germans suspect that, in any case, the USA in particular is moving away from all-out nuclear deterrence toward a strategy that envisages a limited conflict to which NATO would apply a flexible response.[64] Their doubts go back to the Reagan–Gorbachev summit in Reykjavik, where the US appeared willing to accept a proposal to scrap all nuclear weapons, apparently putting national interest ahead of concern about its NATO partners. This is seen as an inevitable evolution of American policy, which appears to be even more concrete in consideration of a recent Pentagon report with the title 'Discriminate Deterrence'.[65] The report recommends a more flexible NATO strategy not necessarily based on the threat of all-out nuclear retaliation. For West German defence analysts, this suggests that the US could be a nuclear sanctuary in a possible conflict with the risks borne by European and especially by Germany alone. They foresee a gradual US disengagement from Western Europe, partly as a result of the economic problems, partly because of a shift of US interest to other parts of the globe. The impact of this evolution on burden sharing in defence for one and on the military pressure on West

German defence spending for another is obvious. The reduced reliance on NATO's nuclear deterrence induces expensive investments in a high-tech military build-up of conventional forces. Therefore a substantial denuclearization in Europe will have significant distributive effects on the alliance and a remarkable impact on West German defence spending.

The prospect of substantial denuclearization and of an upcoming new defence strategy has served to boost the idea of European self-reliance on the security front and to focus attention on the conventional arms threat by the Warsaw Pact. Ahead of the INF agreement European allies had already begun to adjust their defence strategies to the change in the political climate. Members of the Western European Union,[66] for example, have pledged greater European defence co-operation. On a bilateral level, particularly France and West Germany is seeking to build a stronger European pillar within the alliance.[67] Lately military co-operation has even intensified by signing a treaty enabling the formation of a Franco–German army brigade to be based in West Germany under a rotating 6-month command. In addition an agreement was announced to co-produce 400 anti-tank helicopters at a cost of $3bn, the biggest European joint arms venture in recent years.[68] Most important for the Federal Republic's national security, however, was the French hint, that their nuclear coverage might well be extended to include West Germany.

Concerning the conventional arms threat the German as well as the allies' reaction has been double-tracked. On the one hand they try to initiate negotiations with the Soviet Union, aimed at asymmetrical reductions of conventional forces, particularly of tanks and artillery, and on the other hand, to intensify the development of a new generation of sophisticated conventional weapons. The most expensive German procurement in this connection will be the already approved project of the new European-built[69] so-called 'Jäger 90', or European Fighter Aircraft, which is estimated to be worth around DM23bn in today's terms but presumably will burden the German defence budget with some DM52bn during the next decade. That of course will be a major sum on the military budget and will use up funds needed for another main problem for the German Bundeswehr: demographics raise doubts whether sufficient manpower will be available to man the forces of the future. There seems to be no possibility that the Bundeswehr will be able to maintain its present strength beyond the early 1990s. The size of Germany's male population of military age has been dropping drastically during the last years and will continue to do so in the foreseeable future.[70] Under actual circumstances the German army requires an annual replenishment pool of 206,000 new conscripts.[71] Only around 160,000 will be available by the early 1990s, which means that within the next decade the Bundeswehr is almost certain to decline to a force of 400,000 to 450,000 men or perhaps even less. This will be a very costly matter for the German defence budget, for to cushion this development the numerical structure of the armed forces will have to be modified. This particularly will induce tempting financial incentives for a remarkable increase of the 55 per cent volunteer part of the Bundeswehr manpower.[72] To summarize, the military pressure to lift the defence budget substantially above the conceded annual increase of 2 per cent during the next years, will be immense.

At the same time, due to economic difficulties and the uncertain prospects for the end of the 1990s, the coming years are an exceptionally bad time for the growing financial demand for national security. One of the main political consequences of the economic slowdown has been a rapidly increasing public debt with still high downside risks for the years to come and the need for a serious consolidation programme for the federal budget. Considering the forthcoming, heavily contested tax reform, which is accompanied by noticeable tax increases to limit the induced federal budget's deficits, and bearing in mind the need for 'internal compensation', there will be no additional internal revenue for an increase of defence spending. The alternative to increase defence spending at the expense of social welfare programmes appears to be impossible in the Federal Republic.[73]

Social welfare programmes are so closely linked with social peace and the stability of democratic order that they are almost sacrosanct. Many West Germans, remembering the influence of the economic difficulties on the first democratic experiment in the early 1930s, regard the success of the economy and the social welfare system as at least as important for German democracy and freedom as military preparedness.[74] For this reason it is not surprising that the ruling centre-right coalition, although winning electoral success by its unmistakably strong commitments on fundamental security questions, is not willing to make major reductions in social benefits. Under these circumstances the pressure from the economic side will not leave any room for an increase of the defence spending in real terms during the next decade.

Finally there will be a growing and very influential political pressure to reduce military expenditures. Although the West German consensus on fundamental defence issues is still remarkably stable, recent internal foreign policy and security discussions indicate a changing public perception of national security. This has been influenced on the one side by a changing political party structure caused by the success of the ecological 'Green' movement, and a once powerful peace movement, which began to take shape during the neutron-bomb controversy in 1977/78, and which left its traces in West German politics. On the other hand this trend has been recently reinforced by the diminished perception of the Soviet military threat. Though deterrence does not seem to become superfluous, it is more and more difficult to explain to the public the logic behind military preparedness or the necessity and rationale for an expansion of military spending. In consequence, even if the direction of political pressure on national security is the last predictable one, it seems to be quite likely that the pressure to reduce defence spending will accelerate.

In consquence, due to the economic and political pressure on defence spending, remarkable increases in West German defence budgets are most unlikely and should not be part of any consideration on future defence strategies. Moreover, there are few grounds to believe that the conventional force improvements in Germany, apparently dictated by the INF treaty, will exceed any assumed minimal necessity. In addition, proposals concerning the inefficient resource allocation in the military environment, although necessary, are of limited use, particularly in the military sector. This leaves only one road open: to enforce East–West arms control negotiations with the aim to reduce the threat of a Warsaw Pact invasion in Germany and to create a new military balance in Europe at a much lower level.

Notes

1 See e.g. OECD (1987), *Economic Survey of Germany*, Paris; J. B. Donges, H. Klodt, K.-D. Schmidt (1986), *The West German Economy Towards Year 2000*, Working Paper 268, Kiel, Institut für Weltwirtschaft; J. B. Donges, K.-D. Schmidt *et al.* (1988), *Mehr Strukturwandel für Wachstum und Beschäftigung: Die deutsche Wirtschaft im Anpassungsstau*, Tübingen, Mohr-Siebeck; H. Lützel (1985), 'Entwicklung des Sozialprodukts 1950–1984', *Wirtschaft und Statistik*, no. 6, pp. 433–44.

2 See Sachverständigenrat zur Begutachtung der gesamtwirtschaftlichen Entwicklung (Council of Economic Experts) (1981), *Investieren für mehr Beschäftigung: Jahresgutachten*, (Annual Assessment) 1981/82, Stuttgart und Mainz, Kohlhammer.

3 This law commits the Federal and States Government to secure stability of prices, a high level of employment, external balance and a steady and adequate economic growth.

4 In connection with the topic of this contribution this does not hold for military goods and services. Figures provided by the US Department of Defense indicate that, e.g. in 1986, the military trade balance of Germany and the US has been in favour of the US by 114.5 million US dollar. See D. C. Morrison (1987), 'Sharing NATO's burden', *National Journal*, 30 May 1987, p. 1395.

5 See Deutsche Bundesbank (1988), *Statistische Beihefte zu den Monatsberichten der Deutschen Bundesbank* (Statistical Supplements to the Monthly Report), Reihe 4, März 1988.

6 The mentioned trend will have the inverse impact on manpower planning of the Bundeswehr, as will be discussed later.

7 The published figures have been in 1985 195,000, in 1986 249,000 and in 1987 86,000. See Deutsche Bundesbank (1988) p. 14 and OECD (1987), *Economic Survey of Germany*, Paris, p. 14.

8 The economic situation and performance during the late 1970s and the early 1980s was one of the main reasons for the change from a centre-left to a centre-right administration.

9 See OECD (1987) p. 60; Wirtschafts- und Sozialwissenschaftliches Institut des Deutschen Gewerkschaftsbundes (WSI) (1987), 'Die wirtschaftliche Entwicklung

in der Bundesrepublik Deutschland in den Jahren 1987/88', *WSI-Mitteilungen*, vol. 40, pp. 637–55.

10 Prognos AG (1986), *Die Bundesrepublik Deutschland 1990/2000/2010*, Prognos-Report Nr. 12, Stuttgart, Poller.

11 By adapting the Forward Strategy for Europe in 1950 the North Atlantic Council recognized that this would imply the defence of Europe on German soil. Four years later the Paris Agreement regularized relations between the NATO allies and the Federal Republic of Germany. See Nato Information Service (1984), The North Atlantic Treaty Organization, *Facts and Figures*, Brussels, p. 27 and 33.

12 The relatively low budget was due to the NASH-Aid of the USA, which provided as an initial equipment 450 tanks and around 370 aircraft. Actually the defence outlay decreased in 1955/56 because of the reduction of the occupation payments to certain NATO countries.

13 That, for example, excludes any role of German forces in protecting Europe's oil supplies from the Middle East. Once in a while there is a discussion about changing the relevant chapter of the constitution. Recently it was suggested that the Federal Armed Forces should participate at least in the UN security forces.

14 The consequences for the defence budget are obvious. Without nuclear weapons, the extremely high costs of researching, developing, producing, testing and evaluating this kind of complex and technologically sophisticated weapon are avoided. See L. Köllner (1984), 'Die Entwicklung bundesdeutscher Militärausgaben in Vergangenheit and Zukunft', in *Beilage zur Wochenzeitschrift 'Das Parlament'*, B 22, p. 35, and International Institute for Strategic Studies (IISS) (1987), *The Military Balance 1987–1988*, London, IISS, p. 239.

15 See Nato Information Service (1986), *NATO Handbook*, Brussels, p. 27.

16 See J. R. Golden (1983), *NATO Burden-Sharing: Risks and Opportunities*, New York, Praeger, p. 68.

17 The data is based on publications of the Minister of Defence and the International Institute of Strategic Studies. See: Der Bundesminister der Verteidigung (1985), *Weißbuch 1985: Zur Lage und Entwicklung der Bundeswehr*, Bonn, pp. 187–228 and IISS (1987), pp. 64–6.

18 For a detailed analysis of the Bundeswehr Manpower see M. V. Creveld (1983), 'Bundeswehr Manpower Management', in *RUSI and Brassey's Defence Year-book 1983*, London, pp. 47–72.

19 For a discussion of the conceptual and numerical concern of these measures see G. Kennedy (1983), *Defense Economics*, London, p. 46.

20 Germany's contribution in 1987 is almost identical to France's (8.0 per cent) and UK's (8.1 per cent).

21 See Der Bundesminister der Verteidigung (1985), p. 118.

22 The density of armed forces in relation to the population is for example twenty-six times as high as in the United States. See Der Bundesminister der Verteidigung (1985) p. 118.

23 Army General John W. Vessey, the former chairman of the Joint Chiefs of Staff, described the West German predicament this way: 'If you multiply the population of Oregon by 20, give each person a car, arm 1 million of them, bring in another half-million armed foreigners and put a couple-thousand jets in the air, then at least the Oregonians would know what the Germans put up with.' See D. C. Morrison (1987), 'Sharing NATO's burden', *National Journal*, 30 May 1987, p. 1397.

24 The likelihood that Germany's defence outlays will further increase is dim, if considered that the military spending during the last 20 years (1968–87)

increased by 52.2 per cent compared with a 10.2 per cent rise for the USA during the same period (1980 constant prices).

25 Figures released recently by the Pentagon indicate that only around 50 to 60 per cent of the US military spending can be attributed to NATO. See D. Robertson (1986), 'Fair shares in NATO: problems of comparing defence contributions', in *RUSI and Brassey's Defence Yearbook 1986*, London, p. 122.

26 See for a detailed discussion of this classification T. R. Cusack (1987), 'Governmental budget process', in S. A. Bremer (ed.), *The Globus Model: Computer Simulation of Worldwide Political and Economic Development*, Frankfurt, Campus Verlag, and Boulder, Col., Westview Press, pp. 325–458.

27 See for similar discussions on various countries A. Maizels and M. K. Nisanke (1986), 'The determinants of military expenditures in developing countries', in *World Development*, vol. 14, pp. 1125–40; J. C. Murdoch and T. Sandler (1985), 'Australian demand for military expenditures: 1961–1979', in *Australian Economic Papers*, vol. 24, pp. 142–53; D. B. Bobrow and S. R. Hill (1985), 'The determinants of military budgets: the Japanese case', in *Conflict Management and Peace Science*, vol. 9, pp. 1–18; K. Hartley and P. McLean (1981), 'U.K. defence expenditure', in *Public Finance*, vol. 36, pp. 171–92; L. Dudley and C. Montmarquette (1981), 'The demand for military expenditures: an international comparison', in *Public Choice*, vol. 37, pp. 5–31; R. Smith (1980), 'The demand for military expenditure', in *The Economic Journal*, vol. 90, pp. 811–20.

28 See for example E. A. Thompson (1979), 'An economic basis for the national defence argument for aiding certain industries', in *Journal of Political Economy*, vol. 87, pp. 1–36.

29 Dudley and Montmarquette object that within an alliance, however, the probability of enemy attack is unlikely to be related to the increase of a single member's income. For them a more plausible reason is that security is a luxury good whose demand increases more rapidly than income when income rises. Nevertheless our findings for Germany cannot support this explanation. See L. Dudley and C. Montmarquette (1981) p. 6.

30 See A. Maizels and M. K. Nisanke (1986) p. 1130.

31 See for a more detailed discussion D. Fritz-Aβmus and K. Zimmermann (1988), 'The economics of West German defense spending', unpublished manuscript, University of the Federal Armed Forces, Hamburg.

32 Although German armed forces are not allowed to be directly involved in a conflict outside the NATO area, in the case of, e.g., an oil crisis, substitutions between the allied forces will take place with corresponding impacts on defence outlays.

33 See K. Hartley and P. McLean (1981) p. 176.

34 See K. Zimmermann and F. G. Müller (1985), *Umweltschutz als neue politische Aufgabe: Substitutionseffekte in öffentlichen Budgets*, Frankfurt/New York, Campus and F. G. Müller and K. Zimmermann (1986), 'The determinants of structural changes in public budgets: a theoretical and empirical analysis for the Federal Republic of Germany', *European Journal of Political Research*, vol. 19, pp. 481–98.

35 The concept of substitution effects seems to be an appropriate measure of 'where the action is', because the difference between the actual and the expected level of a particular expenditure category represents an indicator of a dynamic process of structural change over time, which can be explained by a set of economic, political or institutional factors.

36 See T. R. Cusack (1987) p. 368.

37 R. Smith, e.g. evaluates intentions as crucial to the expenditure decisions, particularly for small countries. See R. Smith (1980) p. 813.
38 An extensive discussion of both variables, their measurement and significance is provided, e.g., in T. R. Cusack (1985), 'The evolution of power, threat and security: past and potential developments', in *International Interactions*, vol. 12, pp. 151–98.
39 In addition the tendency of the defence bureaucracy to safeguard or expand its organizational scope, ensuring the interest of its members, has to be taken into account.
40 Beginning with the seminal work of Olson and Zeckhauser in 1966, these two elements, and particularly the alliance behaviour issue, have been of great interest to economists. See e.g. M. Olson and R. Zeckhauser (1966), 'An economic theory of alliances', *Review of Economics and Statistics*, vol. 48, no. 3, pp. 266–279; M. Olson and R. Zeckhauser (1967), 'Collective goods, comparative advantage, and alliance efficiencies', in R. N. McKean (ed.), *Issues in Defense Economics*, New York, pp. 25–48; J. M. van Ypersele de Strihou (1967), 'Sharing the defense burden among Western allies', *Review of Economics and Statistics*, vol. 49, pp. 527–36; J. M. van Ypersele de Strihou (1968), 'Sharing the defense burden among Western allies', *Yale Economic Essays*, vol. 8, no. 1, pp. 261–320.
41 See, e.g., T. Sandler and J. Murdoch (1986), 'Defense burdens and prospects for the northern European allies', in David B. H. Denoon (ed.) *Constraints On Strategy: The Economics of Western Security*, Washington, Pergamon-Brassey's, pp. 59–113; J. C. Murdoch and T. Sandler (1984) 'Complementarity, free riding, and the military expenditures of NATO allies', *Journal of Public Economics*, vol. 25, pp. 83–101; J. C. Murdoch and T. Sandler (1982), 'A theoretical and empirical analysis of NATO', *Journal of Conflict Resolution*, vol. 26, pp. 237–63; T. Sandler (1977), 'Impurity of defense: an application to the economics of alliances', *Kyklos* vol. 30, pp. 443–60; T. Sandler and J. F. Forbes (1980), 'Burden sharing strategy, and the design of NATO', *Economic Inquiry*, vol. 18, pp. 425–44; T. Sandler and J. Cauley (1975), 'On the economic theory of alliances', *Journal of Conflict Resolution*, vol. 19, pp. 330–48.
42 Eventually it could even lead to alternative military strategies of an alliance, a possibility which seems not to have been discussed in detail up to now.
43 See R. Cornes and T. Sandler (1986), *The Theory of Externalities, Public Goods, and Club Goods*, Cambridge University Press, p. 261.
44 See NATO Information Service (1984) p. 139.
45 See, e.g., T. Sandler (1977); T. Sandler and J. F. Forbes (1980); J. C. Murdoch and T. Sandler (1982, 1984, 1985). In this section we rely heavily on the joint product model.
46 This has been discussed theoretically and empirically by J. C. Murdoch and T. Sandler (1984).
47 The question remains if this really relieves pressure from German defence spending. Living on the prepared battlefield of the whole alliance does have consequences that do not necessarily lead to a higher defence spending level.
48 A similar demand equation based on the joint product model is more rigorously demonstrated in J. C. Murdoch and T. Sandler (1984).
49 Data for NATO countries are from the Nato Statistical Service. The common definition includes military research and development, military aid in the budget of the donor country, costs of retirement pensions, of paramilitary forces, and excludes civil defence, war pensions and payments on war debts. For Germany a critical statistical year is 1960 because of the budget year change.

50 For transformation into real figures each country's Consumer Price Index (CPI) has been used. The basic data of CPI and the exchange rates of the NATO countries have been obtained from IMF, International Financial Statistics (various issues) and transformed to a standard series. The exchange rates are period average rates (af), e.g. 1.8177 DM per US dollar for the Federal Republic.

51 Not included in the model is a price index for military goods, because data are not consistently available. Nevertheless this will not bias the results, as prices for military activities appear to change at the same rate as prices of all other goods. See e.g. E. Sköns (1983), 'Military prices', in *SIPRI Yearbook 1983*, London, Taylor & Francis, pp. 195–211.

52 The data on GDP as well as on POP and DEF are taken from the Gutachten des Sachverständigenrats (Council of Economic Advisers), because in Germany political decisions concerning economic policy are to some extent based on the data and results of this yearly study of five appointed experts. See Sachverständigenrat zur Begutachtung der gesamtwirtschaftlichen Entwicklung (Council of Economic Experts) (1987), *Vorrang für die Wachstumspolitik: Jahresgutachten (Annual Assessment) 1987/88*, Stuttgart und Mainz, Kohlhammer.

53 The SIPRI data are considered to be the best available, nevertheless they should be used with caution. In our opinion the data on Soviet DS seem to be unrealistic. Recently they have not been published. On Soviet defence expenditures see, e.g., C. G. Jacobsen (1986), 'Soviet military expenditure and the Soviet defence burden', in *SIPRI Yearbook 1986*, Stockholm, SIPRI, pp. 263–74; T. R. Cusack and M. P. Ward (1981), 'Military spending in the United States, Soviet Union, and the People's Republic of China', *Journal of Conflict Resolution*, vol. 25, pp. 429–69.

54 The NATODS1 selection was chosen for several reasons. First, we wanted to exclude exceptional configurations like Turkey and Greece, which are expected to bias the result due to their tension. Second, Canada is excluded as we expect a closer relation between the German DS and the European allies' DS. Third, Iceland does not have any military expenditures and Luxemburg's expenditure is negligible. Last, the data on Portugal and Spain were incomplete. The DS data are taken from NATO official sources, transformed to constant 1980 US dollars.

55 A Nash type adjustment is chosen as suggested and empirically tested by T. Sandler *et al.* in several publications.

56 See J. C. Murdoch and T. Sandler (1984), footnote 13, p. 92.

57 With D1 we wanted to capture the influence of the change from centre-right government (up to 1969) to centre-left (1970–82) and back to centre-right government in 1982. The response on the budget is lagged by 2 years, because of the budgeting cycle.

58 The data for GDS, GDP, DEF and D cover 1961–87, the data for SPILLIN and THREAT cover 1960–86.

59 This included several tests as described e.g., in R. F. Gunst and R. L. Mason (1980), *Regression Analysis and Its Application: A Data-Oriented Approach*, New York, Marcel Dekker, Inc.

60 See F. G. Müller and K. Zimmermann (1986).

61 See for a detailed analysis J. Record and D. B. Rivkin Jr., (1988), 'Defending post-INF Europe', *Foreign Affairs*, vol. 66, no. 4, pp. 735–54.

62 This seems to become particularly true if there is any hope for or even success of East-West conventional arms control negotiations.

63 Considering the recent economic theory of military alliances the realization of the triple-zero option is even necessary for reasons of NATO cohesion.

64 See *Time* (1988) 'Alliance malaise', 14 March 1988, pp. 4–11.
65 The Commission On Integrated Long-Term Strategy (1988), 'Discriminate deterrence', *Report of The Commission On Integrated Long-Term Strategy,* January 1988, Washington, DC.
66 The Western European Union represents a defence forum that brings together Britain, France, West Germany, Italy, Belgium, the Netherlands and Luxemburg.
67 See P. Windsor (1981), *Germany and the Western Alliance: Lessons from the 1980 Crisis,* Adelphi Papers No. 170, The International Institute for Strategic Studies, London.
68 See *Time,* 14 March 1988, p. 10.
69 The four nations involved in the European Fighter Aircraft project are Britain, West Germany, Spain and Italy.
70 See Deutscher Bundestag (1984), *Unterrichtung durch die Bundesregierung: Bericht über die Bevölkerungsentwicklung in der Bundesrepublik Deutschland, Teil 2: Auswirkungen auf die verschiedenen Bereiche von Staat und Gesellschaft,* Bundestags-Drucksache 10/863 v. 5 January 1984.
71 See G. Färber (1988), *Probleme der Finanzpolitik bei schrumpfender Bevölkerung,* Frankfurt, Campus Verlag, p. 168.
72 Women are barred by law from bearing arms but in connection with manpower shortages there are attempts to loosen this regulation more and more.
73 See W. C. Thompson and P. Wittig (1984), 'The West German defense policy consensus: stable or eroding?', *Armed Forces & Society,* vol. 10, no. 3, p. 352.
74 See Thompson and Wittig (1984), p. 329.

References

Bobrow, D. B. and Hill, S. R. (1985) 'The determinants of military budgets: the Japanese case', *Conflict Management and Peace Science* 9: 1–18.
Commission on Integrated Long-Term Strategy (1988) *Discriminate Deterrence,* Report of the Commission on Integrated Long-Term Strategy, Jan. 1988, Washington, DC.
Cornes, R. and Sandler, T. (1986) *The Theory of Externalities, Public Goods, and Club Goods,* Cambridge: Cambridge University Press.
Creveld, M. V. (1983) 'Bundeswehr manpower management', in *RUSI and Brassey's Defence Yearbook 1983,* London.
Cusack, T. R. (1985) 'The evolution of power, threat and security: past and potential developments', *International Interactions* 12: 151–98.
Cusack, T. R. (1987) 'Governmental budget process', in S. A. Bremer (ed.) *The Globus Model: Computer Simulation of Worldwide Political and Economic Development,* Frankfurt: Campus Verlag; Boulder, Col.: Westview Press, 325–458.
Cusack, T. R. and Ward, M. P. (1981) 'Military spending in the United States, Soviet Union, and the People's Republic of China', *Journal of Conflict Resolution* 25: 429–69.
Der Bundesminister der Verteidigung (1985) *Weißbuch 1985: Zur Lage und Entwicklung der Bundeswehr,* Bonn.
Deutsche Bundesbank (1988) *Statistische Beihefte zu den Monatsberichten der Deutschen Bundesbank* (Statistical Supplements to the Monthly Report), Reihe 4, Mar. 1988, Frankfurt am Main: Deutsche Bundesbank.
Deutscher Bundestag (1984) *Unterrichtung durch die Bundesregierung: Bericht über die Bevölkerungsentwick lung in der Bundesrepublik Deutschland, Teil 2: Auswirkungen auf die verschiedenen Bereiche von Staat und Gesellschaft,* Bundestags-Drucksache v., 5 January 1984.

Donges, J. B., Klodt, H. and Schmidt, K.-D. (1986) *The West German Economy Towards Year 2000*, Working Paper 268, Kiel: Institut für Weltwirtschaft.

Donges, J. B., Schmidt, K.-D. *et al.* (1988) *Mehr Strukturwandel für Wachstum und Beschäftigung: Die deutsche Wirtschaft im Anpassungsstau*, Tübingen: Mohr-Siebeck.

Dudley, L. and Montmarquette, C. (1981), 'The demand for military expenditures: an international comparison', *Public Choice* 37: 5–31.

Färber, G. (1988) *Probleme der Finanzpolitik bei schrumpfender Bevölkerung*, Frankfurt: Campus Verlag.

Fritz-Aßmus, D. and Zimmermann, K. (1988) 'The Economics of West German Defense Spending', unpublished manuscript, Hamburg: University of the Federal Armed Forces.

Fritz-Aßmus, D. (1990) *Zur Ökonomischen Theorie der Allianzen*, Bern u. Stuttgart: Verlag Paul Haupt.

Golden, J. R. (1983) *NATO Burden-Sharing: Risks and Opportunities*, New York: Praeger.

Gunst, R. F. and Mason, R. L. (1980) *Regression Analysis and Its Application: A Data-Oriented Approach*, New York: Marcel Dekker.

Hartley, K. and McLean, P. (1981) 'U.K. defence expenditure', *Public Finance* 36: 171–92.

International Institute for Strategic Studies (IISS) (1987) *The Military Balance 1987–1988*, London: IISS.

International Monetary Fund (IMF) (1988) *International Financial Statistics*, Washington, DC: IMF.

Jacobsen, C. G. (1986) 'Soviet military expenditure and the Soviet defence burden', in Stockholm International Peace Research Institute (SIPRI), *World Armament and Disarmament SIPRI Yearbook 1986*, Oxford: Oxford University Press, 263–74.

Kennedy, G. (1983) *Defense Economics*, London: Duckworth.

Köllner, L. (1984) 'Die Entwicklung bundesdeutscher Militärausgaben in Vergangenheit und Zukunft', in *Beilage zur Wochenzeitschrift 'Das Parlament'* B 22: 27–39.

Lützel, H. (1985) 'Entwicklung des Sozialprodukts 1950–1984', *Wirtschaft und Statistik* 6: 433–44.

Maizels, A. and Nisanke, M. K. (1986) 'The determinants of military expenditures in developing countries', *World Development* 14: 1125–40.

Morrison, D. C. (1987) 'Sharing NATO's burden', *National Journal*, 30 May 1987, p. 1395.

Murdoch, J. C. and Sandler, T. (1982) 'A theoretical and empirical analysis of NATO', *Journal of Conflict Resolution* 26: 237–63.

Murdoch, J. C. and Sandler, T. (1984) 'Complementarity, free riding, and the military expenditures of NATO allies, *Journal of Public Economics* 25: 83–101.

Murdoch, J. C. and Sandler, T. (1985) 'Australian demand for military expenditures: 1961–1979', *Australian Economic Papers* 24: 142–53.

Müller, F. G. and Zimmermann, K. (1986) 'The determinants of structural changes in public budgets: a theoretical and empirical analysis for the Federal Republic of Germany', *European Journal of Political Research* 19: 481–98.

Nato Information Service (1984) The North Atlantic Treaty Organization, *Facts and Figures*, Brussels.

Nato Information Service (1986), *NATO Handbook*, Brussels.

Olson, M. and Zeckhauser, R. (1966) 'An economic theory of alliances', *Review of Economics and Statistics* 48, 3: 266–79.

Olson, M. and Zeckhauser, R. (1967) 'Collective goods, comparative advantage, and alliance efficiencies', in R. N. McKean (ed.) *Issues in Defense Economics*, New York, 25–48.

Organization for Economic Co-operation and Development (OECD) (1987) *Economic Survey of Germany*, Paris, OECD.

Prognos AG (1986) *Die Bundesrepublik Deutschland 1990/2000/2010*, Prognos-Report Nr. 12, Stuttgart: Poller.

Record, J. and Rivkin, D. B. (Jun.) (1988) 'Defending post-INF Europe', *Foreign Affairs* 66, 4: 735–54.

Robertson, D. (1986) 'Fair shares in NATO: problems of comparing defence contributions', in Royal United Services Institute for Defence Studies (ed.) *RUSI and Brassey's Defence Yearbook 1986*, London: Brassey's Defence Publishers, 117–44.

Sachverständigenrat zur Begutachtung der gesamtwirtschaftlichen Entwicklung (Council of Economic Experts) (1981) *Investieren für mehr Beschäftigung: Jahresgutachten (Annual Assessment) 1981/82*, Stuttgart und Mainz: Kohlhammer.

Sachverständigenrat zur Begutachtung der gesamtwirtschaftlichen Entwicklung (Council of Economic Experts) (1987) *Vorrang für die Wachstumspolitik: Jahresgutachten (Annual Assessment) 1987/88*, Stuttgart und Mainz: Kohlhammer.

Sandler, T. (1977) 'Impurity of defense: an application to the economic theory of alliances', *Kyklos* 30, 4: 443–60.

Sandler, T. and Cauley, J. (1975) 'On the economic theory of alliances', *Journal of Conflict Resolution* 19: 330–48.

Sandler, T. and Forbes, J. F. (1980) 'Burden sharing, strategy, and the design of NATO', *Economic Inquiry* 18: 425–44.

Sandler, T. and Murdoch, J. (1986) 'Defense burdens and prospects for the northern European allies', in D. B. H. Denoon (ed.) *Constraints on Strategy: The Economics of Western Security*, Washington: Pergamon-Brassey's, 59–113.

Sköns, E. (1983) 'Military prices', in Stockholm International Peace Research Institute (SIPRI), *World Armament and Disarmament: SIPRI Yearbook 1983*, London: Taylor & Francis, 195–211.

Smith, R. (1980) 'The demand for military expenditure', *The Economic Journal* 90: 811–20.

Time (1988) 'Alliance malaise', 14 March 1988.

Thompson, E. A. (1979) 'An economic basis for the national defence argument for aiding certain industries', *Journal of Political Economy* 87: 1–36.

Thompson, W. C. and Wittig, P. (1984) 'The West German defense policy consensus: stable or eroding?', *Armed Forces & Society* 10, 3: 327–60.

Windsor, P. (1981) *Germany and the Western Alliance: Lessons from the 1980 Crisis*, Adelphi Papers No. 170, London: The International Institute for Strategic Studies.

Wirtschafts- und Sozialwissenschaftliches Institut des Deutschen Gewerkschaftsbundes (WSI) (1987) 'Die wirtschaftliche Entwicklung in der Bundesrepublik Deutschland in den Jahren (1987/88), *WSI-Mitteilungen* 40: 637–55.

Ypersele de Strihou, J. M. van (1967) 'Sharing the defense burden among Western allies', *Review of Economics and Statistics* 49, 4: 527–36.

Ypersele de Strihou, J. M. van (1968) 'Sharing the defense burden among Western allies', *Yale Economic Essays* 8, 1: 261–320.

Zimmermann, K. and Müller, F. G. (1985) *Umweltschutz als neue politische Aufgabë Substitutionseffekte in öffentlichen Budgets*, Frankfurt: Campus Verlag.

Chapter seven

Swedish military expenditures and armed neutrality

James C. Murdoch and Todd Sandler

Introduction

Sweden has maintained its neutrality since 1814. Two of its Nordic neighbours – Denmark and Norway – are members of the North Atlantic Treaty Organization (NATO), whereas its eastern neighbour – Finland – is essentially neutral.[1] Swedish defence is of crucial importance for NATO for a number of reasons: (1) Sweden is in a strategic position to monitor Soviet submarine movements through the Baltic Sea; (2) Sweden's northern border is nearby a major Soviet military installation in Murmansk; (3) the Swedish Air Force represents a significant force comparable to that of West Germany and France (Bjøl 1983: 16–17); (4) Swedish armed forces represent a formidable power that could help strengthen NATO's northern flank in times of war; and (5) Sweden may someday choose to join NATO.

Sweden, like Switzerland, adheres to the doctrine of armed neutrality, as recognized by international law.[2] A nation that ascribes to armed neutrality must be self-reliant for its defence; thus, the nation must *not* depend, either implicitly or explicitly, on other countries, including its neighbours, for protection. Armed neutrality also requires non-aligned status, whereby the neutral country does not take sides with respect to conflicts among opposing alliances or nations. Under this doctrine, nations are expected to arm themselves sufficiently to pose a significant threat to any would-be aggressors. During the Second World War, Sweden was the only neutral country in Europe that was not invaded by the Germans.[3] This was due, in part, to Sweden's sizeable arsenal and its northern location, which would have diverted German forces from other fronts.

Strict adherence to defence self-reliance requires a neutral country to be self-sufficient in armament production. In the case of Sweden, it is 80 per cent self-sufficient (Bjøl 1983: 18) and was a net exporter of arms in 1985 (US Arms Control and Disarmament Agency 1987: 136).[4] Neither Denmark nor Norway exports any arms. In addition, armed neutrality is often associated with large reserves of military personnel and a significant civil-defence programme. Large reserves augment the threat posed without maintaining a large portion of the population in uniform; whereas a civil-defence programme demonstrates a neutral nation's resolve to fight if attacked.

The primary purpose of this chapter is to estimate a demand for military expenditure equation for Sweden. In particular, we focus on the self-reliance issue to determine whether Sweden has implicitly relied on NATO allies for part of its defence. We employ nested tests to pinpoint the nature of the dependency during the post-1973 period when some evidence of Swedish reliance is found. A secondary purpose is to estimate a Swedish demand for non-military expenditure in the hopes of uncovering the so-called guns-for-butter trade-off that a central government must face when deciding its military and non-military expenditure. Another purpose is to uncover the intertemporal causal patterns for Swedish military expenditure, Swedish gross domestic product (GDP), Swedish military spillins (e.g. the military expenditure of NATO) and Swedish non-military expenditure using a vector-autoregressive (VAR) model.

The main body of the chapter is organized into five sections. The first contains a review of the Swedish economy and its defence sector. The second sketches the theoretical model for the demands for military and non-military expenditure. In the third, we present the empirical methodology, the data and the estimates for these demand equations. The VAR analysis follows in the next. Concluding remarks and a look towards the future are contained in the last section.

Swedish economy and defence

The Swedish economy: the past

The military strength of a country depends upon more than its stock of armaments, military personnel, infrastructure and current flow of military expenditure. A nation's industrial base, GDP, labour force and resources determine its ability to endure a conventional conflict and to redirect efforts to the military sector in the hopes of achieving a victory. Thus, any analysis of Swedish military strengths and trade-offs must begin with an investigation of its economy. For the purpose of comparison, we also report some key economic indicators for the two Scandinavian members of NATO – Norway and Denmark.

Sweden is more populated than its NATO neighbours in Scandinavia – Sweden has 8.3 million people, Norway 4.1 million and Denmark 5.1 million. In Table 7.1, four economic indicators are listed for 1960, 1970, 1980 and 1985 for Sweden, Norway and Denmark. In terms of real GDP in 1980 $US, Sweden's annual flow of goods and services is approximately double that of Norway in 1985. Since 1960, Norway has grown at a much faster rate than Sweden. In 1960, the GDP of Norway was just over 35 per cent of that of Sweden; in 1985, in was 50 per cent of the GDP of Sweden. Danish GDP has grown at a rate closer to that of Sweden. Given their population levels, Sweden, Norway and Denmark have some of the higher GDP per capita levels for the world. Unemployment rates have been relatively low in both Sweden and Norway as compared with those of other countries. Denmark has experienced a much higher unemployment rate in the 1980s, comparable to other industrial nations in Western Europe.

Table 7.1 Alternative measures of economic performance for the Scandinavian countries by year

Measure	Year	Sweden	Norway	Denmark
Unemployment rate (%)	1960	1.7	1.4	4.3
	1970	1.4	0.8	2.9
	1980	2.0	1.7	7.0
	1985	2.8	2.5	9.2
Real GDP (1980 US $bn)	1960	64.6	22.9	33.2
	1970	101.5	36.3	52.9
	1980	124.1	57.7	66.3
	1985	135.8	68.1	73.5
Balance of trade (US $m)	1960	−110	−110	−210
	1970	300	−1,150	−760
	1980	−2,200	1,900	−2,000
	1985	2,400	4,680	−770
Central government deficit (−) (US $m)	1960	−291	−132	121
	1970	−733	−504	629
	1980	−10,165	−1,093	−1,773
	1985	−13,903	3,854	na

Sources: International Monetary Fund (IMF) (1983, 1987) and United Nations (various issues)

In Table 7.1, the balance of trade is given for selected years. After 1980, all three countries have shown improvements in their current account. The Swedish improvement was due, in large part, to a 1982 devaluation of its currency; whereas, the Norwegian improvement was fostered by the sale of North Sea oil. Central government deficits are also displayed in Table 7.1. This deficit worsened for Sweden for the years shown, whereas the deficit improved in Norway in 1985.

Sweden is a small open economy heavily dependent on its export sector which, on average, accounted for 33.3 per cent of GDP for the 1981–5 period (OECD 1987: 5). Sweden's main exports are machinery, transport equipment, metal products and wood products. With its reliance on export-led growth, Sweden must keep its inflation level in line with those of its trading partners. In recent years, this task has been made difficult, given its low level of unemployment and a concomitant tendency for wages to rise. The 1982 devaluation of the Swedish krona has also created some inflation because of imports of fuel, energy, machinery and intermediate inputs.

Sweden, Norway and Denmark have large central government budgets. In Table 7.2, these countries' percentage of GDP devoted to central government expenditure (CGE) is depicted for 4 years. In 1985, CGE was 46.5 per cent of GDP in Sweden, 25 per cent in Norway and 36.9 per cent in Denmark. Sweden is especially noteworthy due to the growth in CGE since 1960. When local government expenditure is also included, the Swedish public sector accounted for 65.3 per cent of GDP in 1985 (OECD 1987: 9). With such a large public sector, an increase in the percentage of GDP devoted to defence would probably come from a decrease in the percentage of GDP devoted to another budget item, such as welfare. Table 7.2 indicates that the percentage of CGE allocated to military expenditure has fallen in both Sweden and Denmark since 1960. The defence expenditure percentage of CGE increased in Norway after 1980. By the 1980s, Sweden had acquired a massive public sector. Faced with mounting government deficits, Sweden had to make some difficult choices.

Table 7.2 Alternative defence burden measures and the relative size of the central government expenditure (CGE) for the Scandinavian countries and the average for the other NATO countries in Europe by year

Measure	Year	Sweden	Norway	Denmark	Other NATO
CGE/GDP[1]	1960	19.7	17.3	15.7	na
(%)	1970	26.4	22.0	27.5	33.0
	1980	41.0	25.9	34.6	39.0
	1985	46.5	25.0	36.9	na
ME/CGE[2] (%)	1960	20.4	16.9	17.4	na
	1970	13.6	15.8	8.5	10.2
	1980	7.9	11.2	7.0	8.3
	1985	6.4	12.3	6.2	na
ME/Pop[3] ($)	1960	347	188	198	271
	1970	454	325	249	303
	1980	482	408	316	391
	1985	481	505	327	417

Sources: IMF (1983, 1987) and Stockholm International Peace Research Institute (SIPRI) (1974, 1980, 1986)
Notes: [1] Central government expenditure as a percentage of GDP. The other NATO allies are Belgium, France, West Germany, Italy, the Netherlands and the United Kingdom.
[2] Military expenditures as a percentage of central government expenditure.
[3] Military expenditures per person in constant 1980 US$ using 1980 exchange rates.

The Swedish economy: the present

After 1982, the Swedish government instituted a policy of fiscal restraint to curb the budget deficit.[5] The Swedish economy has shown marked improvements as indicated by a falling government deficit, moderate growth, falling unemployment and an improved balance of payment. As a percentage of GDP, the government deficit fell from 6.3 per cent in 1982 to 1.4 per cent in 1986. In 1983 and the following 2 years, GDP grew at an annual rate of 2.4 per cent, 4 per cent and 2.2 per cent, respectively. GDP was estimated to have grown by a more modest 1.7 per cent in 1986. The unemployment rate fell from 3.5 per cent in 1983 to an estimated 2.7 per cent in 1986, giving Sweden one of the lowest unemployment rates in Europe – the average unemployment rate for OECD nations in Europe was 11 per cent in 1986. The balance of payments was in surplus by an estimated 7.6bn kronas in 1986. A fall in oil prices in 1986 helped the Swedish economy, whose oil imports in 1985 amounted to 3.6 per cent of GDP.

Although the Swedish economy has performed well in recent years, a number of factors warrant watching. First, labour cost has been rising faster in Sweden than elsewhere. If this trend does not stop, Swedish industry will lose market shares at home and abroad. The reduced competitiveness of Swedish products is reflected in unit labour cost. Between 1983 and 1986, unit labour cost measured in local currency rose by 8 per cent more than abroad. Even though labour productivity has increased in Sweden, labour cost increases have outpaced productivity. Second, the growth of gross fixed investment dropped from 6.3 per cent in 1985 to 0.3 per cent in 1986, with most of the decline attributed to residential housing and public investment. In Sweden, the engine of growth in recent years has been increases in private and public consumption. If growth were to increase, investment must be stimulated. Third, the share of public expenditure in GDP remained high at approximately 64 per cent of GDP in 1986; this share was over 67 per cent in 1982. From 1982 to 1986, local government expenditure showed little change in its share of GDP: 20.8 per cent in 1982 and 20.5 per cent in 1986 (OECD 1987: 9). Thus, CGE, which includes military expenditure, has been curtailed in recent years.

Swedish defence expenditure

The Swedish defence sector can be compared with various NATO allies by examining alternative measures of defence burdens. Although there is no universal agreement among researchers on the best burden measure, the most commonly used measure is military expenditure expressed as a percentage of GDP. In Table 7.3, this measure is presented for Sweden and ten NATO allies at 5-year intervals starting in 1960. In the 1960s, Sweden allocated approximately 4 per cent of GDP to defence; in the 1970s and 1980s, this figure declined to its current level of about 3 per cent. This decline coincided with the large growth in CGE; the growth of the Swedish public sector was due, in part, to the increase in non-military expenditure such as welfare and transfer payments. This conclusion is also supported by the percentage of CGE allocated to military expenditure, reported in Table 7.2. In 1960, 20.4 per cent of Swedish CGE was allocated to defence; in 1985, only 6.4 per cent of CGE went to defence. In Table 7.3, we see that the pattern of declining defence burdens in Sweden is somewhat similar to that of West Germany and the Netherlands. During the first half of the 1980s, Swedish defence burden in terms of GDP was similar to that of Norway, West Germany, the Netherlands and Belgium.

Table 7.3 Military expenditure expressed as a percentage of GDP for Sweden and some NATO allies by year

Country	1960	1965	1970	1975	1980	1985
Sweden	4.0	4.1	3.6	3.3	3.2	3.0
Norway	2.9	3.8	3.5	3.4	2.9	3.1
Denmark	2.7	2.8	2.3	2.5	2.4	2.3
France	6.5	5.2	4.2	3.8	4.0	4.0
United Kingdom	6.5	5.9	4.8	4.9	5.0	5.3
United States	9.0	7.6	7.9	5.9	5.4	6.7
West Germany	4.0	4.3	3.3	3.7	3.3	3.2
Italy	3.1	3.1	2.5	2.5	2.1	2.2
The Netherlands	4.1	4.0	3.5	3.4	3.1	3.1
Belgium	3.4	3.2	2.9	3.1	3.3	3.2
Canada	4.2	2.9	2.4	1.9	1.8	2.2

Sources: IMF (1983, 1987) and SIPRI (1974, 1980, 1986)

Two additional defence burden measures are displayed in Table 7.2. The percentage of CGE devoted to military expenditure denotes the defence burden on the government budget. Norway's greater relative burden, as compared with Sweden and Denmark, is partly due to the relatively smaller central government budget in Norway. In Table 7.2, the second defence burden is military expenditure per capita. Unlike the other two burden measures, it has increased since 1960 for the three Scandinavian countries as well as for the average of the other NATO allies, thus indicating that military spending has outpaced population. In 1985, Swedish per capita spending on defence was $481, only slightly less than Norway and well ahead of that of the average of the other comparable NATO nations.

Swedish defence forces

The 1986 distribution of military personnel in Sweden, Denmark and Norway is presented in Table 7.4. Swedish active forces are just under twice those of Norway. Conscripts must serve for seven and a half months, which represents a very short period of service.[6] Much of Swedish personnel is allocated to the army. When reserves are included, Sweden can mobilize 9.3 per cent of its population within 72 hours. This military force of 776,000 men is over twice the total military personnel of Norway and seven times that of Denmark. Such massive reserves are a typical attribute of armed neutral nations. Of the three branches of service, the Swedish Air Force has remained strong with 501 combat aircraft, almost half of which are Saab-built multi-purpose Viggens. A new multi-purpose Swedish-built Gripen plane is planned to succeed the Viggens in the 1990s. The Swedish Army contains just four armoured brigades and one mechanized brigade. In recent years, the Swedish Army has relied on 340 ageing British Centurion tanks and 330 new Swedish-built medium tanks (Bjøl 1983: 17).

Perhaps the weakest link in Swedish defences is its navy. This weakness was underscored in October 1981 when a Russian Whisky-class submarine ran aground near Sweden's Karlskrona Naval Base. The submarine, thought to be carrying nuclear weapons, was discovered 12 hours later not by Swedish defences but by a Swedish fisherman! In October 1982, the Swedish navy was unable to capture or sink a Russian underwater craft in the Muskö naval base in Harsfjärden Bay. The two incidents convinced the Swedish government to allocate additional funds to anti-submarine defence in 1984 (*The Economist* 1984: 3).

The relative strengths of the Swedish defence branches are displayed by examining the percentage distribution of military expenditure among the three services. In a recent UN (1981 Table 12: 28) report, Sweden was listed as allocating 33.4 per cent to land forces, 34.7 per cent to air forces and only 14.2 per cent to naval forces. Additionally, 2.6 per cent was allocated to civil defence, and the remainder of the budget was assigned to central support (13.1 per cent) and UN peacekeeping (0.6 per cent). The same report indicated the following breakdown for Swedish defence: personnel (40.4 per cent); operations and maintenance (19.2 per cent); procurement (29.3 per cent); construction (5.6 per cent); and R & D (5.6 per cent).

In 1987, the Swedish government committed the country to a 1987–92 defence budget that pledged an increase in real defence spending (*The Economist* 1987: 21). Much of the planned buildup would go to the navy and the air force.

Table 7.4   Military personnel in Sweden, Denmark and Norway in 1986 (1,000s)

Country	Army	Navy	Air Force	Other	Total active	Reserves	Reserves and active
Sweden	47.0	12.0	8.0	–	67.0	709.0	776.0
Denmark	17.0	5.4	6.9	–	29.3	74.7	104.0
Norway	19.0	7.0	9.1	1.8	36.9	284.6	321.5

Source: International Institute for Strategic Studies (1987)

Demand for military and non-military expenditure: the theory

For the last 20 years, a debate has raged between Norway and Sweden: Norway has accused Sweden of 'free-riding' or relying on Norwegian defences. This accusation has been denied by Sweden; nevertheless, Norwegian suspicions are easy to understand because the decline in Swedish defences after 1960 coincided with Norwegian efforts to boost its defences and with Swedish efforts to augment its welfare state. Geographical considerations also lend credence to Norwegian suspicions because either Norwegian or Finnish territory must be crossed by any land attack launched from the Soviet stronghold on the Kola Peninsula. To examine the free-riding issue, we intend to present some reduced-form equations, based upon a utility-maximizing model, for estimating Swedish demand for military expenditure and non-military expenditure.

A joint product model of defence

The joint product model reviewed here was developed in a series of papers by Murdoch, Sandler and others.[7] Although we summarize the relevant arguments, the interested reader should consult the earlier papers for details. In the joint product model, a nation's arsenal is characterized as providing multiple outputs of varying degrees of publicness. For the basic jointness model, a nation's military activity yields deterrence and a private, defence-related good. Deterrence is purely public between a nation and other nations with mutual defence interests. If, as we suppose here, Sweden and NATO view the Warsaw Pact as a potential adversary,[8] then any deterrence of Warsaw Pact aggression derived from Swedish or NATO military armaments or forces would provide non-rival and non-excludable benefits to the group, thus supporting the notion of pure publicness.[9] The private defence good (e.g. protection of coastal water resources, relief in times of national disaster, control of social unrest or domestic terrorism) is private between nations, but public within a nation. Clearly, multiple public and/or private outputs can be handled easily. For simplicity, however, only one of each output is assumed. By formulating the model in activity space, we facilitate the empirical analysis because military activity can be proxied by military expenditures.

In essence, the joint product model assumes that a nation's military activity, q, yields a private defence output and a public defence output. The former only benefits the ally providing the activity, whereas the latter benefits the entire alliance. Each country's military activity may have different productivities in providing these private and public outputs. These productivities are expected to vary between allied nations because of differences in location, strategic considerations and the composition of a nation's arsenal. For instance, nations with more modern aircraft, better trained troops and more secure supply lines would present a greater threat to would-be aggressors, thereby producing greater deterrence than a less formidable ally. Front-line allies, like Norway, that border an adversary might provide more deterrence than a comparable nation, like Sweden, whose territory lies further from a potential front.

A nation is assumed to consider all possible deterrence decisions of the other nations that it views as allies when choosing its own level of military activity. In particular, the amount of deterrence provided by the 'other' allies, is viewed by each ally, such as Sweden, as the sum of individually rational choices for each ally.[10] Deterrence spillins are the difference between alliance-wide deterrence and the deterrence provided by the representative ally. The level of deterrence that 'spills in' to Sweden[11] is a function of the 'aggregate' military activity $\tilde{Q}$ of the 'other' allies. An increase in the military activity of the other allies will provide greater deterrence spillins to Sweden.

The preferences of Sweden are depicted by a well-behaved utility function that depends on the benefits that it receives from spillins and the purchase of goods. In activity space, this utility function is

$$U = U(r, y, q, Q; E) \tag{1}$$

where r is a private numeraire activity representing privately provided non-military expenditure, y is an activity denoting publicly provided non-military expenditure, q is the country's military expenditures, Q is aggregate military expenditure of the allies, and E is a shift parameter depicting a vector of environmental influences. These influences may be the threat posed by a nation's enemies. Alternatively, demographic factors, such as population, may be an environmental factor affecting a country's need to provide non-military goods and services to its constituency. A change in strategic doctrine may also be considered an environmental factor that influences a nation's trade-offs between military and non-military activities.

Sweden's demand for publicly provided non-military and military activities can be derived by maximizing (1) subject to the country's budget constraint:

$$I = p_r r + p_y y + p_q q \tag{2}$$

where I is the nation's GDP, p_r is the price of the private numeraire, p_y is the price of the publicly provided non-military activity, and p_q is the price of the military activity. The sum of the last two right-hand terms of (2) denotes the central government expenditure. The above maximization problem would yield Sweden's demands for military and publicly provided non-military activity:[12]

$$q = q(p_q/p_r, p_y/p_r, I, Q; E) \tag{3}$$
$$y = y(p_q/p_r, p_y/p_r, I, Q; E). \tag{4}$$

Later (see pp. 161–6), equations (3) and (4) are estimated for Sweden.[13] The following partial derivatives of (3) prove of interest: $\partial q/\partial I$ and $\partial q/\partial Q$. The first measures the effect of a change in Swedish GDP on Sweden's demand for military expenditure and is expected to be positive since defence activity is typically a normal good. We call this effect the 'GDP effect'. The second partial denotes the effect of other allies' military activity on Sweden's demand for its own defence activity. We call this effect the 'spillin effect'. Murdoch and Sandler (1984) have shown that the sign of the spillin effect depends on the consumption relationships of the jointly produced defence outputs and on associated income effects. If the two defence outputs are substitutes, then there is a tendency for the spillin effect to be negative. The smaller is the associated income effect, the stronger is the tendency for the spillin effect to be negative. If, on the other hand, the two defence outputs are complements, then the tendency is for the spillin effect to be positive, but near zero (Murdoch and Sandler 1984: 88–9).

The notion of free-riding is often related to the sign and magnitude of the spillin effect. A nation is said to free-ride or rely on others for its defence when an increase in other nations' military activity induces the alleged free-rider to reduce its own military activity. In terms of our model, free-riding is indicated by a negative and significant spillin effect. If, say, the spillin effect is −1, then every dollar of one's allies' military expenditure replaces a dollar of one's own expenditure. Values of the spillin effect nearer to −1 indicate a stronger degree of free-riding, whereas positive values suggest that a nation has a co-operative defence posture *vis-à-vis* other nations.

We next turn our attention to two important partial derivatives in the publicly provided non-military demand equation: $\partial y/\partial I$ and $\partial y/\partial Q$. The first denotes the influence of a change in Swedish GDP on Sweden's demand for non-military expenditure. If both military and privately provided non-military activity are normal goods, then the budget constraint implies that the income effect $\partial y/\partial I$ must be positive. If the publicly provided non-military activity is an inferior good, then automatic stabilizers (e.g. unemployment payments, welfare payments) may be at work. A government uses automatic stabilizers in a countercyclical fashion, thus confounding the normal income relationship and forcing its non-military expenditure to appear as an inferior good. To account explicitly for these stabilizers, we would have to build a more elaborate model especially in terms of the budget constraint.

The partial derivative $\partial y/\partial Q$ represents the effect that a change in the military expenditure of 'other' nations would have on the non-military expenditure of a country. If, for example, Sweden derived defence benefits from military activities within NATO, then $\partial y/\partial Q$ would denote the change in Swedish non-military expenditure when NATO altered its military spending. When Sweden views NATO's military activities as a substitute for its own, the sign of this effect should be positive owing to the release of income from the Swedish defence sector that can be spent elsewhere.

On recent strategic doctrine

In analysing environment-induced shifts in the demand for military expenditures (i.e. $\partial q/\partial E$) for Sweden, we focus on changes in the strategic doctrine of NATO. Until the early 1970s, NATO relied on the doctrine of 'Mutual Assured Destruction' (MAD), where the opposing alliances forestalled hostilities by threatening one another with massive civilian and industrial losses if they were attacked. The seminal work of Olson and Zeckhauser (1966) demonstrated that MAD induces the larger allies to shoulder the burden of the defence for the smaller allies. In particular, Olson and Zeckhauser hypothesized disproportionate burden shares, in which the wealthy allies (e.g. United States, United Kingdom) allocated relatively greater percentages of their GDP to defence compared with the smaller allies. Statistics in the 1960s lend support to this hypothesis and suggest that the smaller non-nuclear allies free-rode on the larger allies. A degree of free-riding was possible because MAD relied on deterrence.

With MAD, the primary joint product was deterrence, which is purely public to the allies. The MAD doctrine concentrated on nuclear deterrence, thus downplaying conventional forces. But it is these NATO conventional forces that are best able to provide defence spillins or protection to Sweden. Clearly, strong conventional forces in Norway, Denmark and West Germany could provide defence spillovers to Sweden. Under MAD, conventional defence spillovers were less significant for the neutral countries, like Sweden.

In 1967, the NATO alliance switched its announced strategy from MAD to the doctrine of flexible response (Ball 1975). Our previous work indicated that NATO allies did not really respond to the new doctrine until the early 1970s once technological advances in precision-guided munitions permitted the pinpoint accuracy required of counterforce targeting. The doctrine of flexible response allows NATO to respond in different ways to a Warsaw Pact threat: conventional or strategic forces might be used and, in the latter case, missile exchanges might be directed at military or civilian targets. With this doctrine, the European allies must be prepared to defend themselves against conventional aggression in the European theatre, as the initial stages of warfare are expected to involve conventional and tactical nuclear weapon exchanges. No longer can these allies rely solely on nuclear deterrence for their external security. An ally that does not increase its military activity in response to other allies' increased military activities would invite aggression, as an enemy might have a better chance to gain an advantage in a conventional war fought on that ally's soil.

Flexible response makes strategic and conventional forces complementary, because both must be deployed and used in conjunction. Our previous research has established that the smaller NATO allies typically increased their defence spending in response to increases in their allies' military activities after the institution of flexible response. The doctrine's implication for Sweden is clear: conventional force buildups by NATO nations offer greater free-riding possibilities for Sweden. Neighbouring NATO nations, such as Norway, have increased their conventional armaments since the early 1970s and this increase can indirectly protect Swedish sovereignty. We intend to test for increased free-riding on the part of Sweden in the post-1973 era.

Empirical results: demand estimation

Equations (3) and (4) indicate that Sweden's optimal choice of publicly provided military and non-military activity (q and y, respectively) depends on the relative prices of each activity (p_q/p_r and p_y/p_r), the income of Sweden (I), the level of military activity undertaken by Sweden's implicit allies (Q) and some environmental factors (E). In addition to presenting the econometric estimates of these functions, we also describe the data, variables and specifications necessary to test for the source of the spillins to Sweden.

Data and variables

The level of military activity in Sweden is measured by its annual real (1980 is the base year) military expenditure (ME) expressed in $US using the 1980 exchange rate. Nominal military expenditures for 1953–85 are obtained from SIPRI (1974; 1980; 1986) and then transformed into real figures using the GDP implicit price deflators published in IMF (1983; 1987). Average exchange rates on an annual basis are taken from IMF (1983; 1987) and used to convert all of the series to $US. The empirical measure for q is referred to as ME_t. The use of ME rather than some other variable, such as ME/GDP, follows from the reduced-form demand equation, which is based on a utility-maximizing model. Using a variable like ME/GDP as the dependent variable would make the classical assumptions on the error term less likely. The latter variable is legitimate when the theoretical assumptions and/or the underlying utility function indicate its use.

The empirical measure of y, denoted NME_t, is derived by subtracting ME_t from Sweden's central government expenditure. Annual central government expenditure data are reported in IMF, but the data are not strictly comparable from issue to issue. To construct a series comparable with the other data, we use the data in IMF (1983) for the years 1953–82. We apply the percentage rates of change, as calculated from the data given in IMF (1987), to update the 1982 figures through 1985. As with ME_t, the GDP price deflator and 1980 exchange rate are used to express this series in real $US.

Price indices are not available for ME_t and NME_t, and their exclusion from the estimated demand equations could cause serious specification error, biasing the estimated coefficients of the included variables (Johnston 1972: 168–9). Fortunately, there are two reasons for believing that such specification errors are small. SIPRI (1984: 195–211) showed that the price of military activity for several countries appears to change at the same rate as prices in the private sector, indicating that the 'relative' price of military activity is unchanged over time and can be normalized to unity. If this is true in Sweden, then using real military expenditures ($p_q q / p_r = q$) and dropping the relative price term are justified when estimating equation (3). The second reason concerns non-military activity. The GDP implicit price deflator reflects the movement in the prices of *all* components of GDP, including government expenditure. Hence, deflating by the GDP deflator partly controls for the changes due to p_r, and hence p_y/p_r can be dropped from the empirical estimates.

The yearly income of Sweden is measured by the real GDP in 1980 $US and is denoted GDP_t. The data on GDP are taken from IMF (1983; 1987), which reproduces data collected by the UN. UN data are based on the System of National Accounts, which makes the data comparable for all market economies. Whereas several other income proxies including gross national product and net national product could have been used, our previous research indicated little difference in the estimates for these alternative measures.

Several measures of spillins Q have empirical merit. Those considered here are $NOME_t$, the real military expenditure of Norway; $DEME_t$, the real military expenditure of Denmark; $NATO_t$, the sum of the real military expenditure in Belgium, Canada, Denmark, France, Germany, Italy, the Netherlands, Norway, the United Kingdom and the United States; and $ONATO_t$, the difference between $NATO_t$ and the sum of $NOME_t$ and $DEME_t$. The military expenditure data are taken from SIPRI (1974; 1980; 1986) and are expressed in constant 1980 $US using the GDP implicit price deflators and exchange rates from IMF (1983; 1987). The theory does not provide guidance on how to measure spillins or their origin; hence, the appropriate spillin term must be decided empirically. On *a priori* grounds, we suspect that if Sweden is free-riding, the probable source of the defence spillins is Norway. This is especially true under NATO's doctrine of flexible response.

There are numerous influences that could be measured and entered into the empirical models as the environmental factors for the Swedish demands for the military and non-military activity. In particular, we consider annual population (POP_t), an estimate of Soviet military expenditure ($SUME_t$) and two dummy (0–1) variables in the estimates reported below. The population data are obtained from IMF (1983; 1987), whereas the data on Soviet defence spending are from SIPRI (1974; 1980; 1986). As $SUME_t$ is an estimate made by the staff at SIPRI, the empirical results based on these data should be viewed with caution. We use the SIPRI estimates of Soviet military spending since such estimates are generally considered to be the best available.

The first dummy variable ($D1$) is constructed to reflect NATO's change from MAD to the doctrine of flexible response. $D1$ is equal to zero for the years 1953–73 and to one for the years 1974–85. While any of the years between 1968–74 could be justified as a shift year corresponding to the doctrine of flexible response, Murdoch and Sandler (1984) have statistically identified 1974 as the best year. The second dummy variable ($D2$) is constructed to capture Sweden's recent policy of fiscal restraint: $D2$ is equal to zero for the years 1953–82 and to one for the years 1983–5.

Estimates of the demand for military expenditure

Assessing the role and source of the spillin terms in Sweden's demand for military activity is our primarily empirical objective. Our empirical strategy is to estimate a reasonably general specification of Sweden's demand and then impose restrictions in order to identify the source of the spillins. Such restrictions can be tested using a standard F test (Fisher 1970).

An unconstrained empirical form of the demand for military activity (equation (3)) is

$$
\begin{aligned}
LME_t = {} & \beta_0 + \beta_1 LGDP_t + \beta_2 LPOP_t + \beta_3 LONATO_{t-1} \\
& + \beta_4 D1.LONATO_{t-1} + \beta_5 LNOME_{t-1} + \beta_6 D1.LNOME_{t-1} \\
& + \beta_7 LDEME_{t-1} + \beta_8 D1.LDEME_{t-1} + \beta_9 LSUME_{t-1} + \beta_{10} D2 + \varepsilon_t \quad (5)
\end{aligned}
$$

where the ε_t is an error term, assumed to be a normally distributed random variable with a mean of zero and constant variance. The βs are coefficients that can be estimated efficiently with ordinary least squares (OLS) under the assumptions about ε_t.

There are three things to highlight about equation (5). First, the specification is assumed to be linear in natural logarithms. Thus, an L in front of a variable indicates a natural logarithm transformation.[14] Even though our results suggest that the log-linear form fits the data somewhat better than a linear form, the choice of functional form does not appear to affect the results of the relevant tests. Second, the spillin measures are lagged by one period, thereby reflecting the empirical implementation of the Nash–Cournot assumption on behaviour; Sweden (if she responds to spillins) takes the level of spillins as given when determining the optimal level of military activity. Sandler and Murdoch (1987) discovered some empirical support for this type of behaviour for the NATO allies. To some extent, the specification in equation (5) implicitly assumes that Sweden is behaving as a NATO ally in terms of its demand for military activity. Evidence to the contrary would be exhibited by insignificant estimates on all of the coefficients on the spillin terms. Third, the treatment of the dummy variables in equation (5) should be noted. $D1$ is multiplied by each of the spillin measures, while $D2$ is entered into the specification independently. If our prediction concerning the impact of the doctrine of flexible response is correct, Sweden should respond less to spillins during the post-1973 period. The estimates of β_4, β_6, and β_8 (or the appropriate constraints on these coefficients) would hence exhibit negative signs. Since Sweden's recent policy of fiscal restraint is hypothesized to shift the entire demand relationship, $D2$ is entered as an independent variable.

The estimates of equation (5) are presented as model 1 in the first column of Table 7.5.[15] Models 2–5, also presented in Table 7.5, are formulated to test the significance and source of the spillins to Sweden. Model 2 constrains the coefficients on $LONATO_{t-1}$ and $D1.LONATO_{t-1}$ (β_3 and β_4) to equal zero, while model 3 restricts all of the coefficients on the spillin terms (β_3, β_4, β_5, β_6, β_7, and β_8) to equal one another. In model 4, the coefficients on $LONATO_{t-1}$, $D1.LONATO_{t-1}$, $LDEME_{t-1}$ and $D1.LDEME_{t-1}$ (β_3, β_4, β_7, and β_8) are constrained to be zero. Model 5 drops all the spillin terms. Each of these restrictions is linear and can be tested using an F statistic.[16]

The hypotheses, the F statistics, and the statistical conclusions about the tests are presented in Table 7.6. The α levels in the table measure the probability of rejecting the H_0 when in fact it is true. Hypothesis test A indicates that there is some statistical evidence for dropping the LONATO terms from the specification. The results of test B confirm this and also suggest that Sweden does not seem to respond to Danish military spending. Moreover, the conclusion of test C implies that Sweden is concerned with the origin of the spillins; we cannot maintain the hypothesis of equality in the spillin coefficients. Hypothesis tests D and E statistically pinpoint the source of Swedish defence spillins. Test D confirms that Sweden does not appear to respond significantly to Danish military activity. For test D, we maintain model 4 and test it against model 2. Just as in test B, model 4 cannot be rejected. The results of test E demonstrate that Sweden does respond significantly to Norway's military activity. In summary, there is strong statistical evidence that Sweden responds significantly to spillins and that the source of these spillins is Norway's military activity.[17]

Based on the test results, model 4 is maintained as the best specification for Sweden's demand for military expenditures. With the exception of the Soviet term, all the estimated coefficients are significantly different than

Table 7.5 OLS estimates of alternative specifications of the demand for military expenditure, 1958–85

	Model 1	Model 2	Model 3	Model 4	Model 5
$LGDP_t$	0.778 (3.57)	0.718 (2.91)	1.093 (3.61)	0.770 (3.15)	1.257 (4.80)
$LPOP_t$	−3.506 (−3.38)	−3.300 (−2.81)	−2.513 (−1.64)	−3.165 (−2.70)	−2.939 (−2.01)
$LNOME_{t-1}$	0.371 (4.17)	−0.313 (3.45)		0.331 (4.16)	
$D1.LNOME_{t-1}$	−0.360 (−2.10)	−0.235 (−1.29)		−0.102 (−2.08)	
$LDEME_{t-1}$	0.092 (1.17)	0.091 (1.01)			
$D1.LDEME_{t-1}$	0.502 (2.13)	0.129 (0.60)			
$LNATO_{t-1}$			0.052 (0.48)		
$D1.LNATO_{t-1}$			−0.006 (−1.02)		
$LONATO_{t-1}$	−0.206 (−2.35)				
$D1.LONATO_{t-1}$	−0.020 (−2.04)				
$LSUME_{t-1}$	0.007 (0.15)	0.010 (0.201)	−0.032 (−0.53)	−0.005 (−0.12)	−0.089 (−2.53)
$D2$	−0.045 (−1.88)	−0.058 (−2.69)	−0.067 (−2.18)	−0.058 (−2.69)	−0.068 (−2.98)
Constant	5.990 (3.71)	4.701 (2.82)	1.413 (0.68)	4.300 (2.61)	2.194 (1.14)
R^2	0.99	0.98	0.97	0.98	0.96
Residual sum of squares	0.0067	0.0098	0.0190	0.0109	0.020
Durbin–Watson	2.34	1.64	0.96	1.60	1.09
Degrees of freedom	17	19	21	21	23

Notes: The dependent variable is LME; t ratios in parentheses.

Table 7.6 Hypothesis tests for the alternative demand for military expenditure specifications

		Hypotheses	F statistics	Conclusions
A	H_0:	Model 2 is correct	$F_{2,17} = 3.933$	Reject H_0, $\alpha = 0.05$
	H_A:	Model 1 is correct		Fail to reject H_0, $\alpha = 0.01$
B	H_0:	Model 4 is correct	$F_{4,17} = 2.66$	Fail to reject H_0, $\alpha = 0.05$
	H_A:	Model 1 is correct		Fail to reject H_0, $\alpha = 0.01$
C	H_0:	Model 3 is correct	$F_{4,17} = 7.80$	Reject H_0, $\alpha = 0.05$
	H_A:	Model 1 is correct		Reject H_0, $\alpha = 0.01$
D	H_0:	Model 4 is correct	$F_{2,19} = 1.066$	Fail to reject H_0, $\alpha = 0.05$
	H_A:	Model 2 is correct		Fail to reject H_0, $\alpha = 0.01$
E	H_0:	Model 5 is correct	$F_{2,21} = 8.77$	Reject H_0, $\alpha = 0.05$
	H_A:	Model 4 is correct		Reject H_0, $\alpha = 0.01$

Notes: The critical values for $F_{2,17}$ are 3.59 for $\alpha = 0.05$ and 6.11 for $\alpha = 0.01$.
The critical values for $F_{4,17}$ are 2.96 for $\alpha = 0.05$ and 4.67 for $\alpha = 0.01$.
The critical values for $F_{2,19}$ are 3.52 for $\alpha = 0.05$ and 5.93 for $\alpha = 0.01$.
The critical values for $F_{2,21}$ are 3.47 for $\alpha = 0.05$ and 5.78 for $\alpha = 0.01$.

zero in Table 5. The R^2 is high and the Durbin–Watson statistic does not indicate a problem with first-order serial correlation in the error term.

In model 4, the estimated income elasticity of military expenditure is 0.77 (see Table 7.5). Thus, Sweden will increase ME by 0.77 per cent in response to an increase in GDP of 1 per cent, holding the other factors constant. The income response of ME to GDP ($\partial q/\partial I$) can be computed from this estimate by multiplying it by the ratio of ME to GDP. In 1985, this measure was 0.023; hence, a $1 increase in real GDP results in a 2.3 cents increase in real military spending.

The negative estimate for population elasticity may, at first, seem surprising. This estimate indicates that as the population is increasing, holding GDP and the other variables constant, Sweden is forced to allocate more of its budget to social programmes and less to defence. Correspondingly, non-military public expenditure is shown below to be positively related to POP_t. Although the population elasticity is highly responsive (-3.165), the population changes very little from year to year, implying that the empirical magnitude of this effect is quite small.

The estimates on the spillovers from Norway show that during the pre-1974 period, Sweden responded positively to increases in Norwegian military activity. For a 10 per cent increase in Norwegian spending, Sweden would increase ME by 3.3 per cent. Converting this elasticity measure into a partial response ($\partial q/\partial \bar{Q}$) gives 0.93 in 1972; hence, a $1 increase in Norwegian ME is followed by a $.93 increase in Swedish ME.

During the flexible response era, Sweden reduced her responsiveness to spillins. This supports the hypothesis that the new strategic doctrine facilitates more free-riding by Sweden. The spillin elasticity in the post-1974 period is 0.229 ($= 0.331 - 0.102$); the partial response associated with this elasticity is down to 0.44 in 1985.

The Soviet defence expenditure is not significantly related to Swedish defence spending; however, very little confidence can be placed in this finding owing to the nature of the Soviet data. The estimated coefficient on the dummy variable that measures the domestic policy shift toward fiscal restraint (D2) shows that this policy has forced a negative shift in the demand for military expenditure.

There are a number of reasons behind the insignificance of the Soviet data. First, as mentioned, the Soviet data may not be a good proxy for the Soviet military expenditure. Second, Sweden as well as the NATO allies may put more weight on internal budgetary considerations when deciding its military expenditures (i.e. external threat may be of secondary importance). Third, external threat may depend on the Soviet stock of weapons rather than on Soviet military expenditure. Fourth, Soviet military expenditure may be correlated with NATO military expenditure.

Estimates of the demand for non-military expenditure

The estimates of Sweden's demand for non-military public expenditure are presented in Table 7.7. The functional form and independent variables for this specification are the same as those in model 4. The R^2 is again high and most of the estimated coefficients are significantly different from zero – the noteworthy exception is the coefficient on $SUME_{t-1}$. The Durbin–Watson statistic is less than in model 4 but is still within the uncertain range for concluding that first-order serial correlation is a problem. If we were to assume first-order serial correlation in the errors and re-estimate the equation with a correction (Cochrane–Orcutt method), none of the estimated coefficients would change appreciably.

The estimated income elasticity of NME_t is negative and significant at the 0.10 level. This result demonstrates that the impact of the automatic fiscal stabilizers offsets the hypothesized income normality of the non-military public spending. As GDP decreases by 1 per cent, public non-military expenditure increases by 1.6 per cent. This elasticity measure converts into a partial response to income of -0.71 in 1985 (i.e. $\partial y/\partial I = -0.71$).

POP_t has a strong positive relationship to NME. The elasticity measure of 15 means that if population were to change by 1 per cent, public non-military expenditure would increase by 15 per cent. This large figure is rather misleading. In 1980, Sweden's population was 8.31 million; in 1985, it grew to 8.35 million. The percentage change in population over this period is about 0.5 per cent, implying that non-military spending increased by about 7.5 per cent to serve these people.

The estimates on the spillin terms complement our findings above. As Norway increases military expenditure, Sweden is able to cut back on military spending. This cut back releases government revenues for domestic programmes. The implied substitution between budget items is apparently quite large: after 1974, the elasticity measure is 1.104 (= 0.673 + 0.431).

The positive sign on the estimated coefficient for $D2$ signifies that the new domestic policy does not affect military and non-military spending equally. Our empirical evidence suggests that the military sector is shouldering most of the burden of Swedish drive to balance the budget in the 1980s.

Table 7.7 OLS estimates of the demand for non-military public expenditure, 1958–85

Independent variable	Coefficient
$LGDP_t$	−1.630
	(−1.88)
$LPOP_t$	15.168
	(3.65)
$LNOME_{t-1}$	0.674
	(2.39)
$D1.LNOME_{t-1}$	0.431
	(2.49)
$LSUME_{t-1}$	0.108
	(0.70)
$D2$	0.162
	(2.12)
Constant	−21.769
	(−3.72)
R^2	0.99
Residual sum of squares	0.137
Durbin–Watson	1.23
Degrees of freedom	21

Notes: (i) The dependent variable is $LNME_t$; (ii) t ratios in parentheses.

Empirical results: vector autoregression analysis

Background

The results presented in the preceding section depend on the correct specification of the models. If the underlining theoretical structure of our models were incorrect, then our estimates would suffer from specification bias and the interpretations attributed to these estimates would be wrong. As all traditional econometric studies suffer from this possibility, our methodology is no worse (or better) than others. Nevertheless, there are some particularly troubling features that warrant further attention.

When formulating the theory, we assumed that a nation optimally chooses its level of military and non-military activity given its annual income flow. In the real world, however, the distinction between an endogenous and an exogenous variable is blurred. An endogenous variable is determined within a model, whereas an exogenous variable is given and not determined by the model. The assumption of endogenous military and non-military activity and exogenous income ignores the macro-economic effects of public spending on national income. If these macro-economic effects were included, then income would also be an endogenous variable. To build this aspect into the model would require that public spending and income be determined simultaneously and that the estimation strategy be modified.

A second critique of our approach concerns the assumption that the annual data are revealing Nash–Cournot equilibriums. If the relationship between spillins and public spending is more dynamic than our methodology allows, the implicit equilibrium assumption might not be appropriate. Moreover, the Nash–Cournot assumption may be inoperable owing to 'gaming' by the nations, thereby implying that simultaneity exists between Norway's defence expenditures and the military activity of Sweden.

Another potential problem with our empirical analysis is our failure to examine directly the guns-for-butter trade-off. We do not have an estimate of the relationship between military expenditure and non-military public expenditure, because the relative price terms dropped out of the empirical models.

Sims (1980) has proposed the use of vector autoregression (VAR) systems to circumvent these and other problems encountered with time-series data. VAR exercises reduce the 'human input' to data analysis; i.e. VAR analyses require very few restrictions (in the form of structural models) on the data. In a VAR analysis, all variables are treated as endogenous and several time-lags are included for each. The lagged variables facilitate an analysis of the intertemporal relationships or joint serial correlation between the variables, which, in turn, provide some insight into the endogeneity of particular variables. The endogeneity issue and the inherent dynamics of the model can both be examined in a VAR. However, a VAR system is not necessarily derived from a formal theoretical structure. The system can include (say) military expenditure and non-military public expenditure since these are the variables of interest.

Although each of the problems of the traditional approach can be addressed with a VAR system, VAR analysis suffers from several short-comings. First, VAR models are non-structural and, consequently, classical hypothesis testing is not possible. Second, the results from VAR analysis are best considered descriptive of relationships over time. There is a tendency to try to conclude 'causality' between two time-series using the results from VAR analysis. Leamer (1985) argued that the term causality or Granger causality (Granger 1969) should be avoided because the analysis of VARs only reveals (a) the intertemporal precedence (one series changing before another) among series in the past, and (b) the historical response of one series to innovations (or changes) in another.[18] Nevertheless, several authors still employ Granger's causality terminology (Manage and Marlow 1986; Anderson *et al*. 1986; Chowdhury *et al*. 1986) because Granger's definition is based on intertemporal precedence. The term Granger causality does not imply causation in a mathematical sense.

VAR analysis

The VAR system analysed here is a four-equation model with one equation for ME, GDP, NOME, and NME. The system can be written in matrix notation as:

$$
\begin{bmatrix} LME_t \\ LGDP_t \\ LNOME_t \\ LNME_t \end{bmatrix} = \begin{bmatrix} a_{11}^3(L) \; a_{12}^3(L) \; a_{13}^3(L) \; a_{14}^3(L) \\ a_{21}^3(L) \; a_{22}^3(L) \; a_{23}^3(L) \; a_{24}^3(L) \\ a_{31}^3(L) \; a_{32}^3(L) \; a_{33}^3(L) \; a_{34}^3(L) \\ a_{41}^3(L) \; a_{42}^3(L) \; a_{43}^3(L) \; a_{44}^3(L) \end{bmatrix} \begin{bmatrix} LME_t \\ LGDP_t \\ LNOME_t \\ LNME_t \end{bmatrix} + \begin{bmatrix} a_1 \\ a_2 \\ a_3 \\ a_4 \end{bmatrix} + \begin{bmatrix} e_1 \\ e_2 \\ e_3 \\ e_4 \end{bmatrix}
$$

The $a_{ij}^3(L)$ parameters represent the three coefficients on variable j in equation i. The (L) symbolizes the lag operator; hence, each term on the right-hand side of the equations will have three lags. The a_is are the constant terms and the e_is are the error terms. As each equation has the same independent variable set, consistent estimates of the coefficients are obtained by applying OLS to each equation.

Sims (1982) argued that the magnitude of the intertemporal precedence can be described by analysing the variance decompositions of the residuals in a VAR system. Variance decompositions are computed by generating the variances of the forecast (within sample) errors for each variable. These variances are then decomposed into the portion explained by innovations in that particular variable and the portion explained by innovations in the other variables. Evidence that series A Granger causes series B is exhibited in the variance decompositions by two factors: a large portion of the forecast error variance in B is explained by lags in A and a relatively small portion of the forecast error variance of A is explained by B. When series A Granger causes series B, we would conclude that A is exogenous, whereas B is endogenous.

Variance decompositions are presented for the system described above in Table 7.8. The results vary slightly when a different period for computing the decomposition is chosen. The chosen time interval must be of sufficient length to allow the dynamics of the system to play out; 5 years appear adequate for the defence model. As the variance decompositions will change when the ordering of the variables introduced to explain the variance is altered (Chowdhury *et al*. 1986), two orderings are presented. For the first (top of Table 7.8), the forecast error in LME is explained primarily by innovations in LME (48.6 per cent), LGDP (20.8 per cent) and LNOME (20.2 per cent). These proportions change when the ordering is reversed. For the second ordering, LNOME explains 54.1 per cent, whereas innovations in LME only account for 13.5 per cent. In the first ordering, LME is entered before LNOME; in the second, LNOME is entered first. The variable introduced first appears to explain the same variation in the forecast error of LME. This pattern is precisely what we would expect if LME and LNOME are treated by Sweden as substitutes.

LGDP does not appear to be exogenous. Almost 40 per cent of the forecast error variance in LGDP is attributed to LME in the first ordering. The second ordering shows that LNOME again takes on the role of LME, explaining 26.7 per cent of the forecast error variance of GDP. These decompositions indicate that lags of LME (or LNOME) do influence LGDP.

LNOME appears to be exogenous to Sweden. Most of its forecast error variance is explained by previous values of itself. This is true regardless of the ordering. Although lags in LNME explain a large portion of the forecast error of variance of LNME, they do not explain much of the variances from the other variables. Evidence that LNOME precedes LNME is found with both orderings. This indicates that LNME is probably endogenous in the system. LME does not seem to precede LNME.

In summary, we can conclude that both ME and GDP appear to be endogenous. Evidence is also found for the endogeneity of NME. In addition, the VAR analysis suggests that ME and NOME are substitutes, especially in terms of their influence on NME and GDP. The substitution finding is consistent with free-riding and the pure publicness of defence for Sweden and Norway. Finally, the VAR decompositions support the exogeneity of NOME.

Table 7.8 Variance decompositions of the forecast errors of each variable in the VAR system 5 years ahead

Ordering: LME LGDP LNOME LNME

Forecast error in		Explained by		
	LME	*LGDP*	*LNOME*	*LNME*
LME	48.6	20.8	20.2	10.4
LGDP	39.6	52.0	7.4	1.0
LNOME	19.3	6.6	73.8	0.3
LNME	2.5	19.4	39.6	38.5

Ordering: LNME LNOME LGDP LME

Forecast error in		Explained by		
	LME	*LGDP*	*LNOME*	*LNME*
LME	13.5	20.2	54.1	12.9
LGDP	3.6	59.5	26.7	10.2
LNOME	1.1	8.1	86.0	4.8
LNME	3.7	5.8	21.9	68.6

Concluding remarks

A utility-maximizing model was employed to derive a demand curve for estimating Swedish demand for military expenditure. Our estimates indicated that prior to 1973, Sweden was self-reliant for its military expenditure. During the flexible response era after 1973, Sweden began to rely, to some extent, on its NATO neighbour Norway. This reliance is consistent with our theoretical predictions and coincided with the period when there was an unprecedented increase in public sector spending in Sweden. We used nested-test hypotheses to demonstrate that Sweden relied on Norway rather than on Denmark or NATO.

The intertemporal relationship of the variables were then investigated with a VAR analysis. The VAR findings indicated that in our future work we need to handle a simultaneity problem associated with military expenditure, GDP and non-military expenditure. To tackle this problem, we would have to derive equations for explaining GDP and non-military expenditures based upon exogenous variables. In essence, we must construct a simultaneous-equation system that accounts for both supply and demand considerations.

We conclude the analysis by speculating on the effects on Swedish military expenditure if Sweden were to join with Norway and Denmark in a Nordic Defence Pact. Such a pact would be a viable alternative if, say, the United States were to withdraw from NATO. A Nordic Defence Pact would rely on conventional weapons and would offer limited free-riding possibilities owing to the impurity of such weapons. Since Swedish free-riding is with respect to Norway and not NATO or the US *per se*, Swedish defence expenditure should not be significantly affected by a breakdown in NATO. Sweden's free-riding on Norway is very limited in scope and only occurred after 1973; this limited free-riding is likely to continue if a Nordic Defence Pact were formed. In our previous work, neither Denmark nor Norway was seen to free-ride on Sweden (see, for example, Murdoch and Sandler 1984; 1986). Moreover, neither Denmark nor Norway free-rode on NATO: hence, a US withdrawal from NATO should not have a significant impact on these countries' military expenditure. In summary, a Nordic Defence Pact should have little influence on the three proposed participants' defence expenditure. Within such a pact, free-riding is predicted to be minimal and to characterize only Sweden.

Appendix

Table A7.1 Real military expenditures for the NATO allies, 1958–85 (1980 US$bn)

Year	Belgium	Canada	Denmark	France	West Germany	Italy	Netherlands	Norway	United Kingdom	United States
1958	1.73	4.77	0.86	15.56	9.29	4.81	2.89	0.68	21.15	121.88
1959	1.76	4.42	0.81	16.63	14.84	4.96	2.57	0.71	20.77	121.25
1960	1.78	4.39	0.91	17.18	15.83	5.18	2.95	0.67	21.41	117.87
1961	1.80	4.53	0.91	17.68	16.51	5.33	3.39	0.73	21.37	123.22
1962	1.92	4.72	0.84	18.35	20.75	5.78	3.56	0.93	21.86	132.61
1963	2.08	4.38	1.14	17.79	23.32	6.37	3.58	0.98	22.08	130.41
1964	2.21	4.52	1.15	18.12	22.23	6.49	3.81	0.98	22.81	125.83
1965	2.14	4.01	1.21	18.65	21.87	6.74	3.67	1.13	22.73	124.58
1966	2.16	4.09	1.18	18.88	21.43	7.22	3.56	1.12	22.36	147.84
1967	2.26	4.38	1.21	19.83	22.39	7.12	3.92	1.17	22.92	170.31
1968	2.37	4.15	1.31	19.85	19.82	7.22	3.85	1.23	22.60	174.74
1969	2.36	3.91	1.27	19.53	21.24	6.99	4.07	1.28	21.18	167.58
1970	2.52	4.07	1.23	19.40	20.66	7.21	4.16	1.26	20.98	152.06
1971	2.54	4.08	1.32	19.31	21.61	7.98	4.31	1.29	22.05	139.41
1972	2.66	4.08	1.28	19.14	23.13	8.76	4.39	1.31	23.54	138.64
1973	2.85	4.02	1.19	20.38	24.11	8.70	4.36	1.30	23.68	132.36
1974	2.90	4.14	1.36	20.79	25.24	10.09	4.58	1.31	24.44	133.39
1975	3.16	4.09	1.43	21.36	25.10	9.36	4.77	1.46	23.89	129.19
1976	3.38	4.33	1.42	22.37	25.25	9.22	4.75	1.52	24.77	123.66
1977	3.46	4.62	1.45	23.59	25.12	9.71	5.29	1.56	24.15	128.57
1978	3.70	4.89	1.51	24.73	25.81	9.98	5.04	1.69	24.30	129.59
1979	3.78	4.58	1.54	25.41	26.19	10.50	5.37	1.70	25.15	133.35
1980	3.96	4.70	1.62	26.42	26.69	9.58	5.27	1.67	26.78	143.97
1981	4.09	4.87	1.66	27.50	27.61	9.72	5.39	1.68	25.34	155.01
1982	4.02	5.38	1.70	28.16	27.47	10.42	5.35	1.77	26.83	170.10
1983	3.91	5.40	1.69	28.59	27.73	10.59	5.36	1.88	29.41	179.17
1984	3.84	5.89	1.66	28.49	27.57	10.96	5.56	1.81	29.96	188.29
1985	4.01	6.28	1.67	28.40	28.14	11.07	5.46	2.09	31.06	204.95

Source: IMF (1983, 1987) and SIPRI (1974, 1980, 1986)
Note: Adjusted for inflation using the GDP price deflators (1980 = 100) for each country.

Table A7.2 GDP price deflators for the NATO allies, 1958–85

Year	Belgium	Canada	Denmark	France	West Germany	Italy	Netherlands	Norway	United Kingdom	United States
1958	36.30	31.20	20.70	25.20	40.60	15.70	28.80	30.70	17.50	37.00
1959	36.40	31.80	21.60	25.50	41.10	15.70	29.40	31.60	17.80	37.80
1960	36.80	32.20	21.80	26.40	42.10	16.00	29.50	31.90	18.00	38.50
1961	37.20	32.40	22.90	27.30	43.90	16.40	29.90	32.50	18.60	38.80
1962	37.60	32.80	24.40	28.60	45.70	17.40	30.90	29.90	19.30	39.50
1963	38.80	33.40	25.80	30.40	47.00	18.90	32.40	30.90	19.70	40.10
1964	40.60	34.30	27.10	31.70	48.40	20.10	35.10	32.40	20.40	40.70
1965	42.60	35.40	29.00	32.10	50.10	21.00	37.20	34.00	21.40	41.60
1966	44.50	36.90	31.30	33.50	52.00	21.70	39.40	35.30	22.40	43.00
1967	45.90	38.40	32.90	34.50	52.60	22.30	41.10	36.40	23.10	44.30
1968	47.10	39.70	35.20	36.00	53.60	22.70	42.80	38.00	24.00	46.20
1969	49.10	41.50	36.90	38.40	55.90	23.60	45.50	39.60	25.30	48.60
1970	50.80	43.30	39.80	40.50	60.10	25.30	48.00	44.60	27.10	51.20
1971	53.50	44.70	43.00	42.90	64.80	27.10	52.10	47.60	29.70	53.70
1972	56.80	46.90	46.80	45.50	68.30	28.80	57.00	50.00	32.20	56.00
1973	60.70	51.20	52.70	49.10	72.80	32.10	61.80	54.60	34.50	59.20
1974	68.20	59.10	58.40	54.50	77.70	33.00	67.50	60.80	39.60	64.40
1975	76.80	65.40	65.90	61.90	82.40	38.70	75.00	66.20	50.30	70.40
1976	82.50	70.90	71.40	67.60	84.80	45.70	81.10	71.20	57.60	73.60
1977	88.50	76.40	78.20	74.00	88.00	54.50	86.50	77.10	65.60	78.50
1978	92.20	81.50	85.90	81.50	91.70	62.00	91.30	82.10	72.90	84.30
1979	96.40	90.00	92.40	89.80	95.40	71.90	94.70	87.50	83.50	91.70
1980	100.00	100.00	100.00	100.00	100.00	100.00	100.00	100.00	100.00	100.00
1981	105.10	110.50	110.10	111.60	104.00	118.50	105.50	114.00	111.50	109.60
1982	112.40	121.70	121.70	124.40	108.60	137.70	112.10	125.60	120.10	116.70
1983	119.60	128.00	131.70	136.60	112.10	158.80	114.10	133.20	126.20	121.20
1984	126.10	135.30	139.10	146.70	114.30	175.00	115.50	141.80	131.40	125.90
1985	132.60	139.80	146.10	155.20	116.80	190.40	118.80	149.20	139.10	130.10

Source: IMF (1983, 1987)

Table A7.3 Swedish and Soviet data, 1953–85

Year	Sweden Military expenditure[1]	GDP[1]	Non-military expenditure[1]	GDP price deflator	Population[2]	Soviet Military expenditure[1]
1953	2.28	7.71	50.03	21.00	7.19	343.00
1954	2.41	8.55	52.98	21.10	7.23	311.00
1955	2.43	8.40	54.63	22.00	7.26	349.00
1956	2.45	8.92	56.54	23.10	7.32	316.00
1957	2.50	9.28	57.60	24.20	7.37	313.00
1958	2.58	10.33	59.36	24.80	7.42	305.00
1959	2.66	10.89	62.40	25.10	7.45	330.00
1960	2.60	10.12	64.62	26.40	7.48	327.00
1961	2.69	10.28	68.00	27.30	7.52	408.00
1962	2.90	11.11	70.68	28.50	7.56	446.00
1963	3.14	12.05	74.74	28.90	7.60	489.00
1964	3.27	12.81	79.77	30.20	7.66	467.00
1965	3.43	14.54	82.83	32.00	7.73	449.00
1966	3.46	19.11	84.56	34.10	7.81	470.00
1967	3.35	21.55	87.43	35.80	7.87	508.00
1968	3.34	23.14	90.74	36.60	7.91	586.00
1969	3.49	25.03	95.17	37.90	7.97	622.00
1970	3.65	23.12	101.49	39.80	8.04	630.00
1971	3.70	24.09	102.18	42.90	8.10	630.00
1972	3.68	26.41	104.30	46.00	8.12	630.00
1973	3.75	27.49	108.34	49.30	8.14	1,188.00
1974	3.84	30.20	113.09	53.40	8.16	1,207.00
1975	3.77	31.39	115.64	61.30	8.19	1,226.00
1976	3.72	35.07	117.04	68.40	8.22	1,242.00
1977	3.76	38.62	115.57	75.70	8.25	1,261.00
1978	3.84	42.32	117.63	82.90	8.28	1,280.00
1979	3.98	45.86	122.13	89.50	8.29	1,296.00
1980	4.01	46.88	124.15	100.00	8.31	1,315.00
1981	4.11	50.35	123.73	109.50	8.32	1,337.00
1982	4.05	51.82	124.81	118.90	8.33	1,355.00
1983	3.98	56.02	127.79	130.50	8.33	1,379.00
1984	4.01	56.63	132.87	140.50	8.34	1,420.00
1985	4.02	59.14	135.77	150.20	8.35	1,462.00

Sources: IMF (1983, 1987) and SIPRI (1974, 1980, 1986)
Notes:
[1] In billions of US dollars.
[2] In millions.

Table A7.4 1980 exchange rates (local currency per US$)

Country	Rate
Sweden	4.23
Belgium	29.24
Canada	1.17
Denmark	5.64
France	4.23
Germany	1.82
Italy	856.50
The Netherlands	1.99
Norway	4.94
United Kingdom	0.43

Source: IMF (1987)

Notes

1 The Finnish–Soviet Treaty, signed in 1948, pledged the two countries to a mutual defence pact if Finnish soil is invaded. Nevertheless, Finnish loyalties are not with the Soviets. See Bjøl (1983: 7–16) on Finnish aligned neutrality.
2 On this doctrine of international law, see Neuhold (1982: 162–4).
3 When Switzerland was invaded during the Second World War, the Swiss withdrew their forces from the borders. Germany gave up its invasion when it appeared that it would have to fight a door-to-door battle with the Swiss population in the cities. In Switzerland, everyone is part of the reserves.
4 Swedish arms producers include, among others, Bofors (guns and missiles), Saab (aircraft), Hagglunds (tanks) and Kockums (submarines).
5 The facts and figures in this subsection are taken from OECD (1987).
6 Unless otherwise indicated, the facts of this paragraph are taken from the International Institute for Strategic Studies (1987: 88–9).
7 The relevant literature includes Murdoch and Sandler (1982, 1984, 1986), Olson and Zeckhauser (1966), Sandler (1977), Sandler and Forbes (1980) and van Ypersele de Strihou (1967). In an earlier version of this chapter, the mathematical theory was developed explicitly – this earlier version is available upon request from the authors.
8 On this issue, see the discussion in Bjøl (1983: 19–20). In particular, Bjøl stated that 'Swedish officers have openly admitted that the only threat to which Sweden's defence is turned is that from the Warsaw Pact.'
9 A pure public good is totally non-rival in consumption, since its consumption by one individual (nation) does not detract in the slightest from the consumption opportunities available to other persons (nations). Moreover, the benefits of a pure public good are non-excludable; once it is provided, the good is available to all. In contrast, a private good is totally rival and its benefits are excludable. Impure public goods exhibit varying degrees of rivalry and/or excludability.
10 Thus, we invoke Nash behaviour. Our choice of Nash behaviour is defended in Sandler and Murdoch (1987). See also McGuire and Groth (1985).
11 Our empirical section will provide a test of whether Sweden truly behaves as an ally of NATO in terms of its expenditure patterns. If Sweden is not responsive to Norwegian or NATO expenditures whatsoever, then Sweden would truly act as an independent neutral nation.
12 The demand for privately provided non-military activity is not display but would depend on the same right-hand side arguments as equations (3) and (4).
13 If the utility function were attributed to a decision-making coalition within the Swedish government, then a somewhat different approach would be needed. Strictly speaking, only two-thirds of all expenditure are determined by the government; hence, we should subtract the expenditure of good r from the country's GDP to get the government's budget. See Murdoch and Sandler (1986) for details.
14 Our choice of functional form is based on the 'fit' of the specifications. This is determined by examining the residuals and the significance of the estimated coefficients. A complete functional form analysis, based on the Box–Cox transformation, would require more observations.
15 The time series has been limited to 1958–85 for two reasons. First, the VAR methodology, presented in the next section, requires that we enter several lagged variables into the specifications. The years 1953–7 could potentially be used by these lagged variables. Second, we are not convinced that the theory of ally expenditures applies to the European countries during the 1950s.
16 The difference between the unrestricted residual sum of squares RSS (model 1)

Swedish military expenditures and armed neutrality

and the restricted RSS divided by the number of restrictions is distributed χ^2 with the number of restrictions as the degrees of freedom. The mean square error of the unrestricted specification, calculated by dividing the RSS by the degrees of freedom in the unrestricted model (17 for model 1), is also distributed χ^2 with the degrees of freedom from the unrestricted model. The ratio of these χ^2 is distributed F with the corresponding degrees of freedom in the numerator and denominator.

17 This conclusion is stronger than Murdoch and Sandler (1986). The results presented here are based on more years of data, which enable us to locate the source of the spillins.

18 See von Furstenberg et al. (1986) for a recent analysis that follows Leamer's suggestion.

References

Anderson, W., Wallace, M. and Warner, J. (1986) 'Government spending and taxation: What causes what?', Southern Journal of Economics 52, 3: 630–9.

Ball, D. (1975) 'The return to counterforce in the Nixon administration', California Seminar on Arms Control and Foreign Policy, Los Angeles.

Bjøl, E. (1983) Nordic Security, London: International Institute for Strategic Studies.

Chowdhury, A., Fackler, J. and McMillin, W. (1986) 'Monetary policy, fiscal policy, and investment spending: An empirical analysis', Southern Journal of Economics 52, 3: 794–806.

The Economist (1984) 'Sweden: Time for a cull', The Economist, 6 October 1984.

The Economist (1987) 'The Nordic alternative', The Economist, 21 November 1987.

Fisher, F. M. (1970) 'Tests of equality between sets of coefficients in two linear regressions: An expository note', Econometrica 38, 2: 361–6.

Granger, C. (1969) 'Investigating causal relations by econometric models and cross-spectral methods', Econometrica 37: 424–38.

International Institute for Strategic Studies (1987) The Military Balance 1987–1988, London: International Institute for Strategic Studies.

International Monetary Fund (1983) International Financial Statistics Yearbook 1983, Washington, DC: IMF.

International Monetary Fund (1987) International Financial Statistics Yearbook 1987, Washington, DC: IMF.

Johnston, J. (1972) Econometric Methods, New York: McGraw-Hill.

Leamer, E. (1985) 'Vector autoregressions for causal inference?', in K. Brunner and A. Meltzer (eds) Understanding Monetary Regimes, Amsterdam: North-Holland, 255–303.

Manage, N. and Marlow, M. (1986) 'The causal relation between federal expenditures and receipts', Southern Journal of Economics 52, 3: 617–29.

McGuire, M. C. and Groth, C. H. (1985) 'A method for identifying the public good allocation process within a group', Quarterly Journal of Economics 100, supplement: 915–34.

Murdoch, J. C. and Sandler, T. (1982) 'A theoretical and empirical analysis of NATO', Journal of Conflict Resolution 26, 2: 237–63.

Murdoch, J. C. and Sandler, T. (1984) 'Complementarity, free riding, and the military expenditures of NATO allies', Journal of Public Economics 25, 1: 83–101.

Murdoch, J. C. and Sandler, T. (1986) 'The political economy of Scandinavian neutrality', *Scandinavian Journal of Economics* 88, 4: 583–603.

Neuhold, H. (1982) 'Permanent neutrality and nonalignment similarities and differences', in R. A. Bauer (ed.) *The Australian Solution: International Conflict and Co-operation*, Virginia: University of Virginia Press.

Olson, M. and Zeckhauser, R. (1966) 'An economic theory of alliances', *Review of Economics and Statistics* 48, 3: 266–79.

Organization for Economic Co-operation and Development (OECD) (1987) *Economic Surveys 1986/1987: Sweden*, Paris: OECD.

Sandler, T. (1977) 'Impurity of defense: An application to the economic theory of alliances', *Kyklos* 30, 4: 443–60.

Sandler, T. and Forbes, J. (1980) 'Burden sharing, strategy, and the design of NATO', *Economic Inquiry* 18, 3: 425–44.

Sandler, T. and Murdoch, J. (1987) 'Nash–Cournot or Lindahl behavior?: An empirical test for the NATO allies', unpublished manuscript, Iowa State University.

Sims, C. (1980) 'Macroeconomics and reality', *Econometrica* 48, 1: 1–48.

Sims, C. (1982) 'Policy analysis with econometric models', *Brookings Papers on Economic Activity* 1: 107–52.

Stockholm International Peace Research Institute (SIPRI) (1974, 1980, 1986) *World Armaments and Disarmament: SIPRI Yearbooks*, NY: Crane, Kussak & Co.

United Nations (various issues) *Monthly Bulletin of Statistics*, NY: United Nations.

United Nations (1981) *Reduction in Military Budgets: International Reporting of Military Expenditures*, NY: United Nations.

United States Arms Control and Disarmament Agency (1987) *World Military Expenditures and Arms Transfers 1986*, Washington, DC: US Government Printing Office.

van Ypersele de Strihou, J. (1967) 'Sharing the defense burden among Western allies', *Review of Economics and Statistics* 49, 4: 527–36.

von Furstenberg, G., Green, R. and Jeong, J. (1986) 'Tax and spend, or spend and tax?', *Review of Economics and Statistics* 68, 2: 179–88.

Chapter eight

Defence spending in Israel

Alex Mintz, Michael D. Ward[1] and Shimshon Bichler

Introduction

Israel's defence budget is large and its share in the national economy is vast. Data published annually by Israel's Central Bureau of Statistics, show that Israel's defence budget expenditures total almost $6bn per year – about 25 per cent of the gross national product (GNP) and about 65 per cent of total public expenditures. The Israeli military budget consists of two sets of expenditures: domestic defence expenditures and military imports. The former is primarily earmarked for such budget items as compensation of employees in the defence sector, purchases and services from the domestic economy, and construction, whereas the latter consists mainly of imports of weapon systems.

The relative weight of military imports in total military expenditures has fluctuated considerably in the 1960–84 period. In the early 1960s military imports (primarily from France) amounted, on average, to 58 per cent of domestic military consumption. In the aftermath of the 1967 Six Day War, the increase in Israel's military requirements and the shift from European to more expensive, high technology American arms raised this ratio to an average of 65 per cent in the 1967–72 period.

The 1973 war gave a further boost to military imports. Expensive arms deals with the United States in the 1974–7 period contributed to raising military imports to an average of 85 per cent of the domestic figure. Following Sadat's visit to Jerusalem, the Camp David accord and the temporary disintegration of the Arab coalition, the ratio of military imports to domestic military expenditures fell back to an average of 56 per cent in the 1978–86 period.

Domestic defence expenditures also grew rapidly following each of the Arab–Israeli wars. Whereas between 1960 and 1977, there was positive correlation between domestic military expenditures and military imports (Pearson's $r = 0.95$), in the 1977–86 period, a negative correlation existed. Although military imports slightly declined in recent years, domestic defence expenditures remained rather stable. Much of this stability can be

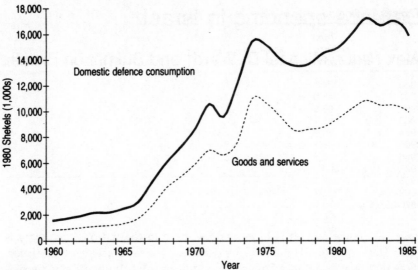

Figure 8.1 Total domestic defence consumption and purchases of goods and services in Israel

attributed to the procurement of military systems from the domestic economy.

Until the early 1960s, the largest share of domestic as well as total military expenditures was accounted for by wage payments. In 1960, domestic military procurement accounted for only 45 per cent of domestic military expenditure. After 1967, however, this share rose to about 75 per cent. In the 1967–75 period, military procurement (domestic and import) amounted to 85 per cent of the total military expenditure. There is a tendency in recent years toward reducing the total military budget, but the share of domestic military procurement in domestic military consumption remained stable, as shown in Figure 8.1. This reflects, to an extent, the structure of the Israeli economy. A substantial part of the business sector has gradually transformed itself toward meeting the demands of the Israeli defence forces. These trends are illustrated by the data in Table 8.1.

This transformation has been especially pronounced in the major industrial concerns where both the level of profit and the rate of profit became dependent on government military orders. In recent years (1985–7), numerous industrial companies, mostly subsidiaries of the largest Israeli holding corporations, recorded losses due to reduction in military orders, leading the Defence Minister to claim that the Israeli army is too small to meet the demands of the local defence industry.

In addition Israel's defence expenditures are strongly influenced by Arab military expenditures. Data show that Arab and Israeli military spending trends move up and down in symmetry. Based on SIPRI data (1987: 234), 6

Table 8.1 Components of defence consumption in Israel, 1960–86

Year	Total defence consumption	Military imports	Domestic defence consumption	Compensation of employees	Purchases of goods and services	Average annual inflation
1960	34.9	8.7	26.2	12.0	14.2	2.5
1961	45.9	14.3	31.6	14.8	16.8	6.8
1962	65.5	27.5	38.0	17.7	20.3	9.4
1963	81.1	34.4	46.7	22.5	24.2	6.6
1964	79.9	31.1	48.6	22.1	26.5	4.9
1965	96.7	36.4	60.3	27.8	32.5	8.0
1966	116.6	38.6	78.0	32.7	45.3	7.9
1967	208.0	87.0	121.0	48.5	72.5	1.7
1968	250.3	86.2	164.0	52.8	111.3	2.1
1969	320.7	120.6	200.0	63.4	136.7	2.5
1970	475.5	218.1	257.0	81.4	176.0	6.1
1971	545.7	210.7	355.0	100.1	234.9	12.0
1972	624.0	256.0	368.0	113.8	254.5	12.9
1973	1,220.0	653.0	567.0	212.8	353.3	20.0
1974	1,640.0	687.0	953.0	274.0	680.0	39.7
1975	2,603.0	1,310.0	1,293.0	384.5	908.9	39.3
1976	2,951.0	1,458.0	1,522.0	482.0	1,040.0	31.7
1977	3,384.0	1,354.0	2,094.0	779.0	1,315.0	34.2
1978	6,020.0	3,070.0	3,290.0	1,221.0	2,069.0	50.6
1979	9,288.0	3,440.0	6,390.0	2,533.0	3,857.0	78.3
1980	24,521.0	10,280.0	14,941.0	5,514.0	9,427.0	131.0
1981	62,441.0	28,264.0	36,292.0	13,162.0	23,130.0	116.8
1982	123,855.0	41,124.0	86,369.0	31,980.0	54,389.0	120.4
1983	277,499.0	73,772.0	208,127.0	77,168.0	130,959.0	145.6
1984	1,576,362.0	566,440.0	1,018,980.0	392,128.0	626,852.0	373.8
1985	5,799,610.0	2,435,559.0	3,396,902.0	1,270,798.0	2,126,104.0	304.6
1986	6,529,222.0	2,076,622.0	4,515,041.0	1,952,342.0	2,562,699.0	48.2

Source: Central Bureau of Statistics
Note: Units: 1000s in current Israeli new Shekels.

out of 8 years between 1976 and 1985 show a correspondence in the direction of percentage increases between Israel and an average of the changes of Egypt, Jordan and Syria. Thus, when the military spending of the confrontation states is going up, Israeli military budgets also tend to go up; similarly, they both tend to be reduced in the same years. SIPRI data show that even in periods of drastic developments in the Middle East (the Egyptian–Israeli peace treaty, the war in Lebanon) changes in Israeli defence expenditures correspond to changes in Arab military expenditures. At the margin, however, Israeli military expenditures are also influenced by political–economic considerations.

The political economy

In contrast to other major arms producing nations in the Third World, such as India (with 280,000 employees in the military industry), South Africa (with 100,000 employees), Brazil (with 75,000 employees) and South

Korea (with 30,000 employees in the military industry), arms production activity in Israel accounts for a very large share of overall industrial activity (Brzoska and Ohlson 1986: 22). Investment in the defence sector accounts for as much as 50 per cent of all industrial investment in Israel. Almost one-quarter of the industrial labour force in Israel is engaged in military-related projects, about one-quarter of Israel's industrial exports (excluding diamonds) originate in the defence sector, eight of the twenty largest corporations in Israel are highly dependent on military contracting and three of the top five Israeli companies are primarily concerned with production of goods and services for the defence sector (Mintz 1988). There is a negative insignificant correlation ($r = -0.05$) between domestic defence purchases (as a percentage of the GNP) and domestic civilian purchases (as a percentage of the GNP) when domestic defence purchases exceed civilian purchases every year as seen in Figure 8.2. What is especially important to note in this figure is that not only is the military portion of GNP much larger than the civilian, but also that there is virtually no variation in the latter.

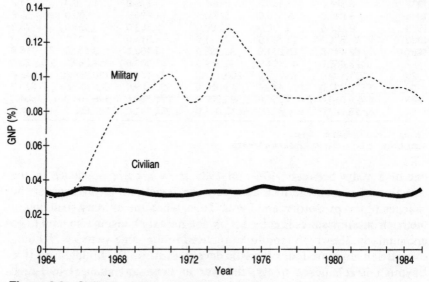

Figure 8.2 Civilian v. military purchases in Israel
Note: All data refer to domestic consumption.

Manufacturing and services of defence items account for a high percentage of employment, revenues and exports in all three sectors in the Israeli economy; ranging at the high end from the government's commercial enterprises, through those of the Labour Federation, to a slightly smaller percentage in the purely private sector.

The high degree of industrial dependence on defence contracting in

Israel has created a situation whereby the Israeli government has been forced in recent years to consider not only the security ramifications of its military procurement policies, but also the economic and political implications of arms production decisions (Mintz and Ward 1989). This was evident in the decision to develop the Lavi aircraft despite opposition from the Ground Forces of the Israeli military and later on to cancel it despite support for the project from the former Commander of the Air Force. Similar concerns were visible in numerous decisions about the exportation of military equipment from Israel. The oligopolistic structure of the defence industry in Israel, where six major companies dominate the market, and the dependence of the government on these major concerns for economic growth, revenues, jobs and exports, has led to a greater sensitivity of the government to the economic well-being of these companies.

Bichler (1986) has pointed out that military expenditures are essential for the economic well-being of major concerns in Israel. Steinberg and Hadar (1988) have suggested that the largest concerns are the main beneficiaries of governmental support for high-tech projects, such as characterize much defence spending. Consequently, military expenditures are expected to increase significantly following a decline in profits of the major industrial concerns in Israel.

Military expenditures are also sensitive to inflation. During the 1960–72 period – years of rapid growth of the Israeli economy – annual inflation was low. The consumer price index (CPI) rose on an annual average of 6.8 per cent. Since the 1973 Arab–Israeli war, the scale of inflation in Israel rose. Between 1973 and 1977, the inflation reached an average of 37 per cent annually. The rise of the Likud party to power in 1977 triggered a rapid increase in prices. Before the 1981 election, prices rose from a 34 per cent increase in 1977 to a 131 per cent increase in 1980. In the election year 1984, prices rose to a peak of 400 per cent. One of the declared goals of the so-called 'government of national unity' was to curb the rate of inflation, both through price control and with the aid of restraining fiscal and monetary policies.

Inflation decreased substantially in 1985 and to double digit levels in 1986 (Central Bureau of Statistics annually). Given the fragile nature of the coalition government in Israel where two major and roughly equal bodies – the Labour and the Likud parties – are struggling to achieve power, recent Israeli elections are highly competitive and incumbents may be tempted to manipulate even the putatively apolitical defence budget (Mintz 1988). Moreover, as the Israeli electorate shifts more intensively rightward as reflected in elections 1973, 1977 and 1981, neither party can allow itself to appear non-supportive and 'unpatriotic' towards defence spending. The pervasive influence of military spending makes it difficult for elected politicians to vote against increases in the budget.

Accordingly, defence expenditures will grow before an Israeli election. As domestic political considerations also influence US aid decisions (Bard 1988; Quandt 1988), changes in US aid to Israel also reflect the electoral cycle in the United States.

Previous studies showed that the Arab–Israeli wars, the military expenditures of the Arab states and the Israeli Defence Forces intensification programmes strongly affect both the domestic defence budget and military imports. Domestic political–economic factors also influence spending when declining corporate profits, increasing inflation and electoral politics strongly affect the domestic defence budget, and electoral cycles in the United States significantly influence US aid decisions, which in turn affect directly Israel's military imports. These various forces are combined in a mathematical model originally developed in Mintz and Ward (1989); it is summarized below and the symbols used are shown in Table 8.2.

Table 8.2 Symbols used in the model

Symbols and descriptions

Endogenous variables

$\hat{y}_1^s$	desired level of domestic defence spending in shekels
y_1^d	actual level of domestic defence spending in shekels
$\hat{y}_2^d$	desired level of US military aid to Israel in dollars
y_2^d	actual level of US military aid to Israel in dollars
$\hat{y}_3^s$	desired level of military imports to Israel in shekels
y_3^s	actual level of military imports to Israel in shekels

Exogenous variables

x_1	extent of war involvement
x_2	percentage increase in military spending of Egypt, Syria and Jordan
x_3	inflation
x_4	Israeli election cycle
x_5	changes in corporate monopoly profits
x_6	intensification programme of Israeli Defence Forces
x_7	US election cycle

Regime switch

s_1	pre-1967–post-1967 switch for US aid

Note: Data are available from the authors.

A model of military spending in Israel

Domestic defence budget

The first topic addressed in the model is that of the domestic defence budget. Our ideas about the causal forces acting on the domestic defence budget in Israel have been analysed and yielded the following results:[2]

$$\bar{y}_1^s = \underset{(\pm 1.99)}{0.0} \ y_3^s + \underset{(\pm 1.17)}{30.07} \ x_1 + \underset{(\pm 28.08)}{736.79} \ x_2 \tag{1}$$

$$\frac{dy_1^s}{dt} = \underset{(\pm .00006)}{.00294} \ \{\bar{y}_1^s - y_1^s\} + \underset{(\pm .0004)}{0.0} \ x_3 + \underset{(\pm 3.18)}{46.28} \ x_4 - \underset{(\pm .0056)}{.0113} \ x_5 \tag{2}$$

Equation (1) portrays the implicit domestic budget requests, or the desired level of domestic spending dy_1^s/dt, as being driven by three forces: defence imports y_3, war involvement x_1 and the percentage increase in Egyptian, Syrian and Jordanian military expenditures x_2 (x_3 is inflation, x_4, the election cycle; and x_5 the change in monopoly corporate profits). Defence imports comprise mainly procurements of new equipment and thereby influence the domestic defence budget by the attendant expansion of maintenance and operations programmes. Accordingly, imports impart upward pressure on the domestic budget. To the extent that the Arab states increase military expenditures, Israeli defence planners respond with similar increases. During wars additional pressure is felt upon defence needs, because war invariably leads to increased allocation to personnel and replacement of military equipment. These pressures lead to increases in the budgetary request.

Equation (1), then, describes the empirical relationship between the military budget requests and three linear additive components: defence imports, war involvement and changes in Arab military expenditures. It represents the desired level, or goal, for spending on the domestic aspects of the military budget in Israel. This formulation feeds into the actual spending patterns, given in equation (2).

Equation (2) describes the adjustments policy-makers make in the domestic budget requests in response to political and economic pressures. The primary mechanism is an adaptive one that drives expenditures y_1^s toward the level of requests defined in equation (1), namely $\bar{y}_1^s$. The actual and desired levels converge at a rate given by the adjustment coefficient, 0.00294. Due to the security threat to Israel and the strength of the Israeli military elite, the level of defence expenditures approved by the Knesset adapts to the requested level of military expenditures.

Turning to the first component of the model, for which the adjusted coefficient of determination is 0.973, it is clear that the overall fit of the model and the data is strong. The level of domestic military spending is adequately reflected by the model, and the major turning points in this series are also captured. Moreover, five of the seven parameters are much greater than their corresponding standard errors, i.e. statistically significant.

The largest impact on 'domestic' defence spending results from the monitoring of Arab military spending patterns, as seen in the large and significant, positive coefficient, 736.79. The weight of the Israeli war on the domestic military budget is also considerable (x_1 is more than 15 times its standard error).

Therefore, it is clear that security concerns of the Israelis play the major role in determining the domestic military budget in Israel. Yet, the onset of the election period (x_4) and corporate profits (x_5) also impart a significant impact on the domestic military budget. Competitive elections make it difficult for incumbents to 'just say no' to requests for increased spending for Israeli national security. One major consequence of this is that periods just before an election witness growth in the government military outlays. This conjecture is strongly supported by the empirical results as reflected by the significant positive parameter 46.28.

The military–industrial–governmental partnership is a prominent one in Israel, and any serious decline in either the level or the rate of increase in the profits of the three defence-oriented monopolies will not escape the attention of the government. Declining profit rates motivate moderate increases in domestic military spending, as shown in the estimated co-efficient, which is twice its standard error. This follows from the conjecture that even in highly security-conscious societies, such as Israel, the government uses military spending to influence the economy, a conjecture supported by our data analysis.

The slow adjustment speed of Israel's domestic spending suggests that the role of accumulated history is quite significant in Israeli defence decision-making. The importance of prior security threats as well as prior domestic political–economic circumstances are not heavily discounted in calculating current defence needs. In line with this we observe that the feedback from Israeli defence imports (y_3^s) to the domestic side of the defence budget turns out to have a negligible impact, being essentially zero, and non-significant. Additionally, inflation (x_3) was shown to have no significant impact on real defence consumption.

Military aid

The second aspect of the model addresses military aid to Israel. The level of military aid that Israel receives, valued in constant dollars (y_2^d) is primarily driven by three forces.

$$\bar{y}_2^d = \underset{(\pm 5.7)}{114.8\,x_2} + \underset{(\pm 123.7)}{0.0\ x_6} \tag{3}$$

$$\frac{dy_2^d}{dt} = [\ \underset{(\pm.005)}{.084}\ \{\bar{y}_2^d - y_2^d\} + \underset{(\pm 17.8)}{226.0\ x_7}]s_1 \tag{4}$$

Equation (3) here represents the establishment of a target for Israeli military aid $\bar{y}_2^d$. This process represents a rough consensus between the US and Israel regarding the legitimate needs of the Israelis. In general, there is broad agreement upon (1) the military threat of Egypt, Jordan and Syria, herein reflected in x_2, and (2) the military needs of the Israel Defence

Forces, as measured by the intensification programmes of the IDF, x_6. Whereas defence expenditures of the Arab countries influence Israel's military expenditures, a reciprocal influence may also complete the feedback (see Hollist 1977 for such evidence). The Israeli military aid target $\bar{y}_2^d$, as negotiated between the US and Israel, responds to changes in Arab military expenditures and putatively to major intensification programmes.[3]

Empirically we found, however, that the intensification programmes of the Israeli Defence Forces did not play an important role in these aid targets, as shown by the negligible value for this coefficient. This was probably due to the contemporaneous impact of the Arab post-war intensification programmes, which are indirectly captured in (x_2).

Luttwak (1984: 131) argues that Israel's weapon system intensification programmes have reflected the force structure goals of the Israeli Armed Forces, as derived from 'evolving operation concepts of war as well as changing definitions of national security'. This stands in contrast to many Third World nations that tend to define their defence needs in *ex post facto* response to their weapons suppliers. As in other countries, however, the military aid target in Israel is virtually always greater than the amount actually being granted.

The evolution of actual military aid (y_2^d) also adjusts to domestic political constraints in the United States. Thus, the timing of increases in aid to Israel corresponds to the electoral cycle in the US (x_7), as well as to the desired aid target $(\bar{y}_2^d)$.

The overall fit of the model to the military aid series is adequate, with an adjusted coefficient of determination of 0.647, but the major fluctuations, primarily caused by war periods, are not adequately reflected in the estimated relationships. Again security concerns are the most important here as seen in the positive, significant parameter for the weight of Arab military spending in establishing goals for US military aid. The empirical results illustrate the sensitivity to the political process, not only in Israel, but also in the United States. The impact of US Presidential election cycles drives up the granting of US military aid to Israel. Actual US aid flows to Israel adjust fairly slowly and the impact of the past does not appear to be very heavily discounted. In addition to the military aid, it is important to note that Israel also receives economic aid of $785m per year from the US. This aid is officially earmarked for civilian projects, yet relieves some of the pressure on the national budget and therefore indirectly helps to finance military programmes (McGuire 1982).

Israeli defence imports

Finally, military imports are adjusted to the amount of military aid granted by the United States. In earlier periods in which there was no military aid being granted by the US, military imports adjusted to the percentage changes in Arab military intensification programmes as reflected in their defence spending, and to IDF intensification programmes. Accordingly, different mechanisms exist for post-1967 (the first term in equation (5)) and pre-1967 military imports, reflected in the second term in equation (6). The variable s_1 is simply a switch between each of these two different aid regimes. The pre-1967 goal for military imports ($\bar{y}_3^s$) was a function of Arab military spending (x_2) and IDF building programmes (x_6).

$$\bar{y}_3^s = \underset{(\pm 96.8)}{235.4} \; x_2 + \underset{(\pm 2852)}{8466} \; x_6$$

(5)

$$\frac{dy_3^s}{dt} = [\underset{(\pm.59)}{1.53} \{\bar{y}_2^s - y_3^s\}]s_1 + [\underset{(\pm.00186)}{.00895} \{\bar{y}_3^s - y_3^s\}]\{1 - s_1\}$$

(6)

The overall fit of the model to the data is quite good, with the adjusted coefficient of determination approaching 0.80. The adjustment speed of Israeli foreign military imports to the level of US military aid to Israel is instantaneous, as seen in the adjustment speed of 1.53. This means that Israel adjusts its total military imports to be almost identical to the amount of aid it receives from the United States.

The ideas presented in this mini-theory of defence spending in Israel have yielded a coherent and robust picture of the broad outline of the military security as well as political–economic influences on the evolution of the military budget in one industrializing nation with a growing domestic defence industry, Israel. The derived model and the actual data are remarkably similar, and the estimated parameters are significant and interpretable in terms of both the model and the history of Israeli defence politics.

Conclusion

Israel presents a 'tough test case' for ideas that suggest the prominence of political economic features in the landscape of defence policy. In fact, some would argue that if there is any country where the defence budget is unlikely to be used as a political and economic management tool, it is Israel since it is surrounded by real enemies with which it has fought real wars. Security considerations were indeed found in this chapter to play a key role in influencing military spending in Israel. None the less, and in contrast to what has been previously known, the electoral competition and concern for the economic well-being of major corporations were also found to influence defence spending, much like in other countries around the globe. The military budget is the Israeli government's single most important fiscal mechanism for stimulating the economy and influencing elections. It would appear that Israeli decision-makers are unable to overlook its political significance.

We do not think that these forces are influential enough to prevent Israel from cutting its military budget should the strategic situation change in the Middle East. We are concerned however, that these forces will become so influential that the Israelis will be prevented from challenging the current security conception.

Notes

1 I am grateful for a small grant-in-aid from the Council on Research and Creative Work at the University of Colorado for the translation of Hebrew materials.
2 The entire model was estimated simultaneously, using full information maximum likelihood techniques. Standard errors are given in parentheses. Data were taken from official Israeli government statistics wherever possible. The data on domestic defence expenditures, defence imports and total military expenditures were obtained from the Israeli Central Bureau of Statistics, whereas data on military aid to Israel were taken from the Bank of Israel's Annual Report. The GDP deflator, annual inflation index and exchange rates were taken from publications of the International Monetary Fund, whereas data on Arab military expenditures were obtained from the SIPRI Yearbook. Data on corporate profits were taken from Bichler (1986). War casualties were taken from Zussman (1983) and the *Israeli Government Yearbook*. Information on the intensification programmes of the IDF was taken from the Hebrew publication *IDF in Its Might* (1982), and was estimated by the authors for the years subsequent to 1982. Variables superscripted with s are measured in constant shekels; those with d are dollar figures; $\bar{y}$ are target levels.
3 The bivariate correlation between Israeli war involvement and Arab military expenditures is 0.70.

References

Bank of Israel (annually) *Annual Report*, Jerusalem.
Bard, Mitchell (1988) 'The influence of ethnic interest groups on American Middle East policy', in Charles W. Kegley, Jr (ed.) *The Domestic Sources of American Foreign Policy*, NY: St. Martin's Press.
Bichler, Shimshon (1986) 'The political economy of defense', MA thesis, The Hebrew University.
Brzoska, Michael and Ohlson, Thomas (eds) (1986) *Arms Production in the Third World*, London: Taylor & Francis.
Central Bureau of Statistics (1982) *Monthly Bulletin of Statistics, Supplement to Vol. 4, Apr.* Jerusalem.
Central Bureau of Statistics (1985) *Monthly Bulletin of Statistics, Supplement to Vol. 36*, Jerusalem.
Central Bureau of Statistics (annually) *Statistical Abstract of Israel*, Jerusalem.
Hollist, William Ladd (1977) 'Alternative explanations of competitive arms processes: tests on four pairs of nations', *American Journal of Political Science*, 21: 313–40.
International Monetary Fund *International Financial Statistics, Supplement on Exchange Rates, no. 9*, Washington, DC, 1985.
International Monetary Fund (monthly) *International Financial Statistics*, Washington, DC.

International Monetary Fund. *International Financial Statistics, Supplement on Price Statistics, no. 12*, Washington, DC, 1986.

Israeli Defense Forces (1982) *The IDF in Its Might* (Hebrew). Tel Aviv: Revivim.

Israel Information Center (annually) *Israel Government Yearbook (Hebrew)*, Jerusalem.

Luttwak, Edward N. (1984) 'Defense planning in Israel: a brief retrospective', in Stephanie G. Neuman (ed.) *Defense Planning in Less-Industrialized States*, Lexington, Mass.

McGuire, Martin C. (1982) 'U.S. assistance, Israeli allocation, and the arms race in the Middle East', *Journal of Conflict Resolution* 26: 199–235.

Mintz, Alex and Ward, Michael D. (1989) 'The political economy of military spending in Israel', *American Political Science Review* 83: 521–33.

Mintz, Alex (1988) 'Electoral cycles and military spending: a comparison of Israel and the United States', *Comparative Political Studies* 21: 368–81.

Quandt, William B. (1988) 'The electoral cycle and the conduct of American foreign policy', in Charles W. Kegley, Jr (ed.) *The Domestic Sources of American Foreign Policy*, NY: St. Martin's Press.

Steinberg, Gerald and Hadar, Shmuel (1988) *Tactics without Strategy: The Rôle of State Subsidies in the Development of Technology-Intensive Industries*, Jerusalem Institute for Research on Israel.

Stockholm International Peace Research Institute (1987 and annually) *World Armaments and Disarmaments, SIPRI Yearbook 1986*, Oxford: Oxford University Press.

Zussman, Pinchas (1983) 'Why is Israel's defense burden so heavy?', in A. Hareven (ed.) *Is it Indeed Hard to be an Israeli?*, Jerusalem: Van Leer Institute.

Chapter nine

Military security and the economy: defence expenditure in India and Pakistan

Saadet Deger and Somnath Sen[1]

Introduction

India and Pakistan both have formidable military power. Straddling large land masses, with the Soviet Union and China as geographical neighbours, linking the geo-strategically volatile regions of the Middle East and South-East Asia, the two countries taken together form a major focus for regional security. In 1985, leaving out NATO, WTO, China, Saudi Arabia and Iraq/Iran (for which precise data are not available), India had the largest military expenditure in the rest of the world.[2] Its armed forces are the fourth largest in the world. Though Pakistani defence spending is far lower, in terms of its much smaller relative size and population compared to India it must also be considered overarmed by any reasonable standards. By Third World standards both nations have a highly sophisticated arms industrial base and skilled manpower. It is believed that both countries are able, if not willing, to produce nuclear weapons and (at least for India) advanced delivery systems. Arms imports remain high and the 1980s have seen a spurt of competitive arms acquisition from international markets. On the other hand, both economies are among the poorest in the world. In 1985, India's GNP per capita was the 17th lowest in the world; the comparable figure for Pakistan was 29th. The dual economy that characterizes the sub-continent is self-evident: advanced industrialization, high quality tertiary education and great wealth co-exist with soci-economic backwardness, inequality and abject poverty.

Nowhere in the world is the inherent conflict between economic development and strategic security as acute as in the Indian sub-continent. The interaction between the 'poverty trap' and the 'security dilemma'[3] is fundamental in the understanding of the military expenditure process. But in a more basic sense the complexities go much further. The tangled webs of Indo-Pakistan security relations go far beyond the narrow realms of defence and development. Indeed they encompass many other dimensions: history, geography, religion, culture and ethos. The most apt description of this complex interaction can be stated as: 'diversity in unity'. There is so much that binds the two countries' societies, economies and peoples. Yet the conflict of the last 40-odd years continues. It is important to remember this background even though this chapter will concentrate on a narrow range of formal issues on military spending determinants.

The chapter is divided into a number of sections. First, we provide an economic background, which, due to size limitations, is selective. Second, we provide a heuristic view of the military expenditure process. A brief discussion on the history of conflicts in the region is also included. Third, we analyse the econometrics results that explain the demand for security expenditures. Fourth, we discuss the economic effects of defence spending and highlight the contradictions between the demands for growth and security. The last section makes some general observations about the future course of events. A technical Appendix (A) sets out a theoretical model that can be used to explain the behaviour of defence expenditure as a proportion of GDP (the 'defence burden'). There is also a data Appendix (B).

The economic environment

The Indian economy

India embarked on a strategy of planning and import substituting industrialization (ISI) almost from its birth as an independent nation in 1947. Given the size of the economy it was thought that the market (in terms of the population and total income) would be large and economies of scale in industry could be exploited. There was already some infrastructure and basic industrialization carried over from imperial days. But there was also a very large section of the population that lacked basic needs. The objective of the Indian planners, using variants of the Soviet planning model, was to achieve rapid growth through domestic industrialization so that the material demands of the rapidly growing population could be met. Government intervention was considered vital since the private sector could not shoulder the burden of the massive tranformation proposed. However, given its democratic structure and the West European-type political constitution, the private sector and the free internal market would have to play an important role in the economy. It was envisaged that the private sector, including the vast agricultural economy, would be used to provide simple mass consumption goods (and food) for the country. Strict import controls were to segregate the domestic economy from external competition.

The first decade of planning and market socialism (1951–61) had mixed results. Though the foundations for industrialization were built, and India was on its way to having a large industrial sector, there were heavy costs. In particular, agriculture suffered and food production and lack of wage goods became an important bottleneck towards sustainable growth. Though the ISI strategy continued well into the 1970s its direction was modified and more emphasis given to agricultural development and the alleviation of chronic food shortages and even famines.

Table 9.1 India: economic data

Year	GDP (1980 Rsbn)	Growth (%)	Inflation (%)	Investment/ GDP (%)	Trade deficit GDP (%)
1960	630.2	3.56	2.97	15.00	12.72
1961	652.65	2.93	4.12	14.90	2.17
1962	671.0	4.70	9.09	15.43	2.09
1963	703.38	7.05	9.06	15.91	1.95
1964	752.98	−1.51	9.30	15.90	2.13
1965	741.6	−0.28	13.37	16.79	2.20
1966	739.53	6.42	8.04	16.75	2.69
1967	786.98	4.09	0.00	15.93	2.30
1968	819.13	5.51	4.22	16.07	1.20
1969	864.25	5.92	3.33	16.05	0.46
1970	915.43	3.15	5.30	15.75	0.17
1971	944.23	0.03	11.16	16.14	0.70
1972	944.5	2.50	18.70	16.71	−0.06
1973	968.15	1.00	17.91	15.70	0.36
1974	977.8	7.36	−2.95	15.62	1.16
1975	1,049.8	3.45	6.67	17.38	1.19
1976	1,086.0	6.55	3.53	18.78	−0.21
1977	1,157.1	6.97	1.97	19.14	−0.26
1978	1,237.7	−2.06	15.57	19.29	0.20
1979	1,212.2	3.55	11.36	19.69	1.29
1980	1,255.2	6.10	9.30	19.79	3.12
1981	1,331.7	4.23	7.87	20.08	3.21
1982	1,388.0	6.80	8.99	20.91	2.65
1983	1,482.4	4.76	6.46	20.96	2.31
1984	1,552.9	5.69	6.87	21.26	1.81
1985	1,641.3			21.86	0.40

Source: International Financial Statistics Yearbook, International Monetary Fund, Washington, DC, various years. Fiscal year data are converted to calendar years where applicable

Table 9.1 gives some crucial time-series indicators of the Indian economy during 1960–85. A comparison series of comparative data (in Table 9.3) for two years, 1965 and 1985, highlights the progress made during the recent two decades. Published data for both countries are in fiscal years (April to March for India; July to June for Pakistan). For the purposes of this chapter all data have been converted to calendar years.

The economic performance during the 1960s was very uneven with some negative growth rates. The latter is unusual in an economy with large-scale industrialization and massive government expenditure. It can be explained by the agricultural cycle whereby a bad (disastrous) harvest could lead to a rapid decline in output given the dependence of the economy on the agricultural sector. The shortage of wage goods (and food) began a relative price increase, which, given the downward inflexibility of industrial wages and prices, led to high inflation. The successive droughts of 1964 and 1965 show negative growth rates for the whole economy as well as exceptionally high inflation. In the absence of food imports and foreign aid the economy would have suffered from major famines and massive deprivation.

Recent years have seen the relative decline of agriculture as a share of GDP, as manufactures and particularly services have grown to fill the gap. In addition, partly as a result of political re-orientation after the death of Mrs Indira Gandhi and partly due to internal economic dynamics, the country has moved away from its stress on import substitution and turned increasingly to export promotion. Even though the trade deficit remains large, due to the imports of intermediate investment goods, exports are now a much higher proportion of GDP. After the so called 'green revolution', essentially a rise in agricultural productivity through the use of new varieties of seeds and fertilizers, the country is now self-sufficient in basic food items and can even export small quantities of wheat and rice.[4]

India responded reasonably well to the oil crisis, an adverse supply shock that bedevilled most economies in the 1970s and early 1980s. The inward looking orientation of the industrial structure, and the adaptability of domestic technology aided by high reserves of skilled manpower, was a blessing in the sense that the economy could cut down its oil imports without major rationing and failure of infrastructure. The low growth of the early 1970s, caused both by war with Pakistan (see later) and the oil price rise, was coupled with high inflation between 1970 and 1973. But the economy bounced back with surprising agility as witnessed by the period 1974–8; low inflation (including a negative one) and high growth continued until the harvest failure and the second oil shock in the late 1970s. India currently produces over 70 per cent of its petroleum needs; in 1980 the figure was around 34 per cent.[5]

At present the economy looks stable with growth rates around 5–6 per cent and inflation rates at similar levels. The exceptionally serious drought of 1987 (reportedly the worst this century) means that GDP growth for fiscal year 1987/88 is expected to be a low of 2 per cent. However, this is an aberration as far as the general trend is concerned. The economy is being increasingly opened up, particularly for consumption goods, and the role of the tradeables sector will play a larger role in the future. The investment share remains very high and with the expected reduction in the capital–output ratio, as industries producing wage goods (like textiles) increase in relative importance compared to heavy industry, the growth rate should be even higher. This is important since per capita income is still abysmally low and in the absence of major income distributional changes poverty remains widespread.

On the basis of aggregate GNP, India ranks among the fifteen largest economies of the world. India also belongs to the group of the ten largest industrial nations of the world. In terms of technical manpower the country ranks third in the world – after the USA and USSR. But in terms of per capita income it is among the twenty poorest nations of the world. It is estimated that 273 million people, about 36 per cent of the population, live below the poverty line. The crucial concept to note here is the size of the country. Thus every aggregate value tends to be high whereas the per capita average is exceedingly low. This perspective must be always remembered in evaluating Indian data; it will become even more crucial in defence-related activities.

The best way to understand both the economies of India and Pakistan, as well as the relation of military expenditure to the macro-economy, is through the concepts of structuralism. Instead of the aggregate nature of the economic system, a common foundation of demand management and supply consideration of classical Keynesian models, structuralist theories emphasize the dualism or dichotomy that characterize less developed countries' (LDCs) socio-economic structures. The best economic way to identify the dualism is through the Hicksian flex-price fix-price distinction. The fix-price system behaves in Keynesian fashion; there is usually surplus capacity and aggregate demand (through inventory adjustments) determines output. Mark-up pricing, through unit costs and the profit rate, determines the price level in this sector. Thus cost inflation is an important ingredient of overall inflationary pressures. The flex-price sector, on the other hand, obeys a Walrasian adjustment mechanism whereby excess demand is sought to be corrected by price adjustment. Output supply depends on technology (and fixed factors such as land or capital) whereas price inflation is motivated by demand.

The traditional structuralist literature labelled these two dichotomous sectors as manufacture and agriculture. A broader distinction seems to be between urban and rural sectors or between large-scale and small-scale producers of goods. The crucial distinction is the ability, in terms of cost, technology and profitability, to hold inventories. Small peasant farmers (the majority) fall within the flex-price sector since they are forced to sell their marketable surplus as quickly as possible. The same is true for producers of small-scale industrial output. On the other hand major industries, and even large land-holders, can afford to wait (at least in the short term) until demand picks up.

The role of military expenditure on the economy, within this framework, becomes complex. It is not simply a vehicle of aggregate demand creation; nor is it just an agent of crowding out. If it creates demand in the fix-price sector (say through the production of armaments) then employment and income here will rise. This creates additional demand for the flex-price sector's output (food, basic consumption) which in turn accelerates inflation there. The feedback through workers' higher wage demands (due to increase in cost of living) produces inflationary pressures in the fix-price sector also. If workers are strong enough (as they usually are in the modern sectors of LDCs) then there may even be a rise in real wages; as profit rates erode as a consequence, the outcome may be a fall in output. Further, a possible decline in profitability will cause a fall in the growth of capital formation; hence the economy suffers in the long run. The problem is exacerbated by the defence sectors since inter-industrial linkages are low and technological spin-offs, for growth and investment, weak.

Another lesson that structuralism teaches us is that balanced growth between the two sectors is the optimum way to increase the efficiency of the economy. Concentrating on the agriculture/manufacture dichotomy, the central problem of underdevelopment often lies in low productivity, low investment and low growth of the agricultural sector. Manufacturing needs agricultural growth as a potential market, inputs for its own product as well as to moderate inflationary wage demands that come from food price rises. A virtuous cycle can be set up by investing in agriculture and thus improving both its and the total economy's growth rates. Unfortunately, private investors and rural landlords in LDCs are rarely interested in investment and technological progress either because of extreme risk aversion or due to lack of a profit maximizing motive. It is generally the government's task to do this type of investment with returns that come in the very long term as well as having social externalities. Yet this type of investment does not have the vote-catching ability of more obvious spending on social goods such as education or health; neither is there the appeal of 'eternal vigilance' propagated by the defence spenders. Cross-section evidence suggests that this type of expenditure tends to get crowded out as military spending increases. The direct stimulus provided by the military for employment or manufacturing demand as well as the probable spin-offs from defence investment, may not be able to compensate for lower agricultural investment by the government consequent to higher military expenditures. In so far as crowding out occurs this particular form may be the most pernicious.

The economy of Pakistan

The theoretical remarks, made earlier, apply also to the Pakistani economy. There are also major similarities in the evolution of the two economies, particularly in the earlier years. The similarity is not surprising given the importance of agriculture, the influence of the weather cycles, the geographical proximity of the countries and their common socio-economic background. Tables 9.2 and 9.3 provide economic data for Pakistan; they reveal both historical change as well as a comparative picture over the two decades 1965–1985.

Table 9.2 Pakistan: economic data

Year	GDP (1980 Rsbn)	Growth (%)	Inflation (%)	Investment/ GDP (%)	Foreign income GDP (%)
1960	106.58	3.15	5.21	13.86	−0.13
1961	109.94	6.73	0.00	14.94	−0.12
1962	117.34	6.25	0.45	16.33	−0.21
1963	124.67	4.33	6.28	17.96	−1.35
1964	130.07	5.63	5.91	16.75	−1.45
1965	137.39	1.40	5.18	15.10	0.34
1966	139.31	0.17	11.74	15.01	1.39
1967	139.55	5.13	4.75	14.54	−0.13
1968	146.71	1.33	2.59	14.16	−0.08
1969	148.66	−0.86	2.52	14.34	−0.06
1970	147.37	0.56	4.92	14.16	−0.08
1971	148.19	3.67	6.74	13.29	−0.01
1972	153.63	6.21	15.66	12.00	0.44
1973	163.17	5.06	23.04	11.84	0.7
1974	171.43	4.60	22.39	13.44	0.88
1975	179.32	4.19	12.15	16.57	1.68
1976	186.84	5.97	10.69	18.53	2.99
1977	197.99	6.40	9.02	17.92	5.33
1978	210.65	6.85	5.48	17.13	7.17
1979	225.09	7.83	10.50	17.32	7.63
1980	242.72	6.57	10.00	16.51	7.98
1981	258.68	6.31	9.03	15.36	8.01
1982	275.00	5.86	5.71	15.48	9.43
1983	291.12	6.69	9.63	15.41	10.16
1984	310.59	7.74	5.86	15.09	8.72
1985	334.63				7.83

Source: *International Financial Statistics Yearbook*, International Monetary Fund, Washington, DC, various years. Fiscal year data are converted to calendar years where applicable.

Table 9.3 Comparative economic data: India and Pakistan

	India		Pakistan	
	1965	1985	1965	1985
1. Population (m)	482.7	750.9	52.2	96.2
2. GDP ($m)	46,260	175,710	5,450	28,240
3. Share of agriculture (%)	47	31	40	25
4. Share of industry (%)	22	27	20	28
5. Government consumption/GDP (%)	10	12	11	12
6. Domestic saving/GDP (%)	14	21	13	5
7. Value added in agriculture (1980 $m)	46,456	61,710	5,007	7,231
8. Value added in manufacture (1980 $m)	16,281	30,035	2,359	5,624
9. External public debt/GNP (%)	15.2	13.5	30.7	31.7
10. Infant mortality rate (per 1,000)	151	89	149	115

Source: World Bank, *World Development Report 1987*, Oxford University Press, New York, 1987
Note: The 1965 population for Pakistan was derived by using a 3.1 per cent growth rate between 1965 and 1985. Figures from standard sources cannot be used as they include that of East Pakistan for 1965.

A number of prominent differences between the two economies must be emphasized. The vagaries of partition, determined by the religions of the two peoples involved, meant that many of the manufacturing industries inherited from colonial days fell to India and were lost to the new state of Pakistan. Incidentally, the same happened to ordnance factories and arms production. For example, in (the old) East Pakistan there was a major jute producing agricultural sector; but the jute mills were mostly in (Indian) West Bengal. Hence, Pakistan was much more dependent on agriculture almost by physical necessity. Even though ISI was also emphasized by the planners here, the door was always kept open for agriculture-based exports. The underlying economic philosophy of inward looking development was always buttressed by elements of international competitiveness. There were less trade barriers; tariffs were emphasized rather than quotas; small-scale industrialization was encouraged primarily for world markets; foreign aid was strongly welcomed and political patronage and influence were bargained for international aid, particularly from the West. This is clearly reflected in the low investment output ratio coupled with high growth (see Table 9.2); foreign aid and small-scale labour intensive industrialization would produce this phenomenon.

The oil price rise was definitely inflationary for Pakistan because cost-push factors, both in oil-based energy and manufactures, produced double digit inflation for the first time. But the country took major advantage of its religious–cultural proximity to the Middle Eastern oil states by substantial exportation of labour. The difference between GDP and GNP in the post-1973 period (see Table 9.2) arises out of substantial factor incomes from abroad, much of it by expatriate labour. As the dual economy was characterized by surplus labour and disguised unemployment it was easy to provide oil-rich economies with the labour force they lacked. In addition, skilled manpower is abundant in Pakistan, given the high level of educational standards, and this was sorely needed in the oil boom countries. Pakistani firms, particulary in construction and services, also contributed substantially to exports, specifically in invisible exports. Interestingly enough Pakistan even suffered from the consequences of the so-called 'Dutch disease'. The influx of exogenous income, and the increase in national wealth (produced by a higher value of exported labour), produced a real exchange depreciation and a shortage of people (particularly the able bodied in rural areas) in the workforce. This caused traditional exports to decline and may cause future problems particularly if the beneficial effects dry up.

The most important phenomenon, from the military–political point of view, was the dismemberment in 1971 of Pakistan into Bangladesh and the old country. This was clearly an example of the most important crisis that Third World countries face – the crisis of legitimacy. Unpopularity and unacceptability of the regime and government were converted to the illegitimacy of the state. Lack of democratic foundations meant that it was difficult to hold together two disparate parts of the country only through religious fundamentalism. The remarkable economic aspect of this primarily political crisis was the incredible resilience of the economy. After having lost about half of the economy (country), output returned and rapidly surpassed the pre-crisis period. The benefits of the (international) oil boom to the Pakistani economy helped considerably in this transformation as well as the strict controls by successive governments.

Currently the economy is growing in healthy fashion with 1987 GDP in current prices at Rs602.19bn. There is greater emphasis on export promoting industrialization, given the current orthodoxy. The debt problem remains of crucial concern; it is a major international debtor and though not in the Latin American class can still create problems of solvency particularly as the Middle-East oil boom is no longer present as a rich source of foreign exchange. Foreign aid remains an important prop for the country particularly after the Reagan administration's assistance. The

Table 9.4 Military data: India

Year	Military expenditure (1980 $m)	Burden D/Y (%)	Budget share (%)	Arms imports (1980 $m)	Arms production (1980 $m)
1960	1,586	1.90	23.14	283.63	0
1961	1,704	2.05	23.0	416.60	0
1962	2,349	2.75	26.45	104.54	0
1963	3,843	4.30	36.29	164.49	0
1964	3,761	3.93	34.85	111.45	37.57
1965	3,667	3.89	35.34	230.59	73.70
1966	3,463	3.68	33.51	353.57	67.92
1967	3,213	3.21	32.02	334.35	169.08
1968	3,344	3.21	34.58	392.01	226.88
1969	3,538	3.22	33.99	517.29	244.22
1970	3,645	3.13	32.26	505.76	247.11
1971	4,338	3.61	32.94	547.27	248.56
1972	4,580	3.81	33.20	952.34	317.92
1973	4,049	3.29	32.02	677.94	278.90
1974	3,766	3.03	29.09	511.15	297.69
1975	4,237	3.17	26.79	186.01	251.45
1976	4,937	3.60	28.91	566.49	365.61
1977	4,843	3.29	26.26	1,139.9	404.63
1978	4,898	3.11	23.75	720.98	278.90
1979	5,196	3.37	25.43	382.01	293.36
1980	5,632	3.53	26.85	1,106.8	423.41
1981	6,016	3.55	26.57	1,438.9	434.98
1982	6,534	3.70	26.11	1,342.0	271.68
1983	6,812	3.61	24.98	1,619.5	362.72
1984	7,190	3.64	23.14	1,033.3	335.26
1985	7,528	3.61	22.45	1,221.4	365.61

Source: SIPRI data base. Military expenditure data are estimates based on national budgets. Arms imports and production data are based on SIPRI trend indicator values. They are not additive since methods of calculation are different. However, the trends are comparable.

Afghan crisis has created certain strains in the economy particularly in the wake of the massive refugee problem (5 million people); but once again foreign aid has alleviated some of the difficulty. The foundations for democracy remain weak; a major political crisis can still destabilize the economy. But overall economic conditions are not unfavourable by historical standards. The major problem seems to be security to which we now turn.

Military security

For poor countries security should not be defined in terms of military and strategic factors alone. The socio-economic dimensions of security are vital in understanding the nature of the security problem. Even though, in this section, we concentrate on military issues alone its implications for the wider debate should be clear.

Table 9.5 Military data: Pakistan

Year	Military expenditure (1980 $m)	Burden D/Y (%)	Budget share (%)	Arms imports (1980 $m)	Regional share (%)
1960	464	4.31	29.12	47.66	22.63
1961	459	4.13	26.09	36.13	21.22
1962	436	3.68	25.12	95.31	15.66
1963	474	3.76	27.63	50.73	10.98
1964	534	4.06	27.68	41.51	12.43
1965	859	6.19	35.02	45.35	18.98
1966	1,003	7.13	39.07	372.02	22.46
1967	817	5.80	36.49	135.28	20.27
1968	839	5.66	36.77	152.96	20.06
1969	915	6.09	38.25	69.18	20.55
1970	998	6.70	41.39	99.92	21.49
1971	1,195	7.98	49.76	310.53	21.60
1972	1,323	8.53	51.81	316.68	22.41
1973	1,184	7.18	43.04	87.62	22.63
1974	1,157	6.68	38.94	191.39	23.50
1975	1,164	6.43	37.00	83.78	21.55
1976	1,167	6.18	36.85	77.63	19.00
1977	1,175	5.88	34.67	343.58	19.52
1978	1,278	6.01	33.32	375.86	20.69
1979	1,375	6.05	33.56	222.14	20.93
1980	1,432	5.84	31.76	380.48	20.27
1981	1,584	6.06	33.36	216.75	20.84
1982	1,832	6.60	35.89	462.72	21.90
1983	1,953	6.64	33.84	250.58	22.28
1984	2,083	6.64	33.12	519.22	22.46
1985	2,314	6.85	34.27	529.59	23.51

Source: SIPRI data base. Military expenditure data are estimates based on national budgets. Arms imports and production data are based on SIPRI trend indicator values. They are not additive since methods of calculation are different. However, the trends are comparable.

Table 9.6 Military capability: India and Pakistan, 1985 (values and ranks)

	India Value	Rank	Pakistan Value	Rank
Milex ($m)	7,493	16	2,378	35
Armed forces (1,000s)	1,515	4	644	9
Arms imports ($m)	2,300	3	480	27
Military burden (%)	3.8	59	6.4	36
Arms imports/total imports (%)	15.5	20	8.2	30
Milex per capita ($)	9	111	23	84
Milex per soldier ($)	4,793	91	6.5	109
Armed forces (per 1,000)	2	116	6.5	62

Source: World Military Expenditure and Arms Transfers 1987, US Arms Control and Disarmament Agency, Washington, DC, 1988

Tables 9.4 and 9.5 give time-series data for the two countries regarding defence spending, military burden, government budget shares, arms imports and production. Table 9.6 provides recent information on force structures and military capabilities. To illustrate the difference in size the ranking of the two countries, in the world league tables, is also provided. For India it should be noted, as before, that the numbers in absolute levels provide remarkably high ranks. In per capita terms, on the other hand, the ranks become much lower. This again emphasizes, in different ways, the notion of the 'largeness' of India and the asymmetries in the two countries' sizes.

India and Pakistan have fought three full-scale wars, and numerous border skirmishes, during the last 41 years as nation states. The precipitous rise in defence burdens, with overshooting in both cases, reveals the importance of these wars in 1965–6 and 1971–2. In addition, of course, India's border war with China (October 1962) contributed to a sharp rise in defence burden in 1963. Clearly the arms race, in the sub-continent, is an important reason for their increasing military expenditure and relatively high defence burden (given the extreme poverty of the region). The first war, over territorial rights of the northern province of Kashmir, took place in 1948. The second, in 1965, was also motivated by the Kashmir dispute; but the major actions of the 22-day war in September were in the Punjab (as well as partly in Sind and Rajasthan). Both these left the eastern part of Pakistan relatively unaffected. The third war, in 1971, took place at both borders and was directly related to the secessionist or independence movement in the erstwhile East Pakistan. It was a humiliating and major military defeat for Pakistan with the loss of its eastern wing, creating the new state of Bangladesh, as well as the loss of a great amount of territory and armour in the West.

Pakistan is almost unique (at least in the twentieth century) in the sense that it is a modern nation state created by an idea – as well as an idea that motivates the workings of that state. Its creation, out of the British Indian empire, was done hastily and was based on religious differences, rather than any fundamental political, socio-economic, geographical or racial differences. Its conflict with India began from birth and was baptized with blood (over 1 million people died and 14 million refugees were created during partition for both sides); it has continued ever since. Its perception has been that of a threatened country with an exceedingly hostile neighbour. However, the most crucial element in that view stems from the sheer size of the adversary. The fact that India is overwhelmingly large, in terms of relative military strength, dominates Pakistan's threat concept.

External military threat and security perceptions for Pakistan come solely from India and nowhere else. In spite of the efforts of successive US administrations (from the 1950s) to portray the Soviet Union as an important threat it is doubtful whether the political and military authorities ever thought of it in that fashion. Superpower rivalry was utilized primarily to enlist support from the US to defend itself from India. In the 1950s Prime Minister Nehru of India began the Non-Aligned Movement (NAM) as a Third World (political) solidarity movement to stand independent of the military rivalry of the two major powers. Using the principle of 'if they are not for us they are against us' the US began a policy of regional security groupings of which Pakistan became a multiple and major member (CENTO, SEATO). Even after the Sino-Indian war (in 1962) when the US provided huge quantities of economic aid, as well as some arms, to India, and Pakistan was naturally suspicious and unhappy, it failed to have a *rapprochement* with the Soviet Union (see SIPRI 1971). Even Afghanistan, in recent years, has been utilized as a convenient method to receive large military aid from the US but which cannot be conceivably used against the Soviet Union.

Regional rivalry, and United States involvement, has forced India to turn increasingly towards the USSR for military support. It is but a quirk of history that the international alignments, in sub-continental regional security, are so explicitly drawn for the long run. Without NAM and the regional military organizations the alliances could have been totally different.

The fundamental point to note is that the central security concept for Pakistan has two dimensions: due to history and size India poses the major (only) threat; whoever is for 'us' militarily (China, US) must be against India and vice versa (the USSR). The dyadic relation is asymmetric. To Pakistan, India is very large and hegemonic. Hence, a very large effort is required to counter that threat. No economic sacrifice is too much for eternal (military) vigilance. There is little extra-territorial/geographical ambition, and international relations are totally motivated by the friends (enemies) of India. As we shall see later, Indian perceptions are much less dominated by Pakistani threats; its security interests lie in many other directions (such as China and the Indian Ocean); though defence is a vital ingredient in the government's welfare function there are also other priorities that can claim equal importance.

Another aspect of the military situation in Pakistan deserves a brief mention. The military has also been directly involved in internal security, which has led to numerous declarations of martial law, a number of military coups and long periods of military rule. The Pakistan army has been both the servant of the state, as well as its master. Thus, democratic traditions are weak. In spite of President Zia ul Haq's recent death, the military remains potentially dominant in the political system. The implication of this stranglehold is that defence spending suffers much less from 'inertia' compared to a civilian dominated democratic political structure (as in India). Hence, military expenditures can be raised more effectively without worries from politicians or internal bureaucratic influences. In a sense the 'rational actor' model, with the military authorities (or their civilian colleagues) allocating government budgets and national product between civilian and defence purposes, is an appropriate paradigm for Pakistan. The various configurations of events, discussed earlier, implies that a neoclassical theoretical structure, with the rational state allocating expenditure subject to environmental (security) and economic constraints, is suitable here.

In terms of force structure Pakistan has generally accorded primacy to the army, which has 450,000 active forces as compared to the total of some 640,000.[5] Reserves are also very large accounting for over half a million forces; the overwhelming number is in the army. Significant arms imports, aided by large foreign military assistance, as well as limited domestic production, has helped the armed forces to build up a sizeable arsenal. This includes 1,600 tanks as well as 381 combat aircraft, many armed with Sidewinder and Exocet missiles.

Given the geo-strategic environment of Pakistan, surrounded by perceived hostile neighbours (India, Afghanistan) along land borders and difficult terrain, it is not surprising that the army is considered vital to its defences. However, increasing importance has been given to the air force over the last one and a half decades. The failure of the blitzkrieg-type operation against India in the 1971 war first alerted the defence planners about the usefulness of a modern air command. Currently, air modernization is somewhat advanced; in particular, its nineteen squadrons of ground attack fighter aircraft (and interceptors) have achieved equal parity with its Indian counterparts even though the Indian air force is overall much larger. Much more needs to be done, however, if armaments balance on the Indian front is to be maintained. In 1987, Pakistan urgently demanded US AWACS aircraft ostensibly to counteract Afghan and Soviet air violations. This may not be met given Indian sensibility regarding such sophisticated equipment and a new technological arms race in the region.

However, it demonstrates Pakistan's interest and willingness to acquire state of the art air defences.

Pakistan is currently concentrating on the navy and a modernization programme seems to be on its way. This must be totally dependent on arms imports given the limited ability of domestic industries. More important, the choice, with other competing and pressing demands, seems to be motivated by Indian naval procurement during this decade.

The catalogue, and evolution, of procurement decisions once again clearly reflects the fundamental fact: Pakistan's choices, both in terms of aggregate expenditures as well as detailed force capabilities, has followed Indian patterns. The arms race is relatively asymmetric. Equally important, domestic constraints do not seem to have a significant effect in shaping defence spending and procurement. Partly this is because of the relatively healthy state of the economy. It can also be explained by US foreign military assistance (FMA); in 1985 FMA of $325m[7] accounted for almost 70 per cent of arms imports ($480m)[8] and 15 per cent of the defence budget. However, the most important factor that overrides economic constraints is the relative power of the military both in government administration as well as in the popular ethos. The military can, and does, get (most of) what it likes.

The Indian case has certain similarities. Defence, and military security, is occasionally akin to Caesar's wife – beyond question. But the strong democratic tradition, the apolitical stance of the military and its reluctance to get involved in internal security matters, greater openness through the often adversarial press as well as the intense pressure for competing expenditures in the public sector, make economic and other environmental constraints more important in the determination of defence spending. Though threat and security still remain paramount, the pull of 'inertia' often reins back excessive and unwarranted outlays.

India's geo-political security concerns are determined not only by Pakistan but also by China, as well as its growing importance as a regional and world power. It now has military commitments on the western and northern frontiers with Pakistan and China; it is also actively involved (50,000 troops) in Sri Lanka. In the 1950s India, pursuing its non-aligned policy, neglected defence and mobilized existing resources for planned industrialization and development. But its naïvety was rudely destroyed in 1961 with the Sino-Indian war when it was manifestly clear that two Third World nations, in spite of great poverty, could still conduct a fratricidal war. Since then, military expenditure, domestic arms production, arms imports as well as force modernization have all continued at a significant rate.

India's armed forces, reported[9] to be over 1.5 million in 1985, are the fourth largest in the world; in terms of arms imports it ranks 3rd; military expenditures give it a world ranking of 16th. It is possibly the Third

World's largest arms producer and, with almost no exports, all output is devoted to domestic military capability.

Almost 90 per cent of the forces constitute the army. It is a formidable fighting force with a range of relatively sophisticated weapons (for local needs). It is thought that the inventory consists of over 3,000 tanks under 46 tank regiments and 2 armoured divisions.[10] The air force is also well equipped with over 100,000 personnel and more than 700 aircraft and 60 armed helicopters. In 1987 licensed production of MiG-27 FGA began. The Soviet Union also supplied its most sophisticated MiG-29 to India and 2 squadrons are fully operational with these multi-role fighters.

The most dramatic development in the 1980s has been the rapid modernization of the navy pushing up arms imports and repairing/refitting capacity domestically. Nineteen eighty-seven saw the delivery of the British Hermes-class aircraft carrier as well as Soviet destroyers (Kashin class). The most publicized event for the last year was the Soviet leasing of a nuclear powered submarine to the navy;[11] this is probably the first time that a Third World maritime power (excluding China) has acquired nuclear-oriented naval technology.

The choice-theoretic reasons for Indian naval modernization, at great cost, are clear enough. India now aspires to be a fully-fledged maritime power, not surprising for a country with such extensive coastlines. The motivation is only partly military. Changes in maritime law[12] and the wealth of the sea have induced countries to claim, protect and defend exclusive economic zones (EEZ) for exploiting the resources of the sea. As India becomes economically more stable, and population pressures increase the demand for resources, it will have to move towards a significant naval presence.

The foregoing analysis points to a significant difference between threat perception, domestic constraints and security relations between India and Pakistan. For the latter, the Indian threat is paramount and overwhelming. Almost all strategic considerations are determined by this unique feature. Even Afghanistan is of minor strategic consequence: as has been claimed 'There have been some clashes along the Pakistan border but so far the most serious threat to Pakistan lies in disorder in and around the refugee camps.'[13] In spite of the weakness of the domestic economy, and the incidence of absolute poverty, the government and state have managed to carry out desired expenditures. In this, help has come from foreign military assistance, co-operation with China and foreign exchange earnings from expatriate labour in the Gulf (including 30,000 contracted military personnel). However, the central reason seems to be the ability of the military to influence the body politic and to legitimize the inevitability of the arms race.

On the other hand, Indian military spending is more subject to checks and balances, both a product of a much larger population with more intense entitlements demands as well as the democratic process. There can be little doubt that the military is a major institutional force; hence its demands need to be taken seriously. The government and the state can still be considered as part of the 'rational actor' paradigm. But domestic constraints are far more important. In terms of international relations, the preoccupation with Pakistan is subservient to the fears of China, the dreams of regional supremacy and the vision of an international role as the 'natural' leader of the Third World. This, therefore, creates an asymmetry in the arms race model.

The second difference, creating another asymmetry, is the variation of size between the two countries. Whatever the index, land mass, national income, population, government budgets, India is considerably larger than its neighbour. Hence these antagonists are significantly unequal in terms of their economic indicators. However, due to the overwhelming threat discussed earlier Pakistan has tried to maintain some form of military parity. For example, Indian GDP, land area and population are respectively about six, eight, seven times higher; but military spending and armed forces are respectively about three and two times as high. The nature of unequal antagonists will feature prominently in the theoretical models that follow (see Appendix A).

Empirical analysis of the military expenditure process of the two countries

Military expenditure for any country depends on the optimal allocation of resources by the state or government. For LDCs, where government participation and intervention (through planning) are crucial, the allocative mechanism becomes even more vital. The choices that are made inevitably reflect the preferences of the government in power. For both India and Pakistan, since the 1960s, security has been of paramount importance. Hence the military expenditure process has often been cushioned from economic problems. The optimal levels of aggregate defence spending, subject to constraints, have often reflected this preference for the primacy of security. The major difference, as analysed above, lies in the democratic process and the involvement of the military in domestic politics. For India, democracy has meant more questions and soul-searching about the economic cost–benefits of defence though not of the central paradigm (that security is paramount). For Pakistan, continuous periods of military rule have meant a much lesser role for 'inertia'.

We therefore propose to use the 'rational actor' paradigm to explain defence expenditures in the Indian sub-continent. This is not to say that bureaucratic/organizational factors are unimportant. The important public choice theory (see Hartley 1987) would also have major implications for defence. However, these become more important at a disaggregated micro-level. At the level of the macro-economy, aggregate military expenditures may conform to government (state) rationality and yet subsume the complications stressed by alternative models.

The other feature of regional defence spending has been its dyadic nature. Though other actors, such as China and the two superpowers, have played interventionist roles the central motivation has been the alleged regional arms race between the two countries. Hence a canonical action–reaction model (supplemented by variables that represent the security/economic environment) between the two countries seems to be suitable as a first approximation.

It is necessary at the outset to specify the way we define an arms race. The fundamental property clearly is the action–reaction process whereby a country responds over time to the other country's threat. A crucial question then arises as to what variables are to be used as parameters in this dynamic process. One point of view is that arms and equipment (weapon stocks) are the relevant variables rather than other elements of the military budget. In other words, the procurement process is essentially driven by the equipment acquisition of countries perceived as a threat. An alternative viewpoint would be that the action–reaction mechanism is represented by the whole military expenditures of the countries concerned. Our models will emphasize this latter view.

The use of an arms race model to explain defence spending can be justified in a number of ways. First, when two countries are rivals from a politico-military point of view an incipient competitive process in military spending can become inevitable (see O'Leary and Coplin 1975). Second, military expenditure increases are often proposed and justified as a response to the rival's defence expenditure. Third, the presence of two dominant players in the security relationship can make each other's defence budget interrelated. Finally, within the government allocative mechanism (where various spending ministries jostle for scarce resources) the existence of the race is often utilized by the defence services to acquire more funding overall.

The empirical model will try to pose and analyse three issues that are of central importance in the context of India and Pakistan's military expenditure process. The relative importance and relevance of military and economic variables in explaining defence spending is crucial. It is also important to note whether the relations are asymmetric or not; in other words are there conceptual differences in the way these two countries view their defence effort. Finally, we need to assess how relevant is the arms race model itself. Alternatively, is there a good case for believing the accepted paradigm that the 'race' actually exists?

As a first approximation therefore, we use the well-known Richardson arms race model to estimate econometrically defence spending patterns of the two countries. Nested tests are utilized to check for the importance of economic variables (constraints) in addition to the basic strategic ones. In differential equation form we have:

$$\dot{M}_1 = aM_1 + bM_2 + X_1 + Z_1 \tag{1}$$
$$\dot{M}_2 = cM_1 + dM_2 + X_2 + Z_2 \tag{2}$$

Here, M_i are the military spending of the two countries; the Zs are vectors of environmental and dummy variables. The parameters b, c represent threat from the antagonists; the parameters a and d represent domestic strategic 'inertia'. The additive constants, the Xs, are core 'grievance' terms that add to military spending even without considering the explicit race and its effects. A dot over a term always denotes a time derivative. To forestall explosive arms races certain general stability conditions are required; these will be checked for the empirical estimates.

It should be emphasized that the above model not only represents a action–reaction model of competitive arms races but can also be derived from fundamental optimizing theory. As Brito (1972) and Simaan and Cruz (1975) have shown, the Richardson arms race model can be derived from intertemporal optimization (using control theory); but their variables (the M_i) are interpreted as missile stocks. In our case, we need to assume that the military stock/expenditure ratio (akin to the capital output ratio) is constant. This is not an unreasonable assumption given the non-substitutable nature of modern defence technology. Then all stock variables can be converted into military expenditure flows and we essentially have the same type of (linear) functions as equations (1) and (2). The only difference is that the coefficients are now contaminated by the two fixed stock/expenditure ratios. But this is not an insuperable problem. Defence technology, for two such close competitors, has many similarities and structures. One country religiously follows the arms acquisition pattern of the other; the armed forces, therefore, tend to end up with similar technologies. Hence a reasonable assumption is that the foregoing ratios are the same. Under these circumstances the model given above can be replicated by a two-country dynamic intertemporal optimization model.

Quite often, however, the levels of military expenditure are not sufficiently illuminating in explaining a country's strategic/military choices. In particular the classic guns-for-butter trade-off needs to be expressed in terms of the opportunity costs of growth reduction through defence allocation. Then, as can be easily shown from a typical growth model, the relevant concept is the military burden, that is, the ratio of military spending to national output.

In a dyadic model, such as that for India and Pakistan, a simple action–reaction empirical model with military burdens as the endogenous variables presents some special problems. This is primarily because the regional conflict occurs among neighbours of 'unequal' size. It is clear from the economic data presented earlier, as well as the relative population size and geographical area, that India and Pakistan can be characterized as the large and small country. This stylized fact of 'unequal antagonists' has an important bearing on strategy, threat and security. The difference comes out sharply when one measures the relative size of the defence effort given by the two relevant ratios – the military burden or the share in the regional total.

Considerations of unequal size imply that the threat perceptions, security consciousness, military reaction functions and economic costs may be asymmetric as between the two agents. The general literature has assumed that the reaction functions are symmetric; a country was identified only by the values of its parameters. In the case of unequal LDCs this will not be the case. For India and Pakistan the asymmetry can be noted in various ways.

Pakistan spends about 7 per cent of its GDP on defence, which India considers an unacceptably high threat. Thus the defence burden of the small country is the relevant threat variable to its adversary. But India spends only about 3 per cent of GDP on its defence; the claim is that because the military burden is only half that of Pakistan the latter should not feel threatened. But from Pakistan's point of view the reality looks different; because India is large and has a high total GDP its burden would have to be commensurately low. Therefore, a low defence burden is not sufficient to assure its adversary that threat is low. In absolute terms India spends over three times as much as Pakistan; thus the former's share in the regional total is 75 per cent or more and it is this that constitutes the threat to the latter. For a large country, the opposition's burden is a threat; for the small country the opposition's regional share is the relevant threat variable. One can easily see that the proxy variables for the unobservables, such as 'threat', are radically different for the unequal antagonists.

Theoretically, it is possible to build complicated analytical models that take into account the various factors discussed above regarding military burdens and shares. Unfortunately, it becomes much more difficult to test them econometrically. The major reason is that we need to quantify weapons stocks as well as flows of defence spending. Data on the former variable, and aggregate measures to use them in macro-models, are not available particularly for LDCs. In what follows, therefore, we restrict ourselves to estimating the behaviour of total military expenditure using data for India and Pakistan. Appendix A describes a theoretical model that may be utilized to explain the dynamics of defence burden and shares.

Before attempting to estimate the variants of the Richardson model, we first have a purely data-based atheoretical evaluation of some of the stylized facts mentioned in the preceding discussions. These are the following: Pakistan has a lower domestic inertia so that its defence spending is relatively independent of economic variables; further, its threat perceptions are dominated ('caused') by the large neighbour; on the other hand, India is more constrained by competing demands for resource allocation and is not always subject to reactive military expenditure; thus, the arms race could be asymmetric.

To check for independence we regress the respective military spending on their three lagged values only and conduct specification tests. The actual results for this third order autoregression are not reported in this chapter but the conclusions are summarized. For Pakistan, the lagged values are significant and the fit is good. But much more important, the specification tests, in terms of checking for serial correlation, normality and homoscedasticity, show that the equation is well specified. For India, on the contrary, there is evidence of serial correlation, non-normal distribution and heteroscedasticity. Thus, for India, the assumption of an independent path of defence spending is not supported by the data. The opposite is true for Pakistan where data-based evidence alone supports the hypothesis of independence from economic factors.

An effective, though atheoretical and data-mining, procedure of noting the action–reaction process is to see whether the opponent's military spending 'causes' the home country's expenditure to respond and change. We therefore check for Granger causality. The three lagged values of the opposition's defence expenditure are added to the list of regressors for the two countries separately and a Granger causality test carried out. The F statistic indicates that Pakistan's military expenditure is not Granger causal with respect to its adversary; but India's defence spending does Granger cause the opposition's defence allocation process. Hence, there is weak evidence of asymmetry.

The foregoing methods, however, have little economic and theoretical implications. It is, therefore, necessary to look at the econometrics of Richardson. The difference equation version of the theoretical specification claims that the first difference of military expenditure is negatively related to its own past level (with the absolute value of the parameter being less than unity). Hence, when the dependent variable is the level of military spending, the coefficient of the lagged endogenous variable should be positive but less than unity. This would also ensure stability.

Among the exogenous variables, the prime candidate is the opponent's defence spending, which should appear with a positive sign. It is not clear a priori whether the current or lagged value should be the appropriate regressor. If the current value is used then the implicit assumption is that the country is responding to 'threat' very quickly. Information is received, processed and utilized fast. Alternatively, the domestic country forms rational expectations, based on the full information set, of its opponent's military spending. These informed forcasts turn out to be substantially correct except, of course, for white noise errors. This representation could be relevant for two close neighbours like India and Pakistan who can predict each other's behaviour reasonably accurately. The similarities of their C^3I as well as military strategies make the assumption of rational expectations a reasonable one. We have used both current and lagged values of the threat variable and report the results separately.

The other military variables that we consider as independent determinants of the defence expenditure process are arms imports and arms production. The former is quantitatively important for both the countries; the latter is included in the regressions for India alone because it has possibly the largest arms industry in the Third World; Pakistan's domestic output for weapons is still low and can be ignored.

A whole host of economic environmental variables can be utilized. We first used the obvious: national income (GDP); presumably its increase will signify an improvement in the economic condition of the country leading to an increase in defence spending. Experimentation with other related economic variables, such as growth rate, industrialization, inflation and so forth, did not give better results. However, it was also presumed that since military expenditure is the exclusive preserve of the government, an indicator of the government's budget constraint would be a useful explanatory variable. The empirical results showed that defence spending was always positively related to total central government expenditure (CGE). But this seems tautologous since for non-inferior public goods one would expect a positive relation almost by definition. Hence, we experimented with the ratio of CGE to GDP, the share of the government in the national economy as an independent determinant of defence spending. This variable represents two rather separate phenomena. First, it is an indication of the relative budget constraint: if the ratio rises then presumably the government is spending more relative to the growth of the aggregate economy. Second, its increase also reflects the growing importance of the public sector in the national economy and could be an indication of expanding state power in the country. One formal problem remains. For many LDCs, total GDP and the ratio of CGE to GDP tend to move upwards with economic development – a variant of 'Wagner's Law'. Thus, use of both these variables in the same equation could produce multicollinearity and possible misspecification. We therefore used only one of the variables in the estimated equations; the choice of which one to use depended on diagnostics and a variable addition test.

The empirical results are given in Table 9.7. Military spending of India and Pakistan is denoted by subscripts 1 and 2. M is military spending; AIMP is arms imports; APROD is arms production; GDP is the gross domestic product; CGESH is the ratio of government expenditure to national output. For each country there are two equations depending on whether current or lagged values of the opponent's military spending have been used as the relevant independent variable. All the estimates are by ordinary least squares (OLS) since the Lagrange multiplier test generally showed no evidence of serial correlation. The diagnostic test statistics, for residual serial correlation, normality and homoscedasticity, are reported in

Table 9.7 Empirical estimates of military expenditures of India and Pakistan, 1960–85

	Equation (3) M_1	Equation (4) M_1	Equation (5) M_2	Equation (6) M_2
Constant	−289	−506	−623	−842
	(−0.67)	(−1.31)	(−2.07)	(3.4)
$M_1(-1)$	0.52	0.59		
	(2.73)	(3.51)		
$M_2(-1)$			0.62	0.56
			(5.55)	(6.3)
M_2		−0.63		
		(−1.12)		
$M_2(-1)$	0.06			
	(0.09)			
M_1				0.1
				(4.0)
$M_1(-1)$			0.08	
			(2.25)	
AIMP	0.06	0.07	0.27	0.20
	(0.18)	(0.21)	(1.66)	(1.44)
APROD	−1.13	−0.83		
	(−1.17)	(−0.85)		
GDP	2.66	3.24		
	(2.64)	(3.36)		
CGESH			41.4	54.0
			(1.86)	(3.06)
R^2	0.9351	0.9391	0.9698	0.9790

Notes: Dependent variables: M_1 (India's military expenditure) and M_2 (Pakistan's military expenditure); t values in parentheses.

Table 9.8 which should be viewed in conjunction with the actual empirical results. Overall, with few exceptions, the equations pass most of the specification tests used for judging the suitability of the empirical model. The fit of each equation is good. Among the four estimated equations, for the two countries, equations (3) and (5) (respectively for India and Pakistan) can be considered the 'best' in terms of an overall evaluation. This evaluation is based on diagnostic checks for (mis)specification, signs of parameters conforming to the theoretical model, as well as the significance of the relevant variables. It is not obvious what levels of significance should be used for simple econometric models, with small samples and few variables, which are expected to capture extremely complex LDC structural relations. For developing countries, small models generally do not perform very well by conventional criteria. In general we have used 10 per cent significance levels throughout this chapter.

For India (see Table 9.7, equation (3)) the inertia parameter is of the order of 0.48 and significant. Thus, an increase of 1 unit of defence spending would reduce the next period increment by about 1/2 units. The effect is important, showing that inertia does exist and serves to restrain

Table 9.8 Diagnostic tests for equations in Table 9.7

	LM version	F version
Equation (3)		
Serial correlation	$\chi^2(1) = 0.63$	$F(1,18) = 0.46$
Normality	$\chi^2(2) = 1.15$	na
Heteroscedasticity	$\chi^2(1) = 2.60$	$F(1,18) = 2.09$
Equation (4)		
Serial correlation	$\chi^2(1) = 0.05$	$F(1,18) = 0.03$
Normality	$\chi^2(2) = 1.17$	na
Heteroscedasticity	$\chi^2(1) = 2.14$	$F(1,18) = 1.69$
Equation (5)		
Serial correlation	$\chi^2(1) = 0.61$	$F(1,19) = 0.47$
Normality	$\chi^2(2) = 0.99$	na
Heteroscedasticity	$\chi^2(1) = 0.08$	$F(1,18) = 0.06$
Equation (6)		
Serial correlation	$\chi^2(1) = 3.07$	$F(1,19) = 2.66$
Normality	$\chi^2(2) = 1.22$	na
Heteroscedasticity	$\chi^2(1) = 0.00$	$F(1,19) = 0.00$

Notes: Lagrange multiplier (LM) test of serial correlation. Normality based on a test of skewness and kurtosis of residuals. Heteroscedasticity test based on the regression of squared residuals on squared fitted values. *F* stands for the *F* statistic.

the military expenditure dynamics though it is not exceptionally strong. The threat variable, emanating from Pakistan's military spending, is insignificant in both estimates; for the current value case the sign also is wrong (negative). India's military spending seems to be largely autonomous of its neighbour's military actions. Domestic economic factors significantly influence defence spending. The coefficient for GDP, at somewhat less than 3, shows a positive relation between national product and defence. However, the coefficient (representing the incremental defence burden) is lower than the defence spending-to-GDP ratio of recent years. The variable CGESH also gave a significant positive coefficient when included. But the equation was very badly specified. It failed all the diagnostic checks and showed evidence of serial correlation, non-normality and heteroscedasticity. This misspecification forced us to reject that equation and conclude that GDP was a 'better' independent variable. Oddly, both arms imports and defence production have no effect on the evolution of military spending; the latter even has the wrong sign.

For Pakistan (Table 9.7, equations (5) and (6)) the inertia effect is weaker; it is of the order of 0.38 for equation (5). This indicates that domestic fatigue at increasing military spending has a rather small effect on the final defence allocation of the government. The threat variable, from Indian military spending, is statistically significant. There does seem to be a reaction mechanism that helps to boost Pakistan's defence spending when the opponent does so. However, the coefficient is not large. In effect, when India's expenditure increases by 1 unit (in constant dollars) then Pakistan allocates around 0.1 extra units to the military. Since the regional shares between the two are of the order of 3:1, it is clear that the larger part of defence spending in Pakistan is motivated by other sources than its traditional foe.

Arms imports significantly contribute to additional military expenditure. It must be stressed that this effect does not imply that the arms were actually paid for through the defence budget. It must be emphatically stated that military spending and arms trade data are not additive. In addition, much of recent arms imports are part of the United States aid package and do not need payment, at least immediately. Yet, there are fundamental structural interconnections that explain why arms imports would raise defence spending. First, clearly, is the direct cause: some arms imports have to be paid directly from the budget. Second, arms imports raise domestic defence costs indirectly: training, infrastructure, repairs and fitting, additional C^3I expenditure to accommodate sophisticated equipments and so forth, are all responsible. Third, if the capital labour ratios are inflexible more procurement may imply more use of well-trained personnel. Fourth, arms purchase may itself be a reflection of the incipient arms race; hence aggregate expenditure will rise simultaneously since threat perceptions have increased. Whatever the reason, this coefficient highlights the high economic costs, in terms of defence spending rise, of weapons importation even though they may have been received as aid, grants or concessionary long-term loans.

As regards economic variables, GDP was consistently insignificant. However, the ratio variable CGESH gave significant coefficients and the estimated equations were also well specified. As discussed earlier this variable could be an indicator of the government's budget constraint. But more important, it reflects the role of the state in economic activity. For Pakistan, as the government (state) became more important, military expenditure also rose. This is an effect of the military regimes that have ruled the country for most of the years under investigation, either directly with martial law or indirectly through undemocratic governments. Overall, economic factors play a minor role in explaining defence spending (GDP and other variables were not significant); but, the role of the state was a crucial determinant both in terms of the economy as well as of military strategy.

One additional estimate, related to our earlier discussion on threat emanating from India's larger size, was also done. Essentially, this shows whether the regional share has any effect on the military expenditure process (see Table 9.9 where SHAR represents the opponent's military spending as a proportion of the region's total). The equations for both countries showed an autoregressive error term that was not significantly different from unity. Hence the first difference of military expenditure $(DM = M_t - M_{t-1})$ was used as the relevant dependent variable. The variable SHAR represents the ratio of military expenditure to the regional total for the other country. Once again, for India, its opponent's share in the regional military allocation had no effects. On the other hand, Pakistan was affected by India's relative strength as given by the latter's share in the regional total. This reflects another type of asymmetric behaviour as between the two countries. Table 9.9 provides the estimates.

Table 9.9 Empirical estimate of the effect of regional shares on military expenditure increments

	India	Pakistan
	DM_1	DM_2
Constant	253.0	−893.0
	(0.44)	(−1.52)
SHAR	−0.76	12.13
	(−0.03)	(1.65)
R^2	−0.434	0.0662

Notes: Dependent variables: $DM_i = M_i - M_i(-1)$, $i = 1, 2$; t statistic in parentheses.

We also experimented with a number of dummy variables: the Chinese threat to India; the role of Afghanistan; the two wars fought during this period, 1960–85. None of the results was changed dramatically and the differences in the values of the coefficients were marginal. The results are not reported in this chapter.

To sum up, we need to understand three issues regarding the military expenditure process of India and Pakistan: the relative importance of military and economic factors; the possibility of asymmetric behaviour; and the existence of an arms race. We summarize each in turn.

For India, economic factors, as well as domestic inertia, which is also dependent on the state of the economy, are essential explanatory factors in understanding its defence spending evolution. On the other hand, threat perception emanating from Pakistan has no discernible effect. Nor does arms import and production influence military expenditure. Thus, certain traditional security variables have little impact. The situation is radically different for Pakistan. The overall security environment, in terms of the Indian threat and concomitant arms import, has an important role to play. In addition, the role of the state in the politico-economic structure of the nation, influences defence allocation. The impact of standard economic variables, such as GDP or growth rates, seems to be minor. This could be due to the all pervading influence of the military in political life, a state of affairs that has continued throughout Pakistan's history though with notable exceptions.

The econometric results also show that the strategic relations are asymmetric. Pakistan is relatively more influenced by its larger neighbour. The threat perception influences Pakistan's military spending in three ways: India's defence spending has a direct positive impact; arms imports rise due to a procurement 'race' that indirectly influences the defence budget; and, a fall in its regional share, leading to a perceived weakness in strength, causes defence expenditure to rise. However, it should be noted that the aggregate effect of all these variables is not very high.

The last question – as to whether an arms race does exist – is the most difficult to answer. The asymmetry noted earlier, implies that the race at best is only relevant to one of the two countries. In spite of the rhetoric, which claims that India is threatened by Pakistan's military power, there is little formal evidence that an action–reaction mechanism is actually present from India's point of view. Rather, Indian defence spending has an autonomous dynamic constrained by the domestic political, technological and economic process. But even for Pakistan, where threat variables are important, the impact of Indian behaviour should not be overestimated. The direct effect of the threat variable is weak (the coefficient is of the order of 0.1); and even the indirect effects through arms imports tell only a partial story since many other influences (Afghanistan, Soviet Union, US influence, procurement cycles, military status, etc.) affect the acquisition of foreign weapons.

Overall, it is safe to conclude that the much vaunted arms race in the Indian sub-continent is probably more a matter of political rhetoric than an empirically supported description of the military expenditure process. Though some evidence exists that defence allocation has been motivated by action–reaction behaviour, its role has been weak and in a more general sense dominated by the influence of domestic factors. Arms control will, therefore, depend more on changing priorities within the countries concerned than by one forever blaming the other for fostering increasing belligerence. This is true for both countries, though more so for India as the larger and more influential partner in the relationship.

The trade-off between defence and development

There is now a large literature on the general relationship between defence and development. The empirical analysis concentrates on the rate of growth because developmental factors are not easily identified let alone tested. Much of it is heuristic but the formal literature has also grown fast in recent years (for a detailed survey see Deger 1986). The impetus to the empirical work, that focuses on the effect of military spending on economic growth, came from Benoit's seminal paper (1978). Contrary to expectation he found that defence spending has a positive effect on the rate of growth of national product (income) in LDCs. Benoit used cross-section data and estimated a single-equation simple tri-variate relation with military burden and investment affecting growth rates.

In a sense most of the econometrics studies on the subject are a response to the challenge posed by the Benoit result. He identified a number of positive and negative channels through which defence is expected to affect growth. The negative effects are standard: resource transfer from investment to defence; and the fact that the government sector (including the military) exhibits no measured productivity increases, hence its relative expansion lowers the growth rate. But Benoit also identified a whole host of factors which directly or indirectly increases growth. He claims

> Defence programs of most countries make tangible contributions to the civilian economies by (1) feeding, clothing, and housing a number of people who would otherwise have to be fed, housed, and clothed by the civilian economy – and sometimes doing so, especially in LDCs, in ways that involve sharply raising their nutritional and other consumption standards and expectations; (2) providing education and medical care as well as vocational and technical training (e.g. in the operation and repair of cars, planes and radios; in hygiene and medical care; in construction methods) that may have high civilian utility; (3) engaging in a variety of communication networks, etc – that may in part serve civilian uses; and (4) engaging in scientific and technical specialties such as hydrographic studies, mapping, aerial surveys, dredging, meteorology, soil conservation, and forestry projects as well as certain quasi-civilian activities such as coast guard, lighthouse operation, customs work, border guard, and disaster relief which would otherwise have to be performed by civilian personnel. Military forces also engage in certain R & D and production activities which diffuse skills to the civilian economy and engage in or finance self-help projects producing certain manufactured items for combined civilian and military use which might not be economically produced solely for civilian demand. (Benoit 1978)

Benoit's econometrics is simplistic since it follows from a rather basic point of view regarding the effect of defence spending on growth. A more complicated formulation would have to take into account quite a few other channels and balance the various influences to produce the net effect. Deger suggests (1986), both from theory and empirical analysis, that the military expenditure growth relation should allow for the following aggregate channels:

1 A direct effect of defence spending on growth through various spin-offs and kick-backs which may on balance be positive (these are essentially the points discussed by Benoit);
2 an indirect effect via the saving rate, reflecting the fact that military

expenditure increases government consumption and reallocates its saving away from productive investment;

3 resource mobilization may also be affected and the propensity of the private sector to save may be diminished as household expenditure goes up to compensate for lower state spending on civilian publicly-funded goods; and

4 open economy considerations that claim that military imports may crowd-out civilian imports and reduce foreign saving entering the country; on the other hand, if military aid is used to reduce domestic burdens or donor countries give more aid to strategic allies then clearly a positive nexus is set up.

Another analytical issue is concerned with the non-linearities (the term is due to Boulding 1974) in the defence-growth relation. Essentially this implies that for a range of countries the parameter (showing the effect of military burden on growth) may be negative; yet, for another range it might become positive. It is not of course easy to identify theoretically which type of country falls within which category. A working hypothesis could be that for small values of the defence burden (relative to the investment base) there may well be positive effects that overcome the growth retardation arising out of lost investment. However, once a 'threshold' is crossed the negative role of resource reallocation and mobilization dominates. Thus we could expect countries with relatively low military burdens to have non-negative parameters whereas countries with high burdens will show the standard negative effects.

The theoretical model, and the multiplicity of channels analysed, imply that a simultaneous equation model is needed. The problem with econometric modelling of this complex relationship is partly data availability; but it is also related to the fact that for identification we need a large number of exogenous variables that are unavailable. For most LDCs, outside planning ministries and CSOs, the required volume of consistent long-run time-series data is simply not available. Cross-section data are, therefore, the most preferred vehicle of analysis. But even here most of the post-Benoit studies tend to use single-equation estimates once again to prove or disprove the claimed positive effect of military expenditure (milex) on growth. This is unfortunate because it goes against the theory, calls for an undesired simplification, leaves out some important avenues through which the relation works and can also lead to specification errors. As Deger has shown in a series of papers, where the data are available on a cross-section basis one should use a more complex model. But unfortunately, serious Third World data problems explain partly the paucity of time-series analysis.

We have faced similar problems with Pakistan data, though not so much with India. To make the treatment comparative and consistent we have opted for a much simpler specification for both countries. The implicit assumption of the economic model is that military spending affects growth in two ways. The first is the direct effect embodying the whole host of spin-offs that Benoit emphasizes. The second is indirect; this works through defence spending affecting investment. Investment in any economy is the sum of the savings emanating from the private sector, the government and the foreign sector (negative trade balance). In so far as military spending affects each of these elements it is bound to have a major role in the investment process. In turn this will influence growth. The treatment here on these multifarious channels is brief; the interested reader can consult Deger (1986) for more details regarding the theoretical analysis.

The postulated model therefore assumes that growth is a function of investment and military spending, both as ratios of GDP. In addition, investment itself is affected by the military burden. Three additional points are utilized in the empirical model. First, due to life cycle effects as well as the assumptions of the Metzlerian target saving hypothesis, we assume that saving, and therefore investment, is also a function of growth. An accelerator type investment function will also give the postulated relation between investment and growth. Second, structural rigidity may preclude investment being productive at the period at which it is done; the installation and use of capital takes time in poor countries principally due to the lack of co-operative factors – the so called absorptive capacity constraint. Hence the effect of investment on growth might come after a lag. Finally, because of a considerable interest in analysing inflationary effects on growth we also include this term for the empirics.

The empirical results for India and Pakistan, using two equations for growth and investment, are given in Table 9.10; it gives the coefficients for the following equations:

$$g = a_0 + a_1 m + a_2 i(-1) + a_3 (\dot{P}/P) \tag{7}$$
$$i = b_0 + b_1 m + b_2 g \tag{8}$$

(here g is growth, m is military burden, i is investment share in GDP and $\dot{P}/P$ is the rate of inflation). Taking both equations together the impact multiplier of m on g is given by a_1; the long-run steady state multiplier is derived from

$$(a_1 + a_2 b_1)/(1 - a_2 b_2).$$

The growth equation (7) was chosen, after a series of experiments, on the basis of theoretical specification, diagnostic checks, degree of fit, plausibility of signs and coefficient value as well as statistical significance. The main criterion was to look for the plausibility and consistency of the economic variables rather than the military one. Hence, for example, if the effect of investment on growth in equation (7) was negative then we would not be able to use it. This seems reasonable.

Table 9.10 Military burden and the economy: empirical results

	India		Pakistan	
	Equation (9) g	Equation (10) i	Equation (11) g	Equation (12) i
Constant	−0.06	0.23	−0.07	0.21
m	1.84	0.67	0.05	−0.80
	(1.17)	(2.35)	(0.07)	(−2.51)
$i(-1)$	0.35		0.65	
	(1.56)		(1.64)	
$\dot{P}/P$	0.35		0.16	
	(−4.02)		(1.67)	
g		−0.001		−0.05
		(−0.014)		(−0.42)
R^2	0.5157	0.9365	0.5376	0.7087
ρ	−0.3(−0.50)	0.98(2.5)	0.6(2.85)	0.4(5.18)
Impact multiplier	+1.84		+0.05	
Long-run multiplier	+2.07		−0.46	

Note: t values in parentheses.

All the four equations are estimated using the Cochrane Orcutt method (CORC) to eliminate possible autoregressive errors. The OLS estimate for the Indian growth equation (Table 9.10, equation (9)) revealed no serial correlation (via the Lagrange multiplier test). Nevertheless we report the CORC results on the basis of general evaluation (as discussed above). Given the well-known problems of estimating LDC growth equations the fit is good for all the equations and the diagnostic checks (for the corresponding OLS estimates) do not reveal many specification problems. For reasons discussed earlier, we use a 10 per cent significance level for rejection of the null hypothesis.

The two countries vary quite dramatically in terms of the economic effects (on growth) of military burden. For India, the impact multiplier from equation (7) is positive, though not highly significant. The long-run multiplier, using both equations (7) and (8), is slightly higher. Overall, the results imply that defence could have a positive effect on the aggregate performance of the economy. It may be thought that the positive impact of defence arises because of substantial arms production that has a strongly positive impact on domestic industrialization, R & D as well as other forms of spin-offs. However, our previous work with inter-industrial data (Deger and Sen 1983) at a disaggregated level for India shows that the claims for spin-off are not supported by the econometrics. A more plausible explanation may be the one given earlier: with a relatively low defence burden the adverse effects do not bite particularly because the industrial and investment base itself is very large. For Pakistan, as we shall see, the case is potentially different; a much larger burden superimposed on a smaller investment base can have detrimental effects.

The results, however, should be treated with caution because the investment equation (Table 9.10, equation (10)) does not seem to be well specified. Given the value of ρ, the first-order autocorrelation term, we also used (separately) the first difference of i as the dependent variable; the regressors then ceased to be significant. Thus there could be specification problems with this formulation. Once again, more large-scale modelling needs to be done; but this is beyond the scope of this chapter. The conclusion for India seems to be that defence does not have a negative effect on aggregate growth; however, a stronger claim cannot be made.

The results for Pakistan are more clear cut. Defence has a small positive direct impact on growth; but the coefficient is insignificant so that positive and negative direct effects are cancelling each other out. But the indirect effects, through investment crowding out, are strongly negative. The final, steady state, impact of defence on growth is negative and very high. The tank and tractor trade-off for the economy is quite crucial. Even though the military expenditure process is not subservient to the demands of the economy, given the autonomous character of the military institutions, the feedback is important. The cumulation of growth retardation may make a long-run arms race untenable, through economic constraints, though in the intermediate term it continues unabated. Pakistan can ill afford a costly sub-continental arms competition with its larger neighbour.

Conclusion

Both India and Pakistan spend large amounts on the military, particularly if one considers their economic problems. There is little econometric evidence of a classical action–reaction process where their main motivation is to respond to the adversary's defence spending and procurement. Domestic factors tend to be more important as well as the behaviour of actors outside the dyadic relation. If an arms race does exist in even a weak sense it is clearly asymmetric with Pakistan responding to Indian expenditure patterns. The adverse economic effects for the Pakistani economy are also substantial particularly in the long run. It is therefore in its best interest to re-allocate resources away from the military sectors, thus contributing to growth and welfare. However, the Indian response must be more favourable and positive arms control measures should emanate from the more powerful neighbour. Recent democratization in Pakistan and more cordial relations among the leaders of the two countries could begin an era of co-operation that may bring an end to the unhappy confrontation.

Appendix A

In this Appendix we try to 'theoretically' model an arms expenditure process between two adversaries in terms of relevant ratios – military burden and regional share – using a differential game model. The alternative, that of optimal control for each country in turn, can also be used (see Deger and Sen 1984); but the present approach is more general. Country 1 assumes the utility function of the adversary from which a reaction function can be derived. Country 2 does the same for its opponent and acts likewise. Being neighbours with similar socio-cultural, economic and military backgrounds, it is often possible to predict the parameters of each other's social welfare functions and react in a game situation. Within this formulation, it is appropriate to look for suitably defined equilibrium concepts and analyse dynamics. By the very nature of arms races, we are considering a non-cooperative differential game with non-zero sum payoffs; we also implicitly need to assume that the two countries cannot make advance commitments on the strategies they would like to employ. Hence, in a defence expenditure model it is quite natural to look for closed-loop feedback solutions.

The most important question in model formulation is how to define optimal behaviour within this game. As these aggressive neighbours do not like to co-operate with each other a Pareto solution is immediately ruled out. The other extreme of a minimax solution, where each country believes that the other is only interested in conflict rather than maximizing its objective function, is rather rare and need not detain us.

The third alternative is the Stackelberg solution. In the Stackelberg case a leader (say the large country) is defined as the player who declares, even implicitly, its game strategy in advance and the follower (the small country) knows this declaration. It must be assumed that the leader will generally utilize the declared strategy. Thus the follower will react in an optimal fashion. As Cruz (1978) has shown, a player is at least as well off playing as a leader, compared with playing Nash (see below).

However, for most LDCs, as in the India/Pakistan case, the conditions required for the Stackelberg strategy may be inapplicable. Due to political instability and fluctuations, as well as changes in regime, it is difficult for the large country to (implicitly) declare and maintain its strategies. Similarly, the small country will find it difficult to accept the declared strategies for the same type of domestic problems. In addition, the prevalence of suspicion will preclude such behaviour. Further, international factors, and third-country influences, are important in determining the environment in which the two-agent model works. As a result of changes in exogenous factors, such as international tensions, etc. the leader may not be able to maintain its strategy nor the follower believe in it. Oddly enough, size *per se* may not be sufficient to clearly define which country is the leader or the follower; the crucial determinant may be independent perception or behaviour. It is possible to have situations where Pakistan, using its influence with the US or the Islamic world, acts as the game leader and follows an independent strategy. However, given the dominating attitude of India as a regional power, it may find it difficult to act as a follower.

We believe that the best method seems to be the Nash solution where unilateral action (at the Nash equilibrium) by any country will harm itself (it will be worse off compared to the equilibrium). Thus neither player will have an incentive to change its game strategy given the game strategy of the other at the Nash equilibrium. Note that a game strategy for a player is defined as a rule for determining its control variable(s) at any point of time as a function of the state variable(s) at that point of time.

In the model that follows we shall exclusively deal with the ratios, discussed earlier, which signify security and threat. The presentation here is brief; more details are available in Deger and Sen (1983; 1984). We consider each country in turn; dynamic optimization results are derived by control-theoretic methods; then we bring them together in the differential game framework.

National welfare (utility) at any point of time depends upon three factors: civilian expenditure (consumption and investment); domestic security depending on military capability; and foreign threat to be defined appropriately later. Civilian spending is GDP minus defence expenditure whereas military capability is enhanced by weapons stocks and arsenals. As we are interested, as discussed earlier, in the relevant ratios, all three factors will be proxied by observable ratio variables.

Consider the small country (indexed 1) that maximizes the intertemporal welfare functional by choosing its military burden:

$$W_1 = \int_0^\infty \exp(-p_1 t)\, u(c_1, s_1, T_1)\, \mathrm{d}t \qquad (A1)$$

$u(.)$ is the utility function of the nation and p_1 is the rate of time preference, assumed constant. The arguments of the utility function are the ratios discussed above; without subscripts these are the civilian expenditures C as a ratio of GDP Y, i.e. $c = C/Y$ ($c = 1 - m$ where $m = M/Y$, the military burden) and the stock S of armaments as a proportion of GDP Y, i.e. $s = S/Y$. For a given amount of national income if civilian consumption rises (military spending falls *ceteris paribus*) then utility rises. If stocks of armaments rise, given size reflected by GDP (Y), then welfare also rises. The threat index, left unexplained here, is simply denoted by T_1; it lowers welfare. Thus the partials of u have the following sign:

$$u_1, u_2 > 0 \qquad u_3, u_{11}, u_{22} < 0 \qquad u_{12} = u_{21} > 0$$

Using the definitional relation that $\dot{S}_1 = M_1$ (a constant depreciation term can easily be added) and noting the definition of s_1 we obtain the

221

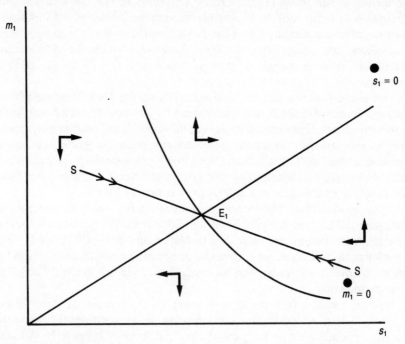

Figure 9.1 Phase diagram one

following relation as the differential equation for the state (stock) variable of the control problem:

$$\dot{s}_1 = m_1 - gs_1 \tag{A2}$$

where g is the constant growth rate of the economy.

Maximizing (A1) subject to (A2) and using the maximum principle of Pontryagin, we obtain two differential equations in m_1 and s_1. They exhibit saddlepath properties (the diagrammatic representation is given in Figure 9.1) and it is clear that the unique path that can lead the country to long-run equilibrium is the saddlepath SS. Equilibrium is defined in standard form: $\dot{m}_1 = \dot{s}_1 = 0$. It can also be proved (by invoking the theorem by Mangasarian 1966), that SS is indeed the grand optimum (the best of all trajectories that satisfy the necessary conditions of maximality) path that the country should follow.

The most important feature from our point of view is that the stable path is negatively sloped. Thus we have, for given threat, a relation of the following type:

$$m_1 = m_1(s_1, T_1) \tag{A3}$$

(the first partial is negative for stability, as in Figure 9.1, and the second partial is positive as expected).

For the large country (indexed 2) also, national welfare depends on civil expenditure, security and threat. Military security and capability, similarly, can be related to stocks of armaments. But, unlike the small country, the relative size of weapons stock is now related to the military expenditure process of the whole region. It is generally observed that when large and small countries coexist at a regional level there is usually an implicit conflict that comes from the tussle for regional balance of power. Assuming that the large country is more powerful (as India is) it wishes to maintain some form of regional superiority or hegemony over the regional bloc. Therefore, it feels secure if its stock of arms (S_2) relative to the total military spending in the region $(M = M_1 + M_2)$ is high. Thus defining its weapons stock as a proportion of total regional defence spending as $t_2 = S_2/M$ we get the relevant security index of the large country.

Another relation we shall need later is that of the regional shares $n_i = M_i/M$. For the large country the military burden and share is related (under fairly general assumptions) by

$$m_2 = \frac{m_1 z n_2}{1 - n_2} \tag{A4}$$

(where z is a constant).

The large country's optimization problem is therefore to choose m_2 (equivalent to choosing n_2 given m_1) to

$$\max W_2 = \int_0^\infty \exp(-p_2 t)\, u(c_2, t_2, T_2)\, dt$$

$$= \int_0^\infty \exp(-p_2 t)\, u1 - \left(\frac{m_1 z n_2}{1 - n_2}\right)\, t_2, T_2 \tag{A5}$$

The dynamic equation for the stock or state variable is given by

$$i_2 = n_2 - b t_2 \tag{A6}$$

Maximization of equation (A5) subject to equation (A6) once again gives two differential equations whose phase diagram is given in Figure 9.2. The essential mathematical characteristics (saddlepoint equilibrium, etc.) are similar to those of the other case but, of course, the fundamental choice framework is totally different. The equation for the downward sloping optimum path SS is

$$n_2 = n_2(t_2, T_2) \tag{A7}$$

Until now the two countries have been analysed separately as optimizing over time their military burden process to get the highest intertemporal welfare subject to the structural differences in their outlook emanating from size differences. Dynamic optimization was carried out under the *ceteris paribus* conditions. We now need to bring the countries together as

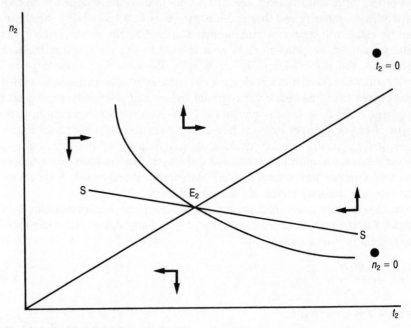

Figure 9.2 Phase diagram two

players in an arms race game. This requires specification of the threat variables, hitherto unspecified. In accordance with our discussion on military security (see pp. 198–204), we assume that for the large country (India) the opposition's military burden is the relevant threat variable; for the small country (Pakistan) the antagonist's regional share of military expenditure constitutes the threat.

Using the postulates of Nash equilibrium, the differential game gives the optimum value of the two choice variables, m_1 and n_2 (m_2) as functions of the state (stock) variables s_1 and t_2. In addition, there are the two dynamic equations for changes in the stocks. Therefore

$$\overset{*}{m_1} = m_1(s_1, t_2) \tag{A8}$$

$$\overset{*}{m_2} = n_2(s_1, t_2) \tag{A9}$$

$$\dot{s}_1 = m_1 - as_1 \tag{A10}$$

$$\dot{t}_2 = n_2 - bt_2 \tag{A11}$$

(An asterisk over m and n indicates optimum values under the postulated conditions of Nash equilibrium.)

Taking time derivatives of equations (A8) and (A9) and substituting equations (A10) and (A11) we get, in the neighbourhood of Nash equilibrium,

$$\overset{*}{m_1} = a_1m_1 + a_2n_2 + a_3s_1 + a_4t_2 \tag{A12}$$

$$\overset{*}{n_2} = b_1m_1 + b_2n_2 + b_3s_1 + b_4t_2 \tag{A13}$$

(The parameters a_i, b_i can easily be derived from the more basic ones in equations (A8)–(A11).)

The mathematical model, in Deger and Sen (1984), demonstrates that the parameters of equations (A12) and (A13) can be signed as follows:

$$a_1 < 0, \ a_2 > 0, \ a_3 > 0, \ a_4 < 0$$
$$b_1 > 0, \ b_2 < 0, \ b_3 < 0, \ b_4 > 0$$

The threats emanating from each other's military expenditure, burden and share have the expected positive effects on the military control variables of the two countries. In the same way, inertia from spending flows have negative effects on m and n. However, the stock effects tend to have counter intuitive effects. The higher the own country stock variable, the greater is the rate of change of its flow variable; this is principally due to the stability conditions. A heuristic explanation is that it takes the economy faster towards the (Nash) equilibrium.

Appendix B

All economic data are taken from the IMF *International Finance Statistics* (various years). Current price values in local currency are converted to 1980 prices (by using the CPI deflators) and then reported in 1980 dollars by using the period average exchange rate for that year.

Military expenditure data for both countries are from the SIPRI data base in current prices and local currencies. They are then transformed to 1980 dollars by utilizing the same method as above.

Data on arms production and arms imports are also from SIPRI. The basic data in 1975 and 1985 dollars are converted to 1980 dollars by utilizing US deflators. However, the methodological basis for these series is fundamentally different from that of the military expenditure series. A good discussion can be found in Brzoska and Ohlson (1988). In general, for any year quantitative data on arms transfers (production) are multiplied by a price vector for 1985; the trade and production information therefore give trend indicators of the volume of arms transferred and produced. They do not show, in any sense, the actual costs involved. Arms trade and military expenditure data should not be added with each other. However, since they both represent volume changes (in constant prices) they can be used as independent regressors to note their respective effects. This is what has been done in the econometric analysis.

Notes

1 The opinions expressed in this paper are entirely those of the authors and do not necessarily reflect those of the affiliated institutions. We are indebted to Ian Anthony, Keith Hartley and Todd Sandler for comments on an earlier draft.
2 See *World Military Expenditure and Arms Transfers 1987*, ACDA, 1988. India's rank was sixteenth out of 144 countries.
3 See Rothstein (1987) for a theoretical discussion of the 'poverty trap' and the 'security dilemma'.
4 *Europa Year Book 1988: A World Survey*, Europa Publications, 1988.
5 ibid.
6 See *The Military Balance 1988–1989*, The International Institute for Strategic Studies, 1988.
7 ibid.
8 See *World Military Expenditure and Arms Transfers 1987*, ACDA, 1988.
9 See *The Military Balance 1988–1989*, 1988.
10 See *Europa Year Book 1988: A World Survey*, 1988.
11 *SIPRI Yearbook 1988 World Armaments and Disarmament*, Oxford University Press, 1988.
12 See Anthony (1988).
13 *The Military Balance 1987–1988*, The International Institute for Strategic Studies, 1987.

References

Anthony, I. (1988) 'The naval arms trade and implications of changes in maritime law', in *SIPRI Yearbook 1988 World Armaments and Disarmament*, SIPRI, Oxford: Oxford University Press.
Benoit, E. (1978) 'Growth and defense in developing countries', *Economic Development and Cultural Change*.
Boulding, K. (1974) 'Defence spending: burden or boon', *War/Peace Report*.
Brito, D. L. (1972) 'A dynamic model of an armaments race', *International Economic Review*.
Brzoska, Michael and Ohlson, Thomas (1987) *Arms Transfers to the Third World, 1971–1985*, SIPRI, Oxford: Oxford University Press.
Cruz, J. (1978) 'Leader–follower strategies for multilevel system', *International Economic Review*.
Deger, S. and Sen, S. (1983) 'Military expenditure, spin-off and economic development', *Journal of Development Economics*.
Deger, S. and Sen, S. (1984) 'Optimal control and differential game models of military expenditure in less developed countries', *Journal of Economic Dynamics and Control*.
Deger, S. (1986) *Military Expenditure in Third World Countries: the Economic Effects*, London: Routledge & Kegan Paul.
Europa Year Book 1988: A World Survey (1988), London: Europa Publications.
Hartley, K. (1987) 'Reducing defence expenditure: a public choice analysis and a case study of the UK', in C. Schmidt and F. Blackaby (eds) *Peace, Defence and Economic Analysis*, London: Macmillans.
International Institute for Strategic Studies (1987) *The Military Balance 1987–1988*, London: IISS.
—— (1988) *The Military Balance 1988–1989*, London: IISS.
Mangasarian, O. L. (1966) 'Sufficient conditions for the optimal control of

nonlinear systems', *Journal of the Society for Industrial and Applied Mathematics (Control)* 4, 1: 139–52.

O'Leary, M. and Coplin, W. (1975) *Quantitative Techniques in Foreign Policy Analysis*, NY: Praeger.

Rothstein, R. (1987) 'National Security, domestic resources constraints and elite choices in the Third World', in S. Deger and R. West (eds) *Defence, Security and Development*, London: Frances Pinter.

Simaan, M. and Cruz, J. (1975) 'Formulation of Richardson's model of arms race from a differential game point of view', *Review of Economic Studies*.

SIPRI (1971) *The Arms Trade and the Third World*, Stockholm: Almqvist & Wicksell.

—— (1988) *SIPRI Yearbook 1988 World Armaments and Disarmament*, Oxford: Oxford University Press.

US Arms Control and Disarmament Agency (1988) *World Military Expenditure and Arms Transfers 1987*, Washington, DC.

Chapter ten

Military expenditures in Argentina, Chile and Peru[1]

Thomas Scheetz

Introduction

South America is a checkerboard of enemies and tacit alliances. Old and simmering conflicts such as Ecuador versus Peru, Peru verus Chile, Chile versus Argentina coexist concomitantly with excellent military relations between Argentina and Peru, and so on. Border disputes have proliferated since the time of independence and currently provide the principal pretext for arms procurement in the region. At the same time the military operational capabilities of these states vary markedly, often even in spite of their having acquired very modern equipment. This chapter will examine three of these countries, very different culturally and economically, but over recent decades involved in arms races for reasons only partially related to these interstate historical boundary disputes. In these countries what is presented to public opinion as the purchase of additional defensive security paradoxically results in less security. All too often the more they spend on security the less they have. Moreover, what the 'national security' regimes like Pinochet's in Chile or *El Proceso* in Argentina claimed was important for the attainment of internal security, actually has been inimical to it, because security is also a function of development and social well-being. For these three countries at least internal (and quite possibly external) security has a negative functional relationship to military expenditure (MILEX). The public and their elected representatives must someday soon arrive at a position where defence questions (especially budgetary aspects) are a matter for public debate, not for back-room secret decisions. After all, countries' potential enemies generally are quite aware of each other's arms stock and operational capabilities. The silence on budgetary questions is defended by the various armed forces as a question of security. Usually it is simply to keep their own citizens in the dark.

This chapter will improve upon international MILEX data sources, thereby reaching more informed conclusions. It will attempt this by inter-country comparison, over time (from 1969 to 1987), and in the context of general economic conditions and spending patterns within the public sectors of the three nations.

This said, an initial caveat is in order. In spite of the efforts by the International Monetary Fund (IMF) to systematize accounting procedures, the quality of the economic data varies from country to country. The attempt here to present three countries in a consistent comparative fashion highlights the difficulties. In the less developed countries (LDCs) the data suffer from the effects of inflation and devaluation. These twin problems are not totally solved by simply putting MILEX data as the numerator and dividing by the GDP or the Non-Financial Public Sector.[2] When a national currency rapidly – but unevenly across time – devalues, it affects MILEX through the arms import factor. A good example of the reverse effects of this is the over-valued Argentine peso from 1979 through March 1981 (the so-called period of the *plata dulce*, i.e. 'sweet money'). Peso-denominated imports appear quite cheap, viewed from national accounts. However, when the entirety of Argentine MILEX is translated into dollars (Table 10.1) the effect is shocking – and misleading. Thus, dividing MILEX (including arms purchases) by GDP or NFPS often understates the true burden on the Argentine economy.

The question of high inflation (very common in Peru, Chile and Argentina in the last 20 years) also directly distorts local data. Normally one uses an average annual inflation rate. But MILEX expenditures are not spaced evenly over the year. Nor are they similar to a normal basket of goods – whatever index is chosen. In the case of Chile five different indices were applied to the data. None was totally satisfactory. Inflation primarily affects the accounting of so-called nominal monetary units and then secondarily the attempt to apply a deflator in order to compare one country's absolute level of expenditure with another's.

Another problem arises on the level of international comparison. Kravis (1984)[3] points out that the real local purchasing power of countries varies inversely with their per capita GDP. Thus the actual purchasing power of the Peruvian Inti is actually greater than that of the Argentine Austral when both are converted to dollars for purposes of comparison. By derivation this factor also distorts the quantity of security, GDP and other governmental services purchased in both countries by similar quantities of money.

And finally, the armed forces of all three countries employ different (and varying) tactics to hide MILEX. Often enough one has to set aside official aggregated public accounting, looking into the budgets for social security, housing, education or the Ministry of Economics. Extrabudgetary accounts (even off-shore ones) are the norm. Interest payments on very sizeable arms-induced external indebtedness are rarely listed as defence expenditure. They are captured here for the case of Peru, partially for Argentina and probably not at all for Chile.

Argentina

Table 10.1[4] represents a reworking of the data presented by Gerardo Gargiulo (1988), former Under-Secretary for Planning and Budgetary Control in the Ministry of Defence. Table 10.2 shows that from the early 1970s the military's share of both GDP and total government expenditure (NFPS) gradually crept upwards, peaking during the years of the dictatorship, self-proclaimed as 'the Process of National Reorganisation' (1976–83), usually referred to as *El Proceso*. A number of regional factors influenced this increase. The year of the highest percentage (1978) was coincidentally the moment of growing tension with Chile over the question of the Beagle Channel (finally resolved in 1985 through the Vatican's mediation). Then later, prior to the outbreak of war over the Malvinas in April 1982 Argentina increased its arms purchases. However, the figures for both MILEX and arms imports for 1979–81 should be taken with a grain of salt because of the effect of the heavily undervalued peso during those years. As mentioned above, dollar figures startle, but must be contextualized. However, providing some credence to the startling MILEX figures, is the statement by the World Bank (IBRD 1985) that the military were overly generous to themselves in terms of pension benefits paid for almost entirely by the Treasury all during the last decade and a half. These costs grew especially during the dictatorship. Furthermore, the figures reported in Table 10.1 for arms imports (and thus by derivation for MILEX) are understated by at least US$ 2.5bn, and probably by two or three times that amount.[5] This was external debt contracted mostly between 1979 and 1981 spent on arms purchases and then passed on to the Ministry of Economics before turning the government over to civilians at the end of 1983.

Another point can be made specifically regarding Argentine defence data, though applicable to all three countries. Recently scholars (for example, Deger 1986: 17) have concluded that military governments do not necessarily spend more on defence than do their civilian counterparts. Improved data on Argentina do not support that view. Over the 17-year period from 1970 to 1986 Argentina spent almost US$87bn (constant 1982 dollars), two-thirds of which were spent during the 8 years of the recent dictatorship. Similar results obtain in the cases of Chile and Peru. So at least in these three countries, the military do tend to increase their share of the pie when they have the leverage to do so, contrary to growing scholarly opinion. It must be admitted though that during the elected government of (Ret. Gen.) Juan Domingo Peron and his wife Maria Estela Martinez (1973–6) the military did increase their share of both GDP and NFPS expenditure. The surprising figures are those for the government of Raul Alfonsin (1984–9). Through a mixture of public antipathy resulting from the massive violation of human rights during the 'Process' and the necessity

Table 10.1 Argentina: total military expenditures and arms imports, 1970–86

Years	MILEX (Am current)	MILEX (1982 US$m)	Arms imports (US$m current)	Arms imports (1982 US$m)
1970	0.000268	1,677.8	120.3	286.4
1971	0.000343	1,719.1	141.9	319.7
1972	0.000564	2,426.6	226.4	486.9
1973	0.001160	4,686.0	339.6	686.0
1974	0.001707	6,322.2	408.0	755.6
1975	0.006443	4,623.3	576.5	972.2
1976	0.039066	4,422.3	579.7	918.8
1977	0.097038	3,534.0	497.2	738.8
1978	0.382230	6,650.8	1,436.0	1,988.9
1979	1.025779	9,909.4	2,163.7	2,752.8
1980	2.152460	13,532.4	2,693.4	3,142.8
1981	4.419559	10,644.5	2,374.0	2,525.5
1982	10.640723	4,108.4	668.1	668.1
1983	50.252666	4,593.2	757.4	729.0
1984	227.152555	3,117.7	183.0	169.9
1985	1,499.289710	2,232.0	155.1	139.5
1986	2,581.242989	2,398.9	162.8	142.7
Total		86,598.7		17,423.4

Source: Gargiulo (1988)
Notes: Am = millions of australes; US$m = millions of US$ (either current or constant, i.e. 1982). The source for MILEX and arms procurement listed expenditures in constant australes of Dec. 1985. For Argentina MILEX includes own resources of the armed forces plus Treasury transfers to the armed forces, National Gendarmerie, Coast Guard, Ministry of Defence, military public enterprises, military pension fund and arms procurement. The Gendarmerie and Coast Guard ought to have been excluded here, but were not. The source data for arms procurement was aggregated for periods of years. The best that could be done was to average the figures for those years. Obviously this distorts both yearly total MILEX and arms purchases. At the end of 1985 there remained a US$ 2.5bn debt of the armed forces. This appears nowhere in the arms purchases figures, as it was impossible to allot. Data for the Treasury contribution to the military pension fund is missing for 1970–8. These would imply something less than an additional 10 per cent added to MILEX for those years. Conversion to US$ was done by using the annual average official market rate of the SIGEP.

of belt tightening measures imposed along with successive futile stabilization programmes meant to deal with the foreign debt inherited from the dictatorship, Alfonsin dramatically cut back on MILEX, though not by as much as has generally been proclaimed. What the data fail to show is the budgetary growth of military expenditures following the Holy Week Revolt in the Army in April of 1987. The downward trend will almost certainly be reversed, as Alfonsin has yielded to military demands for both an amnesty for soldiers accused of torture and repeated salary increases (and in 1988 Argentina again began shopping for arms). In any case even in 1986, MILEX (in real terms) was 43 per cent higher than in 1969, whereas GDP had only grown 23 per cent easily outstripped by Argentina's low (1.6 per cent per year on average) population growth (see the appendices for other macro-economic data on the three countries).

Without some sort of model like that of Deger (1986) it is hard to follow the relation between MILEX and investment. However, we can note the following from the data in Tables 10.1 and 10.2. Over the years, as MILEX

Table 10.2 Argentina: Gross Domestic Product, non-financial public sector, gross investment and MILEX, 1969–87

Years	GDP (Am current)	GDP (% real annual increase)	MILEX/ NFPS	MILEX/ GDP	Investment/ GDP	Investr (% real ann increa
1969	0.008098	4.7	–	–	–	
1970	0.008775	2.8	0.078	0.031	0.212	
1971	0.012518	3.8	0.072	0.027	0.227	
1972	0.020690	2.1	0.073	0.027	0.224	–
1973	0.035485	3.7	0.080	0.033	0.206	
1974	0.048647	5.4	0.073	0.035	0.198	
1975	0.143000	−0.6	0.096	0.045	0.202	1
1976	0.758700	0.0	0.117	0.051	0.216	2
1977	2.093400	6.4	0.106	0.046	0.246	−1
1978	5.234000	−3.2	0.147	0.073	0.214	
1979	14.251000	7.0	0.154	0.072	0.220	
1980	28.336000	1.5	0.150	0.076	0.237	−1
1981	54.752000	−6.7	0.145	0.081	0.194	−2
1982	147.613000	−5.0	0.142	0.072	0.164	–
1983	682.652000	2.9	0.136	0.074	0.143	–
1984	5,281.000000	2.5	0.089	0.043	0.124	−1
1985	39,592.600000	−4.4	0.076	0.038	0.104	
1986	74,309.000000	5.4	0.063	0.035	0.116	
1987	–	0.0	–	–	–	

Sources: FIEL (1985); IBRD (1985; 1988)
Note: The World Bank (and here) deflates using the average between the CPI and the non-farm WPI, 1981 = 100.

has increased, investment as a share of GDP has fallen. In 1973, 1978 and 1981 large increases in MILEX coincide with large drops in the rate of investment growth.

Chile

The data for Chile were developed by the author during a study of the public sector accounts (Scheetz 1985; 1987) at the Contraloria General de la Republica in Santiago. The MILEX data, examined on a greatly disaggregated basis, flatly contradict a number of claims widely made by the Chilean government. The authorities often point to Chile as having diminished its military expenditures and increased social expenditure in education, health, social security, housing and others. This claim is even repeated by international organizations too quick to accept aggregated government accounting. However, the truth of the matter is otherwise. The military (and to a lesser extent the police) have continually increased their real share of the budget at the expense of the social areas (Scheetz 1987: 1069). Using 1969 as the base year, by 1983 GDP had grown by 19 per cent, whereas MILEX had grown by 88 per cent in real terms (Scheetz 1987: 1061).

Salvador Allende was ousted from power in September 1973. As in the Argentine case, the data show clearly that the military once in power significantly increase their share of both GDP and the NFPS, though during the economic recession that followed the coup they too belatedly reduced their real expenditures, albeit not by as much as other economic sectors. This same slowness of reaction to economic downturn is seen in the recession of 1982. It was not till the following year that the military accounts came to grips with economic realities. Similar tardiness can be seen in Argentina MILEX in the recession years of 1969, 1976, 1978 and 1981 (in every case the armed forces chose the wrong moment to increase non-productive expenditures).

Table 10.3 Chile: total military expenditures and arms imports, 1969–87

Years	MILEX ($m current)	MILEX (US$m 1982)	Arms imports (US$m current)	Arms imports (US$m 1982)
1969	2.5	694.2	31.1	78.2
1970	4.5	919.0	83.0	197.6
1971	6.7	1,210.8	70.2	158.1
1972	12.9	1,421.7	65.8	141.4
1973	65.3	1,189.8	98.9	199.8
1974	772.3	1,719.1	155.5	288.0
1975	2,620.6	900.0	79.3	133.8
1976	7,172.3	871.0	102.7	162.8
1977	18,584.8	1,282.0	101.7	151.1
1978	30,303.1	1,325.3	107.9	149.4
1979	48,329.9	1,650.7	200.4	255.0
1980	76,873.2	2,300.0	655.8	765.2
1981	90,077.3	2,457.1	542.7	577.3
1982	102,308.1	2,009.6	263.0	263.0
1983	106,959.9	1,306.6	202.2	194.6
1984	137,785.3	1,299.1	258.3	239.8
1985	188,861.8	1,055.8	272.8	245.3
1986	231,014.3	1,049.4	279.4	244.9
1987	278,371.9	1,079.8	371.1	315.8
Total		25,741.1		4,761.3

Sources: Scheetz (1985; 1986); Republica de Chile, Contraloria General de la Republica (various years)
Notes: $m = millions of pesos. Conversion to US$ was done by using the Nominal Bank Market Exchange rate and the US GNP deflator. The arms import data are of improved quality beginning in 1979. The complex method of extracting the data will be supplied by the author upon request. Earlier arms data simply reflect the 10 per cent allotted by Law 13,196. All Chilean Public Sector accounts for 1973, 1974 and 1976 are of poor quality.

The weakness in Table 10.3 derives mostly from the issue of arms imports. It is fairly well known that the Chilean armed forces have access to at least one extra-budgetary fund destined for arms imports. Since 1958, Law 13,196 (whose unpublished and secret contents) guarantees the military 10 per cent of gross copper sales by the state copper company, CODELCO. These are the figures reported here for the years 1969–78. First, these are yearly balance sheet figures from CODELCO, and thus do not necessarily coincide with arms import expenditures for the year listed.

Table 10.4 Chile: Gross Domestic Product, non-financial public sector, gross investment and MILEX, 1969–87

Years	GDP ($m current)	GDP (% real annual increase)	MILEX/ NFPS	MILEX/ GDP	Investment/ GDP	Investment (% real annual increase)
1969	68.8	3.8	0.114	0.036	0.151	
1970	98.4	1.8	0.125	0.045	0.164	
1971	127.0	9.0	0.122	0.053	0.145	−!
1972	234.5	−1.2	0.120	0.055	0.122	−2
1973	1,147.0	−5.6	0.135	0.057	0.079	−1!
1974	9,199.0	1.0	0.191	0.084	0.212	8!
1975	35,447.0	−12.8	0.143	0.074	0.131	−5!
1976	128,676.0	3.5	0.124	0.056	0.128	!
1977	287,770.0	9.9	0.166	0.065	0.144	1!
1978	487,506.0	8.2	0.161	0.062	0.178	2!
1979	772,200.0	8.3	0.182	0.063	0.178	2!
1980	1,075,269.0	7.8	0.213	0.071	0.210	3!
1981	1,273,123.0	5.5	0.174	0.071	0.227	2!
1982	1,239,122.0	−14.1	0.192	0.083	0.113	−6!
1983	1,557,709.0	−0.7	0.179	0.069	0.098	−1!
1984	1,893,394.0	6.3	0.192	0.073	0.136	7!
1985	2,576,638.0	2.4	0.199	0.073	0.137	−!
1986	3,246,106.0	5.7	0.192	0.071	0.146	1!
1987	–	5.7	0.199	–	–	

Sources: Scheetz (1987); Banco Central de Chile, Boletin Mensual (various issues)
Notes: See Table 9.2. Chilean investment seems highly volatile, deeply affected by political and economic factors.

Second, these must be taken as minimum estimates of equipment imports. The sum of these arms import figures in constant US dollars represents only 18.5 per cent of total Chilean MILEX. This is undoubtedly an uncommonly low figure, even though Chile probably does spend a lower percentage of its military budget on equipment than do the other two nations. The reader will notice how when more reliable data are available (1979–87) the import figures approximately double. Actually, with tensions with Peru on the rise after 1975 and with Argentina after 1978 one would have expected a certain reflection of these situations in arms procurement. This probably did occur, but our arms data does not seem to capture it very well, though the MILEX figures do. The Richardson (1960) arms race model has only partial relevance to the Chilean situation. The arms purchase data are probably underestimated up through 1978, though even the underestimated 1974 acquisitions register an increase that must have worried Peruvians and spurred supporters of arms acquisitions there. Certainly the tensions with Argentina provide the strongest support for arms race analysis. Arms procurement increased notably in 1980 and 1981 as a result of the Beagle Channel conflict. However, when all is said and done it is undoubtedly the internal situation that was the dominant variable in Chilean military thinking, with the issue of salary levels more important than that of expensive equipment. The armed forces' principal effort was aimed at defeating 'the international communist conspiracy's internal ally'. The political foundation of the military government rests on national security state analysis, not on the possibility of external aggression.

Defence specialists often use international MILEX sources to prove their hypotheses. The data here should give some pause for relection. If one compares the Chilean MILEX figures of Table 10.3 with the international data sources (US Arms Control and Disarmament Agency, International Monetary Fund, International Institute for Strategic Studies and the Stockholm International Peace Research Institute) the differences are alarming. Generally (though not always) the figures in the present Chilean case are higher, varying from a small amount up to factors of 300 or 400 per cent. Perhaps the data set closest to that presented here are SIPRI's. However, the Stockholm data contain police expenditures (which should add 35 to 40 per cent more onto our figures). Those here presented have consistently excluded them from all three countries. Perhaps the conclusion is that researchers have to pay far more attention to data quality than they have in the past. The oft heard claim that 'it doesn't make any difference which source one uses; the tendencies are the same', is simply not true. Poor quality data in a well-constructed model do not produce good analysis.

Peru

Of the three, Peru is the poorest country and has the highest population growth rate (2.9 per cent in the 1960s, 2.8 per cent in 1970, 2.7 per cent in 1981 and 2.6 per cent in 1986). Its income distribution is also among the worst in South America. This contextualizes what might appear at first sight to have been extraordinary GDP growth (Table 10.6) during the populist dictatorship of Juan Velasco Alvarado from 1969 to 1975. It also helps explain the political failure of succeeding governments (General Morales Bermudez: 1976–80 and the architect Fernando Belaunde Terry: 1981–5). In GDP per capita 1985 was no better than that of 1964.[6]

Peru always seems on the edge of disaster: the anchoveta failure in 1973, the foreign debt crises from 1976–87, the floods and drought caused by the change of the Child's Current in 1983, the additional corruption brought by the cocaine trade, the continuing guerrilla insurgency of the 'Khmerist' Sendero Luminoso. It is in this context that the Peruvian MILEX have been a strongly negative contributing factor. The worst example was in 1977 when MILEX consumed almost 7.8 per cent of GDP and one-sixth of NFPS expenditure (Table 10.6). Peru was in the midst of the debt crisis. Gross investment had fallen from its peak of two years earlier (from 19.8 to 14.8 per cent of GDP). Unemployment (and underemployment) increased from 8.4 per cent (and 32.7 per cent) in 1976 to 9.4 per cent (and 39.2 per

Table 10.5 Peru: total military expenditures and arms imports, 1969–86

Years	MILEX (Im current)	MILEX (1982 US$m)	Arms imports (US$m current)	Arms imports (1982 US$m)
1969	13.39	869.1	156	392.0
1970	11.20	689.0	137	326.2
1971	10.18	592.2	92	207.2
1972	13.94	774.8	138	296.8
1973	18.55	968.2	173	349.5
1974	18.98	908.4	173	320.4
1975	27.11	1,132.5	208	350.8
1976	41.41	1,176.9	237	375.6
1977	84.16	1,484.7	521	774.1
1978	104.90	929.2	322	446.0
1979	123.67	700.2	206	262.1
1980	277.20	1,119.8	383	446.9
1981	415.25	1,046.0	304	323.4
1982	879.13	1,260.3	505	505.0
1983	1,553.42	915.2	362	348.4
1984	2,413.41	645.8	110	102.1
1985	7,750.43	634.8	227	204.1
1986	12,127.46	761.9	159	139.4
Total	–	16,609.0	–	6,169.9

Sources: Dancourt (1985); IBRD (1973); Banco Central del Peru, *Memoria* (various issues)
Notes: Im = millions of intis. These data have been converted to US$ by using the IMF's exchange rate, line rf in *International Financial Statistics*. MILEX reflects the Dancourt data + 10 per cent for CIF + external debt interest payments. The figures for 1969 are the author's, elaborated in similar fashion to Dancourt's. Dancourt (1985) derives a quite coherent and still higher estimate of MILEX. This is the more conservative estimate presented here. Treasury subsidies (fairly small) to military public enterprises seem to be excluded from MILEX as presented here. Interest payments for the last 4 years are estimates by the author from projections on a running average of disbursed debt.

Table 10.6 Peru: Gross Domestic Product, non-financial public sector, gross investment and MILEX, 1969–86

Years	GDP (Im current)	GDP (% real annual increase)	Per capita (% real annual increase)	MILEX/ NFPS	MILEX/ GDP	Investment/ GDP	Investm (% r ann increa
1969	208.997	4.1	1.3	–	0.064	0.133	
1970	240.666	7.3	4.4	0.189	0.047	0.129	
1971	264.437	5.1	2.3	0.144	0.038	0.150	2
1972	294.683	5.8	2.9	0.145	0.047	0.142	
1973	359.214	6.2	3.3	0.134	0.052	0.157	1
1974	447.505	6.9	3.9	0.094	0.042	0.189	2
1975	550.206	2.4	−0.4	0.106	0.049	0.198	
1976	764.504	3.3	0.6	0.118	0.054	0.179	−
1977	1,073.000	−0.3	−2.9	0.164	0.078	0.148	−1
1978	1,694.000	−1.8	−4.3	0.131	0.062	0.144	−
1979	3,139.320	4.3	1.6	0.083	0.039	0.143	
1980	4,971.855	2.9	0.2	0.093	0.056	0.177	2
1981	8,519.856	3.1	0.4	0.085	0.049	0.221	2
1982	14,150.000	0.9	−1.7	0.103	0.062	0.226	
1983	26,244.000	−12.0	−14.3	0.089	0.059	0.170	−3
1984	58,710.000	4.7	2.1	0.073	0.041	0.161	–
1985	159,259.000	2.0	−0.7	0.085	0.049	0.138	−1
1986	295,866.000	8.5	5.8	0.085	0.041	0.142	1

Sources: Banco Central de Reserva del Peru, *Memoria* (various issues)
Note: Over the period public investment represents between 40 and 60 per cent of the total.

cent). At the same time hidden unemployment (the formerly employed who in discouragement have given up the search for work) grew from 6.8 per cent in 1976 to 10.2 per cent in 1978 (Scheetz 1986). The military could not have chosen a more inopportune moment to force their will on Morales Bermudez. Even the IMF, supposedly given to respect national sovereignty in such matters, commented on the level of defence outlays. MILEX as a percentage of GDP averaged 4.8 per cent during the years of General Velasco, jumped up to an average of 5.8 per cent during the government of General Morales Bermudez, and remained a high 5.2 per cent for the debt- and guerrilla-ridden presidential period of Fernando Belaunde Terry. The Peruvian economy simply could not sustain such unproductive expenditure, a fact immediately recognized by the incoming administration of Alan Garcia when he drastically reduced arms acquisitions in the latter half of 1985.

To explain the causes for these economically destructive levels of expenditure one has to look to the external situation confronting Peru and to the corporate mentality of the Peruvian armed forces. With the ousting of Salvador Allende in 1973 the Peruvian military felt threatened by a traditional enemy, Chile, who now had the activist support of the Nixon administration in Washington, which opposed such ideologically abrasive experiments as that of Allende in Chile, Torres in Bolivia, Torrijos in Panama and Velasco in Peru. Beyond that, and perhaps more importantly, the Peruvian military derive much of their *raison d'être* from the desire to avenge the loss of territory suffered a century earlier in the War of the Pacific. This mentality took firm hold of arms procurement decisions when Morales Bermudez executed a palace coup in August 1975. The increased arms, incomes and perquisites that had begun under an infirm Velasco in late 1973 were further exacerbated under his politically weak successor. With fiscal responsibility thrown to the wind the large-scale arms imports were accomplished by adding to the foreign indebtedness just at the time that Peru could least afford it. This continued until the crisis first reached a peak in May of 1978 when Peru's foreign exchange reserves were totally exhausted and debt service had stopped. But the lesson had not been learned, either by Peru, foreign bankers or arms dealers. In 1983 the navy presented a budget that included plans to build another deep-water port at Chimbote (cost: US$1bn), and an electronic re-equipping of the fleet (cost: US$1bn). The air force also submitted its shopping list that included 26 Mirage 2000s (cost; US$875m). This, of course, was only part of their budget requests (though too, one ought to add that the expenditures would be spread over some years). But the example serves to illustrate that the armed forces, arms dealers and banking intermediaries all were living in an unreal world. In 1984 the Central Government only had US$3.5bn to spend on the entire budget. The nation's purse simply couldn't afford its own armed forces. None the less, all three plans surprisingly went forward.

It was not until Alan Garcia, inaugurated president in late July 1985, that Peru was predisposed to recognize reality. The country could neither pay its debts, nor continue to spend such large amounts on defence. Far from being a challenge to the Western banking system, it was a simple facing of reality.

External friction with Chile stimulated arms increases in 1973 and 1975. But the spurt of 1977 can be explained only by the internal power struggle within the Peruvian Army. Again in 1981 and 1982 MILEX rapidly increased, partially due to the January 1981 frontier incidents with Ecuador. Internally one must point to the growing importance of the guerrilla movement, Sendero Luminoso, the suppression of which was partially handed over to the military.

Peru also seems to present a clear case for the relation between MILEX, per capita GDP and investment. A significantly increased level in MILEX coincided with a fall in per capita GDP and investment during the years 1975–8 and 1980–2 (though investment fell with a lag in the latter period). There is a simple explanation of the causal relationships pertaining here. During both periods Peru's budget was strained by external debt service. As military demands were rarely opposed, cuts were made in public investment (which in Peru's case represents between 40 per cent and 60 per cent of total gross investment) and social expenditures (with the consequent social unrest that ironically the military and police were called upon to suppress).

Personnel costs

Quality information is not available for all three countries in the area of remunerations. The Chilean data set is the best, but information from each of the three throws light on the other two. Column 7 of Table 10.7 is the result of the accounting figures produced by the Contraloria. For those who take the trouble to examine the consolidated balance sheets the military would have them believe that between 53 and 72 per cent of all MILEX is consumed by personnel costs. The first year the military held power, 1974, is really the only believable year for remunerations. Overall, two hypotheses are possible. Either the raw salary data is correct and the total MILEX is falsified, or the salary data hide other expenditures (probably arms procurement). The first hypothesis is the one opted for because it provides greater data consistency.[7] If this hypothesis obtains, this would lend credence to the inadequacy of MILEX data as published by the government. Adding to them arms procurement data and estimates (Table 10.7, column 8) one finds a more realistic measure of the relative weight of personnel costs in the military budget. Note that some exceedingly high years remain, primarily those where the copper tax was used to estimate arms imports. This is just one more indication of the probable

Table 10.7 Chile: defence manpower and personnel costs

Years	IISS listed total active military forces (1000s)	IISS listed conscripts (1000s)	IISS listed non-conscripts (1000s)	Actual number of non-conscripts	General govt. remunerations as % of pub. sec. exp.	Military remunerations as % of min. defence (as listed)	Military remunerations as % of total MILEX	Average annual military remuneration per capita (1982 $m)	Average annual military remuneration per capita (1982 US$)	Defence remunerations as % of gen. govt. remunerations
1969	–	–	–	41,431	24.3	52.8	33.6	0.273	5,355.2	11.9
1970	–	–	–	43,737	27.0	55.0	34.6	0.378	7,419.4	13.6
1971	–	–	–	48,260	17.8	65.7	50.4	0.398	7,815.7	25.6
1972	60.0	–	–	55,992	20.2	64.7	51.6	0.315	6,193.3	25.1
1973	60.0	–	–	44,816	19.9	53.6	34.0	0.222	4,355.0	23.4
1974	60.0	–	–	63,619	15.7	36.7	31.1	0.297	5,840.7	36.5
1975	73.8	–	–	67,388	16.6	57.1	47.5	0.305	5,991.8	38.6
1976	85.0	21.6	63.4	72,405	22.1	59.8	58.4	0.283	5,553.4	32.8
1977	85.0	21.6	63.4	73,858	26.3	65.4	60.2	0.363	7,126.4	35.8
1978	85.0	21.6	63.4	74,000	24.7	61.4	56.2	0.373	7,321.8	34.9
1979	85.0	21.6	63.4	74,000	25.0	70.7	55.0	0.430	8,443.5	37.2
1980	88.0	21.6	66.4	77,240	24.4	*69.7	44.7	0.384	7,534.0	36.1
1981	92.0	31.6	60.4	80,804	20.1	70.3	46.5	0.373	7,320.2	39.2
1982	97.0	31.6	65.4	83,735	20.9	72.4	46.9	0.376	7,393.8	41.7
1983	96.0	33.0	63.0	–	22.2	67.4	47.6	–	–	40.8
1984	96.0	33.0	63.0	–	20.6	66.0	45.7	–	–	41.2
1985	101.0	32.0	69.0	–	17.6	60.8	39.1	–	–	39.4
1986	101.0	32.0	69.0	–	17.1	58.4	36.1	–	–	39.1
1987	97.5	32.0	65.5	–	16.4	62.7	35.1	–	–	40.0

Sources: IISS, various years; Scheetz (1985); Republica de Chile, Institute Nacional de Estadistica (1981); Cortazar and Marshall (1980); Balassa (1984)

Notes: In questions of force levels the IISS is reputedly the best international source. However, their data do not seem usable for close analysis in Chile or Argentina. 'Actual number of non-conscripts' are from Chilean government sources listing those who actively pay into the defence pension fund, i.e. commissioned and non-commissioned officers. The figures for 1980–2 are projections of earlier tendencies. *This figure includes other institutions controlled by the Ministry of Defence. Its effect is to lower this year's average by 3 percentage points. Remunerations to commissioned and non-commissioned officers includes an extremely small amount that is stipended for conscripts. These figures were subtracted and the difference was miniscule. It was decided to ignore conscripts' stipend. The CPI for 1970–4 is disputed. The acknowledged source is Cortazar and Marshall (1980). This has been followed here. See also Balassa (1984). Obviously the choice of index, especially early in the series, affects the size of the reported constant remuneration, whether in pesos or dollars. Military remunerations as a percentage of General Government remunerations may actually underestimate the military's share in general remunerations. It is widely reputed that when working within another ministry officers collect a second salary. Obviously the averaging of officer pay avoids the issue of the possibility of 'rank creep' in the services. The last column includes official Ministry of Defence (i.e. it includes police) and related defence budgeted institutions within the official 'Public Sector'. These personnel costs are divided by the officially listed 'Public Sector' personnel costs.

Table 10.8 Argentina: defence manpower and personnel costs; Peru: defence manpower

Years	Argentina				Peru		
	IISS listed total active military forces (1000s)	IISS listed conscripts (1000s)	IISS listed non-conscripts (1000s)	Personnel costs as % of MILEX	IISS listed total active military force (1000s)	IISS listed conscripts (1000s)	IISS listed non-conscripts (1000s)
1969	137.0	–	–	–	–	–	–
1970	135.0	–	–	48.3	54.7	–	–
1971	135.0	–	–	46.1	54.0	–	–
1972	135.0	–	–	43.8	54.0	–	–
1973	135.0	–	–	46.7	54.0	–	–
1974	135.0	–	–	48.3	54.0	–	–
1975	133.5	–	–	38.9	56.0	–	–
1976	–	–	–	29.7	63.0	–	–
1977	129.9	–	–	29.9	70.0	40	30.0
1978	132.9	–	–	32.8	92.0	–	–
1979	132.9	–	–	33.2	92.0	49	43.0
1980	139.5	92.0	47.5	35.1	95.5	49	46.5
1981	185.5	118.0	67.5	35.4	130.0	51	79.0
1982	180.5	118.0	62.5	26.8	135.5	51	84.5
1983	153.0	108.0	45.0	–	135.5	–	–
1984	153.0	108.0	45.0	–	135.5	–	–
1985	108.0	61.0	47.0	–	128.0	–	–
1986	73.0	35.0	38.0	–	127.0	42	85.0
1987	78.0	–	78.0	–	113.0	69	44.0

Sources: IISS, various years; IBRD (1985).
Notes: The percentages on personnel costs are from the World Bank and do not mesh perfectly with our sources. Missing observations = data not available.

underestimation of arms purchases provided by reliance on that source alone.

Undoubtedly, if one were to compare the budgetary share of military pay with that of the rest of the Chilean Central Government (column 6) even the column 8 figures are startling. The labour intensity of the various sectors of workers (education for instance) would lead one to believe that the relatively more capital intensive armed forces (especially the air force and the navy) would weigh less heavily in the salary percentages. But such is not the case. Moreover, when disaggregated, all three service branches are approximately equally high in the share of their separate budgets allocated to salaries.

After all is said and done, it may well be that the Chilean military are better paid relatively than their counterparts in Peru and Argentina. For the latter the IBRD (1985) lists personnel costs[8] as between 27 and 48 per cent of MILEX (Table 10.8, column 5). Clearly the weight of remunerations will vary from year to year, depending on the incidence of other factors, most notably arms procurement. Table 10.7, columns 9 (constant pesos) and 10 (constant dollar figures) provide a feeling for the absolute level of pay that the average Chilean soldier receives. One has to avoid putting too much weight on these figures because they are the result of the application of indices over years of heavy inflation (see note in Table 10.7). But they do seem to indicate a certain pattern. Military pay took a severe beating in the final 2 years of the Allende government, but quickly recovered when Pinochet came to power. Furthermore, real income has gradually increased over the years. It would be tempting to hypothesize that General Pinochet has maintained his control of the armed forces by an increasing largesse in the area of salaries. Other implications for revival of civilian control of both the government and the armed forces are also obvious. Column 11 adds further evidence in this area. The military have increased their share of the government's entire salary pie remarkably since the fall of the Unidad Popular government in 1973. Indeed the armed forces must account for a large share of the recovery of General Government percentage levels after 1976 as witnessed in column 6.

For the Peruvian case Dancourt (1985) provides what he terms an overestimated indicator of military pay's weight in Central Government salary accounts. His figures run from a low of 27 per cent to a high of 37 per cent of the Central Government remunerations pie. This overestimated range is slightly less than that pertaining in Chile (if one excludes the figures for the Allende years). This probably is fairly close to the truth. The Chilean military are probably better paid than their Peruvian counterparts (though Peruvian salaries and perquisites became a public scandal after 1975). Chile may well be relying on the quality of its officers, since it cannot hope to compete in arms purchases with Argentina. And *de facto* Chile has not kept up the arms race even with the poorer Peru. For instance, Peru has twelve submarines, Chile only four.

The question of force levels is another where international data sources do not inspire confidence. The ACDA figures are simply way off the mark, at least for Chile and Argentina. IISS is slightly better, but still fairly useless for close analysis. Once again the information for Chile is the best available. And there are a few loose numbers available for Argentina that give a feeling for the error factor in IISS figures. Local newspaper sources indicate that Argentina had 92,000 active military forces in 1976, 105,000 in 1980 and 1983, 89,000 (25,000 of whom were conscripts) in 1985 and 94,000 in 1986.[9] Formerly there were around 90,000 conscripts in all three service branches. These fell to 25,000 in 1985 and rose to 27,000 in 1987. These figures suggest that for Argentina the IISS data in Table 10.8 are almost always overestimated (except for 1986). Exactly the opposite occurs with the London-based data for Chilean non-conscripts. Non-commissioned and commissioned officers are regularly from 12 to 14 per cent lower than local figures, which in this case are completely reliable. None of the above figures includes police or paramilitary forces, and so they maintain a precise comparability with those of IISS.

Local defence industries

The defence industries of Argentina, Chile and Peru share a number of common weaknesses. First, though built in an attempt to alleviate arms dependency on foreign suppliers and heavy foreign exchange costs, they certainly do not attain the former and rarely attain the latter. All are very technologically dependent except in the most rudimentary product lines (Argentina perhaps slightly less so than the other two).

Second, their export sales promotion pitch far exceeds reality. For instance, Argentina's TAM tank (German technology) is annually saved from bankruptcy by a generous Treasury subsidy (about US$7m in 1985). It has produced some 350 copies for the Argentine army, but has exported only 16 to Peru. Its sales have been hurt by the possibility that purchasers may not be able to obtain spare parts if the firm closes its doors. Overall, in spite of its size, Argentina's defence industrial complex exported only US$20m in military goods in 1987.[10]

Third, all three countries' industries produce almost entirely for internal consumption. And that production is not even for a market that rationally (with interservice planning) covers the entire spectrum of the armed forces. Rather, each branch of the armed forces in each of the three countries has its own, largely autarkic, production and purchasing units, often for the same good.[11] The lack of co-ordinated interforce defence planning that is evident on a broader tactical and bureaucratic level is also responsible for an irrational division of production units, most of which operate far below the level of economies of scale. In Chile Cardoen and Makina in the private sector and FAMAE (directly under army control) compete with one another in the production of armoured vehicles.

Fourth, and more positively, in Chile and Argentina business relationships are tending to expand beyond simple licensing agreements with foreign arms producers. Argentina and Brazil are moving ahead with plans to produce jointly and market the CBA–23 passenger plane and the IA–63 Pampa trainer. In 1984 Chile purchased 34 CASA 101–B and C kits to be assembled by the Empresa Nacional de Aeronautica, ENAER (controlled by the air force). In exchange Spain ordered forty of ENAER's T–35 Pillan.[12]

Lastly, as in the rest of the public enterprise sector around the world, so too in the defence production sector, there is a move towards privatization. In Chile, for example, this has created tensions between Cardoen (private sector arms firm well connected with the army) and the army's FAMAE over the construction of armoured vehicles. The Peruvian shipbuilder, Servicios Industriales de la Marina, SIMA, is nominally private, but actually navy controlled and subsidized. And both the Argentine navy and air force have developed private sector firms related to their interests, whereas profit-making firms formerly controlled by the army's Fabricaciones Militares are being sold off.

Beyond these generalized trends each country has its own special characteristics. The Argentine defence sector is the oldest of the three and has the broadest product line of all of Latin America. It also has the widest and deepest technological base (excluding Brazil). Fabricaciones Militares (the army's holding company for ownership of, or participation in twenty-six companies) is also overly bureaucratized and inefficient. Members of the board of directors are incapable of controlling the corporation. They are appointed for short, 2-year periods. Basic data on the companies' performance either does not exist or is denied them.[13] Another unique aspect of Fabricaciones Militares is that only about 30–32 per cent of its output is defence material. The rest is for the civilian market. The Treasury annually subsidizes the defence sector (about US$50m in 1985). In addition to FM the other significant defence producers are TAMSE (producing the Argentine medium-size tank), AFNE and Astilleros Domecq (producing and servicing surface ships and non-nuclear submarines) and Area Material de Cordoba, which oversees such air force projects as jets (e.g. the IA–63 Pampa) and rockets (Condor, Martin Pescador, Alacran and Mathogo). There has recently been much international concern over these missile projects, both because of their possible use against the Malvinas and because of supposed future sales in the Middle East. At the present time this second concern is greatly overblown and seems mostly to be based on disinformation by international sources.

The Argentine defence sector closely guards even relatively innocuous data about its operations. But we know that the army's and navy's operations in 1985 employed 34,568 people, had sales (including about two-thirds to the civilian sector, mostly steel products) of US$670m and Treasury subsidies of about US$50m. Information is lacking for Area Material de Cordoba.

Chile's defence sector is smaller, though much more dynamic than Argentina's, though it too is Treasury subsidized (FAMAE received approximately US$4m in 1984). Whereas the current democratic administration in Argentina has vetoed prospective sales to South Africa, Iran, Iraq and Nicaragua from a policy of non-supply to countries involved in conflict, Chile has suffered from no such qualms of conscience. As a result its exports have been fairly successful (Cardoen, well-known for its fragmentation bombs, exported US$100m in 1985).[14]

The other service branches also have their own arms industry. ENAER has been manufacturing small planes under licence. As mentioned above, it is expanding its purview with a negotiated import of Spanish CASA trainers and export of its own Pillan. The Astilleros y Maestranzas de la Armada, ASMAR (the only Chilean firm reporting its number of employees – 4,500 in the mid-1980s), manufactures under licence various small surface ships.

Peru's arms industry is even smaller and far less efficient than Chile's. Once again each of the three services has its respective defence firm. The only one of note is SIMA. In the mid-1980s the entire defence production sector employed about 7,000 people, 5,000 of whom worked in SIMA. By international standards SIMA is hardly efficient, but because its contracts with the government are written on a cost-refund basis it does show a slight profit on its yearly sales of about US$30m.[15]

Comparison of expenditures between Argentina, Chile and Peru

The quality of single country case studies can be improved upon by comparing local information with that from neighbours with whom there exists the possibility of conflict. One hypothesis would be that, *ceteris paribus*, countries' defence expenditure varies directly with the relative size of their per capita GDPs, that is to say, their capacity to dispose of a surplus for a non-productive military apparatus. Obviously this involves the strong assumption that there is a one-to-one relationship between real dollar expenditure and operational capabilities (an economist's argument). But the hypothesis does stand in the cases of the three countries examined here. Argentina's MILEX almost quadruples that of Chile, and Chile's is almost 50 per cent larger than that of Peru. If a country's capacity to defend itself depends on its productivity, then from a soldier's perspective an obvious conclusion ought to be that the best defence – at least in the long run – is a healthy economy, itself the product of productive investment. To that extent defence expenditure is self-defeating. Of course, there do exist 'short-run' defence requirements, that is to say, threats that materialize suddenly and require the display of dissuasive force.

One might also hypothesize that arms purchases would parallel total MILEX, subject to constraints imposed by possible conflicts (and of course other variables such as the political leverage of the military corporation, Richardson-type arms races, the presence of inter-force rivalry or joint planning, etc.). Here again Argentina quadruples Chile's arms procurement, though the figures for both countries underestimate arms purchases, those of Argentina by far more than those of Chile. The surprising situation is that of Peru, which for the same time period out-armed Chile by almost 2bn in 1982 dollars (of course, this sum is really less since part of Chile's arms purchases are not captured). In any case, Chile has largely avoided involving itself in a full-blown arms race.

The strategic conclusion for Chile is, with all else being equal, not comforting. In spite of its mountain border with Argentina it is a country extremely exposed militarily. Further, its two neighbours are both allied against it, the one an overwhelmingly superior economic (and therefore military) power, the other economically weak but heavily armed. Of course, there are other actors in the drama: Ecuador, Brazil and Great Britain, all of whom would (or do) share affinities with Chile against the other two.[16] It behoves Chile to maintain a vigorous diplomatic stance pursuing regional disarmament and concern for its image. This has not been the case, especially during the last 15 years.

Regarding Peru one wonders how long the social situation of the country will permit it to support such a military apparatus. No doubt Sendero Luminoso finds fertile soil in a situation where more productive government social expenditure and investment have so long been neglected. Employing the army, navy and police to suppress the guerrillas, however necessary in the short run, is hardly a creative policy towards solving the underlying long-run problems. The ironic thing is that Peru has been a leader in calls for regional disarmament. Though, of course, most of the ink spilled from the 1974 Declaration of Ayucucho to those of Alan Garcia has come to nought.

Argentina's military spending is open to question from another perspective. Vis-à-vis Chile, Argentina is over prepared. But assuming the possibility of conflicts with Brazil or the United Kingdom, if our economic hypothesis holds, Argentina could at best pursue a defensive position and should rely on diplomacy. This does seem to be the thrust of the current government of Raul Alfonsin. However, the armed forces would still have to be judged as poorly structured to maximize both diplomatic and economic targets. The reason for this imbalance has to do with internal Argentine military–civilian politics. But this leads to another area of discussion where *de facto* the assigned task of each of the three armed forces is not simply that of external defence.

The relations between these three countries would not be complete without some mention of the question of nuclear power. All three have embarked upon programmes of nuclear energy. And because all three are also among the world's most advantageously placed potential hydroelectric producers, the assumption must stand that at the very least certain influential elements within all three societies are looking at the possibility of nuclear weapons. Argentina, and recently Brazil, are among the Third World's leaders in nuclear technology. Indeed, Buenos Aires is advising Lima on the Peruvian programme. An examination of the wholesale costs of electricity generation reveals that electric utility companies such as SEGBA in Buenos Aires would prefer to purchase hydroelectric or thermal from the national net. But they are required to purchase a percentage of nuclear as a way of subsidizing that technology. The argument is made locally that Argentina has developed technological capacity in the area and ought not to discard it thoughtlessly. Undoubtedly this has some merit.

Both Argentina and Chile have reservations about the nuclear Non-Proliferation Treaty and the Treaty of Tlatelolco. Chile's doubts are based on other regional non-signatories, notably Argentina and Brazil. Argentina reserves for itself the right to continue research while other developed countries maintain nuclear weapons. During the Malvinas war the United Kingdom, a full signatory to the Tlatelolco accord, is believed to have introduced nuclear weapons into the area. If so, it would seem that Argentina was justified in its decision. And although it is clear that Argentina does not presently have nuclear weapons, undoubtedly she could acquire them without much effort, economic or technological. This is true of neither Chile nor Peru.

Future contingencies

One of the characteristics of political and economic life in the LDCs is the extreme short-run time perspective. The climate for investment tends to be uncertain when predicting the next 6 months, let alone the next 5 years. The same is true for almost all political and economic variables, including the military.

Of the three countries the most stable economically is clearly Chile. However, in the plebiscite of October 1988 the future presidential ambitions of General Pinochet were defeated. This initiated a period of political uncertainty, where even the strength of the economy may come under question. Without a doubt the role of the armed forces in any future order is under question. When and if civilians take control of the government, at the very least one might reasonably expect cuts in military pay, and possibly trials of human rights violations. These are issues present in the transition to democracy. In the meantime the soldiers are reputedly preparing for the regime changeover by large purchases of arms in 1988 and 1989.

Peru is currently immersed in yet another stabilization effort, each one taking its political toll for the party in power. Meanwhile the country continues to slide backwards economically. Although Alan Garcia has made some headway with reform of the armed forces and control of their budget, one would be overly optimistic if one excluded a growing political role for the military, especially given the disruptive power of Sendero Luminoso and the political strength of the united leftist front in the upcoming elections of 1990.

In Argentina the government of Raul Alfonsin has failed to resolve the economic question. The Ministry of Economics is primarily occupied with the external debt. There has been very little investment in the country during the present decade. Inflation, fiscal deficits and financial speculation seem to be insurmountable problems. Originally the government appeared to be capable of controlling the internal situation within the military, facing the twin crises of human rights trials and heavy budget cuts. President Alfonsin had to confront civilian demands for justice together with military demands for amnesty and a larger budget share (principally salaries, though the operational capability of the armed forces is extremely reduced, given shortages of everything). Originally he underestimated the depth of the problem within the military. He seemed to hope that it would just go away, given enough time. Meanwhile he was constantly emitting contradictory signals to both civilians and soldiers. When the Holy Week crisis of 1987 occurred he ended up yielding to rebel demands. An almost total amnesty (only eleven retired generals remain on trial) was the signal for still further military demands. It now appears clear that the military budget is again on the increase. Alfonsin had proffered 'modernization' and 'professionalization' as solutions to the internal crisis of the military corporation. Probably those ideas will simply translate into the purchase of up-to-date weaponry. Presidential elections take place in Argentina in May 1989. At this point a Peronist victory appears likely, and with it a further strengthening of the role of the armed forces.

Peruvian President Alan Garcia's regional arms control initiative (the 'Lima Declaration' signed on 30 July 1985) is almost surely destined to become just one more failed diplomatic extravaganza. Though all three countries' external debt situations militate against future heavy military expenditures, there are signs in all three that MILEX and arms acquisitions may be on the rise.

As mentioned above, the economic (and resultant social) situation in Peru has reached such a stage that there has recently been talk of a military coup. Simultaneously the attacks of Sendero Luminoso have increased.

The political leverage of the armed forces has grown accordingly. One might reasonably expect arms purchases to follow.

Of the three, Chile is the country least constrained by external debt limitations on foreign exchange availability for equipment purchases. Furthermore, the military, judging that a return to democracy in 1990 will almost certainly imply MILEX budgetary restrictions, has reputedly begun to shop for arms while the situation is still favourable to them. It is also known that certain groups within the armed forces were deeply opposed to the Lima Declaration because Chile would be placed in a disadvantageous position *vis-à-vis* the others.

In 1985 Argentina and Chile signed a Vatican accord resolving the Beagle Channel dispute. On another front Argentina and Brazil have initiated movement towards increased economic integration. These two occurrences have tended to diminish (though not eliminate) Argentine wariness of its northern and western neighbours. Brazil is currently engaged in research aimed at developing a nuclear submarine and nuclear weapons. Simultaneously, the simmering Malvinas question (and Chile's special military relationship with Britain) further complicates any arms control initiative. All sectors of society support Argentine sovereignty over the islands. As diplomacy wanes, armed solutions will become more acceptable. Even granted severe budgetary constraints, the military are none the less pushing for acquisition of more modern equipment. A weakened President Alfonsin has been slowly yielding.

Thus, though financial stringency has limited arms buildups over the last 5 years, there now exist political pressures in all three countries to again begin such purchases. The conclusion with respect to regional arms control would seem inevitable. There will be no significant agreements reached, however much talk goes on.

Appendix

Table A10.1 Argentina: macro-economic statistics, 1969–87

Years	Unemployment (percentage October of each year)	Inflation CPI (year-end %)	Merchandise export FOB (US$m)	Merchandise import FOB (US$m)	Current account balance (US$m)
1969	–	6.3	1,612	1,395	−230
1970	–	22.0	1,773	1,499	−159
1971	–	39.1	1,740	1,653	−389
1972	–	64.1	1,941	1,685	−223
1973	–	43.7	3,266	1,978	721
1974	–	40.1	3,931	3,216	127
1975	3.8	335.1	2,961	3,510	−1,284
1976	4.4	347.5	3,916	2,744	665
1977	2.7	160.4	5,652	3,798	1,290
1978	2.3	169.8	6,400	3,489	1,833
1979	2.4	139.7	7,810	6,026	−537
1980	2.5	87.6	8,021	9,394	−4,767
1981	5.3	131.3	9,143	8,391	−4,714
1982	4.6	209.7	7,624	4,858	−2,357
1983	3.9	433.7	7,836	4,040	−2,461
1984	4.4	688.0	8,107	4,231	−2,391
1985	5.9	385.4	8,396	3,505	−954
1986	5.2	81.9	6,852	4,409	−2,859
1987	5.7	174.8	6,360	5,267	−4,344

Sources: IBRD (1987; 1988)

Table A10.2 Peru: macro-economic statistics, 1969–86

Years	Unemployment percentage (urban)	Inflation CPI (year-end %)	Merchandise export FOB (US$m)	Merchandise import FOB (US$m)	Current account balance (US$m)
1969	10.6	5.7	880	659	–
1970	8.3	5.6	1,034	700	185
1971	7.7	7.7	889	730	−34
1972	7.3	4.2	945	812	−32
1973	7.1	13.8	1,112	1,033	−192
1974	6.6	19.1	1,503	1,909	−807
1975	8.1	24.0	1,330	2,390	−1,538
1976	8.4	44.7	1,341	2,100	−1,192
1977	9.4	32.4	1,726	2,148	−783
1978	10.4	73.7	1,972	1,668	−164
1979	10.5	66.7	3,676	1,954	953
1980	–	60.8	3,916	3,090	−102
1981	–	72.7	3,249	3,802	−1,729
1982	–	72.9	3,293	3,722	−1,609
1983	–	125.1	3,015	2,722	−871
1984	–	111.5	3,147	2,140	−221
1985	11.8	158.3	2,978	1,806	125
1986	8.2	62.9	2,509	2,525	−1,055

Sources: Scheetz (1986); Banco Central de Reserva del Peru (1986)

Table A10.3 Chile: macro-economic statistics, 1969–87

Years	Unemployment (percentage annual average)	Inflation CPI (year-end %)	Merchandise export FOB (US$m)	Merchandise import FOB (US$m)	Current account balance (US$m)
1969	–	29.3	1,173	–	−6
1970	5.9	36.1	1,112	830	−81
1971	5.2	34.5	999	891	−189
1972	4.1	238.6	849	1,000	−387
1973	4.8	605.9	1,309	1,288	−295
1974	9.1	369.2	2,151	1,794	−211
1975	15.7	343.3	1,590	1,520	−491
1976	16.7	197.9	2,116	1,473	148
1977	13.3	84.2	2,185	2,151	−551
1978	13.8	37.2	2,460	2,886	−1,088
1979	13.5	38.9	3,835	4,190	−1,189
1980	11.7	31.2	4,705	5,469	−1,971
1981	10.4	9.5	3,836	6,513	−4,733
1982	19.6	20.7	3,706	3,643	−2,304
1983	18.7	32.1	3,831	2,845	−1,117
1984	16.3	23.0	3,650	3,357	−2,060
1985	13.8	26.4	3,804	2,955	−1,329
1986	13.9	17.4	4,198	3,099	−1,137
1987	12.9	21.5	5,224	3,994	−811

Sources: Cortazar and Marshall (1980); Banco Central de Chile, *Boletin mensual, Sintesis estadistica de Chile 1983–1987. Indicadores economicos y sociales 1960–1982, Balanza de pagos de Chile 1981–1982*; Jadresic, Dec. 1986

Notes

1 This research was assisted by an award from the Social Science Research Council of a MacArthur Foundation Fellowship in International Security.

2 In all three countries the NFPS definitionally includes Central Government expenditures, social security, municipalities and other subnational governing bodies, public enterprises and other budgeting agencies receiving funds from the Treasury. It also includes extra-budgetary defence expenditures where discovered.

3 The work on the International Comparison Project (ICP) appears in many journal articles. Consult Kravis (1984) for a further bibliography. The ICP would imply an inverse relationship between GDP per capita and, for instance, the effectiveness of local military expenditures. That is, the poorer a country, the greater the purchasing power of the local currency. Thus Peru actually receives more 'security' for its outlay than does Chile. And Chile receives more than Argentina for a similar outlay. So, though Argentina appears to spend over four times that of Chile for MILEX, the actual purchasing power of that expenditure is not quite so unfavourable for Chile.

4 Several qualifications apply to all of the tables. First, MILEX does not include police services for any of the three countries studied. Second, all final-year data are preliminary. Third, all tables were converted to US$ 1982 by using the US GNP deflator. Fourth, all public sector data are realized expenditures; none is a budget. Fifth, local monetary unit deflation was calculated using GDP deflators where available. Sixth, Investment is Total Gross Domestic Investment (public and private).

5 Information from a personal interview.
6 In the last 25 years Peru has developed a very large underground economy. Official figures for GDP and investment are surely increasingly underestimated over the period, whereas unemployment is overestimated. Argentina also witnesses this phenomenon, though to a lesser degree. Clearly this factor affects the mathematical relationships between MILEX and GDP, etc.
7 There are three reasons. First, personnel costs among all three branches of the armed forces, plus police (Carabineros and Investigaciones) all move more or less in concert over time. These share relations have been maintained in the official personnel cost data. Second, if significant equipment purchases were hidden here there would be greater volatility in the series as a whole and especially in each branch's personnel costs series. And third, the level of personnel costs that one would expect to find (35 to 50 per cent of total costs) are accounted for nicely by adding the import acquisition costs to officially reported MILEX, especially after 1979 when the import data improve.
8 The figures for both Argentina and Chile exclude most payments into the military pension funds (the Treasury subsidizes the accounts). No information is available for the case of Peru.
9 These were taken from the Buenos Aires daily, *Clarin*, 4 January 1987; 30 November 1986; and 14 August 1985.
10 *Clarin*, 7 August 1988.
11 This is a common complaint in Chile and Argentina. An example is given by an official of Fabricaciones Militares in Aroskind and Fontana (1986: 25).
12 *Defence Today*, nos 91–2, December 1985.
13 Information from an interview conducted with an official of Fabricaciones Militares.
14 *Defence Today*, nos 91–2, December 1985.
15 This figure is from unpublished annual reports. The number is repeated for several years during the early 1980s.
16 Ecuador and Peru maintain a low level of tension over their shared border. Brazil is viewed by many of her neighbours as harbouring expansionist tendencies. Great Britain has recently been arming Chile in exchange for intelligence on Argentina. Thus the first two countries favour Chile by putting pressure on Peru, the last two by putting pressure on Argentina.

References

Aroskind, C. and Fontana, A. (1986) 'El sector de produccion para la defensa: origen y problemas actuales', mimeograph, Buenos Aires.
Balassa, B. (1984) 'Experimentos de politica economica en Chile, 1973–1983', *Estudios Publicos* (Santiago, Chile), no. 14: 49–89.
Brzoska, M. and Ohlson, T. (1986) *Arms Production in the Third World*, Stockholm International Peace Research Institute, London: Taylor & Francis.
—— (1987) *Arms Transfers to the Third World, 1971–85*, Stockholm International Peace Research Institute, NY: Oxford University Press.
Cortazar, R. and Marshall, J. (1980) 'Indice de precios al consumidor en Chile: 1970–1978', *Coleccion Estudios Cieplan* (Santiago, Chile), no. 4: 159–201.
Dancourt, O. (1985) 'Impacto macroeconomico del gasto de defensa, 1970–80', mimeographed, Centro de Investigacion de la Universidad del Pacifico, Lima, Peru.
Deger, S. (1986) *Military Expenditure in Third World Countries: The Economic Effects*, London: Routledge & Kegan Paul.

Fundacion de Investigaciones Economicas Latinoamericanas (1985) *El gasto publico en la Argentina, 1960–1983*, Buenos Aires, Argentina, May.

Gallegos, A., Lozano, A. and Pacheco, J. (1985) *Mapa Economico Financiero de la Actividad Empresarial del Estado Peruano*, Lima: ESAN.

Gargiulo, G. (1988) 'Gasto militar y politica de defensa', *Desarrollo Economico* (Buenos Aires, Argentina) 28, 109: 89–103.

International Bank for Reconstruction and Development (1988) *Argentina: Social Sectors in Crisis*, Washington, DC.

—— (1985) *Argentina. Economic Memorandum*, 2 vols, Washington, DC.

—— (1973) *The Current Economic Position and Prospects of Peru*, Washington, DC.

International Institute for Strategic Studies *The Military Balance*, London, various years.

International Monetary Fund *Government Finance Statistics Yearbook*, Washington, DC., various years.

—— *International Financial Statistics Yearbook*, Washington, DC, various years.

Jadresic, E. (1986) 'Evolucion del empleo y desempleo en Chile, 1970–85: series anuales y trimestrales', *Coleccion Estudios Cieplan* (Santiago, Chile), no. 20: 147–93.

Kravis, I. B. (1984) 'Comparative studies of national incomes and prices', *Journal of Economic Literature*, 22: pp. 1–39.

Republica de Chile, Banco Central de Chile (1984) *Balanza de Pagos de Chile 1981–1982*, Santiago, Chile.

—— *Boletin Mensual*, Santiago, Chile (various issues).

—— (1983) *Indicadores Economicos y Sociales 1960–1982*, Santiago, Chile.

—— (1988) *Sintesis Estadistica de Chile 1983–1987*, Santiago, Chile.

Republica de Chile Contraloria General de la Republica *Estado de la Gestion Financiera del Sector Publico*, Santiago, Chile, various years.

—— Instituto Nacional de Estadistica (1981) *Chile, Series Estadisticas*, Santiago, Chile.

Republica del Peru, Banco Central de Reserva del Peru *Memoria*, Lima, Peru, various years.

Richardson, L. F. (1960) *Arms and Insecurity*, Chicago: Quadrangle.

Scheetz, T. (1987) 'Public sector expenditures and financial crisis in Chile', *World Development* 15, 8: 1053–75.

—— (1986) *Peru and the International Monetary Fund*, Pittsburgh: University of Pittsburgh Press, 1986.

—— (1985) 'Gastos militares en Chile, Peru y la Argentina', *Desarrollo Economico* 25, 99: 315–27.

Stockholm International Peace Research Institute *SIPRI Yearbook: World Armaments and Disarmament*, various years, Oxford: Oxford University Press.

United States Arms Control and Disarmament Agency *World Military Expenditures and Arms transfers*, Washington, DC, various years.

Chapter eleven

Japan's defence spending

Satoshi Niioka[1]

Introduction

Since the beginning of the 1980s, Japan's defence policy has gone through a major change. The government has begun to place high priority on defence spending in its fiscal outlay in an effort to be an 'internationally-oriented nation'. At the same time the guidelines that had worked to block a large defence buildup have been discarded. Behind this change lies the emergence of Japan as an economic power and its greater role as a military ally of the United States. This chapter reviews the implications of Japan's growing defence spending.

Economic and political background

Economic growth and fiscal budget

From 1955 to 1972, Japan achieved rapid economic growth, which helped to increase the nation's finances. As Table 11.1 shows, general account expenditure grew at double-digit rates until fiscal year 1980, and defence spending continued to expand at an annual rate of 10–20 per cent until fiscal year 1979 with the only exception of 9.6 per cent in fiscal year 1965. The sharp increase in government finance and defence expenditure was supported by the increased issue of government bonds.

The national budget law of 1947 prohibited the issuing of government bonds in principle, based on the bitter experience that the government bonds issued in massive amounts during the Second World War helped Japan finance its military expenditure and develop into an ill-fated military power. This rule had an exception: 'Bonds may be issued or money may be borrowed as the financial source of public works, investment or loan within the amount approved by the National Diet' (Article 4, the Government Finance Law). Government bonds issued for these purposes are called 'construction bonds' or 'Article 4 bonds'.

The general account budget stayed balanced from fiscal years 1949 to

Table 11.1 The trend of defence spending (¥100m, current price)

Fiscal year	General account budget	Annual increase (%)	Defence spending	Annual increase (%)	Defence share % in the general account budget	Defence share in GNP (%)
1962	24,268	24.3	2,085	15.7	8.6	1.18
1963	28,500	17.4	2,412	15.7	8.5	1.18
1964	32,554	14.2	2,751	14.0	8.5	1.14
1965	36,581	12.4	3,014	9.6	8.2	1.07
1966	43,143	17.9	3,407	13.0	7.9	1.10
1967	49,509	14.8	3,809	11.8	7.7	0.93
1968	58,186	17.5	4,221	10.8	7.3	0.88
1969	67,396	15.8	4,838	14.6	7.2	0.84
1970	79,498	18.0	5,695	17.7	7.2	0.79
1971	94,143	18.4	6,709	17.8	7.1	0.80
1972	114,677	21.8	8,002	19.3	7.0	0.88
1973	142,841	24.6	9,355	16.9	6.5	0.85
1974	170,994	19.7	10,930	16.8	6.4	0.83
1975	212,888	24.5	13,273	21.4	6.2	0.84
1976	242,960	14.1	15,124	13.9	6.2	0.90
1977	285,143	17.4	16,906	11.8	5.9	0.88
1978	342,950	20.3	19,010	12.4	5.5	0.90
1979	386,001	12.6	20,945	10.2	5.4	0.90
1980	425,888	10.3	22,302	6.5	5.2	0.90
1981	467,881	9.9	24,000	7.6	5.1	0.91
1982	496,808	6.2	25,861	7.8	5.2	0.93
1983	503,796	1.4	27,542	6.5	5.5	0.98
1984	506,272	0.5	29,346	6.55	5.8	0.991
1985	524,996	3.7	31,371	6.9	5.98	0.997
1986	540,886	3.0	33,435	6.58	6.18	0.993
1987	541,010	0.0	35,174	5.2	6.50	1.004
1988	566,997	4.8	37,003	5.2	6.53	1.013

Source: Zaisei Seisaku Kenkyukai (ed.) *Nijuisseiki heno Tenbo – Korekarano Zaisei to Kokusai Hakko [Survey of 21st Century – the Future of Public Finance and National Debt],* Ryuichiro Tachi, 1988, p. 103

1964. After 1965 budget deficits expanded, forcing the government to issue construction bonds within the amount of public works expenditure to finance public works. The amount of such construction bonds increased from ¥665.6bn in 1965 to ¥2,160.0bn in 1974 (Figure 11.1).

The issue of construction bonds was prompted by the business recession in 1965. That year the real economic growth rate was 4.9 per cent, the lowest since 1955, and private business investment declined about 9 per cent in real terms from the previous year. The government overcame the recession through fiscal expenditure by issuing construction bonds, and continued to help economic growth heavily dependent on exports.

In fiscal year 1975, a special law was enacted under which bonds known as 'deficit-financing bonds' or 'special government bonds' were authorized in addition to construction bonds. The issue of deficit-financing bonds was prompted by the rise of prices triggered by the oil crisis of 1973 (and soaring oil prices) and the resultant slowdown of economic growth. The year-to-year increase of consumer prices was 15.6 per cent in fiscal year 1973, 20.9 per cent in fiscal year 1974 and 10.4 per cent in fiscal year

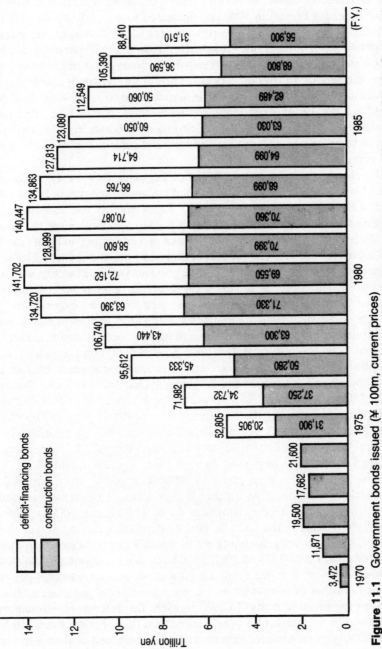

Figure 11.1 Government bonds issued (¥ 100m, current prices)

Source: Zaisei Seisaku Kenkyukai (ed.) *Nijuisseiki heno Tenbo – Korekarano Zaisei to Kokusai Hakko [Survey of the 21st Century – the Future of Public Finance and National Debt]*, Ryuichiro Tachi, 1988, p. 46

1975. The government coped with this recession with a massive issue of government bonds. That year's issue of government bonds amounted to ¥=5,208.5bn (of which deficit-financing bonds accounted for ¥2,090.5bn). The amount increased to ¥14,170.2bn (including ¥7,215.2bn worth of deficit-financing bonds) in 1980 and decreased to ¥12,438.0bn (¥4,135.0bn) in 1985 (Figure 11.1). In the process, the dependence of the national budget on government bonds reached approximately 20 per cent. The issue of deficit-financing bonds made it possible to issue government bonds apart from the quota of public works expenditure, virtually nullifying the provisions of Article 4 of the Government Finance Law, which had been based on the bitter experience of the Second World War. By issuing construction bonds in 1965 and deficit-financing bonds in 1975, Japan was able to increase government expenditure and achieve high growth rates of defence spending.

The change in Japan's defence policy began to show in the early 1980s when the increase rate of general account budget slowed down. In the world-wide wake of administrative reform, Japan set up the second *ad hoc* Commission on Administrative Reform in 1981. To implement the reform, the Ministry of Finance introduced the idea of 'zero ceiling' in fiscal year 1982 and 'minus ceiling' into the process of budget compilation. On this basis, the budget was to be cut 5 per cent from the previous year in all sectors with some exceptions, and since fiscal year 1984 the reduction has been set at 5 per cent for current expenditure and 10 per cent for capital expenditure.

Even under such rigid standards for estimating budget demands set by the Ministry of Finance, defence spending has been treated together with external economic co-operation and government bond expenses as an exception. Indeed, its annual growth rates from fiscal years 1982 to 1987 varied between 5.2 per cent and 7.8 per cent (see Table 11.1). In fiscal year 1981, defence spending's year-to-year growth rate exceeded that of social welfare expenditure for the first time in the post-war period. This change drew general attention as an indication of the shifting priorities in the national budget. Since then, defence and international affairs spending has emerged as the most important item in Japan's national budget.

What priority has been given to defence spending over time will be reviewed by comparing with other budget items. Comparison of budget items from 1955 to 1988 is shown in Table 11.2. From 1955 to 1965 and from 1965 to 1975, the growth rate of defence spending stayed below that of social security spending or of education and science promotion expenditures. From 1975 to 1985 (when Japan's economic growth slowed down), however, defence spending grew at an annual rate of 9 per cent, higher than that of education and science promotion and close to the 9.3 per cent for social security. In 1987 to 1988, the defence spending growth rate stood at 5.2 per cent a year, higher than that of other items. In fiscal year 1988, general account expenditure was composed as shown in Figure

Table 11.2 The general account expenditure (¥100m, per cent current price)

Fiscal year	1955	1955–65 increase rate	1965	1965–75 increase rate	1975	1975–85 increase rate	1985	1986–7 increase rate	1987	1987–8 increase rate	1988
National debt	434 (4.4)	6.6	220 (0.6)	47.0	10,394 (4.9)	25.7	102,241 (19.5)	0.1	113,335 (20.9)	1.6	115,120 (20.3)
Grants to local government	1,374 (13.9)	18.0	7,162 (19.6)	20.0	44,086 (20.7)	8.2	96,901 (18.5)	0.0	101,841 (19.2)	7.1	109,056
The use of NTT[1] stock	(–)	–	(–)	–	(–)	–	(–)	–	(–)	–	13,000 (2.3)
The general expenditure	8,107 (81.7)	13.7	29,199 (79.8)	18.4	158,408 (74.4)	7.5	325,854 (62.0)	0.0	325,884 (60.3)	1.2	329,821 (58.2)
Social security	1,043 (10.5)	18.3	5,183 (14.2)	22.5	39,282 (18.5)	9.3	95,736 (18.2)	2.5	100,896 (18.7)	2.9	103,845 (18.3)
Pension	895 (9.0)	6.8	1,693 (4.6)	16.1	7,558 (3.5)	9.4	18,637 (3.6)	2.5	18,956 (3.5)	0.8	18,798 (3.3)
Education and science promotion	1,308 (13.2)	14.2	4,751 (13.0)	18.5	25,921 (12.2)	6.4	48,409 (9.2)	0.1	48,497 (9.0)	0.2	48,581 (8.6)
Defence	1,349 (13.6)	8.5	3,014 (8.2)	16.0	13,273 (6.2)	9.0	31,371 (6.0)	3.2	35,174 (6.5)	5.2	37,003 (6.5)
Public works	1,635 (16.5)	16.1	7,333 (20.0)	14.8	29,120 (13.7)	8.1	63,689 (12.1)	2.3	60,824 (11.2)	0.0	60,824 (10.7)
Economic assistance	101 (1.0)	32.7	271 (0.7)	21.7	1,925 (0.9)	11.8	5,864 (1.1)	4.2	6,492 (1.2)	5.1	6,822 (1.2)
Small business	26 (0.3)	43.2	217 (0.6)	19.4	1,273 (0.6)	5.4	2,162 (0.4)	3.8	1,973 (0.4)	1.1	1,952 (0.4)
Energy	– (–)	–	– (–)	–	884 (0.4)	21.7	6,288 (1.2)	21.4	4,952 (0.9)	6.8	4,616 (0.8)
Food management	(–)	–	1,055 (2.9)	24.0	9,086 (4.3)	2.6	6,954 (1.3)	9.3	5,406 (1.0)	17.1	4,482 (0.8)
Others	1,670 (16.8)	10.4	5,182 (14.2)	17.9	26,870 (12.6)	4.9	43,244 (8.2)	4.1	39,163 (7.3)	0.6	39,393 (7.0)
Reserve funds	80 (0.8)	20.1	500 (1.4)	19.6	3,000 (1.4)	1.6	3,500 (0.7)	0.0	3,500 (0.6)	0.0	3,500 (0.6)
Total	9,915 (100.0)	13.9	36,581 (100.0)	19.3	212,888 (100.0)	9.4	524,996 (100.0)	0.0	541,010 (100.00)	4.8	566,997 (100.00)

Source: Zaisei Seisaku Kenkyukai (ed.) Nijuisseiki heno Tenbo – Korekarano Zaisei to Kokusai Hakko [Survey of 21st Century – the Future of Public Finance and National Debt], Ryuichiro Tachi, 1988, p. 37.
Note: [1]Government privatized Japan Telegraph and Telephone Public Corp. Its new name is NTT. NTT went public, and the Government realized the profits.

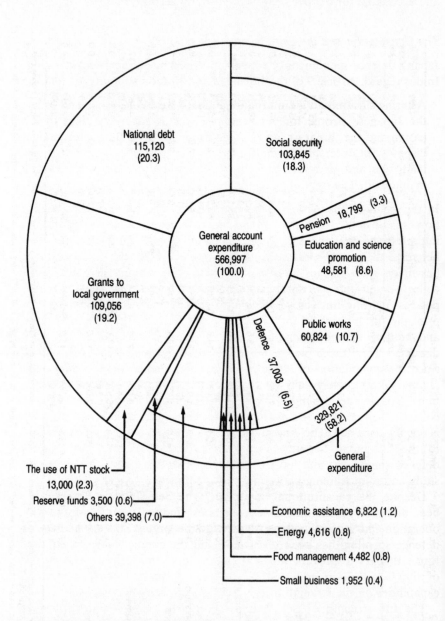

Figure 11.2 The general account expenditure (¥100m, per cent, current price)
Source: Zaisei Seisaku Kenkyukai (ed.) *Nijuisseike heno Tenbo – Korekarano Zaisei to Kokusai Hakko [Survey of the 21st Century – the Future of Public Finance and National Debt]*, Ryuichiro Tachi, 1988, p. 36

11.2, and defence spending reached a level of one-third of social security and accounted for 6.5 per cent of the general account budget.

The Constitution and the Self-Defence Forces

Japan's defence spending is of course influenced by political consideration. In this regard, Article 9 of the Japanese Constitution stipulates as follows:

Aspiring sincerely to an international peace based on justice and order, the Japanese people forever renounce war as sovereign right of the nation and the threat or use of force as means of settling international disputes. In order to accomplish the aims of the preceding paragraph, land, sea, and air force, as well as other war potential, will never be maintained. The right of belligerency of the state will not be recognized.

In the light of this Article, the unconstitutionality of the Self-Defence Forces is obvious. None the less the Japanese government has held to the interpretation that the Self-Defence Forces are not 'military' forces. To help ease the people's misgivings about 'military' buildup, the government has made such pledges as exclusively defensive posture, prohibition of collective self-defence right, triple non-nuclear principle (not to make, possess or bring nuclear weapons into Japan), triple armaments export principle, prohibition of the overseas dispatching of Self-Defence Forces and holding defence spending under 1 per cent of GNP. As will be discussed later, these pledges have been drastically changed or nullified since the compilation of 'guidelines for US–Japan defence cooperation' (January 1978), which laid out the basis for bilateral co-operative operations. Today, the possibility of military action that involves the right of collective self-defence and overseas dispatching of the Self-Defence Forces is openly discussed. The guidelines, as they are said to have given new life to the US–Japan Security Treaty, have influenced the way Japan's defence should be, and led to greater opportunities for joint operation study and joint training between the two countries.

Despite the constitutional stipulation, the Self-Defence Forces have been built up because they have a legal basis in the Treaty of Mutual Co-operation and Security between Japan and the United States. The issue of defence spending has been discussed amid the conflict between political forces that try to prevent Japan's militarization on the basis of Article 9 of the Constitution and political forces that try to build up defence capabilities on the strength of the Japan–US Security Treaty.

The full strength of Self-Defence Forces (an all-volunteer force) is shown in Figure 11.3. As the number increases, the strength of US Forces stationed in Japan declines. As Table 11.3 shows, the full strength of the Self-Defence Forces was 272,762 from March 1987. In 1988, it was over 244,422. The manning rate of 71.1 per cent of the enlisted lower officers of the Ground Self-Defence Forces reflects political conflicts over many issues about the Self-Defence Forces.

Table 11.3 Authorized number and actual number of SDF personnel (as of 31 March 1987)

Division	GSDF	MSDF	ASDF	Joint staff Council	Total
Officers					
Authorized number	22,797	9,569	9,181	131	41,678
Actual number	22,018	9,345	8,849	131	40,343
Manning rate (%)	96.6	97.7	96.4	100.0	96.8
Warrant officers					
Authorized number	3,523	842	780		5,145
Actual number	3,069	792	729		4,590
Manning rate (%)	87.1	94.1	93.5		89.2
Enlisted (upper)					
Authorized number	78,031	22,783	25,769	21	126,604
Actual number	77,054	22,416	25,653	21	125,144
Manning rate (%)	98.7	98.4	99.5	100.0	98.8
Enlisted (lower)					
Authorized number	75,649	12,357	11,335		99,341
Actual number	53,770	11,055	9,520		74,345
Manning rate (%)	71.1	89.5	84.0		74 .8
Total					
Authorized number	180,000	45,551	47,065	152	272,768
Actual number	155,911	43,608	44,751	152	244,422
Manning rate (%)	86.6	95.7	95.1	100.0	89.6

Source: *Defense of Japan 1987*, The Japan Times, Tokyo, p. 289

Changes in defence spending

The history and present state of the expansion of the defence buildup

The present buildup of Japan's defence capabilities is based on the National Defence Programme Outline decided by the National Defence Council and the Cabinet in October 1978. This sets the level of defence capabilities that should be held even in peacetime, as shown in Table 11.4. This target level alone, however, does not show how Japan's defence capabilities have changed over the years. This becomes clear by reviewing the actual defence spending, the history of defence buildup and the process of constructing the defence foundation in three areas.

First is defence grants. As is shown in Table 11.5, Japan used to depend heavily on the military assistance programme (MAP) from the United States. Japan's defence buildup programme had been prepared taking into full account this assistance, which amounted to ¥356.9bn in 1950–7, ¥140.5bn in 1958–60, ¥26.1bn in 1963, ¥49.7bn in 1962–6 and ¥3.3bn in 1967–70. The MAP was cut off in 1971, which implies that the Japanese economy had reached a level sufficient for financing the country's buildup on its own.

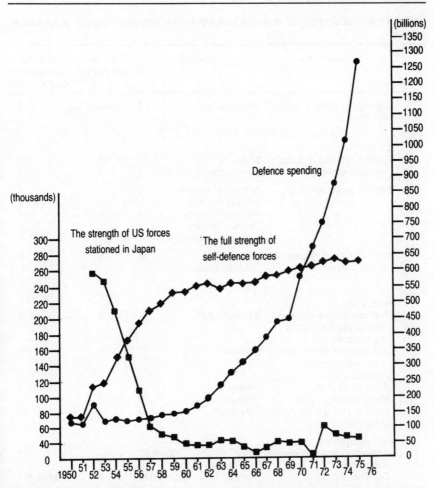

Figure 11.3 The full strength of the Self Defence Forces and the strength of US forces stationed in Japan

Source: Tokei Shihyo Kenkyukai *Tokei Nihon Keizai Bunseki [The Statistical Analysis of Japan's Economy]*, Shin Nihon Shuppan Sha, Tokyo, 1977, vol. 1, p. 114

Second is the method of procuring weapons. There are two points to consider about weapons procurement. The first is whether the defence buildup programme is based on the single-year scheme or the long-term scheme. Since the First Defence Buildup Programme (1958–60), Japan has had medium- and long-term programmes, which were strongly desired by industry on the grounds that:

It is essential for consolidating the firm-rooted self-defense capabilities to prepare domestic production of specific equipment so as to meet

Table 11.4 Attainment of defence buildup in the 'national defence programme outline'

	Classification	'Outline'		Upon the completion of FY 1987	Upon the completion of the programme
	Authorized number of SDF personnel	Unit: 10,000		18	18	18
GSDF						
	Basic units					
	Units deployed regionally in peacetime	Divisions		12	12	12
		Composite brigades		2	2	2
	Mobile operation units	Armoured division		1	1	1
		Artillery brigade		1	1	1
		Airborne brigade		1	1	1
		Training brigade		1	1	1
		Helicopter brigade		1	1	1
	Low-altitude surface-to-air missile units	Anti-aircraft artillery groups		8	8	8
MSDF						
	Basic units					
	Anti-submarine surface-ship units (for mobile operations)	Escort flotillas		4	4	4
	Anti-submarine surface-ship units (regional district units)	Divisions		10	10	10
	Submarine units	Divisions		6	6	6
	Minesweeping units	Flotillas		2	2	2
	Land-based anti-submarine aircraft units	Squadrons		16	14	16
	Main equipment					
	Anti-submarine surface-ship	Ships	About 60	61	62
	Submarines	Submarines	16	14	16
	Combat aircraft	Aircraft	About 220	168	About 214
ASDF						
	Basic units					
	Aircraft control and warning units	Aircraft control and warning units		28	28	28
	Interceptor units	Flight squadrons		10	10	10
	Support fighter units	Flight squadrons		3	3	3
	Air reconnaissance units	Flight squadron		1	1	1
	Air transport units	Flight squadrons		3	3	3
	Early warning units	Flight squadron		1	1	1
	High-altitude surface-to-air missile units	Anti-aircraft groups		6	6	6
	Main equipment					
	Combat aircraft	Aircraft	About 430	396	415

Source: Defense of Japan 1987, The Japan Times, Tokyo, p. 80

Table 11.5 Changes in volume of equipment procurements by procurement method (¥100m current price)

Classification / Year	Domestic procurements (A)	Commercial imports (B)	Foreign military sales (FMS) (C)	Military assistance programme (MAP) (D)	Total (E = A + B + C + D)	Ratio of domestic procurements (%) (A/E)
1950–7	2,415	95	25	3,569	6,104	39.6
1st Defence build-up plan (1958–60)	2,789	109	168	1,405	4,471	62.4
1961	702	63	60	261	1,086	64.6
2nd Defence buildup plan (1962–6)	5,781	424	382	497	7,084	81.6
3rd Defence buildup plan (1967–71)	12,829	662	478	33	14,002	91.6
4th Defence buildup plan (1972–6)	21,588	1,001	617	0	23,206	93.0
1977	5,846	222	194	0	6,261	93.4
1978	7,126	209	1,014	0	8,349	85.4
1979	7,373	394	885	0	8,652	85.2
1980	10,506	567	801	0	11,875	88.5
1981	8,158	604	1,368	0	10,130	80.5
1982	12,425	618	978	0	14,020	88.6
1983	12,673	598	758	0	14,029	90.3
1984	12,791	787	528	0	14,107	90.7
1985	13,417	636	707	0	14,760	90.9

Sources: Defense of Japan 1984, p. 274 and Defense of Japan 1987, p. 310

demand from the Defense Agency. However, as the demand depends on government budgets that are subject to the current political situation, the budget may be reduced or suspended for some reason. Thus the defense industry has a very fragile foundation. For a business corporation to start defense equipment production on a full scale, there must be something highly reliable that eliminates this weakness.[2]

To ensure such a reliable base, four defence buildup improvement programmes were compiled from 1958 to 1976. The first programme lasted for 3 years and the second, third and fourth programmes for 5 years each.

Even after the fourth programme, the idea of a long-term programme has been upheld, though in a different way. Since the National Defence Programme Outline of 1976, the Defence Agency has drawn up weapons procurement programmes to build up defence capabilities. For all fourth programmes, the content and expenditure of defence buildup were shown, but the outline showed only the target and not the necessary expenditure for defence buildup.

The Defence Agency implemented a 5-year weapons procurement programme called the 'mid-term defence buildup programme estimate', together with an expense estimate in 1978. The first estimate covered 1980–4, the second 1983–7, and the third 1986–90. However, this programming formula designed as a reference for the Defence Agency was discontinued in 1985, and today defence buildup is being improved on the basis of the official mid-term defence capability buildup programme (1986–90) prepared by the government. In this, the content and total expenditure of defence buildup for 5 years were officially disclosed for the first time in 13 years since the fourth defence buildup programme. The medium- and long-term weapons procurement programmes were essential for the steady development of the defence industry in ensuing years.

Another aspect of procurement is whether weapons are purchased at home or from abroad. As Table 11.5 shows, the domestic procurement rate continued to increase from 39.6 per cent in 1950–7 to 90.9 per cent in 1985. This shows how steadily the Japanese defence industry has improved its technological level. External procurement (mostly from the United States) is of two types: one is commercial imports through Japanese trading firms and the other is the Defense Agency's purchases from the US Defence Department in the form of foreign military sales (FMS). The total of these two types of procurement (B+C) amounted to ¥161.8bn in the period of fiscal years 1972–6 (¥32.36bn a year). For the following 9 years, fiscal years 1977–85, the figures were ¥31.6bn, ¥122.3bn, ¥127.9bn, Y=136.8bn, ¥197.2bn, ¥159.6bn, ¥135.6bn, ¥131.5bn, and ¥134.8bn. Evidently procurement from the United States has increased rapidly since 1978. Whereas the domestic procurement rate reached 90 per cent, Japan since 1978 has sharply increased imports from the

United States of expensive advanced weapons that are unavailable domestically.

The third area is the type of weapons procured. Table 11.4 indicates that the targets of the outline have been achieved in most areas in terms of quantity. The problem is not the quantity of major equipment but the change in quality. Since fiscal year 1981, procurement from abroad has been increasing chiefly because of the growing sophistication of weapons. By fiscal year 1987, for example, Japan had bought 66 P-3Cs (fixed-wing anti-submarine patrol aircraft) under the plan to purchase 100 of these aircraft after fiscal year 1978 and had purchased 134 F-15 fighter-intercepters under the plan to buy 187 of these aircraft after fiscal year 1978. Such facts attest to the unmistakable improvement in the level of Japan's defence capability. Stable procurement methods and the developed defence industry have helped the rapid upgrading of Japan's armaments since the 1980s.

Japan's defence industry is shown in Table 11.6. Mitsubishi Heavy Industries far outpaces others in entering procurement contracts with the Defence Agency. In 1986, the top five contractors accounted for 53 per cent of the total value of contracts.

Methods and mechanism to expand defence spending

The government pledge to hold defence spending below the ceiling of 1 per cent of GNP[3] was inconsistent with the slow economic growth after 1973 and the increase in defence spending. How have these two seemingly inconsistent requirements been reconciled?

Figure 11.4 shows the change in defence spending by expense item. What draws our attention is the continued increase in the obligational outlay[4] from 21.3 per cent of the total in fiscal year 1979 to 36.0 per cent in fiscal year 1987. The White Paper on defence explains that the obligational outlay tends to increase gradually because of the procurement of large-scale equipment such as destroyers, P-3Cs and F-15s.[5] This obligational outlay, also called 'future obligations', is designed to hold down the first-year payment of weapons procurement and carry it over to later (up to 5) years. This method of appropriation has been used as a way to build up defence while at the same time holding a yearly spending below the 1 per cent of GNP ceiling. This is an exceptional measure under the Constitution which employs the single-year budget system.

The future obligations system, which has been used to achieve the dual purposes of building up defence capability and holding spending under 1 per cent of GNP, is not always favourable to the defence industry. The Defence Production Committee submitted a request to the Defence Agency asking that defence spending be compiled in a way suited for production by the private sector.[6] The request was made because of the

Table 11.6 Ranking of defence agency's contracts (top twenty contractors)

Ranking	Company	Number of contracts	Value (¥m)	%	Main items procured
1	Mitsubishi Heavy Industries	185	235,866	21.4	Aircraft, repair, ships, guidance weapons, rolling-stock weapons
2	Kawasaki Heavy Industries	108	102,736	9.3	Aircraft, repair, ships, guidance weapons, trial products
3	Ishikawajima-Harima Heavy Ind.	55	93,108	8.4	Aircraft engines, repair, ships
4	Mitsubishi Electric	189	92,335	8.4	Guidance weapons, telecommunications equipment, radio equipment, trial products
5	Toshiba	168	60,596	5.5	Guidance weapons, telecommunications equipment, radio equipment, trial products
6	NEC Corp.	291	43,171	3.9	Telecommunications equipment, radio equipment
7	Japan Steel Works	32	23,643	2.1	Weapons, trial products
8	Sumitomo Heavy Industries	26	22,075	2.0	Ships, weapons
9	Hitachi Zosen	27	20,537	1.9	Ships, weapons
10	Itochu Aviation	35	19,470	1.8	Imported goods
11	Mitsui Engineering & Shipbuilding	3	18,048	1.6	Ships
12	Komatsu	57	15,320	1.4	Bullets, rolling-stock
13	Fuji Heavy Industries	30	14,901	1.4	Aircraft, repair
14	Nippon Oil	187	12,875	1.2	Fuel
15	Daikin Industries	58	10,889	1.0	Bullets
16	Hitachi	47	9,976	0.9	Telecommunications equipment
17	Shimazu Corp.	74	9,442	0.9	Aircraft-related equipment
18	Maruzen Oil	193	8,997	0.8	Fuel
19	Fujitsu	94	8,637	0.8	Telecommunication equipment, radio equipment
20	Shin Meiwa Industry	18	7,903	0.7	Aircraft
	Total	1,877	830,525	75.3	

Source: Jieitai Sobi Nenkan [Self-Defence Equipment Annual], Asagumo Shinbun Sha, 1986, p. 540

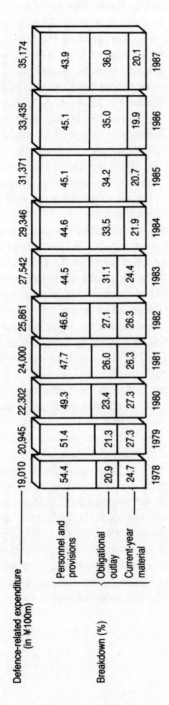

Figure 11.4 Defence-related expenditure classified by expenses
Sources: Defense of Japan 1984, p. 146 and Defense of Japan 1987, p. 150

Defence-related expenditure (in ¥100m)	19,010	20,945	22,302	24,000	25,861	27,542	29,346	31,371	33,435	35,174
Breakdown (%)										
Personnel and provisions	54.4	51.4	49.3	47.7	46.6	44.5	44.6	45.1	45.1	43.9
Obligational outlay	20.9	21.3	23.4	26.0	27.1	31.1	33.5	34.2	35.0	36.0
Current-year material	24.7	27.3	27.3	26.3	26.3	24.4	21.9	20.7	19.9	20.1
	1978	1979	1980	1981	1982	1983	1984	1985	1986	1987

lag that developed between the early-stage equipment investment by companies and payments received by them. The inconsistency between the needs of the defence buildup and the demand for holding it below 1 per cent of GNP has been eliminated by disregarding the latter. The 1 per cent ceiling set up in 1976 was broken through in 1987. Three aspects of Japan's defence spending after this break will now be discussed.

First is defence strategy. A major recent development in Japan's defence policy is the decision of 'the Guideline for Japan–U.S. Defense Cooperation in 1978', under which Japan has undertaken the defence of sea lanes within 1,000 nautical miles of Japanese territory and procured equipment necessary for this purpose, despite experts' criticism that it is an entirely unfeasible and unrealistic idea. In 1987, the idea of air defence at sea was proposed, and the Defence Agency requested purchase of AWACS (airborne warning and control system), a fleet with the AEGIS air-defence system and OTH (over the horizon) radar.

Second are the problems stemming from the standardization of weapons. Japan now deploys F-15 fighters and E-2C, which can properly function and perform when they are connected with the BADGE (base air defence ground environment) system. Armaments are made to function as a system when they are connected with other weapons. However, such standardization causes the following problem. The computer capabilities of the present version of the BADGE system are far behind those of the F-15 or the E-2C. To fill the gap, a new BADGE system, which is said to cost Y=300 billion, must be deployed.[7] The renewal of a component of a weapons system inevitably requires the replacement of others in the system, and this is a further reason for the increase in defence spending.

Third is the problem of R & D. The share of R & D spending in total defence spending edged up from 1.6 per cent in 1984 to 1.84 per cent in 1985 and 1.9 per cent in 1986. The mid-term defence buildup programme (for fiscal years 1986–90) plans to raise this percentage to the 3 per cent level. The increased R & D will help create new weapons, affect the weapons systems and defence plans and increase defence spending. In the past it was inconceivable for private companies to undertake research and develop weapons by themselves without the influence of the Defence Agency. In recent years, however, exceptions to this past rule have occurred,[8] and this will most likely stimulate competition in the development and sale of new weapons. With this constraint removed, the demand for increased defence spending arising from changes in strategies and weapons system and R & D by the defence industry is expected to increase in coming years.

Defence and Japan–US relations

Under the Japan–US security arrangement, Japan's defence spending is closely related to the American military–industrial complex. Japan's defence buildup is thus greatly influenced by the course of the US strategy, defence spending and weapons producing companies. It is meaningful, therefore, to see the recent Japan–US relations in light of: (1) the R & D, production and sale (marketing) of weapons and (2) the burden sharing of defence spending.

Linkage in weapons

R & D

In January 1983, Japan decided on 'the transfer of military arms technology to the US' and in November it signed the exchange notes on the transfer based on the Japan–US mutual defence assistance agreement. This marked a major turnaround in Japan's attitude toward the export of weapons. Until that time, the government had held to the three military arms export principles.

> The Three Principles on Arms Export were declared in April 1967 by then Prime Minister Eisaku Sato. It provided that arms exports to the following countries shall not be permitted: (a) Communist bloc countries, (b) countries to which the export of arms is prohibited under United Nations resolutions, and (c) countries which are actually involved or likely to become involved in international conflicts.
>
> The Government Policy Guideline on Arms Control of February 1976 was announced by then Prime Minister Takeo Miki. The guideline makes it clear that the government will not promote the export of arms, and its gist is as follows: (i) the export of arms to areas subject to the Three Principles on Arms Export shall be prohibited; (ii) the export of arms to other areas shall be restrained; and (iii) equipment related to arms production shall be treated in the same manner as arms. The export of military technologies (transfer to non-residents) shall be treated in the light of the Three Principles on Arms Exports and the Government Policy Guideline on Arms Control of February 1976.[9]

The 1983 policy change was an exception applied exclusively to the United States, and as a result, a team from the US defence industry came to Japan and conducted a survey of the possibilities of technological exchange in October 1983. According to this survey, most of Japan's high technologies that attract American attention are non-military.[10] In Japan there are few cases in which the technology developed for defence purposes is adapted for the private sector, and what draws attention is mostly non-military technology. In July 1987 a government agreement was

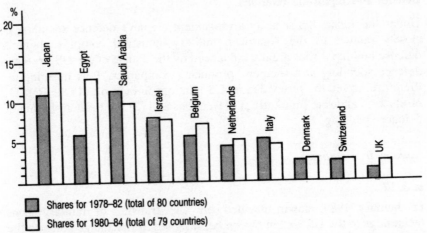

Shares for 1978–82 (total of 80 countries)

Shares for 1980–84 (total of 79 countries)

Figure 11.5 Importers of US major weapons, 1978–82 and 1980–4 (shares are a percentage of total imports of US weapons)
Source: *SIPRI Yearbook 1985*, p. 359

concluded on the participation in the study of SDI. This was intended as a means for the US to absorb the results of Japan's R & D and technology to develop SDI.

Production

US arms are produced using parts manufactured both at home and abroad. Today an important component of weapons is semiconductors, an area where Japan has a strong competitive edge over the US. With the awareness of its vulnerability arising from its dependence on foreign countries for production of certain vital parts, the US Department of Defense issued a report on semiconductor dependency in 1987.[11]

In terms of memory, the Japanese semiconductor industry enjoys an overwhelming share, which is growing steadily. Japan's share of the world's 256 DRAM market is as high as 90 per cent. To cope with the threat from Japan in production of weapons parts, semiconductors in particular, the United States concluded the semiconductor agreement with Japan in September 1986, which called for greater opportunities for foreign semiconductors in the Japanese market and for the monitoring of export semiconductor prices by the Japanese government to prevent dumping. The agreement was prompted by the American military requirement for domestic production of essential parts.

Sale (marketing)

After the Vietnam War, the United States has sought overseas markets to reduce military expenditure and improve its balance of international payments. As a result, US sales of armaments jumped from \$1.5bn in 1970 to \$10.4bn in 1986.[12] The weight of the Japanese market in this endeavour is shown in Figure 11.5. As a market for US arms exports, Japan overtook Saudi Arabia to rank first from 1980 to 1984.

Japan's imports of weapons are shown in greater detail in Table 11.5. Combined commercial import and foreign military sales (FMS), mostly from the US, expanded from ¥41.6bn in 1977 to ¥100.0bn in 1978 and Y=135.6bn in 1983. As a result of the importance of its market for US weapons, Japan's domestic production of weapons has been under constant pressure from the US. A case in point was the scrapping of Japan's plan to manufacture the PXL in October 1972 and the consequent import of the P–3C from the US and its licensed production instead. The plan to produce the FSX (fighter support X) was also cancelled and replaced in 1988 by the plan for joint development between the two countries.

Burden sharing

Burden sharing is being discussed as an issue of international public goods. The Ministry of International Trade and Industry says in one of its recent reports:

> The cost of maintaining and managing the international currency and trade systems as well as the cost of maintaining international security and world politics, and the international economic order in such areas as assistance – that is the burden of so-called international public goods – has been borne chiefly by the United States in the 20th century. In sharing this burden Japan has been behind West Germany, France and Britain. Japan should play a positive role in maintaining the international order by expanding economic assistance, increasing trade through further market opening, and spending more on R & D, basic R & D in particular, thus raising the share of the yen in external assistance and public foreign currency reserves, and by assuming a larger share of the international public goods burden through raising imports and R & D expenditure to the average international level.[13]

With this perception, MITI calculated the indexes of international public goods burden sharing shown in Table 11.7 to make it one of the standards for Japan's burden sharing. As is clear from the Table, the burden sharing index has been prepared with strong emphasis placed on economic considerations. This is not designed to help Japan take action on the present world security system or political system under a new vision. It merely represents an effort to calculate the standard of burden sharing within the policy framework proposed by the United States. This is another example that reveals Japan as a country that cannot have its own foreign policy.

Table 11.7 International public goods: burden sharing index

		Defence v. the world	Defence v. developed countries	ODA	UN expense share	% in public foreign reserves	Export & import	Import	R & D spending
US	1950	0.73	0.98	0.88		0.58	0.43	0.35	
	1960	1.17	1.24	1.05	0.90	1.29	0.37	0.42	
	1970	1.09	1.34	0.97	1.00	1.64	0.43	0.56	1.11
	1980	1.16	1.58	0.78	1.12	1.99	0.52	0.56	1.12
	1983	1.35	1.69	0.87	1.17	2.06	0.54	0.65	1.22
Japan	1950	1.25	1.77				0.96	1.23	
	1960	0.38	0.41	0.45	0.71		1.04	0.82	
	1970	0.23	0.28	0.70	0.80		0.92	0.73	0.78
	1980	0.19	0.25	0.87	1.03	0.31	0.74	0.70	1.02
	1983	0.18	0.23	0.96	1.07	0.30	0.73		0.98
West Germany	1950	1.32	1.76				0.96	1.38	
	1960	0.94	1.03	0.92		0.37	1.43	1.56	0.86
	1970	0.75	1.00	1.01	1.07	1.41	1.69	1.26	0.99
	1980	0.68	0.93	1.27	1.06	1.16	1.32	1.23	0.72
	1983	0.65	0.81	1.12		0.22	1.25		
France	1950	1.38	1.86	6.86			1.44	1.00	
	1960	1.20	1.29	2.71	1.45	0.32	1.96	1.36	0.82
	1970	0.86	1.20	2.50	1.36	0.20	1.45	1.22	0.85
	1980	0.85	1.12	1.80	0.67	0.20	1.09	1.11	0.67
	1983	0.81	1.01	1.65	0.72	0.12	0.94		
UK	1950	1.28	1.69	1.06		8.50	2.20	1.78	
	1960	1.03	1.12	1.17	1.52	4.51	0.98	1.69	0.87
	1970	1.89	1.30	1.10	1.51	2.17	1.49	1.23	0.57
	1980	1.07	1.25	1.00	1.14	0.44	1.23	1.23	0.77
	1983	1.05	1.39	0.87	0.98	0.39	1.09		

Source: Tusho Sangyo Sho Sangyo Seisaku Kyoku (ed.) *Nijuisseiki Sangyoshakai no Kihon Koso [Basic Concept for the Industrial Society of the 21st Century]*, Tusho Sangyo Chosa Kai, Tokyo, 1986, p. 44

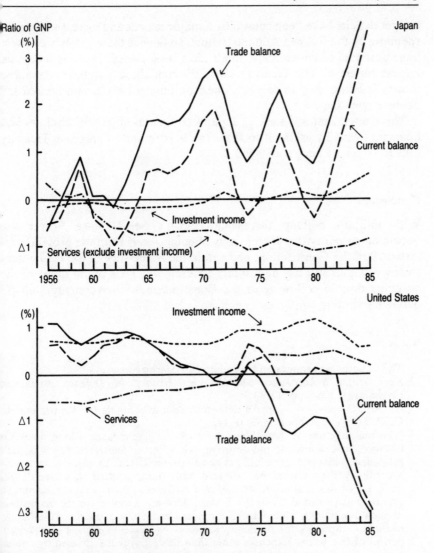

Figure 11.6 Balance of payments (Japan and US)
Source: Keizai Hakusho 1986 [White Paper on Economy 1986], p. 165

Because of the increases in Japan's trade surplus and American trade deficits in the 1980s (see Figure 11.6), there have been stronger demands for Japan to shoulder more of the burdens of defence spending. On the international front, as discussions at the recent Toronto summit of the heads of the seven leading industrialized countries showed, the basis for co-operative economic policy lies in how to reduce the US fiscal deficit and expand domestic demand in Japan and West Germany. The massive US budget deficits have been caused by a major tax cut and increased defence spending by the Reagan Administration. To finance these policy measures, huge amounts of government bonds have been issued. Japan is today the largest buyer of US Treasury bills; through these purchases Japanese money is being used to service American budget deficits and finance US defence spending.

The United States is seeking Japan's co-operation on both military and financial fronts by asking it to share the burden and to purchase Treasury bills to cover its budget deficits.

Conclusion

With military buildup increasing, Japan's Self-Defence Forces are becoming an entity that increasingly alienates itself from the provisions of Article 9 of the Constitution, and within the framework of the US military strategy, Japan still has no military sovereignty. Thus in the midst of the on-going double hollowing of the Constitution and sovereignty, Japan's defence spending continues to expand.

Notes

1 This chapter was translated by Tadatoshi Higashizono.
2 *Boei Seisan Iinkai Junen Shi [10-years History the Defence Production Committee]*, 1964, pp. 172–3.
3 By NATO standards, Japan's defence spending accounts for 1.6 per cent of GNP. *SIPRI, Yearbook 1987*, p. 142.
4 'The manufacture of these large items of equipment takes a long time (for instance, that of aircraft and destroyer takes four to five years, or tanks, self-propelled guns and armored personnel carriers, two to three years), and accordingly they cannot be procured with funds allotted in a single year budget. For this reason, the formulas of contract authorization and continued expenses as provided for in the Finance Law are adopted for the acquisition of such equipment. Under these formulas, budgetary measures are taken to faciliate contracting for the manufacture of equipment covering a maximum period of five years. Expenses other than down payments covered by annual budgets are so called "future obligations", for which appropriations are made in subsequent annual budgets as obligational outlay expenses.'
                    (*Defense of Japan 1987*, The Japan Times, Tokyo, p. 151.)
5 *Boei Hakusho 1986 [White Paper on Defence 1986]*, p. 183
6 *Boei Seisan Iinkai Tokuho [Special Report of the Defense Production Report]*, no. 210, 1985, p. 19.
7 Koichiro Yoshiwara, *Nihon no Heiki Sangyo [Japan's Weapons Industry]*, Daiyamondo Sha, Tokyo, 1982, pp. 87–91.
8 Kazuo Tomiyama, *Nihon no Boei Sangyo [Japan's Defence Industry]*, Toyo Keizai Shinpo Sha, 1987, p. 52.
9 *Defense of Japan 1987*, The Japan Times, Tokyo, p. 177.
10 Akio Sakai, *Nihon no Gunkaku Keizai [Japan's Military Expansion Economy]*, Aoki Shoten, 1987, p. 302.

11 Office of the Under-Secretary of Defense Acquisition, *Report of Defense Semiconductor Dependency*, 1987.
12 *SIPRI, Yearbook 1987*, p. 183.
13 Tusho Sangyo Sho Sangyo Seisaku Kyoku (ed.) *Nijuisseiki Sangyoshakai no Kihon Koso [Basic Concept for the Industrial Society of the 21st Century]*, Tusho Sangyo Chosa Kai, Tokyo, 1986, pp. 42–3.

Index

Abu Nidal Organization 11
acquisition of arms *see* procurement
Action Directe 11
Aden 81
advisors, military: from Warsaw Pact
  countries 48, 50–1, 53
Afghanistan: military expenditure of 46;
  and Pakistan 198, 200, 201, 203, 213;
  (terrorism 11); Soviet occupation of 20,
  25, 36; Warsaw Pact arms exports to 52
Africa: arms sales to 51, 83; French
  military commitment to 100, 101–9
  passim, 114–15nn. 7&9&10; *see also*
  individiual countries
Aganbeygan, Abel 63
aid *see* foreign aid
air force: of Argentina 243; of Chile
  241, 243; of France 98, 99; of German
  Federal Republic 125; of India 201,
  203; of Israel 181; of Japan 260, 262,
  268; of Pakistan 201–2; of Peru 237; of
  Sweden 148, 154; of United Kingdom
  79, 80; of United States 29–30
Albania 61
Alfonsin, Raul 230–1, 245, 247, 248
Algeria 52
Allende, Salvador 233, 237, 241
Alton, T. P. 43
American Battalion 11, 12
Angola 25, 50, 52
anti-ballistic missile (ABM) programme
  29
Arab–Israeli Wars 177, 181, 182
Argentina 228–9; defence industry of
  242–4; economy of 229, 233, 249,
  251n.6; military expenditure of 4, 6,
  229–33 *passim*, 244–6, 247, 248,
  250nn.3&4; (personnel costs 240,

241, 242, 251n.8; socio-economic
  burden of 228); terrorism and 11, 12
armed forces 57; of Argentina 228, 229,
  230, 231, 240–8 *passim*, 251nn.8&11;
  of Bulgaria 47, 48, 53; of Chile 228,
  229, 230, 232, 234–5, 238–48 *passim*,
  251nn.7&8&11; of Czechoslovakia
  47, 48, 49, 50–1; of Denmark 153–4;
  and domestic repression 56, 62–3; of
  France 97–100, 110–12; of German
  Democratic Republic 47–51 *passim*;
  of German Federal Republic 124–5,
  126–7, 138–9, 141nn.12&13, 145n.72;
  of Hungary 47, 48, 49–50, 53; of India
  189, 199, 201, 202–3, 204; of Israel
  178, 179, 181, 182, 183, 184–6; of
  Japan 259–60, 261, 262, 267; military
  governments 230–1, 232–3; of Norway
  153–4; of Pakistan 199, 201–2, 203,
  212, 213; of Peru 228, 229, 230, 237–43
  passim, 247–8; of Poland 47, 48, 49,
  50–1, 56; of Romania 47, 48, 49–50, 53,
  54; of Soviet Union 47, 48, 49, 50, 63,
  64, 67; (and 1917 Revolution 61–2); of
  Sweden 148–9, 153–4; of Switzerland
  171n.3; of United Kingdom 79–82,
  86–7, 126; of United States 10–11, 20,
  24–5, 36, 259, 261; (inter-service
  rivalries 14, 29–30, 33, 34); of
  Warsaw Pact 24–5, 43–4, 45–51, 53,
  67; (and communist parties 54, 57,
  60, 61–6, 67)
arms control: in Indian continent 214,
  219; in South America 247, 248;
  superpower 24–5, 41, 90; (and
  German Federal Republic 136–8,
  140, 144nn.62&63; and US military
  expenditure 14, 23, 29, 33, 35–6)

expenditure 133–6 *passim*);
nuclear forces of 28–9; political
organization of 61–2, 63, 64, 65, 67;
and United Kingdom 79, 84, 90; and
United States 13, 14, 28–9, 36
space forces: of France 98; of United
States 23, 29, 270
Spain 243, 244
SPD (Social Democrats) (German
Federal Republic) 129
START (Strategic Arms Reduction
Talks) 23, 29
steel production 58
Steinberg, G. M. 181
stock market crash (October 1987) 18
Stockholm CSCE agreement (1985) 49
structuralism, concepts of 193–4
Suez 81
Sweden 148–76; armed forces of 148–9,
153–4; economy of 149–52; military
expenditure of 4, 6, 151, 152–3, 170,
176; (demand for 155–69; political
factors affecting 174n.13); and Nordic
Defence Pact 170; terrorism and 11
Switzerland 148, 174n.3, 270
Syria: military expenditure of 15; (and
Israeli military expenditure 178–9,
182, 183, 184–6); Warsaw Pact and
50, 52

Taiwan 46
Tax Reform Act of 1986 (United States)
19
taxation 8; in France 96–7; in German
Federal Republic 122, 139; in United
Kingdom 77; in United States 16–17,
19, 36, 274
technology: in Argentina 242, 243, 246;
in Chile 242; in German Federal
Republic 121, 123, 128; in India 192,
193, 194; in Israel 181; in Japan
269–70; in less developed countries
194, 215; in Peru 242; in Soviet Union
58, 59, 60; in United Kingdom 85;
Warsaw Pact advisors on 48, 50–1,
53; *see also* R&D
terrorism 10–12
Thatcher, Margaret 77
Third World *see* less developed
countries
Tlatelolco, treaty of 246
Togo 102, 114n.9
Total Force Concept (United States) 20

trade balance: of Argentina 249; of
Chile 250; of Denmark 150; of France
96, 110, 272; of German Federal
Republic 119, 120, 121, 123, 129,
140n.4, 272; of India 191, 192; of
Japan 254, 272, 273; of less developed
countries 216, 217; of Norway 150; of
Pakistan 196, 197; of Peru 249; of
Soviet Union 58; of Sweden 150–1,
152; of United Kingdom 76–7, 82–3,
85, 272; of United States 16, 17, 18–
19, 272, 273; *see also* exports of arms;
imports of arms
transport, disruption of 56
Trident missile programme 29, 79,
80–1, 83, 87–90 *passim*
triple-zero option 137, 144nn.62&63
Tupac Amaru Revolutionary
Movement (MRTA) 11
Turkey, 9, 49, 66

unemployment 57; in Argentina 249; in
Chile 250; in Denmark 150; in France
86, 96, 97; in German Federal
Republic 119, 120, 121–2, 123, 128; in
Norway 150; in Peru 235, 237, 249,
251n.6; in Sweden 150, 151–2, 157; in
United Kingdom 76–7, 86; in United
States 16, 18
United Kingdom 66, 76–91; armed
forces of 79–82, 86–7, 126; burden
sharing index for 272; economy of 16,
76–7, 78, 85–6; (trade balance 76–7,
82–3, 85, 272); exports of arms by 83,
85, 87, 203, 251n.16; and France
81, 101; imports of arms by 82–3,
270; military expenditure of 4, 5,
76, 77–83, 90, 153, 174; (demand for
83–5; socio-economic burden of 77,
85–6); and NATO 77–8, 79, 81,
141n.20; overseas commitments of
49, 79, 80, 81–2, 246, 248;
procurement of arms by 81, 87–9; and
South America 245, 248, 251n.16;
terrorism and 11
United States: armed forces of 10–11,
20, 24–5, 36, 259, 261; (inter-service
rivalries 14, 29–30, 33, 34); burden
sharing index for 272; and Chile 237;
economy of 14–19, 27, 33, 34, 36, 60,
273–4; exports of arms by 177, 201,
202, 212, 264–5, 270–1; and German
Federal Republic 124, 131; and